Force of Nature

Three Women Tackle the John Muir Trail

Joan M. Griffin

Black Rose Writing | Texas

The author grants the final approval for this literary material.

First printing

Some names and identifying details may have been changed to protect the privacy of individuals.

ISBN: 978-1-68513-281-1
PUBLISHED BY BLACK ROSE WRITING
www.blackrosewriting.com

Printed in the United States of America
Suggested Retail Price (SRP) $25.95

Force of Nature is printed in Garamond Premier Pro

*As a planet-friendly publisher, Black Rose Writing does its best to eliminate unnecessary waste to reduce paper usage and energy costs, while never compromising the reading experience. As a result, the final word count vs. page count may not meet common expectations.

Author photo courtesy of Marta Franco

Cover design by Laurel Mathe of Mystic Design www.mysticdesign.net

Praise for
Force of Nature

"Epic! *Force of Nature* is like *Wild* meets *A Walk in the Woods*, where breathtaking adventure and humorous setbacks are the narratives nestled in a setting only Joan Griffin can put into words. Griffin's thru-hike of the John Muir Trail is a journey of self-discovery and a testament to the human spirit. In her words: *Fear loses its power in the face of someone who has known courage.* 5-Stars!"

–**Cam Torrens**, Appalachian Trial thru-hiker and
award-winning author of *Stable* and *False Summit*

"A terrific Muir Trail memoir with wonderful descriptions of the trail's majesty and the mental and physical challenges encountered along the way."

–**Ethan Gallogly**, author of the award-winning *The Trail*,
a novel set on the John Muir Trail

"Some people read about it. Others dream of it. Very few do it, and even fewer successfully write about it—for it is a transforming experience. Griffin's *Force of Nature* is not just another *turn-left-here-and-hike-7-miles* guide to the world-famous John Muir Trail. Instead, it is a carefully woven and skillfully expressed collection of real-life experiences shared by friends, old and new. From bluebird skies and sunny days to those with freezing downpours of torrential rainstorms, this small band of mighty women faced each day head-on, with a clear mission to achieve their goal: the entire JMT and the very top of Mount Whitney."

–**Joe Medeiros**, retired national park ranger, John Muir Trail thru-hiker, and
retired Editor-in-Chief, Sierra College Press

"Lace up your hiking boots! Let Joan Griffin guide you over granite mountains, through thunderous storms and wildflower-studded meadows. Shimmering sapphire blue lakes appear as often as strangers along the path, and both will be indelibly etched on your heart. Experiences like these can change a person. *Force of Nature* will inspire."

–**Barbara Olson Lawrence**, artist and author
of the forthcoming *Drawing Water*

"I loved this book. As an experienced backpacker, *Force of Nature* made me ache to get back on the trail again. Joan Griffin captures beautifully: the challenges of this trek; the confidence and strength gained by overcoming difficulties; the natural beauty of the High Sierra; and the joy of becoming one with nature. I admire her journey. Her story is an inspiration to us all, both hikers and non-hikers."

–**Patricia Dove Miller**, author of *Bamboo Secrets: One Woman's Quest Through the Shadows of Japan*

"I found myself both intrigued and inspired by the story of these adventurous women. The vivid visual and sensory descriptions of the scenery made me feel as though I was there. *Force of Nature* was simultaneously restorative and invigorating, inspirational and contemplative. "

–**Sandra Moats McPherson**, lecturer, Sacramento State University School of Music

"Hikers and those who dream about hiking adventures will delight in their literary trek through Joan Griffin's *Force of Nature*. I could vividly picture the majestic JMT scenery, feel the energy of the storms and the ache in my own muscles because of Griffin's descriptive writing. Reading *Force of Nature* took me right back to the backcountry trail and adventure that I love."

–**Jodi Santin O'Keefe**, educator, outdoorswoman, John Muir Trail thru-hiker

"From the first thunderbolt to the last reveal of the range of light, Griffin's magical tale displays her keen observations, wit, and storytelling. *Force of Nature* puts her in the league with the best writers of Sierran literature."

–**Holly Bundock**, writer, naturalist, and outdoorswoman

"Joan Griffin has brilliantly narrated her experience hiking the John Muir Trail. Through this journey of The Three Women, we see how the women are uplifted and restored by the 'hand of unbridled Nature'."

–**B.J. Griffin**, first woman Superintendent of Yosemite National Park, retired, and Public Lands advocate

"Come along on the adventure of your life! Griffin's eye for detail and understanding of what makes us strive will let you experience one of the nation's most challenging trails as if you were there."

–**Dierdre Wolownick**, author of *The Sharp End of Life* and the oldest woman to climb El Capitan

"The Muir Trail lures hundreds of pilgrims into the High Sierra each year. Griffin pulls us along on this two-hundred-mile trek through the heart of the High Sierra. We discover how three very different women pull together, cast aside their differences, and reach a difficult and elusive goal. The trio faced lightning storms, high passes, big blisters, and long days on the trail, but as they continued south, they realized that both the journey *and* the destination really matter."

–**Bart O'Brien**, peak climber with over 300 Sierra summits and pioneer of over 20 Sierra first ascents

"Muir would herald Griffin's enthusiasm for the wonders of the high country, as I do."

–**Mack Shaver**, retired national park superintendent and John Muir Trail veteran

"See the beauty, feel the pain, experience the magic. In *Force of Nature*... I felt the wonder, serenity, and peace I encountered on my own hike, as well as the doubts, frustrations, pain, and even anger... Whether you're looking to relive your own hike, test your readiness to tackle such an adventure, or experience the hike in your clean clothes while lying on your comfortable sofa, you'll enjoy the read."

–**Arnold Marsden**, author of *Muir Trail Magic* and veteran of the John Muir Trail

"*Force of Nature* captures the beauty of the trail and is rich with descriptions of the natural environment, the challenges the women face and fears they conquer."

–**Inga Aksamit**, award-winning author of the adventure memoir *Highs and Lows on the John Muir Trail*

For my son,
Dean Griffin Eckles,
my greatest inspiration and my strongest champion.

May your trails be crooked, winding, lonesome, dangerous,
leading to the most amazing view.
May your mountains rise into and above the clouds...
where storms come and go as lightning clangs upon the high crags,
where something strange and more beautiful and
more full of wonder than your deepest dreams waits for you—
beyond that next turning of the canyon walls.

~ Edward Abbey, *Desert Solitaire*, 1968

Force
of Nature

Contents

Peak Experience   1

Genesis   7

The Sacred E Ticket (Day Zero)   16

First Leg:

    Over The Rainbow (Day One)   24

    Lost And Found (Day Two)   42

    Crossing Over (Day Three)   59

    Gems In The Rough (Day Four)   71

    Down The Staircase (Day Five)   80

    R & R - Rewind & Redux (Day Six)   99

Second Leg:

    Just The Two Of Us (Day Seven)   107

    Trail Sisters (Day Eight)   117

    Climbing To Ten (Day Nine)   126

    Truth Or Dare (Day Ten)   139

Third Leg:

    Kaleidoscope Eyes (Day Eleven)   160

    Serial Encounters (Day Twelve)   177

    Centerpoint (Day Thirteen)   196

Fourth Leg:

    Monsters In Paradise (Day Fourteen)   209

    Walking On The Edge (Day Fifteen)   223

    Lunch At John's Place (Day Sixteen)   231

    Hidden In Plain Sight (Day Seventeen)   251

    Stairway To Heaven (Day Eighteen)   258

    Climbing With Sisyphus (Day Nineteen)   268

    Golden Touch (Day Twenty)   281

    In A Different Light (Day Twenty-One)   293

    A Cowboy, An Egg, and A Question (Day Twenty-Two)   305

Final Leg:

    Lost In Translation (Day Twenty-Three)   323

    The End Is Nigh (Day Twenty-Four)   335

    Sauntering Towards Whitney (Day Twenty-Five)   350

    Sometimes You Eat The Bear (Day Twenty-Six)   357

    Somewhere Over The Rainbow (Day Twenty-Seven)   367

    The Other Side Of The Mountain   376

Peak Experience

Fear not, therefore, to try the mountain-passes.
They will kill care, save you from deadly apathy, set you free,
and call forth every faculty into vigorous, enthusiastic action.
~ John Muir, *The Mountains of California*, 1875

Day Two
July 20, 2006

Donohue Pass — 11,060 feet

We were hiking uphill as fast as our fifty-year-old legs would carry us. Behind us, the sky was a bright California summer blue. But ahead, above the granite mountain ridge we were climbing, it grew gray, then grayer. Still early, it was barely two in the afternoon. Our plan was to be over the pass and setting up camp down in the valley on the other side long before the Sierra's typical evening rains began.

Cresting eleven-thousand-foot Donohue Pass, however, we were shocked to find ourselves face to face with a monster storm lurking behind the ridge. Angry black clouds now rose like towers, filling the sky.

Shoulder to shoulder, we froze. Not only did this army of lightning-laced thunderheads block our forward motion, but it was charging directly at us, riding on an icy wind. There was no time for the three of us to retreat to lower, safer ground.

"What now, ladies?" Cappy shouted over the storm's roar. Her eyes darted about, scanning the terrain.

"Hell! I'm dumping my pack and anything metal I'm wearing," I said. Then pointing, I added, "I'm going to that low spot in the dirt to lie down."

I threw my hiking poles on the ground beside a waist-high slab of granite, unbuckled my pack, and wrenched it off. I pitched my shiny new pack roughly against the rock slab and dug helter-skelter through its contents in search of any and all warm and waterproof clothing, pushing undesired items aside.

"All my warm clothes have metal zipper pulls and snaps," I said. "Is that a problem?" No one answered. Maybe I had not said it aloud. I thought the metal might attract the lightning. In the moment I stood considering, I realized how cold the air and my heart had gone.

Stripping off shorts, I yanked on a base layer, fleece, and waterproof raingear top and bottom, plus gloves and hat. I abandoned my watch and glasses, both metal, zipping them into a small pack-pouch before slipping a plastic rain-cover over my pack.

Huge drops of rain began splatting around us. The wind carried the pungent zing of ozone, a harbinger of lightning, and shoved the rain horizontally with each gust. The black wall of clouds had followed us over the pass, hovering nearly overhead. Gray fingers reached downward from the clouds towards the spot where we dressed.

"It's only a few feet lower here than it was at the top!" Cappy shot back.

"It'll do," Jane assured us in her steady voice. She kept an eye on the rapidly changing sky, as she rifled through her backpack.

Together, we dashed to the deepest of the slight dips in the landscape, really no more than a depression in the ground. Huddled between a tiny snowmelt pond and huge piles of granite boulders, we ran down our lists of sage backcountry dos-and-don'ts.

"I know we're not supposed to stand under tall trees," I said. Not a problem way above tree-line. "We're also supposed to stay away from water and big rocks! So, should I be closer to that pond or these rocks?"

I could not decide; I could not move.

"I don't think it matters any..." A blinding flash of lightning and its immediate crack of thunder stole Jane's words.

"Spread out and get down!" She threw herself on the wet ground ten feet from Cappy. Shocked into action, I dropped into my own shallow dent in the dirt.

After tugging my fleece cap down around my ears, I pulled my rain hood up and cinched it tightly around my face, leaving only a small circle for my eyes and nose. I curled myself into the fetal position, drawing my knees to my chest.

Engulfing us, the sky was battleship gray—the early summer afternoon turned to night. The deluge pounded the ground and drowned out all sound, save the crashing thunder. My gloved hands covered my ears.

Lightning rent the clouds. Terrified, I watched as slivers of electricity, high above us, leapt from cloud to cloud, making intricate webs of light in the darkness. Thicker bolts slashed vertically to and from the twelve-thousand-foot peaks that surrounded us.

I covered my face with my hands. Peeking out between my gloved fingers in momentary bouts of bravery, I slammed closed my finger-shutters with each new assault. Still, I witnessed plenty.

Each time Thor's hammer slammed down, the Earth shook and the air reverberated with thunder. Light and sound struck together, not a nanosecond between them.

Flash-BOOM!

Flash-BOOM!

On and on it went, my heart booming in rhythm.

Flash-BOOM!

At the peak of the storm's fury, frigid winds whipped around us. Rain froze into icy bullets shot from the sky, stinging me through my layers. The clouds grew thick and blinding. Wrapped in a ten-thousand-foot-high fog, I felt alone. I could barely make out the silent lumps that were Jane and Cappy just a few feet away.

What am I doing here? I shouted in my thoughts, trying to hear myself over the storm. *What are three smart women doing in this predicament? We know better than this!*

Prayers, pleas, and promises flew like charged particles from my mind. I urged them upward and outward, hoping they would penetrate the ion-filled sky and find a sympathetic reception with the Powers That Be. I visualized a golden igloo of protective light arching over and around us as we huddled on that small patch of grass in the sky. Whispering my words over and over like a mantra, I held that image of a protective glowing dome steady in my mind's eye.

"Protect us, keep us safe.

"Protect us, keep us safe."

Cold to the bone, even in my layers of fleece and plastic, my body shivered and convulsed. Gritting my jaws could not stop my teeth from chattering. *Has it been an hour? How much longer can I stay curled up here before hypothermia sets in?*

I wiggled and rubbed my extremities in an attempt to raise my body temperature, but to no avail. The shivering and chattering went on and on. The weak link was my feet—I was still wearing my Teva hiking sandals with thick, wet socks.

My ears pricked up. *Is that real? Or just my imagination? Was that a pause?*

I raised my head to watch the sky. The heart of the storm was moving north. We remained wrapped in clouds on the rocky pass, but the violence inched slowly away.

At precisely that moment, Cappy's voice rang out, penetrating the storm's din and my cold-numbed brain. "Let's go! It's moving north! Let's go!"

Galvanized, our three bodies jumped up like one, moving with focused energy. In mere moments, we had packs on. In the same way a distraught mother lifts a car off the body of her child, I tossed onto my shoulders the forty-pound pack I had struggled to hoist and buckle earlier in the day. Faster than I could have imagined possible, we scuttled southward across the broad granite pass, peering through the rain and fog to find our way down the other side.

Frozen feet, impossibly sure-footed, rock-hopped downward over an ancient talus slope, the remains of an old landslide. The trail lay hidden somewhere among the acres of automobile-sized boulders and vast expanses of snow spread across the steep slope before us. Hurtling downhill, I scanned the gray-and-white landscape for any sign of a trail—rock cairns, patches of brown, anything—but saw nothing.

"See that tiny green square at the bottom edge of the talus?" Cappy shouted over the pounding rain and roar of the storm. "That's our destination, Rush Creek." A thin gray ribbon of a river sliced through a postage stamp-sized meadow.

Trail or not, my feet did not care as they fairly flew over the rocky rubble toward that distant spot of green, so eager was I to get down off that damn mountain!

"I have to stop!" I called out, halting on a flat rock slab.

We were only halfway down the mountain, but I could not take another step. My feet had been numb for over an hour, and my legs felt rubbery with exhaustion. With the immediate danger of the lightning and thunder past and my adrenaline surge used up, my feet were lifeless clubs, and I feared stumbling in the rock maze.

Jane and Cappy joined me where I stood.

"I can't feel my feet," I said. "I need to put on my boots and warm up my toes."

The sky, still filled with clouds, had grown lighter and paler. The rain had calmed to sprinkles and showers.

Scanning the sky, Cappy said, "My feet are freezing. I'm changing, too."

While we sat, Jane, who had worn her boots all day, scouted around for some suggestion of a path.

Though the trailing edge of the storm continued to sprinkle on us from high gray clouds, the hour-long run down the mountain had warmed my body. Only my feet remained frozen and unfeeling. I peeled wet socks from my prune-wrinkled feet and massaged my bare toes between gloved hands, encouraging the blood to flow into the pale skin. I tugged on a new pair of plush REI hiking socks and pushed my feet into dry boots.

Before I had tied my laces, Jane called out, "There it is!" Standing on a broad slab of gray stone a few yards away, like a sailor on the prow of a ship shouting,

"Land, ho!" Jane pointed with her hiking pole towards the green spot we had been eyeing all the way down the mountain.

"See how that thin brown line cuts straight across the meadow?" She paused, waiting until our eyes caught up with her words. "Halfway between us and the spot where it disappears into the rocks, you can see a brown patch of trail—"

Cappy and I leapt up to see better.

"—and then another patch a little closer—and a third." All the while, she pointed downward at a series of brown splotches among the rocks. Sure enough, like a connect-the-dots puzzle, the trail stood out from the rock-covered slope as a brown dotted line pointing arrow-straight towards our perch.

"I see it!" Cappy said, a smile growing across her face.

"Wow! It's right there!" I answered.

With warming feet, I felt my confidence return as I navigated the leaps and bounds over and around the heaps of stone. In response, my body stopped gripping itself so tightly, and my breath came easier.

Despite the day's harrowing events, our blundering mistakes, and utter exhaustion, we had survived. We had climbed up and over our first High Sierra pass. We had twice lost the trail, but found it both times. We had responded appropriately to a dangerous situation, partly of our own making, and had come out unscathed.

In the days to come, we would find ourselves repeatedly challenged by the physical demands of the wilderness through which we journeyed. There were more mountains to scale, more rivers to ford, more mishaps to overcome. All that was to be expected, of course. Little did I know that it would be my inner journey—my own personal mountains to climb and rivers to cross—that would prove most daunting.

Genesis

Only those who will risk going too far
can possibly find out how far one can go.
~ T.S. Eliot, Preface to *Transit of Venus*, Harry Crosby, 1931

Safe At Home
2004 — 2005 — 2006

So how *did* three knowledgeable fifty-something women, experienced in the ways of wilderness trails and thorough to the point of obsession in their preparations, find themselves in such a precarious predicament? It started two years earlier.

2004

My best friend Krei and I threw an over-the-top party to celebrate my fiftieth birthday. Scores of friends from every quadrant of my life came dressed for the international theme. I wore a saffron-colored sari. Others wore kaftans and lederhosen, muumuus and Scottish plaid.

Long tables laden with food stood under tents in a pasture. We offered oysters-on-the-half-shell and kabobs and lots of local California wine. Potluck added lasagna and enchiladas, quiche and sushi. One hundred twinkling luminaria marked the path to the party and encircled the field.

After dinner, there were African drummers and Middle Eastern belly dancers. Later, a classic rock-n-roll band played while we danced under the stars of that June night. It was truly a magical way to mark the beginning of the second half of my life.

Late that night, I hugged my dear friend Krei goodbye and bon voyage, as she was preparing to depart on a road trip adventure to Alaska.

A few days later, I was lounging on my couch reading, when my cellphone began to sing.

"Hello."

"Joan..." The husky male voice on the other end paused.

"Yes?"

"Joan. I have awful news." I realized it was Krei's husband. His voice, gruff and hollow, almost a whisper, was barely recognizable.

I sat forward, alert. "Yes?"

"Krei is dead. A drunk driver killed..." Through a whimper, he pushed the word "Dead" out again, before falling into choking sobs.

His words punched. Stunned. My core muscles squeezed my heart. My lungs stopped, frozen. I could not breathe.

No. No. No. This cannot be. I struggled to grasp both air and reality.

Digging deep to control my voice, I asked, "What happened?"

The next thing I remember, I was lying doubled up on the carpet in the middle of my living room floor. I spent hours there. Lost. Adrift. Unmoored. Afraid.

I was a balled-up mess.

A sobbing puddle.

Unwashed despair.

I had lost my best friend, who was also a teaching colleague and travel buddy. But it felt like so much more than that—as if every loss I had ever experienced in my life had come back to amplify this one. I had never been so low, so depressed, so unable to shake myself out of it.

At fifty, the halfway point of my life, I found myself a long-divorced empty-nester. I felt alone and lonely. Powerless and hopeless. Totally despairing. From the heights of extreme euphoria surrounded by family and friends at my birthday party, I plunged into the equal-and-opposite depths of a black hole.

On the outside, I have always been strong, independent, and resourceful. *I am a rock; I am an island.* Now I needed to find a ladder to climb out of my hole. I was scaring myself, and I needed to prove to myself that I was still strong. I was going to need to dig down and pull up anything resembling courage I could find. I needed to get through this.

Still in my pajamas, a few days later, I walked out to my mailbox at the end of the driveway to find it stuffed with several days' neglected deliveries. Among the jumble was a small package. Seeing it, I felt a small jolt of curiosity, the first positive energy I had felt in days. I stuffed everything else back into the mailbox, so I could rip the packing tape from the little box right there and then.

Inside was a sympathy note from a close friend signed with lots of X's and O's, kisses and hugs. "I hope this little gift will help keep Krei close to your heart."

I carefully unwrapped the folded white tissue paper to reveal a necklace—silver charms on a long silver chain. Three flat circular rings, each engraved with a single word. One read STRENGTH, another COURAGE, and the last SPIRIT. I squeezed the chain and those powerful words in my hand and held them to my heart. Tears flooded my eyes and drizzled down my cheeks as I steadied myself against the row of mailboxes.

Days later, I packed my car full of camping gear and ran away to Yosemite. I spent nearly a month camped in Tuolumne Meadows, alternately hiking and reading. I climbed to Clouds Rest and North Dome. I sat amidst the flowers of Dana Hanging Gardens. I wandered through forests and meadows and stood atop granite domes. I took photos and wrote in my journal. All the time, I searched for strength, courage, and spirit.

Of the many books I read, one that spoke directly to my tender heart was *Beauty* by John O'Donoghue, who wrote, "When the mind is festering with trouble or the heart torn, we can find healing among the silence of the mountains..." [1]

Nature heals. Nature inspires. Nature brought me back, however tentatively, to my right mind.

Out of that month of hermit camping came an urgent desire to walk the John Muir Trail. I imagined backpacking that iconic two-hundred-mile trail through the Sierra Nevada backcountry, right from the spot where I stood that summer in Yosemite, southward to Mount Whitney. I trusted that if sleeping under the trees in Tuolumne could begin to heal my spirit, then hiking deeper into the Sierra wilderness for long weeks, communing with nature and standing atop mountains, would be profoundly healing.

It was a huge goal, a commitment, that would require a force of will. And a year of planning, preparing, and training my whole self. There is nothing more hopeful than planning for the future, and I needed hope.

This would give me the chance I desperately needed to prove to myself that I was still strong, still courageous. That my spirit was still alive.

Krei would have approved.

---

[1] John O'Donohue, *Beauty: Rediscovering the True Sources of Compassion, Serenity, and Hope* (Harper, 2004) p17.

2005

I had known Cappy for a dozen years, as the close-friend-of-a-close-friend and as teacher to her now-grown children. We moved in the same circles in our small community, but being busy career women, we had never had time to develop a close friendship ourselves. It was autumn, and Cappy and I were at the home of that mutual friend enjoying a barbecue.

"Cappy, they tell me you and Jim have retired! That's so exciting!"

"Joan! It's great to see you. It's been forever!" Holding wine glasses to the side, we hugged hello.

"Now that you're a woman of leisure, what're you going to do with all your time? I don't picture you two in matching rocking chairs," I teased.

"No rocking chairs," she laughed. "I'd always thought we'd be taking long backpacking trips into the Sierra, the ones I've been dreaming of since college but never had time for. But now Jim's ankles are killing him, and he can't hike, let alone carry a pack."

"That's a shame!" I said.

She shook her head, then smiled. "But you know me, just because he can't go, doesn't mean I can't." There was a real twinkle in her impish eye. "In fact, Jim (he's so sweet and supportive of me) gave me a new ultra-light pack for my birthday, and I've decided I'm just going to do the John Muir Trail one portion at a time. I've wanted all my life to do the whole thing from north to south, but now I'm just going to do shorter segments on my own." She stopped to take a sip of her wine.

"Really, the JMT?" I paused a moment. "You're not going to believe this, but— Why don't you come with me instead and do the whole thing this summer?" I could feel excitement rising.

Cappy went still, her freckled face disbelieving. Then she blinked and broke her own stunned silence. "What? You're doing the John Muir Trail? The whole John Muir Trail?" She was bouncing on her toes, vibrating like she might launch herself into the air.

"Wait. Listen!" I tried to calm her down, but I was pretty excited myself. I could feel a smile stretching across my face. "My friend Sue and I have been planning for over a year—for this summer." I considered putting my hands on her shoulders to hold her down to the ground. "You could join us."

"Really?" Her green eyes grew big, and she touched my arm like she was making sure I was real. Cappy expressed her excitement in her own unique way, shaking her fists like they held invisible maracas.

A few seconds passed, and I watched as she processed the idea. She turned and called across the room, "Jim! Jim!" She dashed over and grabbed his arm. "You've got to hear this—"

Cappy and I talked for an hour. I told her all about Sue and the wonderful JMT adventure we were planning.

"Sue and I have hiked together for twenty years, since the days when we carried our toddlers in our backpacks! We'd originally planned to go this past summer, but the snow was too deep. So, 2006 is our year," I said.

"Last year's snow was record-breaking. You were wise to postpone. Tell me about Sue," Cappy encouraged me. We'd settled onto chairs on the deck where bowls of chips and salsa tempted us.

"Sue's my backcountry hero and guru. She's tall and blond, a real Viking—kind of a cross between the Energizer bunny and a pack mule!" I laughed, thinking of how many times I had followed Sue up a trail to find her waiting patiently at the top. "I have to tell you, Cappy, I would *never* have considered an adventure as extensive as this without Sue."

"I can't wait to meet her." Cappy smiled and leaned closer to ask, "What kinds of preparations have you made so far?"

"I was so disappointed when we had to abandon our 2005 plans that I'm doubly committed this time. I've become a tad obsessive in my preparations." Laughing at myself, I thought about the pile of books and maps I had collected and devoured and all the time I had spent scouring the internet for information about John Muir and the trail named for him. I had read every word on the websites dedicated to the JMTers and gone down rabbit holes researching lightweight backpacking gear and the latest in trail clothing.

"I want to be in tip-top shape, physically and mentally, by D-Day," I declared.

Before I was through, Cappy officially committed to The Grand Adventure Of A Lifetime, leaping in with both feet. We sealed the deal with a toast, clinking together glasses filled with a rich red from Klinker Brick winery.

Over our paper-plate dinner, we tossed around a verbal list of all the things we needed to accomplish before summer arrived:

Apply for the 2006 permit

Research food and equipment

Inventory and weigh our gear

Buy cool lightweight stuff from REI

Read everything we could find about the trail

Get more maps

I told Cappy about my training regimen and how it would increase in the spring. I had joined the local gym and was working with a personal trainer, who had me doing spin classes to strengthen my legs and working with weights to beef up my core. When the weather allowed, I walked and hiked—when it did not, I used the gym's treadmill set at a steep incline.

I told her about the awesome new Black Diamond carbon-fiber hiking poles Sue had found and our scheduled warm-up backpacking weekends in the spring.

2006

The National Park Service letter confirming our six-person wilderness permit arrived in my mailbox in February. By then, I was wearing five-pound ankle-weights everywhere I went, even when teaching in my classroom. Another of my friends and two of Sue's were on board the team, so all our preparations were based on a JMT team of six women, aged forty to mid-fifties.

Suddenly, in March, only four months before D-Day, Sue called to tell me she had to bow out. "What? Why?" I was shocked. This was *our* trip. We were partners—lead actors in this epic adventure story. Everyone else had been eager to join *our* team on *our* trip.

Sue explained how family issues had come up, and she was not comfortable being absent for the whole summer. "This trip is my life's dream," she lamented. Her voice was filled with disappointment.

Of course, our families always came first. I understood completely her decision, but emotionally, Sue's words slugged me in the stomach.

Was I courageous enough? Was I strong enough? Could I take on sole leadership of the expedition? Without Sue to lean into, could I do this? I gave myself a week to study my answers to my questions, and it took me that whole time to convince myself that I could and would continue with the plan. I became tenaciously determined to prove to myself that I was, indeed, strong enough and courageous enough to complete the expedition.

That serendipitous conversation in November with Cappy turned out to be the critical event that saved the trip. Rather than joining Sue-and-Joan's marvelous adventure, Cappy took Sue's spot as "co-captain," and it became Joan-and-Cappy's amazing adventure. I am certain that without Cappy there would have been no trip in 2006. I welcomed her extensive experience in the Sierra and her unflagging optimism. Her strengths and abilities were different from Sue's, though. Without Sue's physical power to depend upon, I forced myself to be stronger. Without Sue's calm, unflappable demeanor, I attempted to find that steady peaceful spirit inside myself.

Cappy jumped right in. We enrolled in a "variety show" course at Sierra College on the history, biology, geology, and artists of the Sierra, each session featuring an expert in a specific discipline relating to the "Range of Light." The highlight for us was the lecture by Joe and Lynn Medeiros, who had hiked the JMT once and were preparing to hike it again[2]. We learned countless indispensable bits of information from them, including realistic pack weight limits and specific locations to ship our food caches. They introduced us to the three-thousand-calorie-a-day "JMT Diet," where one eats constantly and still loses weight.

Sue was the first, but one by one, all the other women dropped out, too. It is difficult to commit to a full month away from home. It is hard to maintain an

---

[2] Sierra College Professor Emeritus Joe Medeiros and 2018 John Muir Association's 2018 *Conservationist of the Year. Class was taught by Gary Noys.*

intense fitness regimen while working. By May, it was just Cappy and me, a six-person permit, a detailed plan, and a growing level of excitement.

I threw myself into building my strength. Loading my backpack up with bags of sand weighing forty pounds, I walked a seven-mile loop around my neighborhood that included the steepest streets in the area. At first, it was only on weekends, with shorter loops during the week, but when school let out in June, it became my daily routine. At first, I felt foolish schlepping my backpack through the well-manicured neighborhoods of Lake of the Pines, wondering if any of the residents would report my strange behavior to security. But then, several neighbors began asking questions and encouraging me. I came to dread those curbside meetings, not because I was still feeling foolish, but because they hindered the strenuousness of my workouts.

In May, after an exhausting spin class at the gym, I was sweating and chatting with Jane, a friend and fellow educator with whom I had long before shared teacher-training classes. With summer approaching, we talked vacation plans. Excited, I described my JMT adventure, now only eight weeks away, and how our group of six women had shrunk to two.

"Could you use a third?" she asked. "Rand and I have done bits and pieces of the Muir Trail over the years. It would be great to go back again."

"I'd love you to join us," I said without a moment's pause.

By the time we walked outside, Jane was committed to joining Cappy and me for the first leg of the trek. Had she not had other plans, she would have joined the entire month-long trip.

Standing beside her car, I said, "We're doing a day-hike Saturday at Hidden Falls. You want to come along and meet Cappy?"

That Hidden Falls hike would be the first in a series of increasingly challenging practice hikes we three would make that spring.

The Sacred E Ticket

Wander a whole summer if you can...
time will not be taken from the sum of life.
Instead of shortening, it will definitely lengthen it
and make you truly immortal.
~ John Muir, *Our National Parks*, 1901

Day Zero
July 18, 2006

Yosemite National Park, Sierra Nevada Mountains of California
Tuolumne Meadows Wilderness Ranger Station – 8680 feet

The unassuming wooden building housing the Tuolumne Meadows Wilderness Office sat alone under tall trees at the end of a long access road. A shrine to the preservation of wilderness, its humble appearance belied its important gatekeeping role.

We were eager to check in and pick up our official Wilderness Permit, so leapt from the car the instant it stopped in the parking lot. As we approached the building, our pace slowed spontaneously and our voices dropped to reverent whispers. Inside resided the guardians whose sacred duty it was to grant or withhold permission to enter protected wilderness. Cappy was first to mount the three steps to the heavy wooden door, pulling it wide like a gate.

Crossing that threshold marked a sacred moment in time. Despite the tangible mass of assembled equipment and miles of practice footsteps taken, until that moment, the expedition was a mere dream.

The interior was bathed in golden light, lit by overhead lamps and rays of late afternoon sun streaming through windows in the western wall. We stood clustered by the entrance. Posters, maps, and photos meant to inspire and instruct those who waited—Half Dome and Yosemite Falls in their Technicolor grandeur, the detailed route of the John Muir Trail (JMT), and an ABC list of Backcountry Wisdom—covered the wood-paneled walls. Solemn and silent, we held back, awaiting our turn at the counter.

As two hikers walked away, Cappy, Jane, and I replaced them at a broad altar-like counter with a scarred, much-used surface. Behind it stood a pair of uniformed National Park Service (NPS) Rangers wearing traditional uniforms of gray shirts and forest-green trousers.

"We're here to pick up our JMT Wilderness Permit for tomorrow," I said. "It's in my name, Joan Griffin."

Silence filled the room as the broad-shouldered ranger looked through his files. I held still, my eyes riveted on his strong hands as he shifted individual papers between his fingers. He was thirtyish, with close-cropped dark hair and a well-trimmed mustache.

"Here it is," he said. My eyes moved from the deceptively simple sheet of white paper he held to his smiling face. His words seemed to break a spell, and the hush dissipated. I felt like I had passed some important test and been accepted into a fraternal organization, the Ancient Order of Wilderness Seekers or something similar. I turned to see Cappy and Jane wearing smiles as broad as my own. Cappy bounced on her toes ever so slightly, while Jane stood straight, resting her forearms on the countertop.

We listened intently to their sage advice, like novices soaking in wisdom from wise gurus—priests of the order NPS. "Are you carrying bear-proof food canisters?" asked the second ranger, the taller, lankier, and older of the pair. He pulled a black canister, just like Cappy's, from a shelf and set it on the counter. We confirmed that we were with simultaneous nods of our heads.

"Good. It's mandatory that you use them at all times along the JMT."

"Yes," we all said, again nodding in unison. I wanted him to know how prepared we were for this expedition, wanted his blessing.

"You must also use the canisters to store all personal hygiene items that might have a scent, like toothpaste or sunscreen, even if *you* think they are unscented," he continued. His eyes were intent, his face solemn. He looked at each of us individually.

The first ranger, who had been quietly watching, added, "This is more about protecting the bears and less about protecting your food. It's very important."

"We understand," I assured him. "We've all used bear canisters for several years."

"Good." The older ranger moved on to the next rule. "Camping is allowed only in designated areas. Be sure you set up camp one hundred feet away from any water source, any lake or stream." He smiled. "That's about fifty of my long-legged strides or sixty of your more petite strides."

We asked about trail conditions and snow depths in the high country and got encouraging answers. The rangers confirmed the series of warm rains in June had melted much of the snowpack. "No," we would not need our spiked crampons to cross icy snowfields. "Yes," we should take gaiters for walking through wet snow. The trails throughout the Sierra Nevada were all passable and in pretty good shape.

"You must keep your wilderness permit with you. Always," the young ranger said. "Rangers out on the trail, especially in highly populated areas, will ask to see your permit, and you *must* be able to show it to them." With a ceremonial flourish, he handed me the single sheet of paper with its official NPS stamp—a certificate proclaiming we had completed our rite of passage. We had been deemed worthy to proceed.

That afternoon, our campsite looked like an REI parking lot sale in miniature. Brightly colored gear and supplies covered every flat surface—boots and socks, a stove with fuel canisters, two tents, cups and spoons, sleeping bags and pads, a huge pile of dry foods in Ziploc bags, gloves and hats, notepads and pencils, vitamin bottles, and maps—all strewn about in no particular order.

Billowing clouds filled the tree-encircled patch of sky overhead. Their steady approach from the west forecast an evening of rain, so it was our last opportunity to sort through gear. Jane staked out one end of the wooden table for her gear, while mine was spread across the other end. Attempting to calm my nerves, I ran my hands over every piece of equipment one last time before repacking it. Attempting was the operative word. My nerves were not calming. Feigning calm, Cappy relaxed in a nearby chair chatting with Jim.

Lists had been made and remade. Packs had been filled and weighed, emptied and filled again. Supplies had been sorted and resorted, packaged and repackaged, moved from one pack-pocket to another. Still, I remained keyed up, anxious, and was doing it all over again for good measure.

"This is a great campsite you found, Joan," Cappy said again. She, Jim, and Jane had arrived the night before, while I had been car camping for three nights. She was right. Tuolumne Campground gets crowded in midsummer and many of the spaces are squeezed together. We were up in remote G section, a distance from the store and famous grill, but away from the masses of campers. The site itself was spacious and quiet. There were no barking dogs, crying babies, or teens playing hacky sack.

"Don't you love it up here?" I separated the clothes I would wear in the morning from those I intended to pack.

"Jane, tell me again, what combination of warm stuff are you taking? I just can't seem to come to a final conclusion." I had a burning desire to keep pack weight down, but I did not want to be cold. "Do I need long underwear *and* fleece, both top and bottom?" I wondered aloud, holding up thick fuzzy pants and top in one hand and thin base layers in the other.

"I'm going to err on the side of warmth," she said, pausing to look at the clothes in my outstretched hands. "It's probably going to rain, it's going to get cold at night, and we're going to get stronger, so the weight will feel lighter as we go." She sounded so confident, so sure of herself.

I had always envied Jane her calm, cool, collected demeanor.

Then she added, "I still can't decide if I should take my hiking pants *and* my shorts, or just my shorts." She was holding up one in each hand. I had already made that decision, having even left my hiking pants home.

Three distinct, yet overlapping, conversations were going on at once.

Unable to decide on fleece and/or long underwear, incapable of making a decision of any sort at that point, I put it off, folded all my warm-fuzzies and my raingear into the tiniest sizes possible, sealed them in Ziploc bags, and set them aside. I picked up the blue nylon bag containing my first aid kit, unzipped it, and ran down my mental list, touching each item in turn—moleskin, tape, Advil, Neosporin, Band-Aids, scissors, tweezers—

"Geez, Joan, what have you got in there? It looks like the whole medicine chest! Are you really going to use all that moleskin?" Cappy called from her chair. "You could cut a couple of pounds just by leaving some behind!"

"I know it's overkill, but it'd be awful to have blisters and no way to fix them." I continued rechecking everything I already knew was there. "Funny, there are some things I've scrimped on, but it's never occurred to me to cut back on this stuff. I'm a wimp about pain!"

Before long, Cappy could not hold herself back, succumbing to the pressure—external or internal, I am not sure. We made space for her pack and stuff bags at the table, and out came all her precious possessions.

"Couldn't resist the fun, could you?" I teased.

"You two were making me crazy! Now I'm second-guessing all my choices!" She spread out her own collection of clothes and gear.

Eventually, decisions were made and our backpacks were strapped closed for the final time. Jane ended up taking both shorts and pants. I carried both fleece and thermals. And as it turned out, those were good choices.

I wrote one final list of everything I needed to do or pack in the morning before leaving—toothbrush and paste, lip balm, sunglasses, fill water containers, make phone calls. As I placed it on the dashboard, Jim announced, "Ladies, it's five-thirty, so we need to leave in ten minutes if we're going to get to dinner on time." He had been quietly observing our preparations, which he found quite humorous.

"Wow! How did it get that late?" Cappy jumped in surprise.

We made quick work of stowing things into tent, van, and bear box. In his important role as one-man support team and chauffeur, Jim drove us to the Tuolumne Meadows Lodge for a celebratory send-off dinner.

I examined the sky again. Like the previous day, the weather had turned gray by early evening. Though it would not be dark for four hours, there was a chill in the air, not a strange occurrence in Tuolumne Meadows, nor anywhere in the High Sierra. The mountains created their own weather patterns. Hot air drifting up from dry deserts to the south collided with hot moist currents driving in from the Pacific and the Central Valley to the west, creating a dynamic weather pattern peculiar to higher elevations. It could be over a hundred degrees under blazing summer sunshine just a few miles in any direction—east in the Nevada high desert and west in California's agricultural fields—while it was raining or hailing, or even snowing up in the mountains.

First come gorgeous days of sun and warmth, without a cloud in the sky. Then for several days moisture builds up in the afternoons, with white clouds rising over the peaks, creating photo-perfect sunsets. When the moisture content becomes too great, those clouds turn dark gray, even black, and the far-off grumbling of thunder warns of coming storms. The afternoon skies open up, creating showers lasting minutes or torrents lasting hours. After a day or three, the moisture is spent, and the pattern begins anew with warm sunshine and the scent of freshly washed air.

Seasoned Sierra hikers know the pattern and watch for its signs. They know when they can stay out hiking, and when it is best to get back to camp or don wet-weather gear. You cannot fight it or avoid it. After a few years, you get pretty good at predicting, but even Sierra veterans can get caught out in the weather.

That evening, as I put my backpack into the van and propped my list on the dashboard, I thought about the coming rainstorm. I hoped it would be a gusher, strong enough to cleanse the atmosphere of moisture. I wanted to wake up to clear skies and have those skies follow us through the first few days of hiking. To that end, I sent out a silent plea to the Universe. *Send us three days of clear weather, please, just three rainless days of sunshine.*

I knew we would face difficult challenges hiking this famous trail—that was a given and part of the allure. My pack was heavier than I had ever carried—forty pounds. The two-hundred-mile distance, even broken into twenty-seven chunks, would require matching my longest single day's hike day after day after day. I had taken great care to plan for all contingencies, plans A, B, and Z. So, despite the anticipated rigor, I was cautiously confident that I would meet the physical challenges of the wilderness trail. It was a different kind of challenge that caused me more apprehension.

I knew this was going to be more than a physical journey. I wanted it to be a meaningful inner journey as well. I wanted to become one with nature, to commune with the natural world. I visualized myself sitting in meditative bliss at every stop—atop domes, beside streams, under forest canopies, and high above tree-line. I hoped all my planning and preparing would release me from worrying along the way and free me to be always in the present moment. Could it be one long walking meditation, like Thich Nhat Hanh describes in *Peace is Every Step*, as a way to inner peace? I hoped for a transformative journey, yet I recognized the irony of my yearnings.

Back across time I whisper, *Be careful what you wish for, dear girl!*

First Leg

Tuolumne Meadows To Red's Meadow
Day One to Day Six

Over The Rainbow

Between every two pine trees there is a door leading to a new way of life.
~ John Muir, Undated margin notes in
Prose Works by Ralph Waldo Emerson

Day One
July 19, 2006

Starting Point — Tuolumne Meadows Lodge Parking Lot — 8680 feet
Yosemite National Park

Our Sierra Odyssey began with limited fanfare on a circuitous dirt path at the edge of a parking lot. We had scoped out the trailhead after dinner the evening before, so that morning we made a beeline towards the jumping-off spot.

Jim parked the SUV and turned off the engine. "Ready or not, we're here," he said, rotating in his seat to face his three excited passengers.

"Let's do this!" Cappy's voice was firm with determination.

"Absolutely," I said. The sureness of my words matched my excitement, but certainly exceeded my actual confidence. Butterflies fluttered about in my stomach. *This is it*, I thought. The long-anticipated moment was upon us. I had spent months planning every detail of this expedition, and now I was about to set foot on the *real* John Muir Trail. My dream was about to be translated into boots on the ground.

"I'm ready." Jane was a purple picture of readiness—grape-colored socks, lavender boot laces, fuchsia Patagonia T-shirt, periwinkle bandana around her neck, and cheeks glowing pink with eagerness. Only her khaki shorts were standard issue.

I scrambled out and headed to the rear door to retrieve my backpack. My right foot propped on a parking bumper, I lifted my pack onto my knee, paused, then swung it onto my right shoulder, sliding my arm into the shoulder strap. Tipping forward, hands behind my back to push the pack upward, I flipped it onto the tabletop of my flat back. Leaning to my left, letting gravity pull the pack, I slipped my left arm into its shoulder strap. Bouncing it forward, higher up onto my upper back, I grabbed both ends of the hip-belt dangling in front of my belly. Straightening, I clicked the buckle closed and snugged the strap tighter on both sides, squeezing my stomach, so the pack sat squarely on my hipbones. I pulled down on the shoulder strap adjusters to cinch the frame to my upper back and clicked closed the chest strap.

"It's up. I'm in," I whispered to myself, pleased I had maneuvered myself into my pack without a hitch.

I had spent weeks winnowing down the weight of my backpack, ridding it of all nonessentials. I had test carried it scores of times. Yet when I wrestled it onto my back that morning, its forty pounds felt frighteningly heavy. *How am I going to carry this two hundred miles?* I thought. *How am I going to manage today's six miles?*

Do not say that out loud! I warned myself. I breathed deeply. I fingered the aspiration necklace at my throat—a silver chain with three flat rings, each inscribed with a single word—SPIRIT, STRENGTH, COURAGE. Touching each talisman calmed the butterflies and focused my mind.

I adjusted my CamelBak water bladder's sipping tube on my shoulder, checked the bandana I had tied around my neck, then reached into the SUV for my hat and hiking poles. Arranging the unusual hat on my head made me smile. Soft and green, it was a billed cap with a detachable flap of fabric that hung down in back to shield my neck and ears from the sun. It was reminiscent of hats worn by the French Foreign Legion in the North Africa deserts, or at least what Gary Cooper had worn in *Beau Geste*.

When I looked up, Cappy was making final adjustments to her pack's straps. Finished, Jane waited, a Mona Lisa smile on her face.

"Ready!" Cappy said, slipping her hands into the wrist straps of her hiking poles. Her eyes crinkled, part of the smile that consumed her whole face. She radiated giddy eagerness, reminding me of a hunting dog on point, frozen gracefully in mid-motion, leaning towards the trail.

The John Muir Trail, our very own Yellow Brick Road, began as a winding path circling the perimeter of Tuolumne Lodge, Campground, and parking lot. A crisp, no-nonsense sign beckoned us forward. Stenciled in white paint on brown, the icon of a hiking man and his arrow pointed the way.

JOHN MUIR TRAIL →

Eager to preserve our final moment on the threshold between civilization and wilderness, we stopped beside the sign for the ritual of posing for photographs— bon voyage tableaus of the three of us balancing loaded packs, all smiles, princess-waving—the sign symbolically front and center. Jim indulged us.

"You're going to walk a little way with us, aren't you?" Cappy asked Jim, looking him in the eye.

"Until my ankles tell me to stop," he said, his black 35mm camera slung around his neck and cap perched on his thick white hair. He was our "wingman" and had done all in his power the last couple of days to support us. His job that morning at the adventure's starting line was to record the moment of our departure in digital pixels. His final job would be to meet us in a month at the finish line, Whitney Portal.

"Look! Here's the *real* trailhead!" Cappy bounced and pointed, her face beaming as she spotted a second sign pointing the way. She had tied her willful salt-and-pepper curls back at the nape of her neck, and her long-sleeved hiking shirt was a pristine white, but neither effort calmed her giddy excitement. Her whole body vibrated.

We quickened our pace towards a broad-shouldered mountain-man of a sign. Old and venerable, its advice deeply carved in thick oak, the sign announced its version of "Follow the Yellow Brick Road!"

JOHN MUIR TRAIL →
PACIFIC CREST TRAIL →
DONOHUE PASS - 11.9 MI →

Again, we went through the ritual of posing at the journey's starting line. Poles planted firmly in front of her, Cappy stood beside the sign. In her hiking culottes, like a cute taupe mini-skirt, and sand-colored brimmed hat, the spitting image of a pith helmet, Cappy was the picture of an Old-World Doctor-Livingston-I-presume explorer-adventurer. She stood center-stage, with Jane and me as bookends.

Still the trail meandered, bending and twisting, avoiding a direct route. A third sign offered direction. *This has to be it,* I thought, *the real trailhead,* and my eagerness grew again. With delicately scalloped edges and capital letters cut clear through burnished iron, like designs in an embroidered sampler, it sang out, "Follow the John Muir Trail!"

JOHN MUIR TRAIL →

Each time a sign had appeared, we thought we had arrived at the threshold, and our excitement rose another notch. Each time, we were mistaken, and the trail continued to wander, making only stuttering progress.

At last, we came to a pair of wide wooden footbridges that together spanned the Lyell Fork of the Tuolumne River, stretching from one large granite boulder to another across the tumbling water. There, finally, beyond the water, the trail untangled itself and set off eastward, following the river's trajectory. There, finally, we strode across the boundary line, entered the wilderness, and began our Sierra Odyssey!

We bade farewell to Jim and his camera at 9:25 am on July 19, 2006, after one last photograph. Arms linked in the center of the first sturdy bridge, wearing our clean and shiny hiking gear, backpacks towering over our heads, we smiled. Looking back at that photo, I see I had already abandoned long sleeves and wore my turquoise tank top over my shorts. Our faces, each partially hidden in the shade of a hat brim, radiated eagerness with broad smiles. For the last time we, and everything we wore, were spotlessly clean. With a final salute to Jim and civilization, we turned to face the wild Sierra.

"We're off to see the Wizard, the Wonderful Wizard of Oz!" I sang, as our boots clomped across the bridge's wooden planks and onto the famous trail itself.

"Follow the Yellow Brick Road—follow the John Muir Trail!" It felt as magical and momentous as if, instead of walking on a dirt path that slipped between rocks and trees, we were spiraling outward on bright yellow paving stones and headed towards the Emerald City!

"I can't believe it! We're on the *real*—the *actual*—John Muir Trail!" Cappy announced when the singing came to an end. "I've dreamed of this for years and years, and here we are!"

I could barely believe it either. Two years had passed since I had first started planning my JMT journey, an expedition that had evolved into a nearly unrecognizable venture—different year, different companions, different equipment—yet my dream had survived all the obstacles and setbacks. The puzzle pieces had come together, and I was striding along the historic path. A month of spectacular possibilities lay ahead. I touched my necklace and felt deep gratitude.

Overhead, lodgepole pines shielded us from the sun. Underfoot, the needle-carpeted ground was littered with ball-sized rocks, fallen twigs, and cones. People traveled that well-worn section of the trail in multitudes—day hikers, weekend campers, and backpackers. We encountered individuals and groups headed in both directions on that busy stretch. Members of a large family, all clad in bright beachwear, toted towels, small coolers, and sand chairs. They were headed for a swimming hole along the Lyell Fork, a spot rumored to have slippery slides of polished granite.

The forest was broken up by open spaces where the trail marched over gray stone slabs or sandy stretches of decomposing granite marked by cairns—small towers of balanced stones (sometimes strangely called "ducks")—or dotted-lines made from long rows of small rocks arranged along the trail's margins. The sun was warm, and the air was tinged with fine granite dust kicked up by hikers crunching along the trail's gritty surface. Then the forest resumed its dominance, and the trail became a brown dirt path in the shade once again.

The forest was quiet, absorbing noise so efficiently that people were out-of-sound before they were out-of-sight. In still moments, when we walked single file, squirrels scampered across the path from one tree to the next, disappearing around the backside of a trunk. Woodpeckers' rat-a-tatting drifted on the forest air.

We were spread out along the trail—Cappy the lead, me the caboose. Even on level ground, I utilized my hiking poles, swinging them in rhythm with my feet—right foot with left pole, left foot with right pole. On a smooth, flat trail, they were not for balance or stability, but to extend stride length by adding a tiny arm-powered launch to each step. Feeling playful, I made a game of speeding up and slowing down, catching up and falling back, along the mostly even pathway.

Together, the river and the trail made a gradual sweeping turn and emerged from the forest into a vast, green meadow that stretched the full length and width of Lyell Basin.

Our pace slowed, then halted.

Side-by-side, we remained silent, taking in the grandeur of the valley spread out before us. My eyes swept across the breadth of the landscape, but found the panoramic view too much to absorb. Like an optical illusion, first it appeared flat, two-dimensional. As my eyes adjusted to the vast depth, the myriad colors began to shimmer, as though light were streaming towards us through a brilliantly colored stained-glass window. Had we come upon an enchanted place?

My eyes teased apart the scene. Tall, tree-covered mountain ridges rose abruptly to either side. Stretching ahead into the distance as converging parallel lines, they defined the eastern and western edges of the valley. A taller granite wall, spotted with snow and topped with serrations, marked the southern end, but that was miles ahead, a distant background. The meadow grasses and sedges that filled the entire valley floor were such a vivid emerald green, they would have tricked an Irishwoman into believing she was home.

In the foreground, wildflowers colored the meadow, too, with dense circles of yellow here and swaths of white or purple there, a dusting of pink, and stripes of blue. Under the influence of a gentle breeze, white wisps of clouds drifted across the sky and everything green swayed and rustled.

"Wow!" I said, nearly inarticulate, my eyes continuing to sweep the sublime scene, trying to separate the details from the bigger picture. Had I walked through the looking glass like Alice?

"It's so classic Sierra—" Cappy's words brought me back to earth. "—but it still takes my breath away every single time I come to the mountains."

Jane walked out into the meadow, bending to look closely at a patch of purple flowers swaying atop long stems all around her legs. She picked just one and brought it back to us, taking care to retrace her footsteps.

"What's that?" Cappy asked, stepping forward, her boots disappearing into the green, to look closely at the small flower Jane held in her hand.

"Sierra penstemon." She passed the flower to Cappy, who took it by the stem and turned to hold it out where I could see. At the top of the stem was a circle of delicate inch-long trumpet-shaped flowers, deep violet on the outside, lavender-tinged-pink on the inside.

"Beautiful. I like the way the purple merges with the pink, so it looks like electric color," I said. Then wondered, "Does that make sense?"

"It does, actually." Cappy laughed. She flipped up her sunglasses and held the flower closer to her eyes.

"Penstemons come in a variety of purplish hues and slightly different shapes. They're common in the Sierra," Jane said. "We'll come across lots of these and various cousins along the way."

"What do you think about a break soon?" I said. "I could use a snack."

"Let's walk another half-hour then stop," Cappy said. "We can picnic in the meadow."

And so we did.

The trail was a narrow track, one person wide, pressed deep into the grassy landscape by the weight and pressure of the tens of thousands of footsteps that had preceded us. The walkway had become a swale, running along below the surface of the ground through which it cut by as much as ten inches. In some places, the trail was so swampy with standing water that we were forced to walk on its verge to avoid wading in slippery mud. Where this had happened often, two or more parallel stripes sliced through the grass.

During years of hiking in the Sierra, I had become enamored of the romantic idea of the trail—that path through the wilderness that is also a symbol of one's journey through life. My grand JMT plan included an artistic goal—I intended to shoot a series of photographs with the trail itself as subject, not just part of the scenery. I had purchased a new digital camera, Nikon's latest compact model, with that project in mind. For months, I had been imagining myself gathering iconic trail shots—the path confidently striding straight towards the horizon, or mysteriously disappearing around a dark curve, or heading into a tunnel made of arching tree branches. There would be pictures of cairns marking rocky paths and granite steps climbing canyon walls. I was not exactly sure what I was going to do with them in the end, but I would come up with something interesting, I was sure.

Our path through the meadow had turned into three muddy trail stripes, triplets cutting parallel lines through the rich green grasses. They would be the first subjects for my trail project.

"Hold up for a minute," I called ahead. "I want this picture." Cappy and Jane indulged me, waiting as I composed the scene.

First, I crouched low and aimed along the trail so the camera could capture the way the footpaths had settled into narrow channels in the meadow. Then I stood tall, allowing the sun glinting on the dampness to turn the mud into ribbons of chocolate-brown satin. I took a third with the toe of my boot just visible in the corner of the frame.

"This is such a fun idea," Cappy encouraged me.

"Thanks." I put my camera back into the deep pocket of my shorts. "Lead on." Again, we set off down the trail, Cappy out front.

The river, which had been hidden from us, revealed only by occasional gurgles and splashes when we had hiked in the forest, came into full view. Broad and deep, slipping along at a saunter, the Lyell Fork seeped past its banks well into the meadow, flexing its springtime muscles and turning the ground marshy. Within its granite channel, the water slid by like the crystal-clear, green-colored glass of a vintage Coca-Cola bottle, revealing golden rock lining its depths and tiny fish playing in eddies.

After Cappy's prescribed half-hour, we paused for a quick rest and sprawled in the grass. I lay on my back, hands pillowing my head. We munched snacks and wondered aloud at the intensity of the colors that surrounded us.

"We are smack-dab in the middle of a rainbow," I said. "Look. I can reach out and touch seven different flowers, seven different colors." I swept my arms slowly and gently, like I was making the upper half of a snow-angel in the grass, brushing just the tops of the stems.

"I can, too. But, other than this pretty penstemon, I can't tell you what any of them are," Cappy said.

"And you and I can only name that one, because Jane just told us!" I laughed. The air was rich with a rainbow of scents, too. The bottom layer came from the rich loamy aroma of the damp earth and the tangy sweetness of grass. On top lay an intoxicating perfume, a mixture of scents from the array of flowers that surrounded us.

"Agreed!" Cappy said. "Though I'm pretty sure this pink one is clover." I looked where she pointed and recognized the pink puffball flowers.

"You get a gold star. That's a clover," Jane confirmed.

I rolled on my side and watched a plump black bumblebee as it slowly worked its way through a patch of Cappy's fuzzy pink pom-poms. It bounced and weaved a drunken path, mounds of gold pollen loaded on its furry legs.

"Lying in a rainbow. I like that," Cappy said. "You have a way with words, Joan. And Jane has a way with plants." She had sat up and was running her fingers through her curls, getting it all going the same direction again and then arranging it into a loose braid at her neck.

"And you're our map expert," I said, assigning credit where it was due. She had a real handle on where we were at any given moment and where we were headed.

"On that note, ladies, it's time." Cappy stretched and twisted her back, then stood to ready her belongings. "I think we've gone almost three miles. That leaves about three-and-a-half to go."

I arched my back until it clicked a couple times, then stood to follow her lead. In minutes, we were back on the trail.

Moving together in a tight knot, we shared stories as we walked on the level ground. It had ducked back under the shelter of trees but kept to the edge of the meadow, so the views remained stunning. So far, our adventure had been a literal "walk in the park." A quarter-mile later, however, that would change abruptly.

"It was a long time ago," I said, "but I've been on this trail before. I was fifteen. I'd nearly forgotten, but somehow, I remember this valley, this particular scene, the meadow grasses and the dark peaks..."

The next instant, I was on the ground. I had stepped wrong and turned my ankle.

Mid-fall, I managed to roll to my left side to minimize my impact with the ground, and I had gotten my hands out in front to keep my head from hitting the dirt. My knees and palms stung, but my left ankle screamed!

I was embarrassed.

I could not get up. I was stuck. Like a turtle on its back, I struggled to right myself under the forty pounds of my pack.

I was *really* embarrassed.

I was walking at the back of our three-person procession, when I crumpled to the ground. I'm not sure if it was my sharp yelp or my dull thud that turned Cappy and Jane around.

"Are you okay?" Cappy asked.

"What happened?" asked Jane as they hurried to retrace their steps.

I held my breath and gritted my teeth to avoid crying out. I fumbled with the plastic buckles that fixed me to my pack. *No tears,* I instructed myself. Once the straps were free, Jane and Cappy together lifted my pack and set it aside. I rolled into a sitting position. I could see my knees, and they were bloody. So were my palms.

When the pain had subsided enough for me to produce some words, they exploded out, "Not again! This did not just happen!" My breath came in gulps, and my heart pounded against my breastbone.

It took a few minutes for the pain to change from stabbing to throbbing. Then, with help from my friends, I stood up on my undamaged leg. I hobbled and minced my way to a nearby log, then sat to assess the damage.

"Better?" Cappy asked. Worry and concern were painted across her tightened face as she studied my own.

"What happened?" Jane repeated her question.

"My left ankle gives out every now and again, usually when I step on a rock or something." I looked around on the ground. "It was probably one of those." I pointed to the place where partially exposed tree roots stretched across the trail like fat snakes. "I heard a definite 'Pop!' when it happened. Then I felt it click back in afterwards."

"Will you be able to walk on it?" Jane asked. Was she worried we would have to turn around?

No way will I give up. No way will I go back, I thought.

"What should we do to help?" Cappy asked.

"I'll be able to walk in a few minutes. I just need to sit here for a bit." I was starting to breathe easier, and my heart had stopped its crashing. "I'll take some Advil and then wrap it, so it won't swell too much."

I pointed Cappy to the zippered compartment where I kept my first aid kit. While I unlaced my boot, she found the pills and the elastic bandage. I wrapped my ankle and replaced my boot quickly to beat the swelling process. Jane dampened my bandana so I could wipe the blood from my knees and hands. Cappy opened the Advil container and brought me water to drink.

Keeping our hands and our minds busy solving the immediate problems kept us all calm. As quickly as the adrenaline had flooded my system when I fell, it receded once the situation was under control. I was able to relax and breathe calmly. I even smiled. Seeing that, Jane and Cappy relaxed, too. Lines of stress softened. Still, we took a few extra minutes to regroup. I touched the rings on my necklace— courage, strength, spirit—I needed another dose.

We set off again, tentatively at first. My companions insisted I walk between them, so they could keep an eye on me, Cappy ahead, Jane behind. Though I hated feeling weak and needy, though I hated being babied, I relinquished control and followed their directions.

We paused by the river's edge in the deep shade of a circle of trees to rest and eat lunch. The circular space on the forest floor was sprinkled with a thick carpet of needles and dotted with cones. Arranged like a living room grouping of sofa and chairs, round gray boulders and a long, thick log offered us comfortable seating.

It was our first luncheon on the trail, so it generated a certain amount of excitement. Which of the myriad foods I had packed should be my first meal? Should I complete the task of pumping water before sitting to eat? Should we take a long leisurely meal break, or press on after a quick stop? Should I unlace my boot and see to my sprained ankle, or leave it snuggly wrapped in my boot? That last question haunted my thoughts as I tried to focus on the others.

Jane and I chose to complete our water-filtering tasks before settling down to eat. It seemed appropriate—work first, then pleasure. From a side pouch in my brown Kelty pack, I pulled a red cinch-bag, the size of a thick paperback, which held my water-filtering pump. I grabbed my CamelBak water bladder and my extra water bottle from their pack-pockets before heading for the river's edge.

Jane joined me where the land slanted towards the water and we scouted for a good spot. We had to walk several yards before we found a small dark blue pool where the river ran deep and slow.

"How about this spot? It looks like a gem," Jane said.

"Perfect," I said.

She sat down on a small rock, assembling her water containers around her. I took a little longer settling my ankle and myself comfortably on the ground. I found a tree root that stood out above the mud where the river's flow had eroded the earth away from it, making a miniature bench that was almost comfortable. I curled one leg around the seat but had to stick the damaged one straight out to the side. If it bent too much, I could feel my heart beating in my ankle, which I did not think was a good sign.

I pulled the cylindrical pump with its two long flexible tubes from the red bag. The black tube, tipped with a mud filter, I tossed towards the water. The filter hit the surface eighteen inches from my foot and sank a few inches, a float keeping it suspended above the muddy bottom. The clear tube I stretched to my CamelBak, placing its end into the top of the three-liter container. With each push and pull of a lever, the pump sucked water from the river, forced it through a dense clay filter inside the cylinder, and pushed it into the CamelBak. Three liters took a few minutes of continuous pumping. Jane kept me company, the tubes in their proper places, and the containers upright, while I levered the water up into all the receptacles, first mine, then hers.

The river gurgled as it entered and left the little pool at our feet. The sun was high overhead, so its rays penetrated clear to the bottom of the river. Schools of small fish hid in the shadows near rocks and sunken branches, occasionally darting out in a game of chase, only to return at some stimulus to the safety of their hiding places. The air around us was moist and cool.

Water containers full, we returned to the circle of trees where we had left Cappy. I perched on the log-sofa while Cappy and Jane assembled themselves on rock-chairs. Opening our bear canisters, we began lunch preparations.

Not many years earlier, bears had been a significant nuisance, even a danger, to hikers in the Sierra Nevada. California's black bears were so smart, so wily, they had become adept at stealing people's food. Working individually or in family groups, they had discovered a plethora of ways to steal unwary campers' food. Mother bears taught their babies to climb out long flexible branches to the spots where bags of food hung from thin ropes. The cubs would bounce on the thin branches until the suspended bag crashed to the ground, or until it came close enough for the mother bear to rip out the bag's bottom. If that did not work, the cub would chew through the rope and the bag would fall.

Hanging bags of food, which for decades had been the prescribed "best practice" to keep bears from moving right into tents, no longer worked. Bears were an even greater danger to themselves than they were to campers. Those repeatedly caught in the act were put down.

By 2006, all JMTers and backcountry hikers were required to carry bear canisters. Some canisters, like Cappy's, are black and require a coin, used like a screwdriver, to open. Others are like large transparent screw-top jars. Mine was like that, a blue plastic jar with a black screw-on lid. Even I had difficulty getting it open, so I knew it was safe from marauding wildlife. Sitting, I had to hold it tightly between my calves, gripping the bottom with the arched soles of my shoes, and use both my hands and my full upper body strength to twist the top open. It was like wrestling with a giant-sized childproof container.

According to the literature that came with my canister, it had been tested on zoo bears. Canisters containing fresh salmon were tossed into several bear enclosures, leaving the animals to puzzle over the containers for days—chewing, tossing, pounding, even throwing them, all to no avail. Only then were the canisters sold to the wilderness-loving public. It did not take long for the wild bears to give up, too. After several years of use in Yosemite National Park, reported cases of bear-human incidents fell precipitously, from fifteen-hundred to under fifty annually.[3] By 2006, it was rare to encounter a bear on the JMT—they had learned there was zero possibility food would be available, so they mostly leave backcountry hikers in peace.

With the canister open, I pulled out a summer sausage sealed in a Ziploc bag. The sausage, once unsealed, would last only a couple of days in our refrigerator-less world, so it would be the first entrée I consumed. With my pocketknife, I cut the long sausage in two, intending to eat only half. Then I pulled out a small bag of crackers. Wielding my knife, I cut the sausage into several thin slices. I counted out an equal number of crackers and then paired them up, one slice of the greasy meat on each cracker. Popping one into my mouth, I chewed and crunched. There's nothing quite like a slice of savory sausage, full of fatty calories, after a morning of intense walking. Between the salt, the fat, and the dry cracker, the treat screamed to be washed down with a long swallow of sweet water fresh from the mountain stream and complemented with a handful of sweet-and-tart dried mango. It does not get better.

Cappy had spent the time while Jane and I were pumping water reviewing our topo maps.[4] Between bites, she explained what we could expect in the afternoon. "After crossing the bridge here," she pointed, "the trail stays close to the river on the other side before it comes back across about a mile ahead."

"How far have we hiked?" Jane asked. "And how much farther to our campsite?"

---

[3] Lisa Morehouse and Marissa Ortega Welch, "A Brief History of Bear-Proofing In Yosemite, From a Garbage Dump to Canisters" (KQED News – The California Report, August 15, 2018). https://www.kqed.org/news/11687093/a-brief-history-of-bear-proofing-in-yosemite-from-canisters-to-a-garbage-dump

[4] *Harrison's Topographic Maps of the John Muir Trail*, a series of thirteen full-color, highly detailed maps printed on indestructible plastic-paper (Tom Harrison Maps, 2005).

"We're over halfway—about four miles—leaving two-and-a-half to go," Cappy said. "It's been really flat so far, but in that final mile, the trail leaves the river and starts to climb up the hillside on this side of the valley." She pointed again.

Wiping my fingers on my bandana, I pulled Winnett's guidebook from its pack-pocket and flipped to that day's trail section.[5] As I was about to read aloud, we were joined at our al fresco dining spot by two other southbound (SOBO) hikers.

A young couple—they looked to be in their late twenties or early thirties—stopped a few feet away from where we sat. Both carried huge packs, which they dropped immediately with heavy thuds. The woman's seemed especially large and somewhat top-heavy.

"I'm Cappy. My friends are Joan and Jane." Playing the role of team ambassador, she had us all deep in conversation within minutes.

The exotic-looking thirty-something man, with dark eyes, brown skin, and a blue bandana tied around his head, walked our way, his right hand outstretched ready to shake. Jane and I were quickly on our feet to meet his overture.

"Great to meet you all. My name is Nicodemo," he said while shaking first one hand then another. "People call me Nemo for short."

Turning to gesture towards his obviously tired hiking partner, he introduced Zoe. Attractive, twenty-something, tall and blond, her athlete's body drooped with exhaustion. Zoe smiled and said her hellos.

"You three walking the whole JMT?" Nemo asked, smiling. He rubbed his shoulders and stretched his back exactly like we had done upon our arrival.

"We are!" Cappy said, while Jane and I nodded our own proud agreement.

"Did you leave Tuolumne this morning?" I asked.

It turned out they had crossed the Yellow Brick Road Bridge just a half-hour behind us and had been following us across Lyell Canyon all morning. There was something particularly exciting about meeting our first trail friends, total strangers who, through the choice of being on the same trail going the same direction on the same day, became instant fast friends. We would bond with several other hikers in the days to come, but Zoe and Nemo would always be our first trail buddies.

Settling back down on our rock and log seats, the conversation continued while we three put away our lunch things, and they got out theirs. We learned that Zoe

---

[5] Thomas Winnett and Kathy Morey, *Guide to the John Muir Trail* (Wilderness Press, 1998).

and Nemo were both brand new to backpacking and had begun this adventure almost on a whim. Zoe was an experienced rock-climber and the trip's planner. Nemo was her enthusiastic, last-minute hiking sidekick.

"Where are you two headed today?" Cappy asked.

"We hope to get to a spot called Lyell Forks. The guidebook says that there are a handful of good campsites there," Zoe said.

"That's where we're headed, too," I said. I was glad to hear we'd have company on our first night out—it would not feel so alone out in the wilderness that way.

As we packed up our final loose ends, they both worked on Zoe's pack, adjusting the straps, trying to get it to fit better, to sit properly on her hipbones. The pack appeared to be too large for her frame and quite heavy besides, and Zoe had already developed some nasty sores and bruises on her hips and shoulders that were making the hike painful. The rule of thumb for pack weight is to carry no more than twenty-five or thirty percent of your body weight. Zoe's pack weighed over fifty pounds, well beyond that limit. We gave a few gentle suggestions about her straps but did not feel comfortable saying any more.

Cappy, Jane, and I hefted our own packs and took off along the trail. The cute puffy clouds that had decorated the sky earlier in the day had multiplied into towering bunches and were quickly turning the sky from blue to gray.

"It's going to rain again this afternoon," Cappy said, scanning the clouds.

"We still have plenty of walking time, but let's make sure to have our tents up before it starts," replied Jane. Like Cappy, Jane's hair was salt-and-pepper, but that is where the similarity ended. While Cappy's fell in long, unruly ringlets she was always attempting to corral, Jane's was thick and straight, cut bluntly just below her chin into a simple bob.

"I hate setting up my tent in the rain. Let's keep one eye on the weather, and I'll walk as fast as I can." I was determined not to let my ankle slow us down any more.

After another hour of hiking, the trail left the river and began to climb up along the edge of Lyell Canyon, hugging the higher ground to the west and hiding under the trees. As the sky continued to darken and sounds of thunder rolled down from the mountain peaks up ahead, we found a pair of campsites on a flat spot above the trail, right where the guidebook said they would be—Lyell Forks Campsite, at just over nine-thousand feet, perched on a "forested bench." It was described as the perfect place to launch a morning ascent of our first big mountain pass, Donohue.

No sooner had we lowered our heavy loads to the ground than a few large raindrops plopped in the dirt. We scurried to unstrap tent parts from packs and retrieve wet weather gear, while also keeping the packs covered to protect their contents from the rain.

The tents went up quickly. That was something we had practiced over and over during our spring and early summer preparatory hikes. It was still technically daylight at only five in the evening, so it felt peculiar to crawl into sleeping bags. But the storm was growing, and Jane and I had no intention of remaining outside. That first night was a test of my packing strategies and my memory, with the rain pressing me to locate things in my pack quickly.

Jane and I retired to our shared tent, careful to leave boots and mud outside, but still under the rainfly. Cappy pitched her smaller tent just a few feet away. We decided to wait a while before cooking, with hopes that the storm would pass, and we could emerge for dinner.

While we waited warm and dry in our nylon cocoons, Zoe and Nemo struggled into the campsite adjacent to ours. With shapeless and dripping plastic ponchos draped over both bodies and packs, they looked like grotesque, navy blue hunchbacks trudging out of the forest.

Cappy, wearing her own raingear and boots, dashed to greet the pair and help them assemble their tent. Jane and I, less gregarious than Cappy, remained inside our warm tent and contemplated how we were going to cook our dinners without having to emerge again.

"Cappy's so nice," Jane said. "Should I go out and help, too?"

"I'm feeling a tad guilty," I said, "but I'm thinking any more hands on their tent would just get in the way—too many cooks in the kitchen."

Watching through the tent's zipper-door opening and the curtains of rain, we saw their tent pop up several yards away. It was a twin to the tent where Jane and I lay watching—a pale gray-green dome trimmed with black and orange.

Cappy returned, her foul weather gear dripping, and climbed back inside her own tent.

The rain did not relent, so we cooked our meals under the tents' rainflies that evening. I sat dry, just inside our tent's zippered doorway, arms extended to the stove setting just outside under the cloth awning. I boiled water and poured it into the cooking bag that held my freeze-dried entrée—beef-and-bean chili. While it steeped in my insulated mug, I moved away from the doorway, so Jane could use my JetBoil stove to heat water for her own entrée.

After dinner, we tucked ourselves in for the night. I was surprised at just how tired my body felt, even as I lay wide awake thinking. I was worried about the morning. I was worried my ankle would swell, and my boot would not fit. I was worried about blisters, too. When I had removed my boots, I discovered that what I thought was just a "hot spot" was actually a pair of nasty, nickel-sized blisters growing on my heel where the edge of the elastic ankle bandage had rubbed my skin raw. The solution to one problem had created another.

You cannot toss and turn when you are sharing a tent. Just rolling over once creates a commotion. Nylon rubbing on nylon is a grating sound. And you are sure to bump against your tent-mate in the tight quarters. So, I lay as still as possible. My mind, however, tossed and turned on its own, creating a commotion inside my head that kept me awake.

Eventually, I did sleep. I know I did, because two or three times in the inky darkness, I was startled awake by a flash of brilliant light and its answering crash of thunder.

Starting Point — Tuolumne Meadows Lodge Parking Lot — 8680 feet
Ending Point — Lyell Forks Campsite — 9000 feet
Highest Point — Lyell Forks Campsite — 9000 feet
Distance Covered — 6.5 miles
Cumulative Miles — 6.5 miles

Lost And Found

Only a few find the way;
some don't recognize it when they do;
some don't ever want to!
~ Cheshire Cat, *Alice in Wonderland*, Lewis Carroll, 1865

Day Two

July 20, 2006

Starting Point — Lyell Forks Campsite — 9000 feet

It was eight o'clock, and the sun had just made its appearance above the high mountain ridge to the east, its rays streaming into our campsite with the intensity of a spotlight. Steam rose from our wet tents in the sudden warmth.

Together, my tent and I performed a slow-motion sun dance around the campsite. Each time the long triangular tree shadows crept across the wet ground and threatened to block the drying rays, I spun the tent back into the full sun. I sat down to eat breakfast, then moved my tent. I washed my face and smoothed on sunscreen, then moved my tent. I carefully wrapped my ankle, then moved my tent. Round and round the campsite my tent and I spun, chasing the light and dodging the long shadows.

Eventually, the nylon dried, and I was able to fold it, roll it, and pack it away.

Jane and Cappy finished their preparations almost in unison. They were packed and eager to set out. My ankle-wrapping and tent-dancing meant I was holding us up.

"You almost ready, Joan?" Cappy asked. She stood with her hand resting atop her pack, like she was deciding if she should hoist it or wait. She still wore her jacket against the cool air, but her curls had been subdued, hat and sunglasses arranged.

"Almost. I need five minutes." I was still bandaging my blisters, cutting moleskin into precise donut shapes to fit over each one, then taping over that cushioning layer with long strips of white first-aid tape. My ankle was tender and stiff, but I was pretty sure the stiffness would ease as it warmed up with walking.

While I finished up—lacing boots, packing away first aid supplies, zipping pouches—Jane and Cappy wandered over to our neighbors' site to check in and say farewell. Tasks completed, I fingered my necklace, lifting the silver circles up so I could read them again—courage, spirit, strength—whispering the words.

Today, it's strength I need most, I thought. *There will be no further falling down*, I instructed myself, before tucking the charms into my collar and heading over to join the chatting group next door.

"I just hope we don't get another storm like last night," Nemo was saying when I walked up. His eyebrows arched towards the red bandana that held back his thick black hair, making his already big brown eyes huge, and he tipped his head back to scan sky. I followed his gaze, sweeping my eyes across the expanse of blue and saw not a single cloud.

"We got soaked on our way here," Zoe said. "These are the only clothes I have that aren't damp," she indicated her long khaki pants and pullover.

"We're hoping to get to our camping spot by mid-afternoon," Cappy said. "That way we can have our tents up before any evening rains."

That statement prompted quick goodbyes. We returned to our waiting packs, loaded up, and were on the trail in a few minutes.

"See ya down the trail!" I called over my shoulder.

All morning, the footpath followed the Lyell Fork as it rose in the direction of Lyell Peak and Donohue Pass. While we climbed southbound (SOBO), the river descended northward. The trail clung to the west side of the lush Lyell Valley floor, preferring the shade of the woods that ran along its edges and climbed its walls like fans in the bleachers overlooking a mile-long soccer field.

Narrow beams of sunlight found their way through the thick canopy of dark green needles and decorated the duff-covered trail with golden spots. The dappling played tricks on my eyes, the shifting spots of light and dark camouflaging potential ankle-turning landmines like small cones, bare roots, and depressions. Cautious, I kept my focus on the spot where I intended to place my next step. Every now and again, I would pause to survey the view I was missing while I walked along looking down at my feet.

The valley grew narrower, the swaths of trees on either side drawing closer, conspiring to squeeze out the meadow between them. Challenging our endurance for the first time, the trail, though not steep, rose steadily. With each step, I used my hiking poles to lift some of my body and pack weight off my left leg to protect my weak ankle from overuse.

We were strung out in a three-person game of follow-the-leader, trading places occasionally, each of us taking a turn as lead and a turn as tail. While normally I enjoyed being leader, that day I preferred staying at the back of the line. When I walked ahead, I could feel Cappy's and Jane's eyes studying my left ankle, watching to see if I was limping or favoring it. I knew my friends were concerned about me, but I am not good at being on the receiving end of doting and worried attention.

Instead of feeling grateful, I felt embarrassed, and my own attention on my ankle seemed to magnify the discomfort. With each flexing of the joint, a moderate jolt of warm pain drew a ring around my ankle, and the stiff heel of the boot chafed the growing hot spots it was supposed to be protecting.

Hikers have different walking styles, like people have different temperaments. I observed Cappy and Jane as they strode ahead. The smallest of us, Cappy was like a pixie with a bounce in her step. Her short legs gave her a petite scampering stride. She could walk steadily, on and on, rarely stopping, her muscular little legs churning right along, relentless, indefatigable, though still covering ground slowly.

Jane, taller than both Cappy and me, had a smoother stride. Compared to Cappy, she appeared to glide down the trail, walking erect and statuesque, her longer legs stretching out in front of her like a dancer carving a wave through the air. Like Cappy, she could walk and walk and walk, rarely stopping.

My pattern was different. I certainly did not bounce like Cappy nor glide like Jane. I often counted my steps into sets of eight—one, two, three, four, five, six, seven, eight—a habit I had developed when I was a kid on swim team and counted my strokes as I swam my workout laps. Unlike my partners, I preferred a quicker pace with frequent brief pauses—for just a minute or two—sometimes for a photo-op, sometimes an oxygen or water break, sometimes to admire the landscape I was moving through. The counting, like a metronome to a musician, kept my steps regular and my progress consistent. That day, the counting also served as a distraction from my left foot.

We stopped for an early lunch and rest in the shade beside the tumbling Lyell Fork. Sitting on a rock on the riverbank, pumping to fill my drinking bladder, I watched the river rush along.

Moving water is a living, breathing creature. Watching flowing water is like listening to a symphony orchestra. If you attend closely, you can pick out the contribution of each note, each instrument, each drop of water, each ripple. Simultaneously, you can enjoy the beauty of the whole composition, the entire river. I would have been content to sit in the shade beside the Lyell for hours, mesmerized by the dynamic colors and patterns of its motion—deep blues, near to violet, transparent aquas and greens, swirling lines and starbursts of reflected silver and gold.

Jane and I propped ourselves by the water's edge on flat stones that sat like a scalloped fringe alongside the moving light and color. In peaceful silence, we watched the water while we pumped to refill our bottles and bladders. I paused a moment to toss a stone into the creek. The widening concentric circles sailed downstream and disappeared. Watching them made me smile. Then I returned to my pumping.

Jane found a round, flat rock, a perfect skipping shape, and flung it across the surface. It skipped once, twice, sinking on the third, sending out into the current three competing sets of circles.

"Nicely done." I smiled. My eyes scanned the ground within reach around me, scouting for another skipping stone. There were none, so I contented myself with tossing another oblong rock into the water and watching its circles sail downstream.

I coiled the pump's tubes and packed it away into its little red bag, then we gathered up the full water containers and joined Cappy, where she sat studying the map and guidebook.

"Learn anything new?" I sat down on a fallen log beside my pack.

"Nothing new. I was just trying to figure out exactly where we are," Cappy said. "I think the real climbing is going to start very soon, maybe just a half mile or so ahead."

For two days we had been watching the looming hulk of Mount Lyell grow closer and taller. Streaked with the white of snow and ice, it stood black and sharp against the sky. It had begun distant and small, but with each step it grew mightier. When the trail retreated to the woods, the mountain disappeared; when it wandered out into the meadow, the peak and its ring of neighbors dominated the valley and scratched the sky.

I ate quickly, so I would have time to attend to my feet before we moved on. My ankle was still tender, but the hotspots on the back of my heel and the pad of my foot were giving me real pains. Peeling off my socks revealed blisters growing atop blisters. The combination of a firmly fitting boot and the elastic bandage I had been wearing to stabilize my tender ankle had resulted in so much rubbing and chafing that several grand blisters were growing where the edge of the bandage pressed on my skin.

When hiking, I had always had trouble with blisters, so I had come armed with reams of moleskin and yards of white first-aid tape. Better to have extra, I'd figured, and that had been a good choice. As it turned out, I might need every square inch of both.

Blisters now populated the pads of both big toes, the ball of my left foot, as well as my left heel, where small bubbles of liquid were ballooning on the surface of yesterday's nickel-sized pink circles. I had never known, when dealing with blisters, if it is better to drain the fluid to reduce the tenderness and chafing, or to leave them inflated to avoid infection. The large blister on the pad of my big toe had popped itself and begun to ooze. It looked gross—crusty and scabbed—so I left the others un-popped and spread a glob of Neosporin across the broken blister.

I had bandaged and taped my feet in the morning with moleskin and white tape, but with each step, my boot had worked to dislodge and destroy my handiwork. The loose, wadded remains of those efforts had exacerbated the injuries.

Sans boots and socks, my feet were enjoying fresh air and freedom of movement. Briefly pain-free, I seriously considered abandoning my flesh-eating boots altogether and walking the trail in my Teva sandals. Without sturdy boots to support my arches and ankles though, I worried I might permanently injure my feet and be unable to complete the two hundred miles. So, second-guessing myself, I decided walking long distances in sandals would be foolhardy.

I am not comfortable with weakness, especially when it's my own. When I had fallen and sprained my ankle, the damage to my pride had been worse than the damage to my body. The fear that I might slow down our progress, that Cappy and Jane would have to wait for me, was more troubling than the shooting pain. I was determined—I would not be needy or weak. I would "keep calm and carry on." This plague of blisters was just another test. I would not let them slow me down, either. I joked about them to disguise my worries. *Was I a weakling? Was my body undependable?*

Starting over, I reconstructed the protective moleskin architecture. Then, I experimented with longer pieces of tape—encircling my feet and ankles so the tape could be attached securely to more layers of tape rather than to my sweaty skin. When finished, I again donned my thick hiking socks and laced up my evil boots.

After lunch, the trail crossed the Lyell on a sturdy wooden bridge, then continued to follow along its eastern edge, climbing through forests of stately trees and small meadows studded with tiny alpine lakes. Inexplicably, the trail emerged from the woods and simply stopped at the edge of the river, which had become a "lakelet," as the *Winnett's Guide* described it.[6] Surrounded on three sides by steep mountains and standing on a wide "beach" of sand and rocks where the trail emerged from the trees, we were confused. A sheer granite cliff blocked the way forward to the south and the east. There was supposed to be a place to ford the river, so we could head west towards snow-covered Donohue Pass looming on the other side. But all we saw was the "lakelet" with no way across or around it. We removed our packs, leaned them against trees, and scoured the beachhead for forensic clues left by those who had gone before us. We were surrounded by footprints and a web of fanned-out trails, but could make neither heads nor tails out of the jumble.

Stymied, thinking we had either walked too far or not far enough, we wandered up and down the lakelet's edge, consulting the map and *Winnett's*, reading and re-reading its directions: "ford just below the lakelet" from east to west. For thirty minutes, we marched around in circles and questioned ourselves. It was a puzzle we could not solve.

As I wandered afoot searching for physical clues, I wandered around inside my head, too, asking questions and searching for clues. We had just embarked on our two-hundred-mile expedition, and already we were lost. Civilization lay only ten miles to our rear, and we were lost. I had barely stepped into the wilderness, and I was lost. Physically lost. Mentally lost. Emotionally lost.

I ended up back where Cappy stood near the packs, staring at the place where the trail had emerged from the trees.

"This doesn't make sense," she said, hands on her hips, brow deeply furrowed.

"I just don't get it," I agreed. I sat down on a rock and scrutinized the lakelet and its far edges.

Jane had walked farther along the lakelet's shore and was just returning to ground-zero. "Nothing," she said. Then silence descended.

The bubble of enthusiasm, which had surrounded us all morning, rapidly deflated, leaving us in despair of ever finding the way across. Time was slipping through our fingers, and we needed to figure out how to proceed.

---

[6] Thomas Winnett and Kathy Morey, *Guide to the John Muir Trail* (Wilderness Press, 1998) p. 21.

From our granite seats, we scanned the mountain and the cliff sides that rose to the west, looking for any sign of the trail leading to the top, and searching for the notch that might be Donohue Pass. If I could just locate the trail anywhere on the mountainside, perhaps I could visually follow it downward and figure out how to get there from where we were stranded. "Can you see any signs of people on the face of the mountain?" I asked. "If only we could see someone hiking, we'd have a clue."

I started at the top of the ridge and swept my eyes systematically back and forth across the mountain, looking for any sign of trail or hikers on the black and white mountainside.

After a few minutes, Jane hopped up. "Look up there, near the ridge line," she pointed. "Can you see people moving across the snow?"

"Where?" Cappy and I asked together.

I stood to get a better view, as though moving two or three feet closer to the mile-distant mountain could bring clarity. I shielded my eyes with my hand to minimize the glare off the snow where I stared.

Jane worked patiently to describe exactly where to look. "Do you see that square notch along the ridge? I see tiny dots moving from left to right just below the sky to the left of that notch." She continued to point with her outstretched arm. "Do you see them?"

I dragged my eyes slowly across the white line of the mountain's ridge just below the sky. My eyes latched onto the colored dots Jane had described. They seemed too impossibly small to be people, mere specks, but they were moving, so they had to be. "I do see them!" I said, adrenaline beginning to wash away my despair.

"There are three of them, right? Two black and one red," Cappy asked. We stood shoulder-to-shoulder at the edge of the water, staring and pointing.

"Right," Jane said. "But they just changed directions. The lead dot is now moving from right to left."

"They must be on switchbacks," I said. Excitement was creeping into all our voices. I felt like cheering. I kept my eyes on them like a tracker beam, intuiting that if I shifted my gaze, I would lose them. I hesitated to even blink, for fear they would disappear.

"They seem to be working their way down, don't you think?" Cappy said.

Despite the great distance to the descending specks, collectively we put great stock in the sighting. It would take a long time for them to descend, but at least we knew there would eventually be a solution to our problem. Alternately pacing and sitting, I followed the dots' slow progress down the distant, snow-covered slope.

Suddenly, as though by magic, an entirely different group of five fast-moving hikers materialized directly across our lakelet. So intent on watching those distant dots, I was stunned by that new group's abrupt arrival.

Moving like a high-speed train with five cars, the group barreled down the previously invisible trail, now as obvious as if it were made of iron rails. When they arrived at the far edge of our watery barrier, they did not slow or waver but simply plunged in. Moving at speed, they crossed the wide expanse, wet up to their hips, striding directly to where we stood watching them, agape.

I was dumbfounded. These hikers had, without hesitation, walked confidently through the water at the precise place we had judged impossible to cross. The leader of the group, a strong, deeply tanned, muscular woman, slowed only long enough for them to answer a few of the questions we threw at them.

"Yep. PCT thru-hikers," the leader said.

Translation: They were hiking north on the Pacific Crest Trail (PCT), having begun in March at the Mexican border and planning to reach the Canadian border in the fall. The JMT overlays the PCT for nearly all the JMT's much shorter two-hundred-mile distance.

Their answers to our queries came in clipped sentence fragments, while they rolled on past us, never actually coming to a complete halt.

"Headed to Tuolumne for the grill and the mail."

"And the showers."

Translation: They were anxious to get to Tuolumne Meadows Backpackers Campground, where hot showers and food caches and the Grill's famous burgers awaited them. Their eyes revealed an intensity. They intended to make those ten miles before the approaching rain set in.

"What's the pass like?" Cappy asked.

"Lots of snow across the top—trail's invisible—but not like southern passes—pretty easy actually."

"You're hiking in sandals?" I asked the woman in the lead.

"Yep. Haven't worn boots for two hundred miles. Makes fording rivers way faster. No stops to change shoes." I studied her moving feet. She wore soggy, sturdy

REI hiking socks, just like mine, inside well-worn Teva sandals, just like mine. *Surely a sign.*

"What's the weather like up there?" Jane asked.

"Big storm's coming. Thunder and lightning."

"Can we make it over Donohue today?" I wanted to know.

"Sure. But hurry." She glanced at her watch. "It's just twelve-thirty. Ya got a couple of hours. It's not even two miles."

While this rapid-fire conversation took place, Zoe and Nemo caught up and stood listening attentively. In mere moments, the PCTers disappeared down the trail, practically running towards Tuolumne and those hot showers. It all happened so fast, like a magical encounter.

"I can't believe they walked across right here, right in front of us," I said, slowly turning my head from side to side in disbelief.

"I can't believe we wasted all that time looking around for what was right under our noses," Cappy said.

"I can't believe they've been walking for five months," said Jane.

"Can you believe she hiked that far in socks and sandals?" I was thinking she had just proved the idea was not foolhardy after all. "Those weren't real people, you know. They were trail angels helping us find our way!"

We kept up the I-can't-believe-ing as Cappy and I rushed to strip off our boots and replaced them with sandals. Then we stepped into the water, trying to emulate the confident, power-walking stride of the thru-hikers. Our steps were more tentative than theirs. Our feet were not so practiced at traversing an uneven riverbed lined with smooth, round cobbles. We had not yet learned to feel balanced while a river's current pressed intently.

Made from barely melted snow, the water was frigid. It sucked the warmth from my toes until they were numb and arrows of sharp pain shot up my shins and into my groin in the short time they were submerged. Wet to the hips, we emerged from the Lyell laughing with renewed determination and headed up the first truly steep ascent we had encountered. Zoe and Nemo followed close behind us.

I took the lead up the narrow, rising trail. It was a joy to walk in sandals. My feet and my spirits were liberated and pain-free. Nothing rubbed or pressed on anything else when I walked. My pain-free feet set a quick pace.

The wet stone footpath shone silver and was dotted with puddles and rimmed by temporary runoff streams. A real stream, the headwaters of the Lyell itself, wide enough to require a sloshing stride or two, crisscrossed the trail repeatedly, at times mistaking the trail for its own bed and running headlong down the same narrow space we were marching up. Without even slowing down, I clicked off a quick shot of a dozen glistening silver stairs clambering skyward.

Halfway up, the trail turned southward, winding through an expansive jumble of huge angular boulders, following a large fissure in the mountain.

When I grew tired, Cappy took over the lead, pushing us to walk faster. The altitude made it more and more difficult to breathe, to find oxygen to feed my leg muscles. Patches of snow appeared among the square boulders, and snowmelt drizzled and gurgled past us. I pushed my legs and my lungs to capacity. I pulled and pushed with my arms and hiking poles. My blisters felt way better, but my ankle still twinged with each climbing step. My calves and thighs were weakening, turning rubbery, and each breath was an aggressive attempt to strip oxygen from the thinning air. Surely, the top of the pass could not be much farther.

The sky ahead darkened from silver to pewter, and the temperature dropped. I was working so hard climbing that I was still warm, but that warmth quickly evaporated off my skin. Zoe and Nemo were no longer in sight. Again, they had fallen way behind.

"I'm not sure we'll make the top before the storm," I said, giving voice to my concerns. I had been anxious for a while, but as I grew more tired, that sensation grew towards fear. I did not want to be caught near the top of the pass in a lightning storm. Both Cappy and Jane were more mountain savvy than me, so I wanted their assurance that all was well.

"We're fine," Cappy called back without slowing down. "It's still early. It's only one-thirty. It never rains until four."

"The sky's getting awfully dark." I used my hiking poles more and more to pull myself upward and take some pressure off my weakening legs.

"I think we're okay," said Jane, "but let's keep a close eye on the clouds."

"Just keep walking fast," Cappy added. "I'm less worried about the storm than I am about making up the time we lost back there. We have to be over the pass and all the way down to Lower Rush Creek today."

I said, "Okay," but what I thought was, *This is not a good idea. We're walking into the face of a storm. I don't want to get killed by lightning.* I hiked as fast as I could—in my mind, I ran—and I watched the path in front of my feet to avoid looking at the sky.

Coming around one enormous pile of bus-sized boulders, I saw a view of the sky to the south opening up before us. Where the sky to our backs remained a cloudless China blue and overhead a steely gray, the clouds ahead loomed huge and black, like a slate-colored curtain just beyond what I thought was the domed top of the pass. The next twist of the path took the sky from our view, but it could not hide the low growl of distant thunder. More and more snow lay beside and across the path, and broad swaths of white spread out all around.

"I'm not sure this is a good idea. This is getting scary." There. I mustered the courage to say it aloud.

"What?" Cappy called back. She had not heard me over the wind and rumble of thunder.

I shouted to repeat myself. No one answered.

"I don't think this is safe," I shouted again. My leg muscles were about played out, I was breathing hard, and I was really cold. I wanted to pull my jacket out of my pack, but I did not want to stop and use up the time. What I really wanted to do was turn around, go back the way we had come, and find a place to shelter from the storm at a lower elevation, but I doubted myself.

"We're almost there. We're not even a quarter mile from the top," Cappy said. "We'll be up and over in just a few more steps and safely down the other side before the storm hits."

How can she be so confident? I was feeling like a real wimp, a fraidy cat. First, I had twisted my ankle. Then there were my blisters. *Am I the only one who's scared?* I struggled to keep my fear in check and my feet moving ever forward.

God, I'm a coward, I thought. *Afraid to go forward and afraid to admit I want to go back.* It was only the second day of a four-week journey, and already I was facing physical and emotional challenges beyond my expectations, perhaps beyond my ability to overcome.

"I think we'll be fine," Jane agreed with Cappy. "But we'll turn back if we need to."

How will we know when we need to? I thought. *I think we need to now!* But I just kept following along, deferring to my companions' greater wisdom.

Again, the trail turned and brought us a clear view of the sky hanging over the rounded ridge ahead. Magnificent thunderheads boiled and churned on the far side of the pass, still at a distance. We pressed on, moving as fast as our tired muscles and gasping lungs would allow. It was a race. We had to get over the top before the storm arrived, and then we could slip safely down the other side. It seemed like the top ought to be around the next bend... or the next... or the one after that.

Donohue Pass was a very broad, flat pass that made a gentle arch, not a point, in the sky. Standing alone, like a sentry on the naked granite directly in our path, stood a worn, wooden sign. Propped up by rocks placed around its base, but leaning precariously amidst puddles and patches of snow, the carved placard marked the elevation at eleven-thousand feet.

"Only fifty-six more feet to the top! We're almost there!" Cappy called excitedly.

In mere seconds, we would be over the top and headed safely down. A bit too early, I breathed a sigh of relief.

A few more steps brought us to the long-sought top.

Close enough to reach out and touch, the monster storm lay in wait, ready to pounce. A bright bolt of lightning streaked from the black cloud to the ground ahead. A second followed. The earth beneath my feet shook with the thunder.

At the precise moment we crested from the north, the monster crested from the south, and we met face-to-face on a collision course.

There would be no descending the mountain now; we had been tricked and now were trapped. The storm filled the entire sky with angry, black, swirling energy. Clouds poured ferociously over the ridge.

The monster had swallowed the sky.

We were next.

Needless to say, we three lived to tell that harrowing storm story. Though at the time, I was not sure we *would* come out alive. Even amidst my terror, I felt embarrassed as I imagined the posthumous newspaper headlines:

"Bodies of Three Foolish Females Found Atop Mountain Pass."
"Stupidity and Lightning Do Not Mix—Three Dead."

The worst, *"Son Asks, 'What the Hell Was My Mother Doing Up There in That Storm?'"*

After hunkering down in our little dips in the ground as the storm raged around us, we were finally released from the heart of the storm. Frozen-footed, we tumbled down from Donohue's dome and across the huge talus slope on the south side of the pass. We were three small bodies—shed by the mountain just like the thousands of boulders we bounced and crawled across. Our rocky descent into the large granite bowl on the southeast side of Donohue Pass ended in the broad green meadow that appeared from the top to be a stamp-sized, green bull's-eye.

The trail across the meadow, made of chocolate-colored mud, was slippery and dotted with deep puddles, while the meadow on either side was soggy and spongy, its grasses even more slippery than the mud. We stuck to the trail until we came to its sudden end.

Bisecting the meadow, Rush Creek lived up to its name. It was awash with the rain that had chased us down the mountain. The muddy brown stripe we followed led to the water's edge, dove into the flooded creek, and then reappeared on the far side, tantalizingly close and frustratingly inaccessible.

Described in *Winnett's* as a "serious ford... difficult in early season," Rush Creek was swollen to twenty feet across and boiling, blocking our path forward.[7] We paused at its edge and studied the water and the trail on the far side.

"What's the plan now? I'm not wading through that." I pointed at the angry creek. "Not when the water's that high." I untied the bandana from around my neck, used it to wipe my face, then stuffed it into my pocket.

"It's pretty deep, but the storm's winding down. The creek'll calm down by morning," Jane said in her calm, reassuring voice.

We had traveled only six-and-a-half miles that day, the same as the day before, and far short of our planned destination. Cappy worried aloud about consequences of not keeping to the schedule. "We need to get further down the trail. We were supposed to be making up for the miles we lost to yesterday's storm. Now, we're even farther behind."

---

[7] Thomas Winnett and Kathy Morey, *Guide to the John Muir Trial* (Wilderness Press, 1998) p. 22.

"Where are we and how far is it to the campsite at Lower Rush Creek?" I wanted to know.

"This is Upper Rush Creek. It's a mile or two to Lower Creek campsite, all downhill," Cappy said. "I'm going to look for a place to ford. There's got to be one."

How can she be so optimistic? I wondered.

She walked back and forth along the creek's edge. Jane joined her, and after a few stubborn minutes, I grudgingly did, too. We searched for a spot where the creek widened out and got shallow, but found none. Jane was calmly accepting of the situation. Cappy was frustrated, but resigned. I was relieved.

Cold, wet, and emotionally depleted, I saw the barrier created by the overflowing creek as the silver lining in the storm that still raged behind us. I wanted to stop, rest, and get my head back in the game. The afternoon's experiences had shaken my confidence. My ego was beyond humiliated, and the shrill little voice in my head, which questioned my ability to do this, was getting louder. A warm meal and a good night's sleep might muffle her.

The lush green meadow, squishy and wet, was littered with gray granite rocks and boulders, not much good for camping. Searching about, we found a flat granite shelf that would just hold our two small tents. It looked down from a small rise south of the trail onto the meadow and creek.

Wave after wave of dark storm clouds continued to roll across the sky pushed along by gusty winds. When one squall had passed, after a pause, another took its place, promising a long night. Pointing to the huge square rock perched on the west end of our stone terrace, Cappy said, "This wall might give us some shelter from the wind that's sure to come with that." She pointed to the next black wall of cloud barreling down on us.

"Before it arrives, we can start to dry our clothes on these bushes," said ever-practical Jane. She took off her outer jacket and spread it over one of the woody shrubs that grew in the lee of the rock wall. Stripping off our wet outer layers, we began to decorate the surrounding rocks and bushes, hoping the air would dry them before the rain began again. It was going to get colder, and we needed to have dry clothes in the morning.

I looked at my watch, "It's five o'clock. I want to be fed and bedded down by six." Jane and I took out the tent and with focused attention built it quickly. Cappy put her coffin-sized tent in the narrow space between the sheltering rock wall and ours.

Then, like a movie run at a speed that was just a bit too fast, with every wave of clouds and large drops of rain, we scurried around, grabbing our drying clothes and throwing them into the tents. When each shower passed, we pulled the damp things back out and arrayed them again to dry. The routine happened over and over, the three of us bustling in circles. At the same time, we wrapped the gear we could not take inside in plastic trash bags, prepared to cook a hot meal, and watched the weather. Even our words were few and efficient, as we divvied up our tasks.

Then we "hit the wall." While grabbing and throwing our less-damp clothes into the tents for the fifth time, giggling brought on by exhaustion began simultaneously with the deluge.

With the tents snuggled closely together, we maneuvered to climb in without bringing the elements with us. Off came muddy boots, soggy socks, and the rest of our wet clothing, which we stored in the sheltered antechambers created by rainflies. Stripped to underwear and shivering, I wrapped myself in my dry down bag and, in a few minutes, became luxuriously warm. Poking only hands and faces out tent flaps, we took turns using my JetBoil under the cover of rainflies to boil water for hot meals and hot drinks.

"I feel like I haven't eaten in days," Jane said as she waited five minutes for her freeze-dried dinner to steep.

"Oh, my. Have you ever tasted food this delicious?" The spicy spaghetti with meat sauce I had chosen was as good as any served in the best Italian restaurant. It is amazing what an effective condiment a voracious appetite can be. I topped off my satisfying meal with dessert made from handfuls of peanut M&M's.

I was finally warm and full, yet it was still early. Though body weary, we all lay wide-awake as the storm raged around us. Cappy had been correct, and we were thankful for the giant boulder that shielded us from the main force of the wind. Despite the barrier, with each gust, the rip-stop nylon flapped and aluminum frameworks shuddered. It sounded like we were riding out the storm adrift at sea in a small vessel, its reefed sails flapping madly, its halyards snapping against the mast. Torrents of rain pelted the straining cloth like waves cascading across the bow.

Snug in my down bag, I pulled out the first fifty-page-installment of *The Devil in the White City* by Erik Larson.[8]

"Shall I read us a bedtime story, ladies?" I asked. Lying on my back, I aimed my headlamp at the first page, expecting an affirmative answer.

"A bedtime story!" Cappy's cheerful voice came through the nylon wall over the sounds of the storm. "Are you going to read aloud to us, Joan?"

"That's my plan." I explained how I had ripped the paperback novel into five sections, each about fifty pages long, and shipped one along with each of my four food caches, keeping part one for our first leg.

"I just love being read to," Jane sighed from her sleeping bag beside me.

"And I really enjoy reading aloud, so it's all good," I said, pleased my surprise had been received with such enthusiasm.

Thus, I began the first of many nightly read-alouds: "'The date was April 14, 1912, a sinister day in maritime history, but of course the man in suite 63-65, shelter deck C, did not yet know it.'" After two intense chapters, with our own night sky awash in the storm's sinister darkness, exhaustion took over. I closed the book.

Starting Point — Lyell Forks Campsite — 9000 feet
Ending Point — Upper Rush Creek — 10,300 feet
Highest Point — Donohue Pass — 11,060 feet
Distance Covered — 6.5 miles
Cumulative Miles — 13 miles

---

[8] Eric Larson, *The Devil in the White City: Murder, Magic, and Madness at the Fair That Changed America* (Knopf Doubleday Publishing Group, 2004) p. 3.

Crossing Over

The sun shines not on us but in us.
The rivers flow not past, but through us,
thrilling, tingling, vibrating every fiber and cell of the substance of our bodies,
making them glide and sing.
~ John Muir, undated fragment of Muir journals, c.1872,
quoted by Linnie Marsh Wolfe in *Son of the Wilderness: The Life of John Muir*

Day Three
July 21, 2006

Starting Point — Upper Rush Creek — 10,300 feet

I slipped partway out of my down cocoon so I could peak through the tent's zippered doorway. The rain had stopped, but the sky lay on the ground, blanketing our meadow in a thick white cloud. Serpentine strands of silvery mist rose lazily from the soggy ground and hung in the air, adding their mass to the cloud layer. In the morning's low light, the meadow was not yet green but merely a shade of gray darker than the sky. Solid shapes near the tent glowed pearl-like with wetness. I watched as the sky began to lighten, highlighting swirls of mist reaching upward like gauzy specters.

The clouds that pillowed us absorbed sounds, leaving behind an empty silence. My ears scanned the air, caught a glimpse of a hush, then stretched out to pull the faint ssshhh of Rush Creek back to me. That sound triggered the image of the previous day's wildly flowing water and the faint metallic flavor of fear. I swallowed and tried to shrug away a shiver.

Donning layers of clothing against the chill wet air—base layer, fleece, and raingear—I climbed out and headed behind a nearby rock to pee. Then I maneuvered my way downward off our shelf, carrying my pump and water containers towards the edge of the creek to filter water for my morning cup of hot caffeine. The job of boiling water felt like an important task that morning, more so than the previous day. I was chilled clear through, and just the thought of holding my hot mug between my gloved hands warmed me and quickened my pace.

When I returned, Jane and Cappy were up and assembling their breakfasts. Cappy liked to start the morning with a bowl of hot cereal, topped with dried fruit, and a mug of cocoa, so her fleece-bundled body was bent over the JetBoil heating two cups of water. Her long unruly curls, loosely braided in back, fell from the knit cap she had pulled down to her eyebrows.

I boiled a second batch of water, enough for hot drinks for both Jane and me. Not a fan of hot cereal, I preferred hearty protein bars. That morning, I munched a tart and creamy lemon Luna Bar, my favorite flavor, while I wrapped my whole body around a steaming mug of spiced chai with an extra shot of instant coffee.

Low clouds continued to weave their way upward into the brightening sky. "Kind of a ghostly scene this morning, don't you think?" I spoke aloud to no one in particular.

"It reminds me of the Scottish moors in old Victorian novels," Jane answered, hugging her steaming mug of black tea.

After a pause, I said, "All that's missing is bagpipe music."

"Now that would be eerie," Jane agreed.

"This spot's prettier this morning than it was last night," I said. "I wasn't in the mood to appreciate it yesterday."

A solid night's sleep had done nothing to soften the anxious voice in my head. In fact, she took on an adolescent tone that morning. *I'm cold. I'm wet. My feet hurt. I hate boots. I'm not having fun. It's not fair.* Her whimpering voice slithered in loops through my mind right alongside the sounds of the river. *I'm scared. I wanna go home.*

Fortunately, no one else could hear my inner thoughts, or I would have been embarrassed as well as fearful. I did have to agree—so far, this hike was not at all what I had envisioned. Fingering the silver loops at my throat and conjuring their aspirational words failed to temper my anxiety.

Breakfast over, I retrieved my wet clothes. I possessed two sets of clothing. The clothes I held in my hands, which had been drenched during the thunderstorm atop Donohue, were still wet. The garments I wore, which I had worn in camp the evening before, were just clammy. Despite all my fleece and wet-weather gear, I was chilled clear through.

We debated what to do next. To move forward, we would first have to ford Rush Creek, which was still running hip deep and wild. That frightened me. Traveling in wet clothes worried me, too. Should we stay or should we go? Could we go? Was the creek fordable?

"I'm sure we can do this," Cappy said. "The creek's way down this morning. And we have several lost miles to make up." She looked at me, her eyes shooting beams of her confidence my way.

I was arranging my wet shorts, shirt, and socks on a woody bush in the emerging sun. "The water is down," I agreed. "But I want to wait until I have one set of dry clothes. I don't think we should risk hypothermia traveling wet." I was shivering from cold or fear or both. *I don't care one iota about lost miles,* I thought.

Jane had one foot in each camp. She was unafraid of fording the creek and could have left immediately with Cappy, but she was also concerned about hiking in damp clothing. "Why don't we let the sun work on our clothes for a little while and then pack up?" As she spoke, the sun made a brief appearance between passing clouds, then was swallowed up again.

Cappy was sure we could cross the creek, sure we should pack up and hike. In the face of her confidence, I felt like a wimp. But I had felt wimpy climbing toward Donohue Pass, afraid of the storm, thinking we ought to turn back, so wimpy that I could not speak in the face of Cappy's confidence like I should have. To make up for my error, that morning I dug in my heels.

I really wanted to crawl back into the tent, pull my nonexistent pillow over my head, and hunker down until the storms passed and the sun was fully out. The desperate voice in my head insisted, *I want to go home. Let's just quit, pack up, turn around.*

If I had not felt so insulted by my own cowardly thoughts, they might have escaped my mouth. I clamped my jaws tight. Fear and pride wrestled for control. *You have been dreaming and preparing for this adventure for years,* I told myself. *You are not going to quit.* So there I was, frozen, locked in a battle with myself.

Cappy's voice interrupted the arguing voices in my head. "Joan, did you hear me?"

I turned to look at her. She was bundled in her jacket, her wool hat pulled down over her ears. Not a single strand of her curls was visible. "I'm sorry. What'd you say?"

"I asked about your clothes. Are they dry?" Her voice was patient and compassionate, but her fidgeting revealed her impatience to go.

"They've improved from wet to damp," I said. "A little longer." I flipped each piece over, like pancakes on a griddle, exposing what had been the bottom side to the air.

As the intermittent sun lifted steam from the wet ground and our gear, I tried to distract myself by concentrating on my injured feet. Step-by-step, I went through the process of shaping moleskin donuts and wrapping my feet in yards of tape. Adding the ankle brace, I pulled on my least wet socks and Tevas. My abandoned boots hung by their laces from the back of my pack.

I had just about convinced my hiking partners to stay through lunch, until our things were completely dry, when, at precisely eleven o'clock, two things happened that changed everything.

First, three men, with full backpacks and hiking poles, came striding along the muddy path fifty yards below our elevated home. They had descended from Donohue Pass, just as we had done the previous afternoon. They paused where the path disappeared into Rush Creek to confer for a moment, looking up and down stream, then confidently walked through the thigh-deep water, making the crossing look easy.

It would have been nice to have talked with them, asked a question or two, but I do not think they even saw us up on our rocky perch. By the time we realized what was happening, they were gone.

Then, just as they had magically appeared from nowhere, the sun finished burning off even the highest clouds, and in the bat of an eye, every last wisp of grayness vanished. The green bowl in which we sat, the blue dome of the sky, and the silver-and-pewter granite of the snow-topped mountains surrounding us simultaneously found their colors and became vibrant. How is it that beauty trumps fear? *Fear? What fear? Afraid? Who me? Isn't this beautiful!*

"If they can do it, we can do it!" I readily changed my mind.

"We are women, hear us roar!" Cappy celebrated.

Jane and I deconstructed our tent, shaking off the last beads of water before folding, rolling, and stuffing it away. We gathered clothing and packed gear. In a half-hour, we were ready. With my fear rolled up and stuffed into a pocket, I shouldered my pack, and we walked down to the spot where the trail got its feet wet.

The moving water was a little less intimidating since we had witnessed it being conquered only minutes earlier. Where it had been gray and frothy the day before, now it was clear, revealing the cobbles that lined its bottom.

"Let's cross one at a time," Jane said. "We can keep an eye on each other and come to the rescue if need be."

We each left loose and dangling the chest and hip straps securing our packs to our bodies. That's a backcountry safety rule for river fording. It is easier to extricate yourself, should you fall into the water, reducing the risk that the weight of your pack will hold you under and drown you.

Cappy ventured into the water first, using her poles to steady herself. She took her time, creeping along, and made it across with no mishaps. "Only twenty steps! Way easier than I thought it was going to be! Come on across," she called. Her expression of relief unmasked her previously hidden concern.

Jane followed with equal care and equal success. The two of them stood on the far shore, smiling and encouraging me.

Bucking up and banishing the wimp within, I stepped in. The water buffeted me from the left, as my feet searched for dependable footing among smooth, round stones. Using my hiking poles for balance, I placed first one, then the other, ahead and outside of my intended path. My pack felt tall and precarious as I leaned left into the oncoming water. Walking in, the water was up to my knees, then my hips, almost to my waist. Halfway, I began walking out of the water, knee-deep, ankle-deep, dry land. I let out the breath I held as a sigh.

"Yay! We did it. Awesome." Cappy was cheerleader. We celebrated with high-fives all around. Not traditional palm-slapping high-fives, our trail version was to clank our metal hiking poles together, like clinking wine glasses in a toast. High-clanks, rather than high-fives.

The moment I stepped onto dry land, I remembered my camera. Tucked safely into the deep right pocket of my hiking shorts—not so safe after all. Pulling it out, I held it up by its wrist cord. It dripped. I dried it off with my bandana. It dripped. I opened it up and dried its guts. It dripped. Nothing I did made one tiny bit of difference. I had drowned my camera.

Day Three, and I had *drowned* my brand new, itty-bitty, amazing, cherished digital camera, the camera I had purchased especially for this trip. I had paid way too much for the Nikon, but had justified the purchase to myself because of my Grand Plan. My Footpath-As-Subject Photo-Journal Grand Plan had drowned with my camera on Day Three.

Let's review: fall, sprained ankle, blisters upon blisters, lost, lightning at eleven-thousand-feet-near-death experience, drowned camera, crushed grand plan. Murphy's Law was the only explanation. Everything that could go wrong had indeed gone awry. What was going to happen next?

That little voice, quiet for a while, was back at it. I was so glad no one else could hear her. *I can't believe you did that. How stupid can you be? How could you forget your precious camera? Now what are you going to do? Your Plan-with-a-capital-P is ruined. Now what? Let's quit now before something truly awful, even fatal, happens. I wanna go home!* Anger was the only thing that kept me from crying.

We continued along the trail, following Rush Creek as it cut across the high meadow and then entered a woodsy forest. The sun remained out and, undoubtedly, somewhere, the world maintained its beauty. I, however, walked beneath my own personal black cloud. My heart ached. All I could do was blindly follow the others at the pace they set. Every few minutes, I would chastise myself aloud, "How could I have done that?"

Finally, after half a mile of trudging along and numerous expressions of compassion from my friends, I apologized, "I am so sorry that I sound so bitchy. I promise, this won't go on for too long. I just have to get this trauma out of my system. Ten more minutes. I promise I'll stop after ten minutes, maybe sooner, if I can."

I remember nothing about that section of the trail. But true to my word, after a few hundred more steps, I sucked it up and stopped complaining. Unfortunately, my inner adolescent-critic voice kept up the internal bitching and chastising for a while, but in the face of the next challenge, even she shut up about the camera.

I was awakened from my pity-party by another Rush Creek crossing. This was a different version, not a fording, but a highwire balancing act. A large log, two feet in diameter, lay high across the creek. The water surged a dozen feet below, foaming over large rocks in its constricted bed. My greatest fear, a long-time phobia, had taken physical form. The idea of walking across that log, balancing with a top-heavy load on my back, over rushing water and sharp tooth-shaped boulders, terrified me to the point of paralysis. It might as well have been a tightrope over the Grand Canyon.

All I could visualize was my body falling headfirst onto the rocks and being swept down river, only to be found days later and miles away, broken, battered, and caught in a snag. "I can't do this," I whispered. The air swam. I blinked my eyes to refocus.

Cappy leapt up and walked swiftly across the bridge, nimble as an Olympic gymnast on the balance beam. Seconds later, she was standing on the far side beckoning us. Jane followed a tad slower, with more caution, but with the graceful strides of a dancer. Then she, too, stood on the far side. Each looked at me across the chasm, expecting I would be following on their heels.

"I can't do this," I said a bit louder. Then, hesitantly, I repeated it a third time, so Cappy and Jane could hear me over the monstrous roar of the water. Or was that the roaring in my ears? "There has to be another way across. There has to be."

I walked some distance down river. Then I returned.

"This is the only way across," I announced. "I can't walk across that log."

I was frozen in place, my legs rooted in the ground, immovable as tree stumps, once again the wimp. Before the whiny voice could get too loud, I came up with a solution. I could not walk across, but I would scooch across the log on my butt.

After explaining my plan to Cappy and Jane, I threw my hiking poles, one at a time, like spears across the gap to them. In the process, my wrist mala, my beautiful white-beaded good-luck bracelet, flew off my arm, arcing gracefully through the air before splashing into the river, an unintended ritual offering to the river goddess.

"Are you kidding me? You want that, too?" I asked the river in complete disbelief, tears welling, but not falling. *You will not cry,* I ordered myself. Holding onto the strength, courage, and spirit rings of my necklace for support, I opened my eyes. "Here goes nothing," I said aloud.

I let loose my pack straps, straddled the broad log like I was mounting a saddle, and began to scooch forward. The log was so wide, and its bark was so rough, that I had to take care to move only an inch or two at a time, lest I shred my legs or tip over sideways.

It took several minutes, and I had to cast my pride into the river to do it, but I managed to reach the safety of the far side. Standing, I gulped air to refill my lungs.

"Thank you both for being so patient with me today," I begged. "I will get better. I promise."

The eager balloon of excitement that had accompanied me on Day One was now completely deflated. Not one ounce of my pride or confidence remained. Like a new recruit at boot camp, I had been brought to my knees by the trail. I only hoped it had a plan to build me back up into a good warrior.

My fellow adventurers were gracious and encouraging, stacking up karma points like stones balanced in a head-high cairn.

The trail followed Rush Creek as it bounced and crashed downhill through forests of giant red-barked fir trees and broad green meadows, occasionally hopping from one side of the water to the other. That, of course, meant that we had to cross and re-cross and re-cross the creek. Sometimes we waded through; other times the path was elevated onto well-placed steppingstones. The crossings I despised the most involved narrow log bridges, though no more scooching was required.

Walking, I watched my feet and I thought. I once read that you could learn to be patient by pretending to be patient. By pretending, fooling yourself and others by your actions, you were actually being a patient person. I wondered if that would work for other virtues, like strength and courage. *Could I pretend that I was courageous?* I pulled my necklace charms from beneath my tank top and rubbed them between my fingers. I wondered, *Can I fool myself into believing I'm brave? Maybe. It's worth trying.*

Finally, the trail left Rush Creek and climbed toward Island Pass, the next morning's challenge. Though the sky was still blue, we could see clouds building over the pass. The growl of distant thunder rolling down toward us made our next choice obvious. There would be no more high-altitude electrical storms for these three ladies. We elected to set up our camp on the flat top of a low granite plateau near one of the small creeks. The plateau was surrounded on three-and-a-half sides by water, a calm still pond, a pair of chuckling creeks, and a grassy marsh.

With our tents erected, we sat back and admired the beautiful grotto-like surroundings. A gentle breeze stirred in the trees, accompanying the musical sounds of moving water. Atop our flat rock sat a higher dome of gray granite. Taking snacks, we climbed to its sun-bathed top to relax and admire the view. From there, we watched the clouds piling up over the southern peaks. My journal entry from that evening reads, "Together, the sun and clouds played a dynamic game of light and color with the sky and mountains as their canvas."

The storm and its rumblings were still some distance away, so we had plenty of time to enjoy the sunshine. Perhaps a little meditation or yoga. Maybe some journal writing. No? What about fending off hungry young marmots? Husky rodents the size of boot boxes, marmots are usually timid creatures who lie around sunning themselves until you get too close, then they run and hide among the rocks. Not these two. These were real risk takers, venturing silently right up beside where we sat, aiming for the little pile of snack foods we had carried up with us.

"Shoo!" Cappy called, waving her hands like she was swatting flies.

"Now you just back off, you little sneak," I warned one of the creatures, looking him in the eyes. He did not appear intimidated.

"Watch behind you! He's slinking around that rock." Jane pointed behind me.

They were a crafty pair. While one approached from the left and drew our attention, the other circled around to the right and sneaked in close. The marmots seemed to have dozens of secret passages in and around the rock-strewn dome, so they could disappear in one spot and pop up from a crack somewhere else moments later. One nearly got to my bag of almonds before I sensed his presence at my side.

"You cannot have my food. Get away from me!" I lectured him, holding my snacks close to my chest and giving him my best stern teacher look.

Those furry creatures were large enough to be a bit intimidating. We took to tossing marble-sized rocks in their direction, aiming close enough to keep them away but without hitting them. The cat-and-mouse game went on for thirty minutes, before we finally convinced them to keep their distance. We remained watchful, however, which meant that neither yoga nor meditation was a real possibility.

A few large drops of rain came just as the sun disappeared inside the clouds. We jumped up for a quick descent, leaving the dome to the marmots and taking refuge inside our tents. To the accompaniment of the rain on the roof, I read aloud from our serial novel: Meanwhile, back in Chicago, "The sky beckoned," and buildings climbed heavenward carried by newly invented elevators until they dominated the skyline, perhaps a bit like the Sierra peaks that encircled us.[9]

The squall was short-lived, and in thirty minutes we reemerged with dinner on our minds. The local mosquitoes had the same thought. Dinnertime! Why had it not occurred to us that water on all sides would also mean mosquitoes on all sides? Before we could make any progress at all with dinner prep, we pulled on long pants and long sleeves, sprayed ourselves with Deet, and even dug out mosquito netting headgear.

"I almost didn't pack this," I said as I pulled the olive-drab net over my hat and head. "I couldn't imagine I would ever wear it." The net was shaped like an extra-large shower cap made of fine mesh, with elastic around its lower edge. My hat's bill kept the net away from my face, and the elastic pulled it snug around my neck, so that it floated like a green bubble around my head. Through the lens of the netting, the world took on a watery green tint.

"It's quite a fashion statement. Very becoming," Jane said from beneath her own mesh mask.

"You think so?" I replied, mugging for a nonexistent camera. "The only reason it made the cut is because it weighs so little. Now, I'm thinking it would have been worth packing, even if it weighed a full pound!"

"Our little friends really like your white shirt, Cappy," I said. "There are hundreds of mosquitoes on your back, way more than either Jane or me."

---

[9] Eric Larson, *The Devil in the White City: Murder, Magic, and Madness at the Fair That Changed America* (Knopf Doubleday Publishing Group, 2004) p. 23.

"They look like moving black polka-dots," Jane said. Cappy looked down to inspect her shirt. When she raised her arm, the dots lifted off, hovered a moment, then returned to their spots on the white fabric.

The whine of so many dive-bombing varmints nearly drowned out the human conversation. "Let's be careful climbing in and out of the tents, keeping them zipped as much as we can. The last thing we need is one of these little monsters moving in and serenading us to sleep," Cappy said.

We ate our dinner inside again. Scores of mosquitoes buzzed and did their prowling dance on the surface of the tents. Only a couple managed to slip in while we climbed inside, and those were quickly dispatched, smashed on the ceiling. "Do we give off a delicious aroma? Or is it body heat that attracts them?" I wondered aloud between bites of savory beef stroganoff.

"Good question," Jane said. The creatures surrounded the tents like an army in siege. Their antics were interesting to watch behind the safety of the nylon barrier.

Tummies full, Jane and I lounged on top of our sleeping bags. We listened through the nylon walls while, next door, Cappy went over maps and reviewed our position and the next day's route. "The original plan had us crossing Island Pass today and camping at Thousand Island Lake tonight," she reminded us. Instead, we were camped one-and-a-half miles below the pass and would not get to the lake until late the next morning. I could hear either frustration or disappointment in her voice. I could not see her face through the tent walls, so I was not sure which it was.

"So, we're already a day behind schedule on day three?" Jane asked.

"That's right," Cappy said. "We've got to make up the distance." It sounded like she was taking the delay personally.

"The weather has really set us back, Cappy," I said. "Don't worry. Give us a few dry days, and we'll catch up with ourselves." It was my turn to give assurances.

"There is a silver lining," Jane said. "We'll be up and over the pass first thing in the morning, long before any storms are brewing."

"True," Cappy's concession came through the nylon wall. She did not sound appeased.

After we had reviewed the changing itinerary, I put on my headlamp to take a close look at my camera. I opened its battery compartment and used my bandana to wipe every crack and crevice dry, then did the same with the slot that held the memory card. Crossing my fingers, I slid the power switch to the on position.

Nothing.

I flipped a second switch to view photos that had already been taken. The little screen flickered. I held my breath. The image of the trail climbing up silver stairs towards Donohue Pass blinked onto the two-inch screen. It was the last picture I had taken. I exhaled, pressing the arrow key to flip back in time through two dozen stored photos. It went all the way back to the very first photo of the three of us posing beside the initial trailhead sign in Tuolumne Meadows.

My excitement and hopes expanded to fill the tent with little squeals. But my bubble popped in the next minute when, holding my breath again, I flipped the switch back from viewer to camera. The screen erupted into white-on-black jigger-jagger patterns, dramatic lightning bolts—the camera's death throes—before going permanently black. I groaned, turned off my headlamp, and put the camera aside.

"G'night, my friends," I said, rolling on my side to face the blank tent wall.

"Goodnight," they each responded.

"Tomorrow will be better, Joan," Cappy said.

"Good thing," I said. Then, after a pause, "I'm sure you're right."

Before I could sleep, I lay thinking for a while. Becoming "one with nature" was turning out to be more difficult than I had anticipated. I had lost my bracelet, my camera, my pride, and my Grand Plan. But, with my companions for support, I would continue to face my fears, and I was (sometimes) even enjoying the beauty that surrounded us.

Tomorrow will be better. I will be courageous. I will be strong.

Starting Point — Upper Rush Creek — 10,300 feet
Ending Point — Davis Lake Trail Junction (Grotto Camp) — 9680 feet
Highest Point — Upper Rush Creek — 10,300 feet
Distance Covered — 2.5 miles
Cumulative Miles — 15.5 miles

Gems In The Rough

The snow is melting into music.
~ John Muir, *John of the Mountains: The Unpublished Journals of John Muir*,
Edited by Linnie Marsh Wolfe, 1979

Day Four
July 22, 2006

Starting Point — Davis Lake Trail Junction (Grotto Camp) — 9680 feet

The millions of mosquitoes to whom we had been introduced the previous night greeted us again in the morning. "Leave me alone!" I waved my hands around my face. It was hard to see what I was doing with little black spots flitting back and forth in front of my eyes.

"Just ignore them," Cappy said with a calm disdain. For some reason, they did not hover around her.

"Why are they all over here?" I was working double-time to pack up.

"She's just not as sweet as you and me," Jane laughed. She was hustling, too.

"Must be true," I agreed and hoisted my heavy pack, slipping my arms through the shoulder straps and buckling the belt. Moments later, we were off towards our second big pass, Island Pass.

The trail worked its way back-and-forth on switchbacks that carried us up the steep face of the ridge. Sometimes it crossed wide stretches of granite studded with erratics, those ancient glacier-abandoned standing stones. Other times it climbed through the open forest floor in the shade of towering straight-backed lodgepole pines.

We paused for a breather at a U-turn halfway to the top. Warmed up and far above the mosquitoes, Jane and I abandoned our long sleeves, me for a bright blue tank, Jane for her hot pink tee. Cappy always hiked in the same loose-fitting, long-sleeved white shirt. Leaning against a large dark-colored boulder, I drank water and popped a peppermint in my mouth.

"This trail reminds me of the trail to Loch Leven." Jane referred to a trail near home we had used as a practice hike a few weeks earlier. I looked ahead to the footpath crawling up the mountain's north face.

"Absolutely. Same trees, same switchbacks," I said. "And just as steep."

The crown of ten-thousand-foot Island Pass was a broad, flat dome dotted with several small ponds, tarns that had been gouged from the rock by a passing glacier as though with a giant ice cream scoop. The morning air was clear and still, so the ponds were perfect mirrors reflecting the intense azure blue of the sky and the silver and pewter of the rocky formations around their edges. Small patches of snow dotted the grassy fringes of the tarns wherever there was shade.

Striding across the broad pass and looking ahead, we were brought to an abrupt halt by the breathtaking panoramic view. Southward, the entire earth before us was one massive black bowl, its rim constructed of monstrous black peaks—craggy and sharp enough to scrape the sky. Extensive swaths of snow blanketed the hips and shoulders of Banner Peak, the tallest of the rough volcanic peaks dominating the wide valley. Its tremendous mass seemed to rise vertically from the very shore of Thousand Island Lake, though really it was some distance beyond.

Its deep water the darkest blue, the huge lake was dotted with the islands that gave it its name—some mere stones tossed into the water, others large enough to support trees. There was something epic about the rock valley—dragons or griffins would have looked quite at home guarding the lake's shores.

"I've read so much about this place—longed to see it my whole life," said Cappy, her voice reverent. "How beautiful!" She swept her arm to take in the vast landscape.

"It's stunning," I agreed. "The colors so intense. The shapes are massive." From our ten-thousand-foot vantage point, the view was breathtaking, and for a time I remained transfixed, unable to relinquish it.

Shaking ourselves loose from the view, we continued to walk along the eastern rim of the valley, Cappy bouncing along in the lead. At a smooth rocky promontory overlooking the vast lake like a VIP stadium box, we stopped for an early lunch. Legs dangling over the edge of the small shelf, we watched the lake far below. Ripples generated by a light breeze turned moving patches of water into the silver glitter of reflected sunlight.

The same breeze moved through the surrounding evergreens, creating a repeating psithurism—an approaching melodic murmur giving way to rhythmic overhead swishing and delicate whispers of retreat. I held my food wrappers down so they could not dance away with the wind.

"What color would you call that?" I asked, referring to the lake. "Is it midnight blue? Or ultramarine? I want to write about it in my journal tonight." There was a pause.

"I think it's the color of those old-fashioned blue glass medicine bottles," Cappy said. "Does that have a name?"

"Medicine bottle blue?" I dug through my mental files. "Might that be cobalt?"

"What about sapphire? Or lapis?" Jane said. She had spread her lavender neckerchief across her lap like a tablecloth and was spreading peanut butter on crackers and eating them slowly one by one.

"You're both right," I agreed, "but I think the jewels are the better analogy." I leaned back on my pack after finishing my tuna and crackers and began chewing on dried mango. "Sapphire it is."

"I read something interesting in the guidebook," Cappy said. "For the next eighty-five miles, all the water we see—lakes, rivers, and all the melting ice—will flow clear to the coast and right into San Francisco Bay."

"I can't imagine this wild mountain water would feel at home in The City," I said, thinking about the two hundred miles that must lie between our spot on that rock and the Golden Gate.

While I put away my lunch fixings, Jane and Cappy took out their cameras and began clicking away at the lake and the surrounding mountains. I reached into my pocket for my camera, before remembering I had destroyed it. Disappointment welled up in my chest as I sat camera-less in the midst of such photogenic scenery—a gigantic view impossible to capture in a four-by-six-inch frame—but I would have attempted the feat anyway. If only.

I lay back, head pillowed on my hands, and looked up to watch the sky. A few puffy white clouds sailed in slow motion across the blue expanse, and I let their simple beauty carry away my grumbling thoughts. Without the convenience of a digital memory card, I would strive to imprint the images of craggy mountains and sapphire water in my brain's analog memory cells and carry them home that way.

Cappy exchanged camera for map and began pointing out the landmark peaks beyond the lake. "That whole wall of mountains over there is the Ritter Range." Her arms swept the distant sky. "The closest one, with a squared top, is Banner Peak. The sharpest one—peaking over Banner's left shoulder—is Mount Ritter." One hand pointed at Banner, the other at Ritter. "Beyond them, that saw-toothed group are the Minarets." She swung her arm, indicating the distant scalloped ridgeline.

For some reason, hearing all those labels irritated me. I sat up, leaned into the scene, imagined the array of islands as a fleet of black ships menacing a small blue harbor and the craggy black castle towering over it, tuning out the naming exercise.

Before leaving, I picked up a small sharp-edged chip of granite—gray with white speckles, the size of a nickel only square. I turned it over in my hand, admiring the sparkle its white crystals made in the sun. *If I can't take photos, I'll take a tiny slip of stone,* I thought, sliding it into my shorts' pocket.

The hot, dusty footpath mapped the lake's northern and eastern shorelines, skipping past several filled campsites. Heading south, the trail became the golden chain in a necklace of glistening lakes. We climbed up and down a series of mild rises, each time descending into a granite bowl with its own lake, every one a different jeweled hue.

Petite Emerald Lake, to our east, was chatoyant—a cat's eye, its blue-green color radiating from deep below the surface. It sat in a form-fitted red rock bowl and was fed by a pair of miniature glaciers that came right down to the water's icy edge. Misnamed Ruby Lake was more opal than ruby—the midday sun and warm breeze turned its surface a rippling, reflecting mixture of greens and blues. Garnet Lake, with its dozens of miniature islands, was either more emerald than Emerald Lake or the warm golden-pink of a raw garnet, depending on the angle of view.

Our water containers on empty, we looked for a shady spot near the edge of Garnet Lake to filter water and fill our containers. We settled for a lonely stunted tree on a rocky peninsula stretching out like a muddy big toe testing the water. After eating a second lunch, I checked the wrapping on my ankle and the tape on my feet.

Cappy went for a swim in the cold water. "Jane! Joan! The water's delightful. Join me!" she called as she burst upwards from the surface and shook the water from her face. She had dunked her entire body, and her mane hung sleek and shiny down her back.

"It's way too cold for this girl. You be sure to enjoy it, though!" I had no intention of submerging myself in ice water, but I was tempted to wade up to my knees like Jane was doing. The water would have felt good on my tender feet. I held myself back, though. If I got the bandages wet, I'd have to completely reapply them.

While Cappy continued to splash and stroke back and forth near shore, Jane joined me in the small patch of shade created by the shriveled tree.

"I wonder what happened to Zoe and Nemo," I said, suddenly thinking of our first trail friends. "They're young and strong. I keep expecting them to go roaring past us." The last we had seen of them was when we had all five crossed the Lyell Fork together. Very quickly they had fallen behind as we had climbed up towards Donohue and into the face of that horrible storm.

"They couldn't have been too far behind us when we got stuck on Donohue," Jane said. "I hope they're okay."

"I hadn't thought of them being in danger," I said. "I just wonder why two strong kids are lagging behind three 'old ladies.'"

"That is odd, isn't it?" Jane said, her face thoughtful. "I don't think we could've missed them. Do you? They'd have had to walk right past us."

"Another fun bridge! Oh, boy!" I said when I spied what was ahead. I was flooded with dread, and my stomach tightened around the food I had just eaten.

A slender bridge spanned Garnet Lake's outlet creek. Built from two straight and narrow tree trunks strapped together like a pair of chopsticks, it was supported, in the center of the creek, by what looked like a tower made of shoebox-sized Lincoln Logs. The wide stream ran swiftly, with the bridge suspended only a few inches above.

"You okay with this one?" Cappy asked.

"I'm okay," I assured them, putting on my most nonchalant face to camouflage my rising fear. If I could project courage and strength, perhaps I would feel them.

Jane went across first, and I observed her closely, wanting to emulate her every movement. The bridge was just wide enough for her to place one booted foot on each of the logs, but no room to plant the tips of her hiking poles. She held both poles in her left hand and walked across, slow and sure, her eyes on her boots and the bridge one step ahead.

"You want to go next?" Cappy asked. "Or do you want me to go?"

"You go ahead. I'll watch you." I took a step to the side and she pranced across, faster and steadier even than Jane.

"You can do this, Joan," I told myself in a whisper so soft neither of the others could hear me. "You can do this." I moved my poles to my left hand, unbuckled my hip and chest straps, and took a couple of slow, deep breaths. I could feel Jane's and Cappy's eyes on me, observing me as intently as I had observed them, but I did not look up.

I started with my right foot, placing it with care on the right log. It was old and smooth, its bark worn away. Moving my weight onto that foot, I was committed, and shifted my weight onto the bridge. My left foot found its place beside the right. I stood on the starting end of the narrow bridge, like a competitive diver preparing to begin her step-step-step-hurdle-bounce approach to her dive. With another deep breath, I stepped out with my right foot and moved forward.

"Keep moving," I whispered. As when riding a bicycle, it is easier to maintain your balance when you are moving forward. I never looked up nor at the water. I riveted my gaze to the logs in the small space just ahead of my feet, which moved a few inches forward with each step. The end of the log bridge appeared. I stepped down to solid ground.

"You did it!" Jane wore a smile on her face and in her dark eyes; she touched my shoulder.

"It wasn't that hard!" Cappy said. Little did she realize.

"I *am* getting better," I admitted. "I wasn't so wobbly that time." I stopped for a drink and to let my heart slow down before we went on. It seemed such an irrational fear, but I was humbled every time I faced a river crossing.

Water, both running and frozen, marked the entire length of the climbing trail. As if the day had not already romanced us with intoxicating panoramic views, the afternoon climb ended at a saddle of high rock that offered us yet more. Ahead lay a narrow green valley dominated by distant range after sharp peak after towering mountain, all beneath an infinite blue sky.

A giant old talus slope and a hot and dry descent spread out below the ridge where we stood. At the talus's edge, meadows then forests took over. Wildflowers were riotous in the meadow. A rainbow salad of mixed colors—pink, yellow, blue, lavender and deep violet, red, orange—flanked the trail, a serpentine brown ribbon through lush grasses and sedges.

Along the shady edge of the woods, the flowers were equally numerous, equally colorful, but entirely different. We paused for a brief rest within one colorful stretch—just long enough to drink water and survey the plant life surrounding us.

"I've been on so many guided wildflower hikes. So many times, I've been taught the names of flowers. Why can't I remember more than a few?" I wondered aloud. I pointed to a group of spiky scarlet blooms. "Like this one. I recognize it—Indian paintbrush. But this yellow one—I've seen it a million times, but I've no clue what it's called. It's frustrating."

"I'll bet Jane knows them all," Cappy said. She was right. During the many summers Jane, her husband, Rand, and their kids had spent living and working at

Sierra fire lookout stations, she had taught herself the names of all the flowers and trees and birds. "Why don't you tell us the names of some of these?" Cappy invited, casting her arm around to the flowers.

"You sure? Some people find that irritating," Jane said, wanting assurance. Jane was a strong woman with extensive knowledge, but she was also reserved. In all the years I had known her, I had never seen her feathers ruffled nor heard her crow.

"It makes me crazy when someone does that all the time," I admitted, "but I love it when I get short doses. Really."

"You're right. That's paintbrush," she pointed at the spiny red flower before turning to another. "You remember this one." She held an iridescent blue tube-shaped flower, whose interior shone bright pink, between her fingers. "It's mountain penstemon, the higher elevation version of the one we saw in Lyell Canyon. It's a big family. They come in lots of shades of blue and purple and pink."

"What's this?" I asked. It was a low plant with woody stems topped with pale purple puffball flowers. I bent to pick one.

"Pennyroyal. It's in a category of plants called aromatics. Like sage or lavender, its stems and leaves produce an aromatic oil." She picked a stem with several narrow gray-green leaves. "It's got a sharp scent, not sweet, but pleasant."

I brought the stem I held to my nose. "Nice. It's similar to sage," I said, "Or incense." I slipped the flower into the front of my shirt so I could take in its aroma as I walked. Pennyroyal would become my favorite flower in the coming days, its scent a frequent companion.

"Over here is wild garlic." A tall slender stem topped with a round, multi-petaled, lavender flower stretched above the green masses at its base. "You can pick one of these long scapes"—it was a hard bud on the end of a tall stem—"and chew on it while you walk." She picked one and took a little bite to demonstrate. "It tastes like you'd expect garlic to taste, only sweeter and milder."

"I love garlic." I picked one. Cappy did, too. I chewed as we moved on, our break and our brief botany lesson over.

In early evening, we stopped near Ediza Trail Junction to make camp alongside a fast-moving creek. No sooner had we put down our packs than two threatening swarms swept in—high above, winds carried billowing battleship-gray clouds that filled the sky, while in our midst, thousands of carnivorous mosquitoes descended.

We scurried to construct our tents whisper-distance apart—an assembly process we had gotten down to two minutes of choreographed and coordinated movements. We beat the rain and outmaneuvered the bugs with our speed. We donned warm clothing and assembled the cooking gear under the rainfly's protected "front porch." The mosquitoes vanished the moment the rains began, first as a few fat plops of water, then a heavy shower accompanied by distant flashes of lightning and echoes of thunder. We were getting better at managing our cooking and housekeeping tasks through the challenges of weather and insects, learning the music and the dance steps.

Tucked in, I read aloud from our serial bedtime story. Chicago's city fathers and architects were discovering the depth and breadth of the monumental task they had committed themselves to accomplishing, transforming a swamp into a majestic White City worthy of hosting the world at its 1893 World's Fair.

Our own journey was carrying us away from cities, into the majesty of true wilderness, and I was daily discovering the magnitude of the challenge we had undertaken. For so long, the John Muir Adventure had been my romantic notion. I had not expected it to be easy. I knew I would face tough physical tests. The reality was so much more. The first four days had been filled with lightning storms and blisters, mosquitoes and scary river crossings, wet clothes, a drowned camera, pain, fear, and self-doubt.

There had also been transcendent beauty that defied capture or description, peacefulness, and genuine companionship. The unpredictable reality, I was finding, was bigger in every conceivable way than my imagination could have conjured.

Starting Point — Davis Lake Trail Junction (Grotto Camp) — 9680 feet
Ending Point — Ediza Lake Trail Junction at Shadow Creek — 9000 feet
Highest Point — Island Pass — 10,205 feet
Distance Covered — 7.4 miles
Cumulative Miles — 22.9 miles

Down The Staircase

Wild rivers are earth's renegades, defying gravity,
dancing to their own tunes, resisting the authority of humans,
always chipping away, and eventually always winning.
~ Richard Bangs & Christian Kallen, *River Gods*

Day Five
July 23, 2006

Starting Point — Ediza Lake Trail Junction at Shadow Creek — 9000 feet

"Ladies, we have a decision to make," Cappy said early in the morning. She had been scouring the map and guidebook again as we ate breakfast under a blanket of low, gray of clouds.

"Between here and Red's Meadow, the John Muir Trail and the Pacific Crest Trail split apart to follow different routes. And they intermix with a couple other trails, the River Trail and the Shadow Creek Trail. We need to choose just one route." She had finished her breakfast and worked on dismantling her tent while she talked. "Do we want to stay on the JMT? Or do we want to jump over to one of the others?"

She went on to describe what the guidebook said about each option. The description of the JMT was not pretty. She paused working to read a couple quotes. The book warned we would be "tackling a dusty, switchbacking climb" and "descending loose pumice" and walking past "overused" camping areas.[10] The route Cappy preferred stuck to the river's path away from most of the volcanic dust and rocks.

We debated the pros and cons of each while preparing our gear and ourselves. Should we be "true" to the JMT, or should we venture off and choose the more attractive route?

I taped my feet as we talked, trying to duplicate precisely the previous day's wrappings, which had provided my first pain-free day. Again, I intended to wear my sandals with socks. Again, my boots would hitch a ride dangling from my backpack.

In the end, Jane and I deferred to Cappy's greater knowledge and stronger feelings. That turned out to be a brilliant choice. The combination of the Shadow Creek Trail and the River Trail was both a visual delight and a wild adventure.

It began as a gentle hike through a lovely forest with the trail following along the banks of a raging Shadow Creek. The water swept back and forth between steep, black rock walls and bounded over boulders that tried to block its way. It foamed and splashed and called out in the roaring voice of a great beast. The bellowing and thrashing stopped suddenly when the water spread out into aptly named Shadow Lake. Still, blue-gray water sat in a rocky bowl and reflected, like an antique mirror losing its silvering, the exact, inverted images of the trees lining its edges.

---

[10] Thomas Winnett and Kathy Morey, *Guide to the John Muir Trial* (Wilderness Press, 1998) p. 24.

At the lake's other end, its outlet, the creek continued and so did our trail, until together they encountered the edge of a steep cliff.

The river did *not* execute a graceful swan dive from top to bottom, slipping smoothly, toes pointed, into the basin far below. Rather, it leapt headlong off the wall, caroming, bouncing, and crashing off every bump and ledge on the steep stone walls, plummeting at a reckless pace. We stood peering over the precipice, watching the river fall into the abyss.

Our trail followed the river, taking a parallel plunge downward towards a junction with the San Joaquin River out of sight nearly a thousand feet below. Chiseled from the rust-and-charcoal-colored rock, a staircase hugged the canyon wall alongside the falling water like a fire escape clinging to an old brick building. The steps, moist with spray, shone with the slick wetness.

"Looks slippery." Cappy said what I had been thinking. I could almost see the gears in her head turning as she stood perfectly still and surveyed the challenge ahead.

"Reminds me of the Mist Trail in Yosemite," Jane smiled. It did resemble that popular, wet trail that rose from Yosemite Valley past Vernal Falls to Nevada Falls. As though Jane had waved her magic wand, by comparing the steep, wet-blackened trail to one we'd each hiked several times, the anxiety that had filled the air receded.

"Hiking sticks, extend," I deadpanned in my best imitation of a military command while unclipping the locks and pulling my telescoping poles out another six inches. Testing their length, I stood upright atop the first step, without bending forward, and tapped the poles' tips on the flat of the next step down. Descending with the poles outstretched in front of me, I could remain stable on my feet, even as the trail fell away and my pack clung top-heavy to my back. Beside me, Jane and Cappy clicked their poles into equally lengthy dimensions.

Pulling back several curly wisps of hair that were dangling in her face, Cappy undid and redid, in one swift and practiced move, the tie at the nape of her neck, recapturing the strays. "What do you think is the best way to approach this?" she asked. We both turned towards Jane to hear her reply.

"Take it slowly and really use your poles to lower yourself down," Jane said. "Your upper body can take some of the pressure off your knees and toes."

"We should spread ourselves out a bit, too," she added, spreading her hands wide in gesture. "If I fall, I don't want to start a human domino cascade."

"What an awful visual!" I imagined the spectacle of arms, legs, packs, and poles bouncing down the staircase like three entangled Slinkys, but it did make me laugh.

"I hadn't thought of that!" Cappy turned to look down the cliff towards the river.

"I'm glad you're with us, Jane," I said. "You're our levelheaded backcountry guru."

Jane smiled and shook her head, her thick pageboy hair waggling ever so slightly. Anyone other than Jane would have added an eye-roll. She just sighed, accepting my comment for the genuine admiration it was.

"Who's going to give us sage advice and keep us out of trouble after you leave us?" I asked. Jane's one week with us was more than half over. Her departure from Red's Meadow in two days would leave a hole in our team.

We began to pick our way down the staircase, with Cappy in the lead and Jane in the middle. I waited while Jane took three steps downward before I began lowering myself into the chasm. I anchored each hiking stick on the granite one step below my feet, then reached down with my right toes. I lowered the weight of my body and pack using the muscles in my left leg. I thought about Jane's advice and directed the muscles in my shoulders and arms to contract in time with those in my left leg.

Once there, I discovered the step's top was too broad for one stride. So, after taking two baby steps, I repeated the process. After only a score of these slow downward levitations, my left leg complained with a slight quiver, and my right foot hit the bottom with a small jarring thunk. With a little soft-shoe shuffle, my legs exchanged roles, so that it became my right leg's job to perform the lowering and my left foot's to touch down.

The trailblazers who had built this stretch of the trail had done a Herculean job, sculpting it from granite with hand-held tools lugged in on their backs, but they must have been men of Herculean stature as well, for the steps they carved were half again as tall and wide as would accommodate one of humble mortal proportions. My stride fit neither the rise nor the run of the staircase. Each step downward ended with a small drop that was followed by a mincing two-step to position myself for the next drop.

This awkward gait required a laser focus. I could walk, or I could admire the harsh beauty of the rock and the water, but not both at the same time. Multitasking while descending could be fatal. Even the sound of the water had receded into white noise, as I focused on the clicking of my hiking poles and the clunking and sandpaper scratching of my own footfalls on rock.

"I'm calling a Kodak moment." Using an outdated euphemism for a rest stop, I called out to Jane, who passed my message on to Cappy.

Cappy slowed. Jane and I caught up. We paused on the stairs, stacked up one just above the other.

"Why is it," I wondered, "that the prospect of going downhill sounds so lovely, but the reality of it is so painful?"

"Downhills beat up my body," Cappy agreed. "Each step jams my toes into the front of my boots."

I was glad to be wearing my open-toed Teva sandals. My blistered toes were already tender enough without the added violence Cappy was experiencing.

The sheer canyon wall that rose straight into the sky defined the left edge of our path. To our right, on the far side of the river, the canyon's other wall was its twin. It looked like the canyon had been formed when a narrow slice had been cut from a giant layer cake, revealing multicolored striations of varying thicknesses and textures in hues from caramel and dark chocolate to gingerbread.

Between the walls high overhead, the narrow swath of visible sky was a cloudless, pale blue. The sun stood directly overhead, staring down on our heads and shoulders. To the right of our feet, the trail's edge dropped as straight as gravity to the water below.

The sound of the water, a dull background noise while I had walked, separated itself into its multitude of parts when I gave it my full attention. Like a chorus in surround-sound, the soprano splashes and splats mixed with alto gurgles and deep bass roars and moans, all of which reverberated off the vertical walls.

The water separated and rejoined itself over and around protruding rocks and threw itself into the air. I welcomed the mist that fell on my skin. Though it lasted only a moment before evaporating in the heat of the midday sun, it cooled my hot, sweaty body.

A young fir tree, gnarled beyond its years, grew right out of the canyon face directly across the rocky abyss from where we stood. Dark green needles and burnished rock, wet from spray, sparkled in the sun. "How do you suppose that little tree got started growing there?" I pointed with my pole across the space.

Cappy turned to look where I pointed. "Amazing! A real testament to life."

Looking around, I became aware of numerous small plants clinging to the rocks. I pulled a tender stem from a silver-green shrub growing from a crack where my step met the rock wall to my left. I crushed it gently between my finger and thumb before putting it to my nose. Its pleasant spicy aroma tickled and made me smile. I took several more deep whiffs. "Jane, what's this?" I held up the greenery and pointed to the little shrub beside me. It smelled familiar, and I knew Jane would find it in her mental catalogue of native plants.

She looked closely at the silver-green plant, reached out to touch it, and then said, "Lavender—a particularly compact version that likes these hot rocky places."

I put the cutting back to my nose and breathed it in. Its tanginess completely drowned out my own strong scent. Four days of hard walking had passed since we had last enjoyed showers, and we had each developed a piquant aroma. You know you stink when your own unique odor rises up and sends your nose into an automatic curl. I grabbed a second sweet-smelling twig and stuffed them both down the front of my shirt, like a Medieval maiden warding off the plague.

Despite the starkness of the canyon walls, there was an abundance of flowers and small aromatic shrubs growing from the cracks along the trail's verge. As the trail became a little less steep, a little less precarious, Cappy and I quizzed Jane on all the flowers within reach.

"Could you give us another little lesson, Jane?" Cappy asked, her eyes alight with this sudden idea.

"You're sure you really want to get me started again?" Jane laughed, looking from one to the other of us for confirmation.

"As long as there's no test at the end," I said. "Maybe this will be the time the names stick!"

Cappy agreed. "I enjoy hearing the same lessons every year!"

"Okay, but stop me when you've had enough," Jane said.

To be safe, we came to a complete stop at each new flower, and our descent slowed to a crawl.

"This peach-colored one is monkey flower. See its little face?" She picked one blossom, held it out, and gently squeezed it so the petals moved and the flower made "faces" at us.

Jane named every plant we encountered. Many flowers came with an anecdote or a bit of history or botany lore. The deeper we climbed into the shade of the canyon, the more plentiful the plants became, turning the stark environment into a hanging garden. Jane gave each flower a proper introduction and that evening she would help list them all in my journal: Mariposa lily, mountain pride, ranger's buttons, and monk's hood. Larkspur and delphinium. Columbine, pussy paws, and goldenrod. Forget-me-nots, wall flowers, and cow parsnips. Cappy and I oohed and aahed with each revelation.

"Here's another edible one." Jane handed me the long hollow leaf of a wild onion. "Chew on this while you walk. You'll find it refreshing."

So now I was stuffing some plants in my shirt and munching on others. Time flew as Jane's guided flower walk carried us effortlessly down the trail, and abruptly, we found ourselves at the bottom of the thousand-foot drop.

Deep in the river's broad canyon, away from the splash of the falling water, the trail grew dry and dusty. Paused in the shade of quaking aspens, we found ourselves in another debate. The map showed two ways of getting to Red's Meadow, where food shipments, showers, and a cafe awaited us. Option One required us to walk six miles to Red's Meadow. Option Two took us about a mile to Agnew Meadows, where we could grab a shuttle bus to Red's instead. It seemed we were back in civilization.

"I think we should take the shuttle," Cappy said. She removed her pack, sat down on a fallen log, and spread the map open on the ground in front of her. She pointed to each of the meadows on the map, and then to the spot where we sat. "We're all tired, and I'm really looking forward to those showers." Cappy looked tired. The creases around her eyes darkened them, snuffing out the twinkle I usually saw there.

"But that's cheating," I said. Though equally rung out by the day's difficult descent, I was feeling stubborn. "Worse than a shortcut, we're actually skipping a few miles of the trail. I vote for the longer walk." I rotated the map to look more closely at the topo lines the trail ahead would cross. "It seems like a pretty flat walk, not a lot of ups and downs."

"Jane needs to get to Red's to call Rand and let him know where exactly to pick her up," Cappy said, attempting to pull Jane into the disagreement.

"We're still going to get there this evening. She can still call him. It'll just be a bit later," I said. I felt strongly that we should walk each and every step of the trail, that taking the shuttle bus would somehow discount our accomplishment.

While Cappy and I politely, but insistently, presented our arguments, Jane remained silent. She was leaving us at Red's. She had only planned on doing the first leg of the trail, so a couple of miles one way or another was not an issue for her.

"It's not cheating," Cappy said. "Lots of PCT thru-hikers use the shuttles."

"You're right about what other people do, but it feels like cheating to me. You made a great choice this morning, Cappy, when you pushed us to take the Shadow Creek Trail—it turned out to be a beautiful route. But this time, I really disagree." I stood back up.

"Okay, you win," Cappy said. I think she relented in the afternoon's debate, because she had gotten her way earlier in the day. Or maybe she gave in because she did not have the energy to argue any longer.

The gorgeous morning trail gave way to a hideous path. It was dry, it was hot, and it was ugly. Each step tossed clouds of dust into the air. After a short distance, our feet and legs were coated in the powder-fine grit. There were no shade trees. Hip-high vegetation, bordering the narrow path on both sides, reached out with prickly wooden stems to scratch at our bare legs.

Each step was a labor, and my pack stuck to my sweat-soaked back. More sweat trickled between my breasts, soaking my sports bra, then ran lower to make a dark ring around my body where the hip belt held my pack to me. I pulled out my hidden lavender stem and tossed it aside.

After trudging a mile-and-a-half, we stopped for lunch when we found a rare wide spot, a gritty turnout by the side of the dirt trail. In silence, we ate fast, barely breathing between bites, and drank large quantities of water to replace the perspiration that poured from our skin. Cappy pulled out the map to check our progress.

For the hundredth time I used my already dusty bandana to wipe away the sweat and dirt coating my face. I removed my cap. No curls remained—my damp hair was plastered to my head. I combed my hair back with my fingers, tucking it all up and into the cap as I replaced it.

Finally, I looked directly at Cappy. "I'm sorry I pushed for this path," I said. "Yet again, Cappy, you were right. This is awful. I wish I'd listened to you. If we had not come so far, I'd suggest retracing our steps."

"Thank you." Cappy held my eyes with hers. "I appreciate that." She grabbed the map again and spread it out to show our dusty spot beside the trail.

With a half-smile, she said, "You'll be glad to know we have an opportunity to undo the problem coming up here in a quarter of a mile or so."

"What do you mean?" asked Jane. She leaned in to see the map.

"Here, look." Cappy pointed to a few places on the map. "This is where we are. Here's Red's, and here's Agnew."

There was a trail cutoff that would take us back to Agnew Meadows where the shuttle stopped. In changing direction, we would lose only a half-mile, and we would still be able to take advantage of the shuttle option. The decision was immediate and unanimous.

Within an hour, we arrived at Agnew Meadows to find not only the bus stop, but also a *real* bathroom with flushing toilets and running water to wash our hands and faces.

"What a delight!" I emerged from the small building wringing out my all-purpose neckerchief and wiping my neck and shoulders with its cool dampness.

A bus stop sign displayed the shuttle schedule, and the next bus would arrive in fewer than ten minutes. A uniformed employee, wearing a bright red cap and matching red company shirt, appeared out of nowhere. He talked with us as we waited in the shade by the restroom. "Over there—" He pointed across the street at the best spot to wait for the bus. "—the driver will be sure to see you and stop."

Moving across the road, however, meant re-hoisting my pack, and never had it felt so heavy. Really it was not, as I had eaten most of my food stock, but it felt like it contained a bag of rocks. The long, hot hike had zapped me of all the energy I had absorbed from the morning's rainbow-colored trail.

That lovely gray-haired gentleman must have thought we looked pathetic in our disheveled and exhausted state. A real knight-in-shining-armor, he insisted on helping each of the distressed damsels lift her pack onto her back. Like it was filled with goose down, he picked mine up and held it high while I slipped my arms through the straps. Then he lowered it gently onto my shoulders after my hip belt was securely buckled.

"Good luck." He smiled as he waved goodbye, climbed into his pickup truck, and drove away. Blink, and he was gone. Another trail angel had come to our rescue at the precise moment we needed him.

Red's Meadow wrapped us in the smothering embrace of civilization, bombarding us the moment we stepped off the shuttle with the sights, sounds, and smells of summer vacation crowds. Sunburned faces and banana-scented suntan lotion. Fluorescent t-shirts and Hawaiian-print shorts. "Mommy, Mommy!" and "Hurry up!" Straw hats, sunglasses, and the clip-clop of flip-flops on the packed dirt.

My first instinct was to flee back to the safety of the wilderness, but instead, together, we sought refuge in the shelter of a tall tree, the centerpiece of the swirling courtyard.

After only five days in the relative isolation of the trail, even the moderate commotion of this outpost overwhelmed my senses. People moved around us— children darting ahead of their parents, dogs tugging on leashes, more people in two minutes than we had seen in five days. I felt disconnected from my surroundings, isolated and alone in the crowd. It reminded me of that surreal feeling of looking up from a good book that has held me engrossed for hours to find that for a moment, I am lost between two worlds.

With our backs to the sturdy tree, the camp store stood to the left, a jumble of bikes propped up near the door. People emerged holding bottles of soda and rainbow-hued Popsicles. To our right, a rustic cafe emitted familiar aromas. *Was that apple pie? Could I really be smelling French fries?* Straight ahead a sign pointed us to the backpackers' camp a quarter-mile beyond.

I shook my head and rubbed my eyes. *What first? Should I pick up my food cache at the store? Sit down to a real meal at the cafe? Set up camp? Take a shower?* With each step in the hot sun, all afternoon, I had daydreamed about a chocolate-dipped ice cream bar. My body leaned, half turning toward the camp store, where an ice cream freezer stood pulling me like an ice-cold magnet.

"Let's go find a campsite." Cappy's voice broke into my thoughts.

"Don't you want to get your supply box?" I asked. "The store's right here."

"I don't want to carry the box and my pack at the same time," she said. "We can claim a site, drop off our packs, and then come back."

How logical, I thought. "Good idea," I said. I shrugged my pack higher up on my back, took a long sip of lukewarm water from my CamelBak, and began to move towards the sign with its arrow aimed towards the backpackers' sites.

"We should put up our tents, too," Jane added as we walked three abreast across the courtyard. "It's going to rain."

She was right, too. The skies to the north and west were bulging with dark clouds. The thunderstorms had found us again. That would make it six days in a row, unusual in the Sierra. I hoped it was the last storm for a while.

The path to the campground took a slippery, soggy route across a meadow saturated from several days of rain and edged with blackberry bushes. The trail sank deep into the squishy ground. Where the path was completely submerged, long narrow planks had been laid out, sometimes stacked two and three atop one another, forming a drunken boardwalk that zigzagged haphazardly across the meadow. Though the lumber successfully showed the direction of the footpath and kept us from sinking into the mud deep enough to lose our shoes, it did not keep our feet high and dry.

Tired and top-heavy with packs, we walked in a careful parade along the unstable timber path. Halfway across the field, I foolishly planted my sandaled foot off-center on a wobbly board. The nasty troll under the bridge tipped the plank on its edge and tried to toss me off into the mud. To keep myself upright, to avoid launching into the mud, my arms wind-milled, while my dancing feet and my pounding heart did an undisciplined, high-speed duet.

Finally, my balance restored, I was able to take my eyes off my feet and look at my hiking partners. Terrified at the thought of just how close I had come to adding a very muddy disaster to my growing list of mishaps, I was slow to realize the humor. My partners, on the other hand, judged me comical almost immediately. "We can't start laughing now," Jane warned, stifling her own escaping chuckle. "Wait until we're back to solid ground."

"No worries," I assured her. "I've too much adrenaline flooding my arteries to laugh just yet." Jane shook her head. Cappy was probably rolling her eyes, but I missed that part.

Jane turned and led the way, one careful footstep at a time, until our parade came to the end of the planks and stepped off onto the lush green terra semi-firma. Turning to look back the way we had come, across the length of a football field, I half expected to see a troll winking at me from his hiding place beneath one of the planks.

The trail ended at the backpackers' camp, curving among the dozen or so small tree-shaded sites. In contrast to the hustle-bustle of Red's main courtyard, the campsites were silent. Most were empty. Two contained tents and equipment, but no people. A Steller's jay cleaning crew, making a sweep of the vacated sites, hopped on and under wooden picnic tables and around the steel bear-boxes, scavenging for edible droppings left by previous human occupants. The birds kept their keen eyes on us as we approached, but did not relinquish any ground.

At the end of the camp trail, where the path headed across a stream and into the woods, we turned back to survey the sites we had passed. "Which spot shall we claim?" Cappy asked. "I like this one on the end." She unbuckled her pack.

"I agree. Fewer neighbors, more trees—and the sound of moving water," I said, slipping off my pack and propping it against the large, metal bear-box. It felt good to be rid of the weight. I arched my back to stretch my muscles, leaning left and right, feeling my back snap-crackle-and-pop as it loosened up.

Jane's pack was off, and she was already loosening its outer straps to get at her portion of our tent. While we had traversed the boardwalk, the black battleship clouds had swept in and were nearly above us. "If we're lucky, we can get the tents up before the rain starts," Jane said, as she clicked together the bungeed tent poles. Hustling, we had both tents up in moments.

"We're getting good at this," I said.

Large drops of rain began to plop, first one, then several, into the dirt, making little asterisks in the dust, the opening salvo from the storm's leading edge. I pulled my raingear and a large, black plastic trash bag from outer pockets on my pack. After donning rain jacket and hood, and stuffing money and ID into my pockets, I slipped the plastic bag over my pack, pulling it snuggly all the way to the ground.

Finished, I asked, "Ready?"

"Ready," they both responded.

The trip back across the zigzagging boards was much easier without the top-heavy tower on my back. No trolls played under the planks, even when we stepped over our own muddy footprints. Our pace was quick—we covered the distance from camp to store in half the time.

What first? Dinner? Food packages? Phone calls? I thought as I walked along. "Shall we get our boxes from the store first? Or eat a real meal in the cafe first?" I said aloud.

"I can't wait to call Jim." Cappy marched along at the head of the group. "I think I saw a pay phone in front of the store."

"A restaurant meal sounds so good right now," Jane said. "Especially fresh fruit." Jane followed Cappy, her eyes on the wood where she placed her feet.

We talked right past each other, more thinking aloud to ourselves than having a conversation.

"Jane needs to get ahold of Rand right away." Cappy's voice barely reached all the way back to me.

Head down and hood up, I kept my eyes on my feet, making sure I stayed far enough behind Jane to never step onto a board Jane was still traversing.

"I want a salad, a really big salad. But first, I want ice cream." I was completely under the spell of my body's cravings. Right then, three thousand calories did not seem nearly enough for one day.

The boardwalk ended abruptly, and a few feet later, the trail deposited us in front of the small camp store. Cappy grabbed the screen door handle and pulled it open wide. The wooden frame was weathered and the metal screen dented in several places. The hinges squeaked and groaned, announcing our arrival and making the tinkle of the attached bell unnecessary, then slapped itself closed loudly behind us.

Inside, tall shelves along the walls were stacked ceiling high with every kind of outdoor supply and tool imaginable. Additional shelves, creating narrow aisles through the small store, were laden with a camper's or hiker's every possible need, from axes, Band-Aids, and cold cereal, to repair kits, stove fuel, and t-shirts sporting images of wild animals and emblazoned with "Red's Meadow Resort." The sheer quantity of brightly colored stuff assaulted my eyes, yet somehow, at the same time, the abundance was attractive. I would come back later to see if there were any disposable cameras hidden in the jumble.

What to do first? I was torn between grabbing an ice cream bar or going to the counter to retrieve my precious box of cached food and personal supplies. Without hesitation, Cappy stepped towards the counter to join a line of half-a-dozen others. The crowd made my opposite decision easy.

Jane and I stood together at the ice cream freezer carefully surveying the selection. Häagen-Dazs Vanilla Chocolate Peanut Butter. Chocolate Dark Chocolate. Coffee Almond Crunch. Dreyer's Cookies 'N Cream. The Original Klondike. Whole Fruit Bars. Good Humor Strawberry Shortcake and Drumstix.

"What are you gonna get?" I asked, hoping for decision-making assistance.

"Hmmm. Not sure yet. I want to savor the choosing," Jane replied, without taking her eyes away from the cold box.

I slid open the small freezer's glass door and snatched up a Coffee Almond Crunch bar, Jane chose a Klondike, and we both headed for the counter, where Cappy was already near the head of the line. Waiting my turn, I concentrated all my attention on enjoying the creamy, crunchy confection in my hand.

Teenagers, children, couples, lone adults, all in casual summer attire, moved around the store. Some were scruffy long-distance hikers like us, dressed in the uniform of dusty trail wear and hiking footwear. Others, guests at the resort, were attired in colorful shorts and t-shirts, even bathing suits.

Cappy turned from the counter empty-handed and strode towards us. "My food package isn't here!" She had removed her hat and was nervously pushing errant wisps of curly hair from her face. A crease had deepened between her brows.

"What?" I asked. That was not good news. "How can that be?"

"The woman said to check back tomorrow. There will be another delivery in the morning." She shrugged. "But I mailed it over two weeks ago. It should already be here." Her usual impish countenance sagged.

"Don't worry," I encouraged her. "We'll figure this out." Inside, I wondered if it would be that easy.

"I'll meet you two outside." Cappy retreated towards the door, which ushered her out with a creak.

Jane paid for her snack then followed Cappy.

It was my turn. "Hi. I'm hoping you have a box for me." I gave the woman behind the counter my name, and she headed into the back room to find my food cache.

Waiting, my hands kept busy folding and refolding the ice cream wrapper into precise geometric shapes, while my brain perseverated on the fate of my box. *What would I do if my box were not there?* A missing supply box would be the last straw for me. If my box was not there, I'd just pack up and go home with Jane.

The store clerk returned after a few very long minutes with a familiar cardboard box in her hands. "This yours?" she asked, aiming the address label towards me.

"Yes! It's mine."

A wave of calm flowed through me as I greeted the box like an old friend. Pulling it to my chest, I said, "Thank the gods, you made it. I was worried about you!" With my left arm wrapped protectively around the package, I paid for my ice cream with the right.

"Thank you!" I told the clerk. I tossed my origami wrapper into the trashcan by the door, and clutching my treasure to my chest, I exited the store. I found my two companions beneath the towering conifer at the center of the courtyard. Jane reclined on a bench in the shade, while Cappy stood at an old-fashioned black pay phone recounting the tale of the missing box to Jim.

Spotting me with my food parcel, Cappy pointed at it, raised her eyebrows, nodded and smiled. Then she told Jim, "Joan's box is here!" In a higher pitched voice, she added, "Why isn't mine?"

My excitement over the prospect of opening my box was dampened by Cappy's lack of one, so I joined Jane on the wooden bench and held it unopened in my lap.

"Let's eat!" Cappy said, sounding her optimistic self again, as she hung up the receiver. Jane and I leapt up, and we all headed across the courtyard to the restaurant.

We assembled ourselves around a table beside a window. I carefully placed my precious box on the table's fourth chair then sank into my own. After sitting on logs and rocks and dirt for five days, the support of the simple wooden chair felt luxurious. Red's Meadow Cafe was bright and cheerful in a rustic country way, built of logs and river rock. The menu offered a variety of standard American fare.

I asked the waitress, "How big is the salad that comes with an entrée?"

"It's small, about like this," she said, her hands making a six-inch circle. "They're really good, made with all fresh ingredients."

"I am lusting after a large green salad," I said, "so I want to order two with my dinner."

"Lusting!" The waitress laughed. "I've never heard that before."

"Thoughts of crunchy greens have been consuming me all day!" I added. As good as my chosen trail dinners were, they lacked the crisp textures and bright flavors of fresh vegetables.

"I don't know that I have been lusting, but I think I'd like two, also," Cappy said, holding up two fingers, like a peace sign.

Jane set her menu on the red-and-white checked tablecloth and said, "Make that three pair."

In addition, we ordered burgers and fries, with fresh apple pie for dessert, and when they were delivered, we stuffed ourselves silly. The hamburgers were good. The fries, dipped in brown mustard, were good. The salad was an indescribable sensual pleasure, the first one—and the second one. Crispy lettuce greens, crunchy cucumber slices, and sweet tomato wedges topped with chunky bleu cheese dressing generated groans of pure pleasure, then satisfied chuckles.

Thoughts of the absent box, the drowned camera, my ankle and blisters, and mosquitoes rested on the floor beside us. I would pick them back up when we had finished our supper.

Before heading back to camp, I stopped at the pay phone to check in with family. First, I called my folks to let them know we had safely arrived at our destination. Mom and Dad were following our daily progress on the highlighted paper map and itinerary I had given them, so I knew they were anticipating a call. With one of them on each phone extension, I provided a tame version of our first days of hiking—with all the high points, but none of the difficulties. I could have told Dad all the details—he would have vicariously enjoyed our challenges. Mom, however, was a master worrier, so extreme censorship was my only option with them both on the line.

Then, I called my son, Dean, and told him the *real* story. Since he was an accomplished outdoorsman, I shared the vastly more interesting true story—including the Donohue storm, the river crossings, and the camera drowning. I recruited him to help me solve my camera problem by arranging with our friends John and Janiene to find my old camera and mail it to me at our next resupply, Vermilion Valley Resort (VVR).

We walked back to the backpackers' campsites under dark gray skies, carrying enormous slices of apple pie wrapped in foil and my unopened supply box. As we traversed the meadow this third time, the sprinkles continued. Thunder sounded a warning salvo in the near distance.

"So much for the shower plan," I said. "I've been craving a shampoo almost as much as that salad." Just the thought made my scalp itch.

Cappy agreed, "No sense in getting clean only to slop through the mud again."

"Tomorrow morning will be better for showering anyway," Jane said. Nothing ever bothered Jane.

While walking, my mind kept returning to Cappy's food predicament. *What's she going to do without her supply box? She needs to have at least four days of food when we set out tomorrow,* I thought. That would get her to VVR, where our next supply boxes would be waiting. Like me, she had spent a huge amount of time and energy planning and packing the contents of her shipment. Beyond that, where I had purchased all my meals, Cappy had cooked, dehydrated, and packaged all her own meals. *Before this day is over,* I thought, *she's got to replace everything.*

At the campground, we discovered most of the sites occupied. "It's The Three Women!" someone called out. Zoe and Nemo, our young trail friends, waved us over. They stood by a picnic table spread with dinner preparations, their tent a few feet away. Reacting to the sprinkles, they were removing clothes they had draped on a line to dry.

"We are soooooooo glad to see you!" Nemo spread his arms for a welcoming embrace. His damp black hair was held back with a blue bandana, and he had abandoned his boots for the comfort of sandals.

"We're really glad to see you!" said Cappy. We all hugged like old friends long separated.

"Nemo and I were worried about you during that big storm up on Donohue," Zoe said, smiling. Having just returned from the showers, she was bundled in fleece and working a comb through her wet hair.

"And we were awfully concerned about you," I said. "We thought you were right behind us, but never saw you again. Where'd you camp that night?"

"We'd been following you gals all day, but you kept pulling away until we couldn't see you anymore." Zoe shook her head. "We were nowhere near the top when that storm came over the pass. God, it was huge! We turned around and high-tailed it back down the mountain."

On a signal from Zoe, Nemo ran to get something from their tent. He returned holding up a pair of green hiking shorts in one hand and a bright orange hand trowel in the other. "Look what we found! Do they look familiar?"

We all laughed. "I wondered where my poop-scoop went!" Cappy reached out to take the little shovel. "Where'd you find it?"

"Those're my shorts," said Jane. "I realized I'd dropped them up on Donohue. I never expected to see them again."

"That's right where we found 'em," Nemo said, nodding, and tossing them to Jane, "just short of the eleven-thousand-foot sign. The bright orange shovel caught my eye. We thought it might be yours."

"When Nemo picked it up, the shorts were lying right next to it," added Zoe, spreading her hands to measure two feet. "We've been asking everyone on the trail if they'd seen The Three Women. Northbound hikers told us we were following right in your tracks, but we couldn't seem to catch up."

"Finding your gear near the peak frightened us! Is that where you were during the storm?" Zoe asked.

"Not nearly as frightened as I was being up there!" I said. Then we took turns recounting our Donohue storm story. Zoe and Nemo, eyes big, heads shaking, listened in silence.

When we had finished, Nemo changed the topic and the mood. "Did you know that some people call you The Golden Girls?" he asked. "But most of us call you The Three Women. It's your trail name."

"Cool! Getting a trail name is an honor!" I looked first to Cappy and then to Jane. Cappy's smile crinkled her face from brow to chin, while Jane's pleasure bloomed as a soft glow. I knew my own face was bright with the warm happiness I felt inside.

So far, the tall trees had shielded us from the light rain, but the squall was growing and wind began to throw rain at us. The Three (Golden) Women escaped, dashing twenty yards to our tents. I put my food cache and our foil wrapped apple pie into the bear-safe then crawled into the tent. It had rained every evening since we had walked onto the trail five days earlier. We had gotten used to it, but it was still a nuisance, especially at bedtime.

In the confined space of our shared tent, Jane and I bent and twisted ourselves out of damp clothes and into sleeping bags, while next door, Cappy arranged herself in her single-person tent. Wet gear in the tent's vestibule and shed clothes at my feet, I pulled out our bedtime story, *The Devil in the White City*.

Our tents stood abreast of one another, fabric walls nearly touching, so we could talk easily and Cappy could hear as I read, even over the rain's patter. I snuggled into the depths of my down bag and thought of the cardboard box I had tucked into the bear-safe for the night. *First thing tomorrow I'll open it,* I thought. More than food, I was eager for the clean socks and underwear I had sent to myself.

"A Trail Name!" I whispered with reverence and satisfaction. "You know, a true trail name must be bestowed. You can't name yourself." Liking the official sound of it, I said again, "We have a Trail Name!"

"I feel like there's a community building out here, and we're a part of it," Cappy said through nylon.

"Me, too." I touched the words on my necklace, remembering how I was going to pretend to be strong and courageous. "We're not alone out here anymore."

Starting Point — Ediza Lake Trail Junction at Shadow Creek — 9000 feet
Ending Point — Red's Meadow Resort, Mammoth Lakes — 7500 feet
Highest Point — Ediza Lake Trail Junction at Shadow Creek — 9000 feet
Distance Covered — 7.2 miles
Cumulative Miles — 30.1 miles

R & R — Rewind & Redux

If we had no winter, the spring would not be so pleasant;
if we did not sometimes taste of adversity, prosperity would not be so welcome.
~ Anne Bradstreet, c. 1670

Day Six
July 24, 2006

Red's Meadow Resort — Layover Day — 7500 feet

Lying in my sleeping bag, the sun bright through the tent's thin walls, I turned to Jane. "G'morning!" I said. "You know, we are faced with another difficult decision."

"Good morning to you, too! What difficult decision is that?"

"We have to decide what to do first—breakfast or shower?" I said.

"I don't know. I hadn't gotten that far in my processing yet. What are the pros and cons?" Jane replied, smiling, her voice still morning soft. Her down bag was pulled up to her chin against the chill air. Her thick hair encircled her face.

"It's a dilemma," I said. "My scalp itches and my body's pungent, so I'd love a nice hot shower right away. However, as cold as it is, the warmth of the shower will dissipate in less time than it will take me to dress in my clean clothes." I rolled over onto my side to see Jane better. "I'd like to wait until I can savor that hot shower even after I'm out of it."

"That's one argument," Jane said, humoring me.

"Besides, I'm betting there are lots of early birds already in line, already using up that hot water—so, I cast my vote for breakfast at the cafe, followed by hot showers."

"You make a compelling argument." Jane raised her eyebrows and nodded.

I felt more optimistic and lighthearted that morning than I had since twisting my ankle. We had planned a layover day at Red's, and I intended to make good use of that time. I would replenish my pack and myself, clean up, heal up, and make a fresh start on my adventure. JMT Adventure: Take Two!

I worked my way out of my bag and into yesterday's clothes. There were clean underwear and socks waiting for me in the cache box, but I would save those until after my shower.

Crawling out of the tent, I discovered Cappy, her toiletry supplies under her arm and tiny towel over her shoulder. "You're up," she said. "I decided not to wait. I'm going to the showers."

Change of plans, I thought.

Jane crawled out. I pointed to Cappy's receding back. "Difficult decision made," I said. "We're showering first."

I retrieved my food canister and cache box from the large metal bear safe and sliced through the box's packing tape with my pocketknife. From the supply box, I pulled out fresh panties, a tank top, and socks. From the food canister, I pulled my toiletries. I piled trial-sized tubes of shampoo, conditioner, shower gel, moisturizer, and sunscreen on top of my little chamois towel. I added my comb. I had only one pair of shorts, which I was wearing. I wrapped everything protectively inside a light cotton sarong and returned the leftovers to the bear safe.

"Let's eat!" Cappy's voice startled me. I turned around to see her striding back to camp looking exactly like she had looked ten minutes earlier when she had walked away towards the showers, except now she was frowning.

"I thought you were showering," I said, "but you're still dry."

Unzipping her tent, Cappy threw the clothes she had been carrying inside. "There's a long line. We'll come back later." She set her shampoo and soap inside the bear locker.

"Great. I'm looking forward to an omelet," Jane, unfazed, agreed, grabbing her fanny pack from the table. "Let's check the store again for your box while we're there."

"The next mail delivery won't be there until almost noon," Cappy stated, moving towards the trail again.

"Maybe there's a different person working today, someone who'll have a different story," I suggested.

Returning from breakfast, still without Cappy's box despite a second inquiry at the store, we were surprised to see a large crowd gathered around Zoe and Nemo's campsite. In an attempt to lighten their too-heavy loads, they were offering their over-abundance of foodstuffs to anyone who wanted them. Spread across the picnic table was a plentiful display of trail foods—granola bars, instant oatmeal, dried fruit, dehydrated meals, crackers and cookies, peanuts, packages of hot chocolate, and candy.

Most SOBO hikers shared their problem at this point in the journey, having too much food rather than too little. People over-plan, not knowing how quickly they will walk, how much ground they will cover, or how much they will eat. I had done that. I still had that one extra just-in-case day's worth of food I had packed for the first leg in my bear can. And there was another just-in-case in the cache box I had yet to unpack.

As it turned out, our just-in-case day had arrived in a different form. With Cappy's resupply box having gone MIA, the extras became necessities. Jane and I could each give Cappy our extras from the first leg, but she would still need to acquire three more days' worth of food.

Zoe's and Nemo's little backpackers' garage sale was a perfect solution to Cappy's problem, and Cappy's problem was a perfect solution for theirs. She immediately began selecting the things she wanted.

"I want both of these meals," she said. "And this oatmeal and hot chocolate, too." She began to pull out her money pouch to pay for the food. "How much do you want for all this?"

"No, no," Nemo said. "We don't want your money, Cappy. This is a gift. We don't need it, and you do." He put his hand up to signal his unwillingness to take her money.

"Are you sure you won't take it? You might need it later," she insisted gratefully.

"Absolutely not," agreed Zoe. "You can buy us beers at VVR instead, if you want."

"Perfect," Cappy agreed. However, I suspected we would not see our trail friends at VVR. That was four or five days hence, and their youth was certain to carry them far ahead, no matter how much rejuvenation we gained from our day off. Actually, I was surprised they were taking a "zero day" at Red's, too. I had expected them to be on their way early that morning, though I was pleased we would get a little more time with them.

The crowd at the "food garage sale" included a young man we had not met before. Ryan was lean, almost skinny, and dirtier than the rest of us, if that was possible. I think it was because his hiking clothes and gear all seemed old, and mismatched, like everything he carried was a hand-me-down. Ryan's blond hair was longish, hanging down his neck and into his eyes. He kept pushing it back from his face with soiled hands. With long slender fingers, he grabbed several bags of food off the table, placing them into a drawstring cloth bag.

Cappy mentioned needing to purchase some specific kinds of food that Zoe and Nemo's stores could not provide. It was Ryan who told us about a huge barrel at the cafe filled with leftover food free to those in need. It turned out many SOBO hikers, who had made the same abundant over-calculations we had, deposited their extra food in that barrel for anyone who needed to take it. That was really good news for Cappy.

"I'm definitely going to check that out," Cappy told Ryan. Her full smile had returned.

"We just came from the cafe and didn't see it. How'd you know about it?" I asked.

"It's in the corner, but if you ask, they'll point it out." He turned to look at me. "I'm walking north, and I heard about it from some south-bounders I camped with a couple nights back."

He had been on the trail a lot longer than we had, having started a few weeks earlier down at Whitney. When asked, Ryan spoke quickly, with some bravado, about his travels so far. He was hiking the opposite direction to the rest of us, so he had already crossed country we had yet to see, and we were eager to hear his descriptions. We would be climbing to higher elevations and encountering both snow and snow melt, so we quizzed Ryan.

Continuing to wear his smile, Ryan radiated as he described how he was spending his summer. He had left school. He had no job. He had lost his apartment and his girlfriend. He had sold his car for cash, borrowed necessities for backpacking, and began walking the John Muir Trail. He carried no water filter, no bear canister, and little food. "I put my mattress and all my other stuff in a friend's garage and just took off to find some adventures," he told us. "It's a cheap way to live, man!" He pointed at his pack where it leaned against a tree, its frame dented and pack stained. "I have everything I need on my back, clothes, shelter, a bed. What I don't have, I can find. Water in streams and lakes. Food in barrels along the trail. And friends. I've met friends every day. Just like you guys!"

With his announcement, I realized who he reminded me of. Fearless, friendly, happy, generous, full of bravado, and breaking so many rules of the trail, this was Huck Finn reincarnated. The JMT was his Mississippi River, and he carried his raft on his back.

"Have you had any difficulty crossing snowfields or fording rivers?" Nemo asked, voicing a question we all carried.

"Yeah, Dude, there was one place I lost the trail for a while under the snow. It was crazy! You know what sun cups are? Anyway, I came across a couple of PCT hikers that seemed to really know where they were going, walkin' really fast, ya know. I think they had GPS, and they were wearing crampons—I mean they were bookin' it. So, I just followed 'em. No worries," Ryan explained.

"Where was that?" Nemo asked again.

"Muir Pass. It was radical!" Ryan bobbed on the toes of his boots while he talked, his muscles flexing and relaxing with each bounce.

"What about Silver Pass?" Cappy broke into the conversation, her face tight, eyes focused, as she listened to Ryan's trail descriptions. We would get to Silver Pass before Muir.

"Silver had snow, too, but only on the north side. It was cool. I just skied down the mountain," he laughed and flipped the hair from his twinkling eyes.

"Skied?" Zoe nearly whispered.

"Yeah, it was crazy! I just skied down on my boots. Ya just run off the top and keep on runnin' until ya start slidin' and before you know it, you're at the bottom."

Crazy, for sure, I was thinking. I was more concerned about crossing rivers than snow, so I asked about upcoming fords.

"Dude, there are some real wild rivers to wade through," he said. "There's even a waterfall to walk through."

"A waterfall?" Nemo asked.

"Yeah, Dude. I heard somebody fell off that one, but I don't know if that's true or not. And Deer Creek Crossing was crazy, too. Clear up to my waist. I thought I was gonna have to swim across or somethin'. But I just ran across instead. And here I am, Man. Lived to tell the story," Ryan grinned widely and bounced around as he talked.

As we headed back to our campsite, our hands filled with Cappy's new food supplies, her relief was obvious. Though she had been outwardly nonchalant, almost dismissive about it, I knew the missing box had been causing her distress. Her face was squeezed a bit tighter around the edges, and she was more antsy than usual.

We spread the food out on our picnic table, so Cappy could take stock of what she had and what she was still missing.

"What a great find!" Jane said. "All of this *and* the barrel."

I was chewing on the information in Ryan's stories. "How much of what he said do you think was accurate description and how much was hyperbole?" I looked at Cappy, since it was she and I who were headed towards the passes and fords he had described.

"I'm going to guess it's fifty-fifty—Dude," said Jane, her face and eyes expressionless.

Making eye contact, we smiled, then laughed until I had tears running down my face and had to sit on the picnic bench. I hoped she was right.

Arranging her new food into the metal bear box, Cappy suggested we try the showers again. I reassembled my clothes and shower supplies and was ready in a flash. When Cappy saw my assortment of little bottles and tubes, she started to tease me about the extra weight I had been lugging around, but I did not let it ruffle my feathers. I would soon be clean from head to toe.

It is often the case that when one spends time mentally constructing an imagined version of something one strongly desires, the reality simply cannot satisfy. So it was with the showers. A damp, unlighted, cinderblock room, about six-by-six, sported a shower nozzle in one corner and a hook in the opposite corner. The room was cold and dark. The floor was wet and slippery with muddy footprints. I was not sure where to set my things, or how to keep them dry while I got wet. The water started out warm and got cooler as I washed. I succeeded in shampooing and conditioning my hair while it was still warmish and that felt wonderful. Then I managed to suds my whole body while the water temperature was only cool. I rinsed myself as fast as I could, before grabbing my dirty clothes. I washed them quickly in what had become icy cold water.

Shivering, I wrung the excess water from my cleanish clothes and set them in a pile in the cleanest and driest spot I could find. I wiped myself down with my chamois and wrapped my hair in my sarong to keep the cold water from drizzling down my back. I donned fresh underwear, a clean tank top, my only pair of shorts, and my sandals.

"That was fun," I said when I arrived back at the campsite to find Jane and Cappy already there. I carefully laid out my clothes to dry, then sat to apply moisturizer to my face and sunscreen to everything else. I hung my head upside down and ran first a comb and then my fingers through my clean curls to fluff them up before they dried. Finally, I wiped the new "clean" dirt from my bare feet and redid my bandages before slipping on fluffy new hiking socks.

I was ready to begin again.

Second Leg

Red's Meadow to Vermilion Valley Resort
Day Seven to Day Ten

Just The Two Of Us

Those who contemplate the beauty of the earth
find reserves of strength that will endure as long as life lasts.
There is something infinitely healing in the repeated refrains of nature—
the assurance that dawn comes after night, and spring after winter.
~ Rachel Carson, *Silent Spring*, 1962

Day Seven
July 25, 2006

Starting Point — Red's Meadow Resort — 7500 feet

The Three Women sat at the wooden picnic table beside our tents, enjoying breakfast. "What time do you need to meet the shuttle?" Cappy asked Jane between bites.

"I need to take the nine-thirty bus," Jane said, cupping her mug of hot tea and breathing in warm vapors. "Rand's going to meet me in town at ten."

"That gives us plenty of time," I said, "but I really wish you weren't leaving us. We're stronger and braver together—or at least I am." I would miss Jane. Not only was she good company and easy to be around, but I found her low-key personality steadied me. And the way she took everything in stride was a nice contrast to Cappy's energetic intensity.

"Who's going to identify all the flowers for us?" Cappy asked.

Flower names are nice, I thought, fiddling with my necklace rings. But it was Jane's backcountry savvy and the way she unconsciously employed it to mentor us through lightning storms and water crossings that I would miss most. I would no longer be able to borrow a little of her confidence when I needed it.

Breakfast finished, I pulled out my first aid and toiletry kits to begin my morning rituals. For my blisters, I'd switched from first-aid tape to silver duct tape, as it repelled wetness better and seemed to last all day without needing repairs—my feet would resemble foil-wrapped burritos when finished. Doctoring done, I slathered on sunscreen and donned hat and sunglasses.

Jane and Cappy swapped tent parts. Jane would be taking Cappy's tiny cocoon-of-a-tent home with her, leaving us to share my two-person tent.

"Everybody ready?" Cappy adjusted her hat and the wrist straps of her walking sticks. A few errant smudges of white sunscreen dotted her forehead and chin.

I surveyed the campsite, checking in the bear box and under the table to make sure we were not leaving anything behind for the Steller's jays. "I'm not only ready, I'm cleaner and lighter," I said and picked up my own sticks.

Jane led us away from camp and across the narrow boardwalk a final time. Both the shuttle bus and the JMT departed from the courtyard.

Dropping her pack outside the store, Cappy popped in for one last check on her missing food box. Jane and I stood nearby to wait, scanning the mural-sized map of the trail painted on the store's outer wall. The location of Red's Meadow was marked with a big red star. Our next food drop at VVR was marked, too. Bears, eagles, and marmots populated the border illustrations, all of them with welcoming cartoon faces—a Disney-like interpretation of the JMT's route through the Sierra.

We drifted from the store towards the shuttle bus stop sign. "I'm going to check on Cappy," I said, leaving Jane and walking back to the store.

Standing in the doorway, I heard the bus pull up to the curb. I stuck my head in the door and called, "Cappy, the bus is here! Jane's leaving!"

I spun around to see Jane stuff her backpack into the storage area underneath the khaki-colored bus and climb aboard. Waving madly at her silhouette in the tinted window, I dashed toward the bus as it pulled away from the curb. She never saw me.

Cappy arrived at my side and said, "I can*not* believe I missed her leaving," as the bus disappeared down the narrow road. Expelling air like a deflating party balloon, Cappy's shoulders slumped, and she shook her head. "I didn't even get to say a real goodbye!"

"It happened so fast," I said.

We walked back toward the store and our waiting packs, loaded up, and walked off towards the point where the southbound JMT reentered the wilderness. Reduced from a trio, Cappy and I would be a duo for the remainder of the journey.

"You know we're going to have to abandon our trail name, don't you?" I said as we walked. "We've only known about it for two days, and already it's obsolete."

"We can't be The Three Women anymore," she agreed.

"Somehow The Two Women doesn't sound as poetic," I said.

"It doesn't have a ring to it, that's for sure."

"Too bad The Golden Girls didn't stick," I said. "I liked that name."

"Me, too. I think we're pretty *golden*." Cappy smiled.

Black charcoal-encrusted remains of tree trunks dotted the landscape like headstones standing askew in an ancient cemetery. The skeletons of fire-blackened trees had snapped and toppled to the ground in random piles, like a malevolent game of pick-up-sticks. The earth we trod upon—a mixture of gray ash from recent fires, sand-like grains of pumice, and chips of obsidian, the black glass from ancient volcanoes—scrunched beneath our feet. Between the oppressive heat, the monotony of the gray-and-black burn-scape, and the acrid sulfur smell of a fiery destruction, I wanted to hit the fast-forward button and make a quick escape from that apocalyptic world. Instead, I picked my way, walking with care through the minefield of broken rock and hunks of charred wood.

Eventually, Cappy and I emerged from the dead zone, our backsides shrouded in gray veils of fine ash tossed up behind us with each step. In shade at the edge of the woods, we paused to look back the way we had come.

Crowds of fireweed—their flame-colored blossoms balanced atop long, slender green stems—gathered like an advancing army all along the boundary between living and dead trees. With those vibrant flowers in the foreground, the view of the desolate landscape was transformed into a place of stark beauty. "Perspective is everything," Cappy commented, pulling her tiny camera from her pocket.

"It's like replacing the lenses in my sunglasses with rose-colored ones," I agreed.

The previous day, I had purchased two twenty-four-shot disposable cameras. They were nothing like the camera I had lost—both the quantity and quality of the photos being limited—but I was determined to shed my camera grief by coaxing out a few good images.

I squatted down to get a better angle with one of the cardboard cameras. Attempting to capture a wisp of this unexpected beauty within the confining dimensions of the tiny plastic viewfinder, I adjusted myself until the black-and-white scene was framed within a magenta fringe. Before I stood, I selected a lump of lavender-gray pumice, the size of a misshapen marble and pitted with holes, and put it in my pocket beside the chip of granite I had chosen at Thousand Island Lake.

We walked together that day, taking turns being leader and follower. She had led us the first gray mile; I took over as we entered the shade of the old forest. Through the course of the next few days, we would carefully, often wordlessly, renegotiate the jobs, the roles, the balance of power on the trail now that Jane was gone, and we had become a pair.

After walking in the heat of an open meadow, soaking in the intensity of the sun on my head and shoulders, my feet and I wanted a rest. My stomach signaled that I was hungry, and I realized it was nearing lunchtime. Walking a few strides ahead of Cappy, I stopped and turned. "Are we there yet?" I asked, trying to be funny, but really, I did not have the slightest idea where we were relative to anyplace else. Cappy was the bearer of all trail information; I just went where I was pointed.

I liked that feeling of walking while lost in time and space, so deeply immersed in that moment, that environment, that I had no idea what time it was or how much distance I had covered. It was like putting on earphones and being swept away by beautiful music—when it's over, you are surprised to look up and see that an hour has passed and all those musicians and their instruments have vanished.

"Not yet, Honey. Almost," Cappy humored me. "I think our lunch spot is just around this next bend."

It seemed to me Cappy preferred, perhaps needed, to know precisely where we were at all times. She had long ago taken possession of the thirteen topo maps and trail guidebook I had brought. She studied them intently and frequently. I think she memorized the details of each day's trek—the names of every landmark, the twists, turns, and elevation gains of the trail. Her way was in stark contrast to my way of enjoying our sojourn. Being able to let that all go, to walk along nearly hypnotized by breathtaking surroundings, was the benefit I gained from her insistence on being navigator.

I wondered if I provided something similar to Cappy, something that enhanced her experience? *Did she ever get lost in the moment when she walked? Did she see the nameless things that surrounded us? Were we even experiencing the same journey?*

Sure enough, just as Cappy had predicted, when the trail drew us closer to the creek, a circle of cottonwoods created an oasis of green-tinted shade, a curtained pavilion that called seductively to our two-person caravan. The heart-shaped leaves of the cottonwoods gave off a gentle ssshhh-ssshhh of welcome, as a breath of air rose off the bubbling creek. The combination of breeze and shade had me so pleasantly distracted that I did not notice, until I was practically upon them, Zoe and Nemo already sitting in the shady circle finishing their lunch.

"Hey, guys! Thanks for saving us a spot!" Cappy said, her deep-toned laughter erupting. She dropped her pack against a tree and plopped herself down on a log carefully cut and arranged by a trail crew.

Nemo was up and putting away his food. "How far you going today?" he asked. He pulled off the red bandana draped over his head like a doo-rag, refolded and rearranged it so it looked exactly like it had before to hold his black hair out of his eyes.

"Cappy says we're going to camp at Deer Creek Crossing tonight," I said, setting my pack on the ground and retrieving my lunch.

"About three miles ahead," Cappy specified, like I knew she could.

"In that case, this'll be the last time we see The Two Women," Nemo said. "We're putting in another six miles today."

"It's still early, and we've been making good time," Zoe added, sounding much more sure of herself.

"I'm glad your sores are healing up, Zoe, but it makes me a little sad to see you two go," I said.

In the short time we had been on the trail, Zoe and Nemo had become the BFFs of our trail friends. They had been our first JMT buds and the team we had leap-frogged with most. We'd shared meals and drinks and stories, too. We'd even had opportunities to worry about one another. Though we had only known the pair a few days, they had become intimates. Now that Zoe's hip sores were healing, it seemed only natural their youthful strength and stamina would outpace us.

"So, I guess that means goodbye!" Cappy held her arms wide to invite a farewell hug. Nemo took the hint, wrapping his long arms around her tiny body to squeeze. Zoe and I followed suit, with me on my tiptoes to reach her taller frame to hug a final farewell. Sweeping packs onto their backs, they stepped on the trail, leaving Cappy and me to settle down to a peaceful lunch and lengthy rest.

"Two goodbyes today," I said. "First Jane. Now Zoe and Nemo." Again, I felt a pang of loneliness. "It's just you and me, kid." I tilted my head and sighed a little laugh. "Makes me feel lonely."

"We're a good team, Joan," Cappy replied, skipping over my emotion. "We'll be just fine."

"No doubt," I said.

After I had eaten, I unrolled my sleeping pad and lay down on the ground. I propped my head on my folded jacket and my stockinged feet up on the log where I had sat, letting the blood flow down towards my torso. That was becoming my daily post-lunch resting pose. I closed my eyes, shaded them with my hat, and listened to the soothing sounds of flowing water and rustling leaves. I took a few slow, deep breaths, concentrating on relaxing my whole body, especially the overworked muscles in my lower back and legs. I let my mind wander back to savor the day's beauty.

I was brought back to wakefulness by the sound of papers rustling. Cappy had spread the day's map across her lap and was examining it. The guidebook lay open at her side.

Locating the very spot where we sat in the shade by the creek, she leaned towards me and held the map out so I could see it. "Here's where we are now—and there's Red's." She used her finger to point out first one spot then the other on the map.

Taking the bait, knowing Cappy wanted to talk about the day's plans again, I asked her how far we had come and how far we had yet to travel. "It's six-point-one miles from Red's to Deer Creek Crossing. We've already walked three miles, so we're halfway there." She pointed to a little red dot at the spot where the brown line of the JMT crossed a blue line labeled Deer Creek.

"What's the plan?" I asked, open to whatever she wanted. I looked at my watch; it was one-fifteen.

"It's three miles. Let's walk for an hour and see where we are then," she said, folding the map back into tight rectangles.

"Perfect," I agreed. We tended to walk between two and three miles-per-hour, depending on the terrain, so I was thinking an hour might get us all the way to the campsites at Deer Creek Crossing.

Up and moving, she pointed, and I walked on.

The campsite was a large right-triangle sitting at the point where the trail intersected the stream. Side A was the trail, side B the stream, and side C the hypotenuse, was the boundary that separated us from forest. The land was flat, mostly dirt, and shaded by a few statuesque grandmother trees. Fallen trees had been artfully arranged by powerful forces into a hexagon, providing us with seating and a sense of structure in our wall-less space. We set up our two-person home-away-from-home within that hexagonal enclosure.

"Only one tent tonight," I said, kicking a few cones away before flipping the ground cover out across the dirt.

"It feels odd without Jane," Cappy said.

Lonely was the word I had been thinking at that moment. "We're going to have to reshuffle all the camp setup tasks, since she's skipped out on her assigned jobs," I replied.

The two of us had never set the tent up together, so it took a little longer. Finished, we settled into a still early evening. It would have been cocktail hour had we been in the right neighborhood, but there were no pubs or wine bars for miles in any direction. The low sun cast a warm golden light into our space under the trees—like a cozy fireplace glow.

Laying my sleeping pad on the ground and padding my back with my fleece, I pulled out my journal to catch up on my stories. A lot had happened at Red's that I had not found time to jot down. Always hungry, I munched on nuts and dried cranberries while I wrote. Cappy moved into an open space, where she could practice her tai chi in the cool shade. Her long evening shadow moved slowly, creating shifting geometric shapes where it intersected with the straight lines cast by trees.

In my journal, I wrote, "Today we remounted the JMT heading south into the Heart of the Sierra." And, "Tonight is the 7th night in a row I shall fall asleep to the music of running water. How will I sleep at home without those water sounds?"

A pair of ground squirrels came to investigate my lounge area. Did they smell the pecans and Craisins? One hopped up on the log, standing on all fours, then sitting erect, its tail a fluffy question mark and its face pure innocence. "Oh, aren't you cute?" I whispered, not realizing I had fallen for its ruse.

While I admired Thing One, even chatted him up a bit, his accomplice was slowly sneaking up behind me. Thing Two had sneaked along behind the log I was leaning against, invisible to me. It crept stealthily towards my open bag of fruits and nuts.

I heard the tiniest of plastic rustles when it reached out for the Ziploc bag. I shifted my gaze to the right, and our eyes met. Thing Two and I both jumped. I gave a little yelp, and Thing Two spun on his four heels and was gone over the side of the log with a flash of bushy tail. I laughed aloud, startled by my own yelp and tickled by the tricksters' near success. What a feast those two little Things would have had if I had been a second later in catching on to their scam!

Our campsite at Deer Creek Crossing was an excellent place to sit and watch the world go by. Travelers, both thru-hikers and weekend adventurers, hiked past us, heading in both directions on the JMT "highway." People-watching along the trail, I felt like an anthropologist observing members of my tribe, admiring and learning from them. Young or old, NOBO or SOBO, usually nameless, my admiration came from our secret-society-like bonds of community and common purpose. Whether pilgrim, wanderer, or explorer, they were my blood and kin.

An older woman, in her early seventies and traveling alone, stopped to talk for a moment. Yes, she was traveling solo. Yes, she had done it before a number of times. No, she never felt lonely or afraid. She was dressed in odd layers, a shawl wrapped over a long-sleeved blouse with buttoned cuffs, long socks that nearly met her long shorts at the knee, and a faded lavender bandana topped with a straw sunhat. Reaching to the carabineer on her pack's hip belt, she detached an old-fashioned stainless steel Sierra cup.

"I haven't seen one of those in years," I said when I saw the dented silver cup in the shape of a shrunken pie tin with its wire handle.

"I've had this one since my early backpacking days when I was just a kid," she told me. Expecting her to sit and pump water, I was surprised when, balancing herself with a hefty wooden walking stick, she bent forward and dipped the cup into the bubbling water adjacent to the trail crossing and proceeded to drink it all down.

"Don't you filter your water?" I asked.

Swallowing the last bit, she wiped her mouth with her sleeve and looked at me. "Been drinking straight from streams in the Sierra for sixty years. Never gotten sick. Not gonna change now," was her reply. She clipped the cup back to its carabineer, rearranged her long gray hair and her faded bandana, and strode across the stream and on down the SOBO trail. Like a gypsy, she was gone.

Walking north, the opposite direction, two men, perhaps a father and his grown son, appeared just before our dinnertime. They toted matching blue internal frame backpacks that appeared brand new like their shiny black boots. Otherwise, they were outfitted quite differently. The older man sported long sleeves, long pants, both well used, and a wide-brimmed hat decorated with souvenir pins advertising previous adventures. He had definitely done this before and was an experienced outdoorsman. The younger man, on the other hand, was outfitted in the latest REI fashions and high-tech materials with prominent labels from Patagonia and Northface. I wondered if this was a father-son, male-bonding trip encouraged by Mom.

They paused for a moment to ask how far it was to the next camping spot.

Heck if I know, I thought. "Cappy," I called, "these gentlemen have a question about the trail I'm sure you can answer."

Raising her head from where she had buried it in the hiking guide, Cappy was all ears. Just as I'd thought, she gave them the answer they were looking for, "It's about three-quarters of a mile north. When we walked through there earlier, it looked like a nice spot to camp, clear and shaded."

With a pair of enthusiastic thank-yous, they turned to hike on. "We can do that!" said the older man.

As the sun settled down to rest on the edge of the sky, we heard the faint high-pitched whine of incoming swarms. When the first thirsty insect landed on my forearm, I slapped it away and leapt up to don protection—my blue long-sleeved Patagonia top, green windbreaker, and black wind-pants. I pulled long socks over my feet, gloves over my hands, and mosquito netting over my hat. Then, I sprayed DEET over cloth-covered arms and legs. No sooner had I settled back down, hoping to complete my writing before dinner, than I was engulfed in a black cloud of miniature predators. And to think I had seriously considered leaving the quarter-ounce mosquito net behind just because it looked funny!

It did not rain that night. It did not even cloud up. I took that as a sign, an omen of pleasant days ahead. I did not speak my thoughts aloud for fear of jinxing them, but if this were typical summer Sierra weather, Week Two would be fair. We could be hiking under bright blue skies and sleeping under the stars for several days and nights.

Starting Point — Red's Meadow Resort — 7500 feet
Ending Point — Deer Creek Crossing Camp — 9100 feet
Highest Point — Deer Creek Crossing Camp — 9100 feet
Distance Covered — 6.1 miles
Cumulative Miles — 36.2 miles

Trail Sisters

Go out in the woods, go out.
If you don't go out in the woods nothing will ever happen
and your life will never begin.
~ Clarissa Pinkola Estes, *Women Who Run With The Wolves:
Myths and Stories of the Wild Woman Archetype*, 1992

Day Eight
July 26, 2006

Starting Point — Deer Creek Crossing Camp — 9100 feet

Our morning walk took us gradually up more than five miles along the forested sheer edge of Cascade Valley. Knowing how unsafe it can be to hike while sightseeing, Cappy and I stopped often in the shade of tall conifers to scan the sweeping panorama. Looking down into the canyon's broad U-shape made it easy to imagine a mighty glacier tirelessly scraping the valley out of the granite mountain. Far below us, Fish Creek ran down the center of that U, carving a smaller V-shape along its bottom.

"I can see why it's called Cascade Valley," Cappy said. "Look at all those beautiful waterfalls!" She swept her arm from left to right, taking in the long canyon wall opposite from where we stood side-by-side.

Several small hanging valleys were visible, each sliced off by that ancient glacier as smoothly as if by a knife. The open-ended valleys were lined up like a row of open windows. Their rivers, slender lacy ribbons, plunged like so many Rapunzels had tossed their white-blond tresses down from their towers.

"Those hanging valleys are like massive dioramas," I said, wishing I had binoculars. The truncated valleys gaped at us, showing off luxuriant shamrock green meadows suspended a thousand feet in the air. "They look like lost worlds."

"I'm sure you could get to them. There have to be trails into each one from the west side." Cappy forced realism onto my fantasy.

"Cappy, you burst my bubble." I laughed. "I was envisioning dinosaurs and unicorns in their own isolated kingdoms."

The trail continued to tread along the verge of the canyon, weaving around ancient trees that grew right to the edge. Across the way, the same trees were reduced to a thick green carpet that covered the ridge top. We stopped again to gaze across the canyon.

Below our shady perch, small birds, swallows perhaps, with wings swept sharply back, darted from their nests along the face of the canyon's wall, sailing in circles, playing chase, and catching bugs. At eye level, a pair of red-tail hawks soared on updrafts, drifting in wide arcs on golden wings and calling in high-pitched whistles. Those same updrafts brought waves of warm air to my face, suggesting a hot afternoon to come.

"This pristine view makes me wonder," Cappy said, "is that what the entire continent looked like when the Europeans showed up to 'discover' it." Cappy turned away from the view and made air-quotes around the word discover.

"Most likely," I said. "I'm glad we've managed to preserve some of it. Our Sierra is so beautiful." I knew we had to keep moving, but it was hard to tear my eyes away from the magnificent scene and the raptors still riding the thermals and whistling to one another across space. The sky was clear except for two vapor trails, thin white threads pulled across azure silk by silver needles, reminding us we stood firmly within the twenty-first century.

"Here's where we turn," Cappy said at the point where a creek came tumbling down from an intersecting valley to our left.

"Our red dot?" I asked, referring to the tiny red circle on our map that marked this turn in the trail. Cappy had shown it to me over breakfast and again over our morning snack.

"Yep. Duck Creek. It's draining out of Duck Lake up there somewhere." Cappy pointed.

My empty stomach gurgled, insisting lunchtime was approaching. I checked my watch—twelve-thirty. "Is this a good lunch spot?" I suggested.

We had found our rhythm, becoming religious about sticking to our daily schedule. Earlier, we had made a mistake—minimizing the time we paused for lunch and snacks, thinking we would make better time by walking at a steady pace for an extended time, stopping only long enough to eat and drink. We had found ourselves drained by the afternoon, often unable to make the distances we anticipated and had gotten behind schedule. Those lost miles had begun to pile up, and we would eventually have to make them up.

We had figured out that by stopping for a long lunch break, where we actually lay down and rested, we could hike longer in the afternoon and make greater daily distances. In our new pattern, we divided each day into four two-hour hikes: starting at eight-thirty, we stopped for a twenty-minute snack break at ten-thirty, devoted a full hour to lunch and reclining at twelve-thirty, broke off for another twenty-minute snack around three-thirty, and finally stopped to set up camp about five or five-thirty.

After a long swig of water flavored with tangerine Gatorade, I laid out a row of Mary's Gone Crackers on my canister's lid, topping each one with a thick dollop of peanut butter I squeezed from its tube. Atop each mound of peanut butter, I placed three dried cranberries to create trailside PB&Js. Chewing, I savored the combination of sweet and salty, crunchy and chewy.

"I sure hope John and Janiene can find my old camera," I said between bites. It was old and had a low pixel rating, but it would be better than the disposables from Red's.

"They will," Cappy assured me. "I'm sure your camera will be waiting for you when we get to VVR."

I hoped she was right. I had not even bothered using the cardboard camera to photograph the vast panoramas that had captivated us all morning. Any photo would have minimized the view to a pair of indistinguishable stripes, a sky blue one hovering above a forest green one. Besides, with only a few shots on each camera, I intended to be selective.

I unrolled my sleeping pad and stretched out on my back, feet elevated. Looking straight up, I could see the dark silhouettes of a million crisscrossing pine needles fracturing the blue sky. The incense of pine filled the still air under the trees—a crisp cool scent like a mint for the nose. It was almost powerful enough to neutralize my own rich aroma—a mixture of sweat and sunscreen that always followed me down the trail.

I pulled the bill of my hat down over my eyes, drew in and released a few relaxing breaths, and allowed myself to drift off into that quiet place halfway between sleep and wakefulness.

A batch of switchbacks carried us over a small rocky peak and down into a pretty, little bowl-shaped valley—the Purple Creek drainage. Filling the bottom of the bowl was Purple Lake, which we circumnavigated until we came to the point where Purple Creek's water flowed out. Where trail, lake, and creek met, we sat down to rest on the duff-covered ground. Small granite rocks created a circle at the foot of a cluster of young trees whose slender shadows were thrown out onto the water by the afternoon sun. The walls of the valley were a deep bluish-black that gave the shallow lake a magical purple cast—a dark periwinkle or lavender. The sun's rays coming in from the west turned the delicate ripples on the surface of the purple water into golden glitter.

While I changed into clean socks and Cappy checked the maps again, a pair of tall, slender women-of-a-certain-age strode up to our trailside rest-stop and paused.

"Helen! Hannah!" Cappy leapt up to greet them. "I didn't expect to see you two again. I thought you'd raced on ahead."

The nearly identical sisters we had first met at Red's Meadow were celebrating "little sister" Helen's fiftieth birthday by hiking the JMT. We had found instant camaraderie when we had discovered in our first conversation that, beyond being of the same generation of California Girls, we all hailed from the same neighborhood in Northern California's Gold Country, living only minutes from one another.

"Fancy meeting you two here," I said, looking up from my boot project. "Did you get your pack repaired okay?"

Helen carried a classic, thirty-year-old Kelty pack she had owned since her college days, not dissimilar in design from my newer and lighter version. For nostalgic reasons, she had insisted on using her old pack and not purchasing a new one for their celebratory expedition. Unfortunately, the stitching on her hip belt had torn away only a couple of days into the hike, making it unusable. By the time they had arrived at Red's, it was causing her crippling discomfort, all the pack's weight hanging off her shoulders instead of setting solidly on her hips.

"I'm so grateful!" Her smile communicated relief. "We took Red's shuttle into Mammoth, where we found a shoemaker, a little old guy who had the right sewing machine for repairing thick webbing." She turned and pointed to her belt so we could see where new webbing was stitched with thick black thread. "It's as good as new," she added. They were the only shiny pieces on the pack—everything else was faded and scratched with use.

"If we hadn't found him, Helen would have had to buy an expensive new pack," her sister continued the story, "and I would have been able to say, 'I told you so!'"

"Instead, it cost me only twenty dollars," Helen added with a wry victory smile.

"I guess neither our aging bodies nor our aging equipment are as strong as they used to be," Cappy said, and we all laughed.

"Ain't that the truth?" I agreed, thinking of my tender taped feet.

"See you ladies down the trail," Hannah said. They waved goodbye, as their matching ballerina-like bodies moved gracefully away.

"Happy trails," I called to their departing backs.

A few minutes later we followed their footsteps up a series of hot, dusty switchbacks. Then we surmounted a small pass and came face-to-face with yet another stunning view. Distant peaks of black rock, their tops bedecked in thick snow, pierced the sky to the south. From that vantage point, Virginia Lake, in her green valley, came into view.

The trail descended gradually to the wide green meadows surrounding the lake. Strewn with boulders poking their heads above the tall grasses and dotted with clusters of trees, the little valley was home to a popular backpacking campsite. Several groups of thru-hikers had already settled in—the largest gathering of backpackers we had come upon.

A half-dozen tents—small nylon domes in tan, green, and blue—were spread out across the broad meadow surrounding Virginia Lake. Three more sought the shelter of trees a little farther from the water. Campers had taken care to separate themselves, keeping a polite distance between campsites. As early as it was—barely five in the evening—more hikers were sure to join us.

Having learned the value of being at a distance from water and the mosquitoes that hovered over it, Cappy and I chose a level spot near a copse of trees fifty yards from the lake. Close by, under the trees, a young woman, a solo hiker, was setting up her sleeping spot. After erecting our tent, we waved, and then, being good neighbors, we walked over to introduce ourselves.

"I've heard about you two," she said. "You used to be The Three Women, now you're down to two." It was amazing to me how word traveled among the JMT thru-hikers. "I'm Stella." She offered her hand, and we shook.

"We'd heard there was a pretty young woman with really short hair solo-hiking the trail. That must be you," Cappy said in her earnest way, eyes wide.

"Good to meet you, Stella," I added, "It's nice to put a face and name to that bare description."

Stella was in her mid-twenties, with delicate features. She had cropped her hair to a half-inch especially for the hike, giving her a cute-as-a-button Kewpie-Doll-look. A faint New England accent gave away her origins.

"You're not a California girl," I said. "Where are you from?"

"Connecticut. I just finished my graduate degree, and I'm 'trying to find myself' out here before I enter the *real* world," she answered, using her fingers to make air-quotes. "At least, that's how my parents began explaining it to their friends after I told them my plans." She smiled sheepishly as she revealed an awful lot about herself in one sentence.

"That's what we're doing, too," I said, "finding ourselves. We may be in a different stage of life, but we're still looking." We all laughed. Cappy and I each had children her age, but life's quests are lifelong pursuits.

Stella was carrying ultra-light gear that included no real tent, only a thin rain-fly she had propped into a triangular-shaped tube to keep off precipitation and bugs. I wondered how effectively that minimalist contraption worked against crafty mosquitoes. We excused ourselves to get to our evening chores and let Stella finish her own campsite preparations.

The dampness of the meadow and its proximity to the lake was going to make the little valley into mosquito heaven the moment dusk arrived. I was determined to finish all my evening chores quickly so I could avoid being caught out when bugs took to the air. Anticipating swarms, I changed into wind pants and stuffed my mosquito netting and my gloves into my jacket pocket, before heading down to pump water. Cappy was set on squeezing in a swim in the frigid water before it got too late.

No sooner had I found a high and dry perch on the water's edge than the aerial attack began. As the sun sank behind the mountains to the west, the high-pitched whine rose in my ears. I pulled netting over my face and slipped on gloves. The green sleeves of my windbreaker became nearly black with eager bugs, but its plastic lining protected me from their probing beaks. Those Virginia Lake mosquitoes were worse than any others we had experienced, maybe worse than all the previous evenings combined. The air was thick with them and seemed to vibrate with their jerky movements. When I raised my arm, they parted slightly, like a school of fish parting for a moment when a shark moves through their mass. Then they reformed, filling in the gap with their black bodies.

All the while, Cappy continued to swim; how she could stand it, I do *not* know. As long as she remained submerged, she was safe from the flying predators, but her face and her arms, exposed above water, were fresh meat to be consumed at will.

However is she going to get out and get dressed without being devoured? I wondered, sitting safely inside my faux-HAZMAT suit filtering water.

Cappy burst from the water and snatched up her washcloth-sized backpacking towel. Swiftly and still sputtering, she pushed her feet into sandals and whipped on layers of clothes. Her damp hair had been released from its captive braid and was aswirl around her face. She wound it into a knot to stuff into her soft mosquito-netting helmet. Holding her socks, she said a combined hello-and-goodbye before pushing her way through the bugs towards our tent.

As beautiful as her million silver-and-pewter curls were, they required attention, and Cappy was forever pushing them out of her way. Even when she had maneuvered it all into place and secured it with a clip, some piece invariably made a break for it and waved around in the breeze. Every time I watched Cappy wrestle with her long tresses, I was happy I had had mine clipped short in preparation for the hike. I could never have shorn them the way Stella had done. *You have to be really young to pull that off,* I thought. Cutting my own hair back from shoulder-length to a mere three inches had been a tremendous leap of faith for me. I had also permed it into loose curls, so caring for it between infrequent washes was a breeze— I simply dampened and scrunched it. It stayed out of my face, off my neck, and might have even looked cute peeking out from under my cap.

Stella, dressed against the onslaught much like me, walked over from her campsite, water bladder and pump in hand. "Mind if I join you?" She sat when I welcomed her.

"Isn't it a beautiful evening?" I said, scanning the sky to see only wisps of clouds. "Two in a row with no rain."

"It's wonderful!" Her eyes followed my skyward gaze. "This is how I imagined the Sierra would be—without the bugs, of course."

We were both quiet while she arranged herself. Organized, she asked, "What do you know about trail conditions ahead?"

"Not much, only what I heard at Red's. There's a good-sized snowfield this side of Silver Pass," I answered. "People said we wouldn't need crampons, which is good since I didn't bring mine."

Stella's laugh was delicate and musical. "Nor did I. They didn't meet my 'ultra-light' standard." She concentrated on working the handle on her water filter for a minute, until her second container began to fill, then she went on, "I heard from a PCT guy yesterday there are sun cups there now. Have you heard that?" she asked, a little crease of concern showing between her arched brows.

My containers were both full, and I had coiled the tubes and packed the little machine away in its drawstring bag while we talked. Flicking away mosquitoes that had lighted on the net in front of my eyes, I said, "I've read about sun cups, but I've never seen them before. I read they're frustrating to cross. I'm glad to have a heads-up—not be surprised."

She smiled, packing up her own things. "We all need to look out for one another, but as a solo female hiker, I want to make absolutely sure I reach out to all the women on the trail. We're a tribe of sisters out here, and we need to honor that relationship we inherited." Even in her gentle, well-bred voice, Stella spoke with the passionate conviction unique to idealistic young women.

"Agreed," I said, reaching out to touch her shoulder. "We must honor and look out for one another."

"See you in the morning." She stood, and I watched her walk back towards her little triangular tent among the trees.

Starting Point — Deer Creek Crossing Camp — 9100 feet
Ending Point — Lake Virginia — 10,330 feet
Highest Point — Lake Virginia — 10,330 feet
Distance Covered — 9.1 miles
Cumulative Miles — 45.3 miles

Climbing to Ten

The goal of life is to make your heartbeat match the beat of the universe,
to match your nature with Nature.
~ Joseph Campbell, *A Joseph Campbell Companion*, 1992

Day Nine
July 27, 2006

Starting Point — Virginia Lake — 10,330 feet

"I love the smell of DEET in the morning!" I announced in Cappy's direction. I was spraying my legs and arms and the back of my neck with Off Mosquito Repellant, sending up a cloud, all the while holding my breath to avoid the bitter chemical.

Swarms of the voracious biters made performing my morning rituals both trying and comical. Drinking coffee, eating breakfast, brushing my teeth, washing my face, and applying sunscreen—all while wearing mosquito netting over my head and gloves on my hands—was a real challenge. Add to that the wiggling necessary to answer nature's call, bare-bottomed in the bushes, without getting bitten on a sensitive spot, meant it took longer than usual to prepare for the day's hike.

"You're making some ugly faces over there," Cappy called from where she sat, tying the laces on her boots, nearly ready to go.

"I inhaled some. It tastes awful!" I said, realizing my face and eyes had performed a spontaneous scrunch inside the netting. I blew out between pursed lips, trying to get the taste off my tongue, then tightened the last Velcro strap on my sandal and stood to leave.

"Doesn't it make you wonder which is worse, the problem or the solution?" Cappy said.

"You're just jealous because they like me better than you."

While Cappy had on the clothes she wore every day—taupe hiking culottes and long-sleeved white shirt—I alternated between two bright tank-tops layered with one of two thin, long-sleeved pullovers. That morning, I pulled on a blue top over my lime tank. The morning air was cool, but I pushed my fleece into my pack. A couple hundred yards of hiking up the first hill wearing the jacket, and I would be overheated. To remove the jacket later, I would have to stop to remove and replace my pack. Better to start out cool and jacketless to avoid the hassle.

"It looks like everyone's in a hurry to get away this morning," Cappy said.

I looked up. Not only were the bugs up and moving, so were the people, no doubt roused by the predators' shrill whines. In an unusual mass migration, everyone camped around Virginia Lake and at nearby Purple Lake converged on the point where the trail met Virginia Lake's outlet stream. Dozens of people hit the single-file creek-crossing at the same time, creating a traffic jam. It was the only exit option, so required patient queuing.

Donning socks and sandals at our campsite had been a shortsighted error on my part. I had not realized that we would be wading through the stream; I had envisioned a log or rock-hop crossing. With a sigh of mild frustration, I pulled off my socks and sandals, replaced the sandals, walked across the calf-deep stream, then sat to wrestle my socks and sandals on over my now-damp, duct-taped feet.

All the while Cappy waited, her hands resting atop the handles of her hiking poles as she watched hikers parade past. Each time I apologized, she responded, "No big deal," or "Don't worry about it," showing more patience than me.

In the time it had taken me to make the switch, the crowd had dissipated, with hikers sorting themselves by speed. The faster hikers hustled off into the distance, with the slower strung out behind.

"We look like a flock of sheep being hustled down the trail with sheepdogs nipping at our heels," Cappy said.

We stepped onto the footpath at the tail end of the group in time to watch the leaders disappear over the hill. That was the last we saw of the crowd. In fact, we would see only one or two hikers all day long.

After skirting the lake's edge, the trail took a gentle climb through forests to a saddle ridge before dropping down flower-edged switchback after switchback to the bottom of the canyon called Tully Hole. The same huge quantities of water—snowmelt from higher elevations that swelled the rivers and attracted mosquitoes—also fed a vast kaleidoscope of flowers. Wherever sunlight reached the soil, color bloomed. Bright petals swayed atop tall stems in knee-deep ribbons along the trail's verge. More blossoms spread out low to the ground in dappled spaces under the trees, gathered in sheltered crevices among rocks, and were woven into thick emerald carpets of sodden meadows.

The previous day, hiking along the rim of Cascade Valley, we had looked down from great heights to admire distant Fish Creek as it flowed down into the massive valley. Twenty-four hours, seven miles, and a huge descent later, what had been a distant ribbon of glistening silver was now a thundering river deep in the V-shaped valley it had painstakingly carved.

"How're we *ever* going to cross that river?" I called over the river's roar. Standing a scant number of switchbacks above the turbulent flow, we paused to watch. "*That* is not fordable."

"There's a bridge—I think," Cappy said, remembering her reading.

"Ye gods, I hope it's a *real* bridge—not some old log laid down across the water," I said.

"I'm sure it's a *real* bridge," Cappy assured me in a voice like the one I use to encourage my reluctant students—part compassion, part humor. "A river this big *demands* a real bridge."

We paused again after another two switchbacks and stood side-by-side looking downward on Fish Creek. *That is not a creek*, I thought. *That is a river—a wild and crazy river.*

"Look—there—" Cappy pointed with her outstretched arm, her hiking pole dangling by its wrist strap. "Can you see it?"

"What?"

"The bridge, of course!"

"Where?" I surveyed the river's length, the view partly blocked by trees growing on the steep slope below us, until my eyes found the structure—a long, solid-looking span built of thick beams, wood or steel, I could not tell at that distance. "That's a pretty hefty bridge!" Anxiety turned to eagerness. This I could do with ease.

"After you," I motioned for Cappy to lead the way. I could tell by the bounce in her step she was as pleased as I was by the bridge's studly appearance. We bounded down the path toward the growing symphony of the river.

The bridge was a burly steel span, wide enough that with my arms outstretched I could not touch both sides at once, and long enough that it connected the rocky walls of the V-shaped canyon high above the spray of the water that streamed past. We paused at its center. I looked at the river—first upstream, then down—in awe of the wild and powerful water that continued to carve the rocky canyon into its image.

Leaning on the chest-high railing, I patted it gratefully. In the past, I have occasionally come across backcountry trail maintenance crews. They do backbreaking work in the remotest wilderness, all without power or machinery. They haul in their equipment and tools and then lug it all back out when they have finished. But this bridge was extraordinary. "I wonder how they got the tools and materials all the way out here to build this," I said.

"Not by helicopter—canyon's too narrow." Cappy leaned beside me. She pulled her eyes from the river to admire the structure. "Mules?" she suggested. "Wasn't it back in the Thirties? Or do you think this might be newer?"

"I find it amazing someone went to all that trouble to build this gorgeous footbridge just for the likes of us. This was obviously meant to last forever."

Out of both questions and answers, we took photos of ourselves on the bridge with Cappy's good camera. In the background, the water foamed and rushed high above its summertime banks, reaching into the bushes and shrubs growing among the rocks along its banks. Then we followed the trail southward up and out of the canyon.

With Silver Pass looming ahead as our afternoon's calling, it became our focus of conversation. The pass sat at nearly eleven thousand feet. Trail Legend held that its north-facing slope, the one we would have to traverse on our way to its crest, was still deep in snow. Not fluffy snowman-making snow, but ice-encrusted snow. In the cool of morning, the snowfield would be frozen into a slippery sheet of concrete, but in the afternoon sun it would become a fragile frosting over deep, wet slush. My talk with Stella suggested it might also be dotted with water-filled sun cups.

In preparing for the trip, one of the topics I had researched online was snow along the JMT. The previous year, 2005, we had postponed our adventure as twenty feet of snow had buried the trail even late into the season. In 2006, a series of tropical storms—the Pineapple Express—had swept in across the Pacific from Hawaii in late June, reducing the thick layer of snow to a manageable depth. However, the trail on north-facing slopes, which are never warmed by the summer sun, remained frozen under vast snowfields.

We had debated the need to carry crampons—thin sheets of metal arrayed with metal spikes that strap to the soles of hiking boots. The spikes dig into the icy crust with each step, providing traction on steep expanses of snow. I had brought mine as far as Tuolumne Meadows, but left them behind after consulting the rangers at the permit station.

That day, word on the "street" suggested crampons might have come in handy on Silver Pass after all. The rumors seemed to begin with brief exchanges between SOBO JMTers and NOBO PCT thru-hikers, then evolved with each retelling into dramatic "trail legends" foretelling of looming obstacles like treacherous snowfields dotted with sun cups on the way to Silver Pass. The veracity of each legend's warning was always a bit sketchy—"I heard from someone whose friend talked with a PCTer—" So we were never sure how much credence to give the legends or accompanying advice.

Switchbacks climbed upward to Squaw Lake, the halfway point along the climb towards Silver Pass and our afternoon rest stop. Squaw Lake was a petite tarn—a glacially carved granite bowl. Its blue surface was dotted with erratics— odd, out-of-place rocks dropped by an ancient receding glacier. The landscape was sparse, the only vegetation being stunted grasses and sedges growing like shag carpeting across the flat bottom of the bowl right to the water's edge. The perimeter of the alpine meadow, where larger rocks had been shoved aside into piles by the same glacier, sported stunted shoulder-high firs whose slender silver trunks were gnarled and twisted with age and exposure to the elements.

"You're not really getting in that icy water, are you?" I already knew the answer. Cappy had been threatening all afternoon to swim when we got to Squaw.

"The water is refreshing," she said.

Frigid, I thought.

Already up to her knees, she stood contemplating the deeper bluer water farther from shore. Cappy held her arms out—away from her body and not touching the water—stepping carefully deeper and deeper. In one sudden motion, she bounced on her toes, threw her arms up to clasp her hands together over her head, and arched through the air to slide through the shining surface. She disappeared for a moment, leaving behind only spreading concentric ripples. Cappy burst from the water, partly cheering and partly gasping. Tipping her head back, eyes closed, her hands swept her curls back from her face. Stroking her way back towards shore, she smiled triumphantly.

"You should come swimming. It feels so good to wash away all that trail dust and sweat."

"Not a chance," I called from my toasty warm rock.

While Cappy paddled around with obvious delight in water that had been ice only hours earlier, I decided to find a way of wetting my hair. I walked into the lake up to the middle of my calves—the water so cold it burned my toes. Like shots of iced electricity, ripples of pain ran up from the soles of my feet and along my shinbones. I am sure the blood in my legs fled upward to escape. Bending at the waist and sticking my head vertically downward into the water, I dunked only the crown of my head. The intensity of the cold on my scalp was shocking—I gasped and my eyes began to water. I forced myself to continue. If Cappy could submerge her entire self in the lake and like it, I could tolerate a little cold on the top of my head.

My fingers massaged the wetness into my scalp. I would rather have shampooed, but even the best biodegradable shampoo should never be used in the pure water of Sierra. A good dunking would satisfy. I wrung out my hair, squeezing the curls to get rid of excess water. I slipped my old blue bandana from around my neck and used it to towel my hair dry. Flipping my head up and back, so I was standing straight, I rubbed and scrunched and fluffed my curls into place, a few rivulets of water trickling down my neck. Even in the sun I shivered.

Escaping the water as fast as I could on numb toes, I found a spot on a broad flat rock where I could sunbathe. From there, I watched as Cappy completed her splashing. She emerged from the water into the warm air, her skin glowing pink and her lips blue. She used her tiny towel to rub her limbs briskly and bring warmth back into her skin.

"Join me," I called. "It's nice and warm up here." The surface of the sunbaked stone sent threads of heat into my chilled body.

Cappy plopped down on the warm granite. "That's so refreshing. I feel so alive in the cold water. I wish you'd try it next time." She arranged herself on the rock to collect warmth from above and below.

"Not gonna happen. I don't enjoy it. I find it painful and not the least bit pleasurable." I pulled out my snack and Gatorade.

As a kid, during a decade's worth of daily swim team workouts, I had spent many an hour swimming laps in chilly pools. Then later, I had been doused repeatedly with cold Pacific Ocean water while racing catamarans for another decade. I had experienced more than my fair share of cold water and never learned to enjoy it. As a mature adult, I had vowed to avoid cold water for the rest of my life.

"This perfect little bowl with its perfect little lake is exactly what I'd expected the high country to look like." I held my arms out dramatically, taking in the entirety of the granite bowl.

"And, best of all, we have it all to ourselves!" Cappy said. While we had been there, not a soul had passed by.

"This could be a page in a wall calendar." I brought my hands together in front of me to make a small rectangle, a frame, and viewed the scene through that viewfinder.

Silver Pass rose ahead, a six-hundred-foot climb above Squaw Lake along a series of steep switchbacks that snaked back and forth across the north face of the mountain. As we got closer, what had appeared from below to be delicate spots and splashes of snow grew into wide, intimidating fields of ice-coated snow. We were able to navigate easily around the first patches we encountered by going off trail into dirt or onto rocks. But as our elevation increased, the patches grew until they entirely covered the steepening slopes, and the trail became invisible, buried in white.

The slippery surface ahead was pitted with the infamous sun cups—scores of ice-water-filled bowls. I had never seen a sun cup before, but I had seen photos online, so I recognized them immediately. My stomach dropped. I had read the punch bowl-sized divots formed across the surface of the snow when snowfields were repeatedly warmed and refrozen. The bowls filled with ice water each day and refroze solid each night.

The terrain ahead was so irregular that simply walking a straight line would be impossible. Rows of footprints led uphill, sometimes running in parallel stripes, sometimes fanning out around gaping holes and rocky obstacles, or zigzagging around sun cups like drunken sailors.

"We'll just take it slow and careful," Cappy said, hoisting her pack higher on her back.

"Right. Stick together. No risky moves," I agreed. I took the lead, moving in a start-and-stop fashion. I paused every three or four steps to scan the terrain ahead for the safest route that wouldn't end in a dead-end. Then I moved forward, only to stop and plan again.

I planted my hiking poles securely, slamming them into the snow one at a time, just as I planted my feet firmly and securely. I kicked my toe or my heel into the ice several times to break the fragile ice coating. That way, the tread on my Tevas could find a grip on the sloping ground before I shifted my weight from one foot to the other. Always keeping three points firmly on the ground, I lifted only one foot or one pole.

Once, having worked painstakingly forward, I discovered the path was too steep, and I had to retrace my steps downward a short way to find another way. Turning around, I looked downhill. My heart leapt into my throat, and I had to look away for a moment. Below me, the mountainside was a giant white slide that ended on rocks more than a hundred feet below. To avoid that destabilizing view, I focused on the snow directly in front of my feet. Descending those few feet had to be accomplished by sidestepping a half-step at a time.

Moving upward again, I slipped once when my right foot cracked through the sun-rotted icy surface of the snow. My sandal-and-sock-clad foot plunged into the slushy, crunchy snow beneath the ice, then skidded downhill before catching on a piece of ice that was a bit thicker and stronger. I was pitched forward onto my left knee, my teetering backpack threatening to push me onto my face. Only my hiking sticks kept me from burying my face in the snow. My arms, bent awkwardly upward, maintained a hold on those poles through force of will. Gasping at the unexpected suddenness of my crash and the sharpness of the cold on my snow-buried foot, I remained intentionally motionless long enough to slow my heart and think through the process of getting up again. Before moving, I took a mental inventory of my extremities.

Behind me, I heard Cappy call out, her voice loud and high pitched, "Joan! You okay?"

"I'm good," I said as calmly as I could, not wanting to waste energy on conversation beyond that necessary to reassure her.

Pressing with steady, slow firmness, coordinating both arms and both legs and engaging every core muscle I could find, I rose in slow motion to a stooped standing position. Bringing my right leg back into line with the rest of my body, I stood up taller, keeping my poles planted widely. I breathed deeply and did another mental scan of my parts and pieces. I was pleased to discover everything was in order.

"All's well!" I called back to Cappy, who was now just a few feet behind me. "Be careful. It's really slippery. and the ice is fragile here."

I moved cautiously forward again, picking and choosing my footholds with even greater care than before.

"Yee-Hah!" someone hollered from high above us.

"Woo-Hoo!" came another whoop answering the first.

I froze in place and scanned the way ahead. Wild yelps came rolling down the mountainside towards us. I watched in a mix of horror and amazement as two brightly clad young men flew feet first down the snow-and-ice-covered slope we were so assiduously struggling up. They flashed past us, skiing partly on their boots and partly on their backpacks, veering this way and that, as the terrain steered for them, pitching and bouncing over humps and through sun cups full of water. Squealing in delight, they disappeared far downhill, crossing in a few seconds time the same distance we had required thirty minutes to conquer.

"Did you see that?" Cappy laughed. "That's what Ryan was describing at Red's!"

"I would never do that," I said. "That's crazy!" but I was laughing, too, as the shot of adrenaline their first whoops had induced spread out through my blood.

Minutes later, in a thrilling moment, I simply popped up onto the top of Silver Pass. Unlike Donohue, which had been a broad, rounded hump-shaped dome, Silver Pass had a sharply pointed top, like the crest of a roof. One minute I was still climbing, and the next I was standing at the very top, like I had stepped on the last rung on a ladder that ended at the top of the world. Forward and backward, I was able to look out and down.

Turning to observe Cappy's approach, I called down to her, "We're here! It's the top!"

She looked up. The physical strain of the climb showed on her face, but she smiled broadly. Quickly, she returned her focus to her feet and the steps in front of her.

I continued to watch her climb and saw the exact moment when she slipped, much like I had done. Unfortunately, when her foot broke through the ice skin and began to skid, it found no purchase and continued to slip. Cappy ended up slithering downward several feet on her knees and hands. Her poles, hanging from their wrist loops, skipped wildly on either side.

I held my breath until I saw her downward movement stop. From my perspective at the top, the angle of the slope looked steeper than I had imagined while climbing upward. I was glad I had refrained from looking down earlier. I was glad I was standing at the top with my feet planted firmly on granite.

"Cappy! You all right?" I yelled down to her.

Silence.

I held my breath, waiting for her response. All my senses perked up, antennae bristling. I began to unstrap my pack to be ready—for what exactly I did not know.

After a few very long moments, I heard her voice drifting my way. "I'm good."

I sighed, chuckled at her sense of humor even in crisis, and called back, "Please, be careful." And then, "You're almost there."

For several minutes, Cappy climbed upward without mishap. Then we stood together on the top of the world admiring the three-hundred-sixty-degree view. While climbing that glass mountain, I had been focused on the space immediately around me. The rest of the universe had receded from my consciousness, evaporating into white noise, while every fiber, every cell, every neuron worked in unison to fulfill my immediate intention. At the top, with the force of gravity, the universe simultaneously pressed in upon me and expanded around me, tugging on my heart.

The sky, vivid in its blueness, its clearness, hung like an inverted bowl over our heads. "My first impulse is to take a picture." Cappy held her small digital camera in her hand. "But there's really no point."

"Beauty like this is impossible to capture," I agreed. "No way to get the three-hundred-sixty-degree intensity of it." We continued to stand and breathe it in.

"I know photographs won't do it justice, but I'm going to take a few anyway," Cappy said. Holding the little silver box up to her eye, she took a series of shots, moving the viewfinder from left to right across the panoramic view.

"We'll both be glad you made the attempt." I encouraged her. "Later, your pictures will trigger the real scene in our minds."

Silver Lake sat just a quick half-mile hike down the south side of Silver Pass.

"This is a TEN!" I announced when the lake came into view. "Cancel what I said at Squaw Lake—that was only a nine-point-five. *This* is exactly what I had imagined the High Sierra would look like." My backpack still on, I turned in a slow circle, taking in the details of the landscape.

We stood in another small granite bowl. A wide shallow pond sat surrounded by scores of smaller versions of itself, serene little pools and puddles in rock, like a queen surrounded by her assembled court. Round stones, like giant marbles, lay scattered about in and around the water. The late afternoon sky, periwinkle blue polka-dotted with white clouds, was reflected in the perfect mirror of the small pond—and in each of the cups and pools arranged across the granite bowl. Like holograms, each pool, cup, puddle, and pond held the entire sky and surrounding mountain peaks—the mirrored surfaces broken only by the little marble islets.

My pores seemed to absorb the effervescent beauty, like a sponge absorbing spilled Champagne. Any remaining anxiety dissolved into an expanding, foaming sense of beauty. I felt joyful, transfixed, and infused with contentment. Can one feel calm and fizzy at the same time? I must have gone on and on about it. Because a decade later, Cappy tells me I went kind of nuts over Silver Lake. I do not remember doing that, but I do have that hologram image hardwired in my brain. All I have to do is close my eyes—and it's right there.

In the Heart of the Sierra, it takes a long time for day to give way to night. Dusk comes early to these high-elevation valleys, hours before it descends on the flatlands to the east and west. When the sun dips behind the tall mountain ridges, the valleys are cloaked in shade, but the sun continues to light the sky overhead long after it stops warming the shadowed ground. For two hours we lounged, adding layers of fleece as the shadows grew deeper.

Weary after two days of strenuous hiking, we climbed into our sleeping bags long before the clear sky was dark enough for the Evening Star to show her face. Before giving into sleep, I reviewed the day in my mind as I fiddled with the rings on my necklace—strength, courage, spirit. Though humbled by all the challenges we had faced, I was satisfied, even proud of myself. The fears and insecurities that had loomed so large the first few days of the trek were fading in the face of recent accomplishments. Trust was growing between my mind and body. My mind could depend on my body to be strong enough—balanced and steady. My body could depend on my mind to be strong enough—clear and steady, too. It seems odd to think of them as separate entities, but that is how it felt, like they had been in conflict but were now working together as a team.

Nature was having a hand in the inner changes I was feeling. So many things had gone wrong early in the trip, and I had survived them all—some more gracefully than others, some more confidently than others. And here we were at the end of a wonderful day, camped in a beautiful place, and I was feeling satisfied.

"Could it be," I whispered, "that we've outlasted Murphy's Law and only good things lie ahead?"

Starting Point — Virginia Lake — 10,330 feet
Ending Point — Silver Pass Lake — 10,384 feet
Highest Point — Silver Pass — 10,895 feet
Distance Covered — 7.2 miles
Cumulative Miles — 52.5 miles

Truth Or Dare

If there is magic on this planet, it is contained in water.
~ Loren Eiseley, "The Flow of the River", *The Immense Journey*, 1957

Day Ten
July 28, 2006

Starting Point — Silver Pass Lake — 10,384 feet

I tossed my backpack up onto my back with one easy motion.

That's right.

TOSSED. BACKPACK. EASY.

My pack had become an integral part of me, rather than a piece of luggage strapped awkwardly to my back and shoulders. Like a camel has its hump, like a shark has its fin, I had my pack—we were *one*. Not only had its shape become my shape, its weight my weight, I knew exactly where, in its myriad of inner and outer pouches, each and every one of my possessions was hidden. Packing, unpacking, accessing, and carrying had all become second nature.

It was that satisfying knowledge that gave me growing confidence. And confidence I would need, as this was the day we would face and ford Silver Creek— Trail Legend Number Two.

We had heard rumors about the treacherous Silver Creek water crossing for two days. It seemed every hiker on the JMT had something to say about the Silver Creek Waterfall. Those headed north, mostly PCT hikers, mumbled warnings as they strode swiftly past. Fellow SOBOs, gathered at trailside rest stops, comparing what they had heard and attempting to assemble the data points into a cohesive story.

The gist of Trail Legend Number Two had the sweet meandering Silver Creek growing into the powerful Silver Creek Waterfall. It was said the waterfall landed directly on top of the JMT, pounding downwards to sweep travelers off their feet and down the face of the mountain. The story inspired a dozen questions and no answers. I wrote in my journal about the Trail Legend:

The river is full and fast, they said.

You have to pass under a waterfall, they said.

It's dangerous, they said.

It might be impassable, they said.

With an odd combination of confidence and trepidation, we set out that beautiful morning. Twice we crossed the creek in thigh high water. We stopped everyone we saw to ask about Silver Creek and its waterfall crossing. The NOBOs, muscled and tested from nearly four months on the trail from Mexico, all seemed to confirm what we already knew but offered little advice about how to approach the crossing beyond, "Be careful," before rushing north.

"Obviously all these people survived the crossing, so could it really be that bad?" I asked Cappy, my mind working on the problem.

"They're all so much bigger and stronger than we are. Remember yesterday, at the lunch stop, that bearded guy said people had gotten knocked down the hillside and hurt?" Cappy worried out loud.

"If it was just one group telling that tale, I'd think they were pulling our legs," I said. "But *everyone* seems to be telling a version of the same story."

"I know," Cappy agreed. "That makes me worry."

We had had this conversation a half dozen times, trying to wrap our brains around the obstacle to come up with a plan. I told myself to not think about the waterfall anymore, but that was like telling myself to not think about pink elephants.

I tried thinking instead about where we would be that night. We would catch the four o'clock ferry across Edison Lake to VVR where luxuries awaited us—showers, telephones, bunk beds, a restaurant, and supply store. *Ice cream bars!* Beyond the shower, I looked forward to the two boxes waiting for me—a big one with my food and supplies and a little one containing my old digital camera. All we had to do was survive the Silver Creek Waterfall Crossing. *Oops!* There I was thinking about it again.

To further distract myself, I thought about that second box containing my new-old camera. Keeping it charged was going to be a challenge—I would have to be diligent about keeping it turned off between shots.

When I ran out of distractions, visions of the waterfall crossing returned again and again.

The gentle trail ahead turned into switchbacks that would take us steeply downhill alongside the plunging Silver Creek. Before descending, we stood on a granite hump at the cliff's edge, where the cascading creek first leapt off and fell. I looked over the side to watch the water falling and bouncing for hundreds of feet. Cool air rushed up from below, amplifying the roar into a cacophony.

"Somewhere down there, we have to cross under all this water," Cappy shouted above the din. We looked down the mountain for some indication of where the trail and the creek met again, but could not see past the tumbling water and its cloud of spray.

I raised my open hands to signal that I shared her disbelief.

It was well after our morning break when the trail stopped dropping, leveled out, and became a nearly flat path, a shelf cut across the face of the granite canyon wall. Trickles of water from snowmelt higher up made their way haphazardly downward, darkening the bronze-colored stone. Trees stood tall, and we walked in their shade. Moisture-loving ferns and shrubs carpeted the ground alongside the trail.

According to Cappy's map, we were just steps away from our face-to-face meeting with Trail Legend Number Two. The same creek we had admired two hours earlier leaping into thin air was about to reappear as its alter ego, the crashing end of the waterfall.

I walked, searching ahead, trying to bend my vision around each curve to catch a glimpse of the watery obstacle. Emerging round one of those curves, striding toward us, was a figure straight from the pages of *Outlander*. Had we been transported to the Scottish Highlands? Or had he walked through a time warp into the Sierra?

He stood over six feet, with broad shoulders that made his backpack look like a child's toy. His hair and beard were a thicker, longer version of the curly ginger fur that covered his muscled limbs.

"Hey, ladies!" his deep voice greeted us from a dozen feet ahead. A broad smile spread across his friendly face as he approached from the south. "I'm Bear!" His PCT trail name was an apt moniker—he *did* resemble a big cinnamon bear, rippling with muscles.

"Hey," we both responded. This was our last chance to learn something helpful about the fast-approaching crossing.

"Can we ask you about the waterfall?" Cappy said before he could vanish.

"Why sure, Little Lady," he beamed, his gold-green eyes twinkling under bushy brows. "What is it you want to know?"

A floodgate of questions burst from both of us.

First Cappy, "How far is it? How high is it?"

Then me, "Does it really fall on the trail? Is there any way around it?"

"Whoa there. It's not so difficult as all that. If you do exactly what I tell you to do, you'll be safe," he assured us, putting one paw-like hand on Cappy's shoulder and the other on mine in a reassuring gesture.

Bear remained there in the center of the trail with us for nearly ten minutes while he gave us step-by-step directions for approaching and passing safely through the infamous waterfall ford. He gestured with his hands and used his body to demonstrate proper stance and movement, like a sensei in his martial arts dojo instructing his students in The Way. And we were good students, scrutinizing every movement and hanging onto every word.

It boiled down to three things: First—Pass through one at a time, enter slowly and get through quickly, so you are not inside too long. Second—Stay way to the left, with your shoulder right up next to the canyon wall so you are behind most of the water. Third—Unbuckle your pack, so if it goes over the edge, you do not go with it.

"Oh, Bear! Thank you so much!" Cappy and I spoke over the top of one another, telling him how grateful we were.

Relief and a smidgen of confidence began to return. *We can do this*, I thought.

We waved farewell to Bear—our Trail Angel Sensei, whose appearance was so perfectly timed it felt like Trail Magic—and watched him disappear around the curve headed north.

Less than a-quarter-of-a-mile down the trail, we put his advice to the test.

The siren's voice of the water reached out to us, drawing us in long before it was visible. Cappy and I walked side-by-side, slowing our pace, stretching our vision to find the first sign of what had taken on the personality of a water-breathing dragon. The trail curved slightly to the left as the canyon wall curved.

I saw a flash of white and reached out to hold Cappy's arm.

"Is that it?" I whispered.

We took a few more steps, my hand still on her arm.

"Yessss," Cappy said, breathing out what had become obvious.

We stopped in our tracks to watch the living thing dance atop the rocky ground shining wet from the mist. The roar at the top of the cliff two hours earlier had been loud. At the bottom, where the water drummed on the stone, it was deafening yet beautiful—in the way live dance music is floor-poundingly beautiful, even as it makes your ears ring.

The fire hose of water fell straight down the cliff from above. It bounced once—right on the footpath—and fell again. The trail was swallowed by the bouncing froth. Shards flew. Foam boiled. The gush roared. Twenty feet ahead, the footpath reappeared. This was it. The Trail Legend was true after all. We really did have to walk through a waterfall!

"Stay left," Bear had said. "Lean into the cliff, then walk straight."

I stood on wet rock, watching the water. Calculating, building courage, touching my necklace, I prepared myself. "Okay," I said.

"On the count of three," I breathed.

"One...

"Two...

"Three!"

I plunged forward, head and shoulders down. My feet found solid footing. The torrent flew over my head and past my right shoulder. The back spray of frigid water engulfed me—more airy foam than water. I gasped. I shrieked in shock—then in delight!

It was not difficult, after all—like wading through thick bubbles. It was exhilarating, thrilling, wonderful! I slowed down to savor the last steps of my stroll through a waterfall.

Cappy waited behind, watching from the other side. I found her eyes and waved across the white dragon's back. "Come on!" I yelled, raising both arms in the air in triumph.

She waved and hollered in return, her voice swallowed by the roar, her meaning making its way across without it. She celebrated my triumph with me.

"It's fun!" I hollered, knowing she could not hear me. I took out my disposable cardboard camera and carefully took aim at Cappy—engulfed in a halo of foam against a backdrop of golden rock.

After she emerged, we stood, wet and ecstatic, looking back at conquered Legend Number Two and laughed. We clinked poles in metallic high-fives and stood for a long time admiring the mighty and graceful falls.

Where minutes earlier I had seen only its power and the danger, I saw majesty—turquoise and white cascading downward over golden rock, polished to marble and carved over eons by torrents and trickles into sensuous curves.

A large American flag on a small pole moved lazily in a current of air lifting off the lake. Propped up on a large granite slab the shape and color of a sandy beach, the Stars-and-Stripes marked the water taxi's pickup point. We could have chosen to walk seven miles around Lake Thomas A. Edison to reach VVR. Wisely, we chose instead to ride the little ferryboat straight across the lake. Cappy and I awaited its four o'clock arrival, relaxing with a dozen travelers.

We chatted with a father and son from Atlanta and another pair from San Francisco. Cappy relished in the socializing, moving about, talking with other hikers, learning about their jobs and schooling, their families and backgrounds. I watched as she immersed herself into animated conversations punctuated with gestures and expressions. She was in her element, and I knew she would be able to later tell me the name, hometown, and occupation of every person with whom she had spoken.

I am generally a people-person myself. I love good conversation and talk eagerly with new acquaintances. I did a fair bit of chatting while we waited, but was soon overwhelmed and longed to return to the peace of the wilderness. By way of retreat, I leaned back on my pack, pulled my hat forward to shade my eyes, and observed. Allowing the sounds of voices to blend into the wind's musical psithurism working through the trees overhead, I was able to find stillness. I thought back over recent days' highlights.

I thought about water, and all the ways Cappy and I had experienced water on this expedition. Had we fallen asleep to the lullaby of moving water every night on the trail? I thought so. I wondered if our night at VVR might be the first night I would sleep without watery music. My mind moved on to all the places where the trail had crossed water. We had done it scores of times now—on sturdy bridges, on carefully arranged river rocks. We had waded across, too, ankle-deep, knee-deep, and hip-deep. And of course, my least favorite method, we had balanced on logs.

I thought of the first of those deep crossings, way back when we had lost the trail before Donohue Pass. That day, I had been scared and watched with envy as veteran hikers plowed confidently across. Today alone, we had done that twice—plowed across, thigh-deep, with confidence, without hesitation. *Now that's change!* I told myself.

I almost cringed, remembering how I had scooched along the giant log laid across Rush Creek on my butt. This day, I had skittered easily across logs half that size. Which brought me back to the waterfall—the grandest crossing of them all!

You've come a long way, baby! I thought.

The people noises grew louder and were joined by the approaching growl of a motor. The ferry pulled up to a small dock—the gangplank for our boarding. Stretching my back and shoulders, I stood and hoisted my pack. Cappy came to retrieve hers, and we joined the casual line that snaked down to the boat.

Passengers sat shoulder to shoulder on benches in the center and around the perimeter of the boat, backpacks propped against knees. Conversation, over the sounds of motor, wind, and the boat slapping on the water, was impossible beyond the person directly beside me, which was Cappy.

"I've been thinking." I leaned close to Cappy's ear so she could hear me. "I think that the wildest thing in the world, wilder than anything alive, is falling water."

She looked at me quizzically, her head cocked, brow raised.

"Think about the waterfall," I added, watching her eyes when the wind was not blowing her hair into our faces.

Cappy nodded and gave me a thumbs-up. "Poetic," she shouted. We turned to face into the wind, abandoning conversation and letting the air fly past us.

Disembarked and filled with anticipation, we walked with the crowd towards the rustic combination store-restaurant-bar—eager to retrieve our packages, eager for a real meal with wine, eager to arrange for bunk beds and hot showers.

"Cappy! Joan! Over here!" What we had not anticipated was seeing our trail buddies, Zoe and Nemo.

Following their familiar voices, we detoured around the store to enter the restaurant's open-air patio instead. Standing up from a table loaded with beer bottles and half-filled glasses, Nemo and Zoe strode in our direction. Nemo, always the gallant, was first to reach us and enveloped us both in a powerful bear hug. Zoe came up next to him, grinning widely.

"What're you doing here?" Cappy asked. "We thought you'd be long gone by now."

"What a wonderful surprise!" I said at the same time.

"We're having so much fun hanging with this gang," Nemo said, indicating the smiling group of hikers gathered around the table, "we decided to take another zero day."

As Nemo resumed his seat, Zoe spoke more softly just to Cappy and me, "What he *really* means is my hip and shoulder sores are slowing us down, so he's giving me an extra day to heal up before we set out again."

I turned my head to make eye contact and raised an eyebrow to signal silent questions—"Are you okay? It's still that bad?"

She gave me a barely perceptible nod, communicating, "Ask me later."

"Okay," I said, concerned.

Encircling the heavy wooden table on the deck of the bar-restaurant was a welcoming host of JMT hikers. The two young solo hikers we knew—Stella and Max—and several others.

"Join us!" Stella smiled, indicating a seat.

"We still have our backpacks." Cappy pointed over her shoulder to where we'd leaned them against the porch beams.

"Is it true JMT hikers get a free bunk bed to sleep in?" I asked the group at large.

Leaping up again, Nemo said, "I almost forgot! I saved the last two bunks for The Two Women!"

"The last two?" I asked.

"Ssshhh! Grab your packs and follow me. I'll tell you the story while we walk," Nemo directed.

We slung our packs onto our shoulders and fell into step with our chivalrous leader. He guided us to a group of small buildings standing off by themselves.

"How'd you know to save us beds?" I asked, unclear on why we had to whisper.

Nemo slowed to let us catch up. "We'd heard The Three Women, now The Two Women, were headed this way today, from two other lady hikers, sisters, I think, who were here last night. I forget their names, but they said to say hi when you got here."

"Hannah and Helen," said Cappy.

"Yep, that's right," said Nemo. "A large group of hikers came on this morning's shuttle-boat and took all but two of the beds. So, Zoe and I put a bunch of our stuff on those two bunks to claim them for you, which is technically against the rules. That's why I was whispering back there." He winked in a gesture of mischievousness.

"You broke the rules to assist two damsels in distress," I said. "Thank you. I've been dreaming about a real bed. I'd have been disappointed if they'd run out." I briefly thought about all the hikers on our four o'clock shuttle. A smidgen of guilt tickled my mind but was quickly dismissed as overreaction.

"Here we are, Fair Ladies," said our Knight in Shining Armor as he pushed aside the cloth doorway to a tent-cabin that held eight beds, four high and four low, and lots of scattered gear. He swept away the stuffbags and jackets that had staked our claims and tossed them onto his own bed. "You two get settled then join us back at the bar for some dinner and drinks. The restaurant food is really good," he said as he strolled out the door.

The room was sparse—beds and gear piles the only contents. A bare bulb hung from the ceiling. Filtered light came in through a mesh window that opened with a zipper, but the room was filled with cool shadows.

Leaning my pack against the bunk bed's metal post, I fished around for my wallet, slipping it into the pocket of my shorts. "You want the top or bottom bunk?" I asked.

"I'll take the bottom, if that's all right," Cappy replied. She tossed her sleeping bag onto her bare mattress.

"As much as I want a glass of wine, I need to shampoo my hair first. I wonder where the showers are," I said, pulling things from my pack. I laid out my mummy bag on the upper bunk, marking my territory.

"A glass of wine sounds wonderful, doesn't it!" Cappy agreed. "But a hot shower sounds even better."

"First things first. I need to go to the store to get my boxes. I want to see if the camera made it. You coming?" It was getting chilly, so I pulled on my fleece.

"I'll get my money," Cappy said. "I want to use their pay phone to call Jim and let him know we've arrived." She wore a relaxed smile as we walked back up the hill towards the store and restaurant. I did, too.

I opened the screen door and stepped in, and Cappy followed. The tiny, brightly lit store was filled with people, several at the long glass counter where the register stood, and others in the two long, full aisles. Shelves loaded with the chocolates and salty snacks thru-hikers craved stood next to a refrigerated display of soda and energy drinks. I opened the glass door and extracted a Diet Pepsi, which I immediately popped and drank in long satisfying gulps.

I grabbed two small rolls of duct tape, though I knew there would be first aid tape in my box. "The way I've been going through this stuff, I'm going to grab extra," I said to Cappy, only to turn and realize she was not beside me. She was at the counter asking about the phone. I followed, placing my rolls of tape and empty soda can on the counter.

Cappy held a portable phone in her hand. The resort had no pay phone, just this landline. Campers charged their calls to credit cards or called collect. Cappy chose the latter, knowing Jim would be home to accept the charges. He was, and she carried the phone away from the crowd to get a smidgen of privacy.

I told the gentleman behind the counter my name and explained there would be two boxes for me. After "the curse of the missing box" had struck Cappy at Red's, I was feeling a little apprehensive about my own packages.

When he returned, he carried three boxes: the familiar box I had packed for myself and two smaller cardboard boxes addressed in Janiene's hand. *Why two?* I thought. I paid for my tape and soda and carried my packages to the side to wait my turn for the phone. Too curious to wait, I cut open the little boxes with my pocketknife.

As expected, one held my Canon QuikShot with its rechargeable battery and electrical plug swathed in bubble-wrap. The camera had served me well for several years; and though it had a low pixel rating, it took excellent photos. However, it required regular recharging, not very practical in the wilderness, which was one reason why I had invested in my beloved new Nikon. *May it rest in peace.*

The second small box contained a second Canon QuikShot and a handwritten note. Recognizing the shortcomings of the rechargeable camera on the trail, my friends John and Janiene, at the last moment, decided to send me their own camera, too, so I would get twice the mileage between charges!

I smiled, feeling grateful, then held the twin cameras high, one in each hand, and called out, "Cappy, look what I got in the mail!"

When she turned her head, I realized she was still on the phone with Jim. Seeing the cameras, she raised her eyebrows and smiled, then walked in my direction. "Joan's backup camera came," she told Jim. "In fact, she has two cameras now!"

Cappy knew how much I had been suffering. My practical intention had been to ration the daily photos I took with my disposable cameras, but I found it impossible to resist trying to capture the incredible beauty we passed through. I had managed to save one final shot to document the Legend of the Waterfall Crossing that morning. Cappy had generously allowed me to suggest a photo here and there for her to take, but even that required personal restraint on my part.

It was my turn to use the phone. First, I called my mom and dad and again provided them a censored summary of events—focusing on the beauty of the wildflowers and the night sky and skipping over the mosquitoes and the high water. "You'll be careful, won't you?" Mom said when we finished the call.

When I talked to my son Dean, he got to hear the best bits—beginning with sun cups and ending with our walk through the waterfall. "Did you get your camera?" was his first question. Grateful for his help, I assured him I had. "Have fun!" he said before hanging up. Finally, I called John and Janiene to thank them for rescuing me from my camera-less state and for their brilliant idea of sending two.

With the phone to my ear, I watched as the man behind the counter returned carrying Cappy's supply box. Cappy let out an excited little "Yip!" and held the box up for me to see. I pumped the air and felt a warm surge of relief.

Saying goodbye, I pressed the red end-call button and paid for my telephone time. We carried our supply boxes outside to a picnic table, and I cut them open with my knife. The boxes might have contained gold coins the way we ran our hands lovingly through their depths—I wanted to inspect every item in my box.

On top was the third installment of *The Devil in the White City*. Then came fresh clothes—a hiking tank top, the kind with the internal bra that makes hiking so comfortable, a long-sleeved polypropylene top, clean hiking shorts, a blue bandana, fluffy hiking socks, and panties. In the morning, I planned to mail my dirty clothes home in the same box. Beneath the clothing, a Ziploc bag held travel-sized containers of shampoo, conditioner, sunscreen, moisturizer, and lotion, a new spiral notebook and mechanical pencil to continue my journal, and *lots* of food.

In early June, during our first practice hike in the mountains near home, Cappy had laughed when I revealed my plan to include new clothes and tubes of skin care products in my supply shipments. She had insisted the little "luxury tubes" would add too much extra weight to my pack and thought shipping fresh clothes was impractical. Second-guessing myself, I had weighed all the little containers—they had not even amounted to a half-pound. So, I had stuck with my gut feeling and my original plan.

That evening, it was the shampoo, conditioner, and body soap I greedily sought from my box. I had been daydreaming all day about a hot shower—my scalp itched and my body was sticky and gritty from the trail. Cappy and I walked back to the tent cabin, our treasures tucked under our arms.

In addition to one free night in the bunk beds, VVR made hot showers available to all JMT and PCT thru-hikers. There was a single shower stall, however, so trail-dusty people had to jockey for position and wait in line. I was at the line's tail, following Cappy, so when it was my turn, the water in the cramped closet of a shower was merely lukewarm, not frigid, but nowhere near hot.

No matter. It was a luxury. Since I was last, I took my sweet time, shampooing thrice, soaking my hair in sweet-smelling conditioner for a long five minutes, lathering and sudsing until the water ran clear. I even shaved my legs with a disposable razor. After drying with my handkerchief-sized chamois towel, I wrapped my short hair in my sarong, and slathered myself with a scentless moisturizer.

Then, and only then, did I don my clean clothes—a pale blue tank over taupe hiking shorts, topped it with a long-sleeved, mint green polypropylene, and slipped on new socks with my Tevas. What a delight to feel so fresh!

I arrived back at the restaurant to find a gaggle of happy hikers around the long wooden table on the patio-bar. Plunder from a variety of meals covered the table. Some plates were newly filled and held towering burgers and mounds of fries. Others were stripped clean, only the smears of ketchup or blue cheese dressing hinted at what had been consumed. The glasses had multiplied since I had walked past earlier. Max and Stella looked up from an intense conversation to smile and motion me to join the group. Cappy and Zoe scooted over to make room for me.

"What's good to eat?" I asked the group as I sat and looked at the jumbled array of plates and glasses. "Looks like you've been enjoying *real* food."

Stella, in her precise musical voice, said, "I'm loving this huge chef's salad with bleu cheese dressing. Huge. It's really fresh." I did not know if it was the beer or the food, but she looked relaxed and happy. "That's my suggestion."

Max smiled as he watched Stella speak, his dark eyes following her movements. Pointing with a bitten piece of garlic bread at a nearly full plate of spaghetti buried in a deep red sauce, he said, "I recommend the pasta." Then added, "Savory."

Cappy set down her glass of red wine and turned in my direction. "I'm glad you're here, Joan." Her voice danced—animated and excited. "Wasn't that shower wonderful?" She had loosed her mass of hair, letting it dry, and curls floated around her head.

"Delightful," I said. "I know I'm five pounds lighter, so much mud ran down the drain!"

Cappy handed me a menu. "I haven't ordered yet. I've been enjoying the wine though—a California zin. I've been watching everyone eat and smelling the aromas. I'm feeling like one of Pavlov's dogs."

"You were sweet to wait for me." I touched her shoulder and smiled. "What are you ordering?"

We both ordered meat and salads—two things hard to come by out on the trail. And plenty of wine. I am generally not a big meat eater and rarely ever have red meat, but craved the quality of fat and protein only a big hunk of beef can provide. I ordered a steak, very rare, and a large dinner salad.

The salad and wine came quickly. After days of dehydrated meals, the fresh crunch of lettuce and cucumbers and the tang of juicy tomatoes were heavenly. Everyone else at the table had already experienced the pleasures of their first meal off trail. Stella and Max had arrived on the morning ferry, and Zoe and Nemo had arrived the day before. They watched in amusement as Cappy and I moaned with our first fresh bites.

Most of the diners moved off soon after they finished eating, leaving the six of us—Zoe and Nemo, Max, Stella, Cappy and me—sharing stories. I was only half aware of time passing as twilight intensified into darkness and a half moon rose overhead. With little light pollution, the stars came out by the millions.

We talked for hours, moving well past cursory introductions to meaningful depths. Why are you here on the JMT? What purpose does this adventure serve? Are you finding what you sought? What will you do after you get back to the real world? Where is your life headed? We were products of different geographies and different generations, yet those questions and answers connected us, like individual threads each of unique beauty, woven into a tapestry of greater beauty still.

Max, a thoughtful young man from Oregon who spoke with the language of a poet, confessed to being on a modern-day spiritual pilgrimage. He had chosen to walk the path solo, the better to find what he was searching for. "My life is on the cusp of change, and I have big decisions to make in the months ahead." His head was bowed and several locks of his black hair shielded his eyes and expression from view. No one else spoke but just waited out his long pause.

"My folks want me to go to law school—continue the family legacy. My father's always talking to me about economic security and career advancement." Max paused. He pushed his hair from his face, revealing deep espresso-colored eyes. "But I *need* to be an artist." His voice was both reverent and full of resolve.

"What kind of art?" Zoe asked. Our earlier boisterous cross conversations had given way to a one-speaker-at-a-time practice in deep listening. All ears waited for Max to go on.

Both elbows on the table, the long, slender fingers of both hands extended as though holding an invisible balloon in front of his face, Max said, "I have more decisions to make. This fall I have to submit my portfolio to MFA programs." It was easy to imagine those strong, fine-boned hands wielding a paintbrush or molding clay.

"I'm an only child, and I don't want to let my father down, but I can't make that sacrifice." Sadness flickered across his features. Then he sat up straight and smiled. Holding up his near empty glass, he offered a poet's toast, "To the magic of the journey!"

I lifted my wine to clink the other five glasses held high. "To the magic of the journey!"

"What about you Zoe?" I asked. "What's your story?"

We learned that tall, athletic Zoe was a card-carrying member of the Teamsters Union. "I work as a Longshoreman in the Port of LA," she said matter-of-factly, as though it were the commonest vocation in the world for a modern young woman.

"What?" a group-gasp arose. I wondered for a moment if I had misheard her. She did not fit my movie-generated stereotype of a Longshoreman, being neither burly nor hard-swearing, but statuesque and easy-going.

Zoe laughed and her blond ponytail swayed, sharing her delight in our surprise. "I drive an eighteen-wheeler up to a container ship. A massive crane removes a couple of metal trucking containers from the freighter and loads them onto my truck. I secure them and deliver them into the storage lots. I do that over and over all day long, driving in convoluted circles." I imagined it was a little more complicated than that.

"So, why the JMT?" Stella asked. Leaning in, focused on Zoe, she took a small sip from her beer, her littlest finger extended as she lifted the bottle to her lips.

"Adventure is the simple answer," Zoe said without a pause. "A personal, physical competition," she offered after another beat or two. The light was low, but it seemed like a rosy blush colored her cheeks. She must have felt the heat, because she touched her face with her hand. The group waited, wanting more flesh on her story.

"I have done a lot of hiking and rock-climbing, and as a gamer, the JMT just seemed like moving on up to the next level." Emerging from her shell, she was revealing herself to be both fun loving and competitive. The spotlight moved around the table, as though one of the beer bottles were being used as a game spinner to select the next speaker.

We learned from Nemo that he was a waiter at a mom-n-pop restaurant in a quaint beach town in Southern California. A hand-talker, gesturing this way and that, he told us all about the town and cafe, assuring us they served "the best pancakes and waffles you've ever tasted" to locals and beach-going tourists. With his charming smile and flirtatious personality, I imagined he made good tips.

Zoe was one of his regulars. "She came in all excited one day, telling me about this cool trip she was doing." He looked her way smiling. "That's all she talked about for weeks." Spreading his arms out wide to show how obvious his next action had been, he added, "Finally, I couldn't stand it anymore and asked to tag along—" When he smiled, he looked like an Italian movie star. "And the rest is history!"

Laughter swept round the table. Glasses went up again, as Nemo toasted us all, "To Trail Friends!"

The game spinner landed on Cappy next, then me. Stella would be last in our backcountry game of Truth or Dare. Just being present at that table meant we'd accepted the Dare, already committed to our own personal versions of the JMT challenge. That evening, the game was simply Truth, each of us sharing our Personal Legend.

"Have you read *The Alchemist* by Paulo Coelho?" I asked. Max and Stella had—the others had not, so I quickly explained. "One of my favorite quotes about finding and fulfilling one's path in life comes from that book. Tonight's conversation and the way our paths have brought us together reminded me of it just now." I looked around the table, hoping they'd find the words inspiring. "'To realize one's Personal Legend is a person's only obligation. And when you want something, all the universe conspires in helping you to achieve it,'" I quoted the Old Man's advice to the young shepherd who searched for his purpose.[11]

"We're all on the same trail, walking the same direction, but each of us is experiencing a different journey, each of us has a different destination," that was my take on the purpose of that evening's communal experience. "Somehow, in unknown ways, we are each contributing to everyone else's journey, too." The wine gave me courage to express those thoughts aloud to a group of friends, nee strangers, but I was speaking from the heart.

"Speaking of the universe, I've got a John Muir quote that I think pairs nicely with the Old Man's words," said Max. "You've all heard it, I'm sure. 'When we try to pick out anything by itself, we find that it is bound fast by a thousand invisible cords that cannot be broken, to everything in the universe,'" he smiled.[12]

"I think everything happens for a reason," he went on. "I chose to walk the trail, so did each of you. We had no way of knowing we'd be sitting here under those stars," he pointed to the now entirely black sky and the millions of twinkling pinpricks, "at this table with these people." He indicated all six of us. "That's where the magic comes in."

Cappy and I took our turns sharing. She lovingly described her three children, nearly the same ages as Max, Stella, and Zoe, and how proud she was of them and their chosen lives. She extrapolated that pride onto their whole generation of young adults. She told stories of her own youthful backpacking adventures right there in the Sierra during the Sixties and Seventies, and how, in her retirement, she felt called by the beauty of the Sierra wilderness. It seemed like she was time traveling, using the John Muir Trail as the conduit.

I told my tale, too—though, I suppose, I told only half of my truth. I left my grief and the ghost of Krei out of my tale completely. I did not show them my necklace—I did not want to break its spell by mentioning the loss of my dear friend. I didn't want to weigh down the buoyant spirit connecting us to the stars that evening. Instead, I described how the idea of the JMT adventure had morphed from dreamy romantic ideas into a detailed concrete plan and then a reality.

"I began with plans and preconceived notions about the experience I'd have on the trail and how events would unfold, what the scenery would look like and how

---

[11] Paulo Coelho, *The Alchemist* (Harper San Francisco, 1995) p. 21.

[12] John Muir, *My First Summer in the Sierra* (1911) p. 110.

I'd feel. From the first day, in fact, from well before the first day," I said, "natural forces have put pressure on my whole experience, forcing me to change the plans, rearrange my expectations, and even alter my beliefs about why I'm here."

I was thinking how confused that sounded but was deeply aware that night, listening to everyone else's stories, that my own intentions were evolving every day I walked. "Was I simply looking for adventure? Seeking a meaningful spiritual retreat in the wilderness? Had I arranged a mid-life personal challenge? A photographer's art project? Was I trying to prove something?" I could not really answer my own questions, except to say, "Probably so," to all of them.

I had not noticed when he had gotten up and left us, but I realized when my turn at baring my soul was over, Nemo's place at the table sat empty. I wondered where he had gone.

From Stella's stories, we learned she was a New Englander from an "old money" family, her manners and speech, infused with refinement, giving witness to that upbringing. Her detour to hike alone on the JMT was preparation for embarking on a new endeavor. She had finished her graduate work at a fine university, one of the Ivies, and wanted time and space to prepare herself for a role with an international NGO in war-torn countries. Stella talked of service to the world, of hunger and disease in far corners of the planet, of war and peace and how to eliminate the former and replace it with the latter. Her spine was as straight as a lodgepole pine, and her Sierra-sky-blue eyes flamed with hot intensity when she spoke about making world peace her life's mission. Underneath her controlled demeanor, she was a firebrand.

I was fascinated. Six people. Six plans. One trail, one path. Six journeys that would end in the same place, but at different destinations. I was also impressed. These were good people. I was humbled and proud to be a part of this nomadic community.

It had gotten late. We exchanged good nights and promised to see one another on the morning water taxi that would take us back to the JMT and perhaps at breakfast as well. The youngsters would all be moving on, outpacing Cappy and me. The morning would undoubtedly be the last time we would see them.

Heading back to the tent cabin, I detoured towards the restroom with Zoe. The half-moon was bright enough we did not need our headlamps. A small light glowed over the restroom door, pulling us that direction.

"Where'd Nemo go?" I asked. "And what were you trying to tell me earlier about your extra layover day?"

"I'm not sure where he went, but he has a bee in his bonnet," she began. I could not see her face well, but her voice was tight and level, like she was controlling it.

"The sores on my hips are *not* getting better," Zoe continued. "I'm bruised purple, and the bandages don't seem to give enough protection from my pack's weight and the constant shifting and rubbing. I've tightened the hip belt as tight as it will go, but it's just too damn big for me." The control left her voice, and I heard it catch.

"I wish I could help," I said, racking my brain for a practical solution, a way to cushion her sores. "Can I see them?" I thought maybe I had something in my first-aid kit that would help.

She lifted the bottom of her shirt to expose one hip and pulled back a gauze bandage. I aimed my headlamp at the dark spot on her skin. They looked like bedsores, red, swollen, and scabbed over. They were angrier than I had imagined they would be.

"Yikes!" I said. "Those are deeper than simple abrasions. I bet they hurt down to the bone."

"The ones on my shoulders are a lot smaller and not so tender. But the ones on my hips just keep getting ripped open."

"We've got to figure out a different kind of padding. Let's think about possible cushions," I said, visualizing something soft and squishy stuffed under her pack's hip belt.

"Nemo's come to the limit of his patience. He's pressuring me to walk faster, so we can make up all our lost distance. He's set a new goal of twelve miles a day. But the farther I walk in a day, the worse the sores get and the more pain I'm in—which just slows me down more. Each step hurts."

"Sounds like an impasse. A-rock-and-a-hard-place kind of dilemma. He insists on hiking farther—but you can't," I was thinking aloud.

"I don't know what to do. He's my friend, but he's not acting like it." She sounded sad.

"I always thought you two were a couple," I said.

Zoe chuckled. "No. Not my type. We're just friends."

I chuckled, too. "Not being a couple makes your problem simpler. It's just about the hike, not about a committed relationship."

"He's being so pushy." There was hurt in her voice. "Sometimes, I think I should just hike out and go home. I could try another year with better equipment. Other times I think, wait, this is *my* trip. Nemo invited himself along on *my* trip. He shouldn't get to take charge." I heard the strength returning to her voice—anger was good for that.

"Why don't you two split up?" I asked.

Silence. "What?"

A light bulb went off in my head. "Why can't he just hike at the rate he wants to hike and you hike in your comfort zone? He could go off solo, like Max and Stella. You could slow down and hike with Cappy and me—we're slowpokes."

"I couldn't do that." There was surprise in her voice.

"Sure, you could," I said. "Think about it."

We had finished at the restroom and were approaching the tent cabin. A few gentle snores drifted from the cloth doorway, so we silenced ourselves and climbed into our own bunks. I had to climb up and over Cappy's sleeping form to get to mine.

I lay awake. I had plenty to think about. *Why* was *I here? Really, what* were *my driving motivations? Had they evolved? Is Zoe lying awake, too? Is she thinking about my proposal? How can Cappy and I adjust ourselves to accommodate Zoe?* I knew Cappy would be pleased with the idea but was not sure how Nemo would react. There were practical considerations, too. I fell asleep making a long mental to-do list.

Starting Point — Silver Pass Lake — 10,384 feet
Ending Point — Vermilion Valley Resort (VVR) — 7670 feet
Highest Point — Silver Pass Lake — 10,384 feet
Distance Covered — 7.5 miles
Cumulative Miles — 60 miles

Third Leg

Vermilion Valley Resort to Muir Trail Ranch
Day Eleven to Day Thirteen

Kaleidoscope Eyes

Tell me, what is it you plan to do
with your one wild and precious life?
~ Mary Oliver, "The Summer Day", *New and Selected Poems,* 1992

Day Eleven
July 29, 2006

Starting Point — Vermilion Valley Resort (VVR) — 7670 feet

Nemo stood at the point where the spur trail from Edison Lake met the JMT, the point where we would again turn southward. He lounged under the wide boughs of a huge evergreen tree, casually allowing its rough reddish trunk to support the weight of his backpack. Startled to see him, my pulse quickened. Moments before, my attention had been spread wide, taking in my whole environment—now I held Nemo in my focus. I slowed just a bit to return myself to calm, took a couple of deep breaths, and organized my thoughts.

I had wanted to talk with him. In fact, I had been contemplating ways of getting him off from the group, so I could start a conversation, but I had not anticipated running into him so soon. The Universe has a way of creating convenient coincidences, and this was one of them. I wanted to be calm and composed and bring the illusion of wisdom to the conversation.

Upon hearing my approaching footsteps, he pulled his gaze from the dirt at his feet and glanced up at me. His dark eyes communicated boredom, not the concern I'd hoped to see.

"Hey, Nemo. Nice spot you found," I said. "Can we talk a minute?"

"Sure." He shrugged, though the word lacked any sign of enthusiasm.

"Zoe's really struggling, you know."

Nemo stood straighter and took a step in my direction. He looked down at me. Though still early on a bright summer morning, we stood deep in the forest. Tall trees cast shadows so intense that we cast none at all, or rather, ours were swallowed whole. Nemo's coffee-colored eyes were made darker yet by the shade. I had always thought him exotically handsome, but today that was marred by the faint scent of hostility, like I was Little Red Riding Hood to his Wolf. He was no longer playing his White Knight role.

I wondered if his intimidation was intentional or unwitting, while I consciously stood my ground and maintained my space on the trail. As casually as I could affect, I unbuckled my chest and hip belts and swung my pack onto the duff at the side of the path. Turning my back to Nemo, I tipped my pack against a knee-high granite boulder.

Returning my eyes to Nemo, I said, "Zoe's pack is too heavy, and the sores on her hips are causing her real pain."

"She's walking too slow—even after a full day of rest." He made a show of looking at his watch. "It's already late. At this pace, we'll never make twelve miles today." With a loud sigh, he removed his own pack and set it on the opposite side of the trail from mine. He began to pace around the small space we shared.

"I know you've given yourself a deadline to get to Whitney, but it doesn't seem like she can keep up with you."

"No kidding." He glowered, looking back the direction we had both come. "I need to be to Whitney Portal by the sixth of August."

"Is that a deadline you've had from the start, or is that a new plan?" I asked, already knowing the answer. Zoe had told me they had set no firm end date when they had begun their hike. She had planned an open-ended adventure, and he had tagged along with an equally open schedule.

"There's someone I have to meet in LA on the seventh," he said, neither looking at me, nor answering my question.

"Look. Would you think about something for me today? Would you think about the idea of going on alone, solo, so Zoe could hike with us?" I watched closely for his reaction. I had pondered it so long now that I was *sure* it was a good solution.

"What?" He shifted to look right at my eyes. I think my question took him by surprise. "How would that work?"

"It would be easy to do," I said, having figured out important details the night before. "Since Jane left us at Red's, Cappy and I have a vacancy on our three-person permit. You could take yours and Zoe's permit and walk ahead as fast as you want. Zoe can stroll along at our old-lady pace, and we'd be a threesome again." I had said it aloud, and it did not sound crazy in the least.

We both turned to look back as Cappy's and Zoe's voices drifted our way, their bodies still hidden by the curve in the trail. They were chatting away as they emerged from among the tree trunks.

"I don't know if I want to hike solo," Nemo said, hurrying to close our conversation.

"Just think about it. It could be good for everyone," I urged, looking straight into his deep eyes and using my best "wise woman" voice.

I hefted my heavy pack, swung it onto my back, bounced it higher, and snugged the hip belt. The approaching pair waved enthusiastically, but it was obvious by her stiff movements Zoe was smiling through pain.

Waving back, I called, "Look who I found! And he found the JMT!"

Consciously shifting my tone, I asked Nemo, "What've you heard about today's Ninety-Nine Switchbacks? Do you think there really are ninety-nine? Or is that exaggeration? I heard they seem to go up forever."

He pulled his eyes away from Zoe and looked at me. "What'd you say?"

"Do you think the rumor's true? Are there really ninety-nine switchbacks to climb today?"

"I heard that again at breakfast," he said, as Zoe and Cappy joined us. "But I can never tell if trail stories are real warnings or just practical jokes someone makes up to freak everybody out."

We all stepped together onto the JMT, turning south and heading for those switchbacks. All morning, Zoe hiked with Cappy and me, while Nemo strode on ahead. We last saw him mid-morning when we caught up to him at a small pond. We stepped off the trail for a snack stop and were surprised to find him sitting there.

His impatience on full display, Nemo stood to depart before we even sat down. "Zoe, I'll meet you at camp," he said flatly, then insisted, "Gimme the tent. It'll lighten your load, and I'll have it set up when you get there." He stood, his pack propped against his leg, and watched her with smoky eyes.

"All right. I guess," Zoe said. She unstrapped the tent from her pack and handed him the bundle.

He snatched it, cinched it onto his pack, then turned and walked off. He did not look back, not even when she called, "I'll see you there." With a small over-the-shoulder wave, he was gone.

Questions hung in the air, filling the uncomfortable vacuum Nemo left behind.

Once seated and eating, Cappy asked, "What was that about? Why's he suddenly in such a hurry?"

"He's always wanted to walk faster than I could go, and he's been getting more impatient daily. But something changed at VVR. It seems he met someone at a party the night before we left home for Yosemite." Zoe's shoulders sagged. "At VVR, he called home to get his voicemail messages and was jazzed when he found one from that person. Now, he's in a hurry to get home and hook up." Zoe shrugged, suggesting she found him incomprehensible.

"So, let me get this straight—Nemo's in a hurry, wants to rush through this amazing life experience, so he can get home to meet up with a new lover?" Cappy, up and pacing, tried to translate.

"Yep. That's the long and the short of it." Zoe had her water purification system in her lap and was refilling her container from the small pond.

"But this is *your* trip," I said. "Since he hitched a ride with you, by what logic does he get to tell you to alter your plans?" I checked my foot tape while we talked.

"That's the million-dollar question." Zoe nodded and sighed a half-laugh. "Now he's miserable to be around. All he wants to talk about is hiking faster and farther. He doesn't understand I just can't. Even if I wanted to—which I don't—I can't hike any faster."

I took a deep breath. "Zoe, why don't you just hike with us?" I repeated my proposition of the night before. "We have a three-person wilderness permit. You could join us, and we'd be The Three Women again."

Cappy assured her we had talked about the idea that morning and were in complete agreement. "Zoe, you'd be a wonderful addition to our team. Please, tell Nemo to take off on his own, then walk with us. We're a lot more fun than he is, anyway!"

"You know I'd really like that. I love you girls, but I don't know if he'll agree," she hedged, looking from Cappy to me and back again. "I don't want to impose, either."

"What's to agree? If he wants to walk fast, solo is his only choice." I paused my packing up to look at her. "He doesn't want to walk slowly—you can't walk faster. He has to make a decision." It seemed so obvious to me. I hoped the idea would grow on Zoe—and Nemo would come to his senses.

"It's no imposition!" Cappy insisted. "I'm excited about it!" Her eyes were bright with eagerness. She accentuated her words with that unique fist-shaking gesture of hers.

As we walked on down the trail, we brainstormed all the details necessitated by such a team trade, going over all the equipment and food supply issues we could think of. We had come up with Plans A, B, and C, so that when we saw Nemo again, Zoe could be very convincing.

Distracted by the conversation with Zoe and the thoughts running through my mind, I was oblivious to the passing landscape. When I realized I had slipped from paradise into my head, I built up a distance between myself and my companions. I walked ahead several yards and let them continue to chat without me. I took deep breaths and focused on the sensations of my feet pressing down on the trail—heel, ball, toe, heel, ball, toe—and the force of the earth pressing back on me, supporting me. I allowed myself to absorb the beauty of the scene surrounding me. Tall evergreens, deep green and innumerable, carpeted the mountain slopes ahead of me. The dark brown trail cut through fields of grasses and shrubs, approaching the forest.

When I arrived at the point where the footpath turned sharply upward, the same place where field gave way to forest, I stopped and turned to watch my companions approach. Zoe towered over diminutive Cappy, her long, slow strides juxtaposed to Cappy's quicker, shorter steps. Cappy was chattering away, deep into a story, only pausing when they got close to where I stood.

"Here we go!" I said, indicating the steepness of the trail with a tilt of my head. "Do you think there *really* are ninety-nine of them like the Trail Legend says?"

Squinting into the shadows of the trees, trying to make out where the trail led, Cappy said, "I still don't know what to think, and not knowing makes me nervous."

"Can we look at the map again?" Zoe asked.

Taking out the topo map, Cappy pointed to the trail's blue line as it crossed through thin black line after thin black line in quick succession. "See how the contour lines are all bunched together? That's our path, over two thousand feet straight up." The closely packed lines looked more like an artist's dark shading than individual elevation contours. It had not changed since earlier that morning.

I readjusted my hiking poles for the ascent, shortening them by four inches to an efficient climbing height. Cappy put away the map and worked on her own poles.

"Let's count 'em!" Zoe's voice was playful. "It would be fun to keep a running tally of the switchbacks we complete."

I smiled—we were again a trio. Nemo was long gone, with no fanfare, and Zoe's companionable tone suggested she'd emotionally changed teams, becoming one of us. It felt so comfortable I had not noticed the moment her loyalties had shifted.

"Great idea," Cappy said. "Ninety-nine is a huge number—we need a strategy of attack."

I'd been thinking about chunking up the climb so it would not seem so daunting. "Assuming there *are* ninety-nine, let's break the climb into thirds and stop to rest after number thirty-three," I said.

"That's do-able," Cappy said. "I like it."

We clicked sticks together in agreement. I led, Zoe followed, with Cappy as rear guard.

The broad, smooth trail was deep in the forest's shadow. Conifers towered over an open forest floor, peaceful and quiet. A breeze moved up the mountain through the treetops. Approaching from the west as a gentle high-pitched whispering, the wind's melody swelled into a deep-throated swoosh as it passed directly overhead before disappearing. Occasionally, woodpeckers high in the canopy hammered out a sharp rat-a-tat-tat. A few times, out of the corner of my eye, I caught a glimpse of a small bird darting from one tree to another.

I kept my head down, eyes focused on the trail. Sunlight streamed through the trees in laser-like beams to play light tricks, dappling the trail with thousands of dark and bright spots. Small stones, cones, and dark-colored divots, camouflaged by the shifting dots of light, became an ankle-turning minefield. To admire the grand horizon behind and below us, I forced myself to stop. *When walking walk, when viewing view,* I thought, paraphrasing the Zen proverb.

I set a slow, steady marathon pace, one I hoped we could maintain to the top. When the incline was gentle, each hiking stick synchronized with the opposite leg—left pole moving forward with my right leg, right pole with my left. My stride became longer, an undulating fluid movement, powering me along without speeding up my steps. My breaths came slow, smooth, and deep. When the trail grew steep, however, the poles moved together, reaching out to grab the earth. My arms and shoulders pulled and hoisted my torso, relieving my legs and hips of some of the climbing burden. My strides shortened, but their speed and rhythm remained the same. My lungs pulled at the air, stripping every inhaled breath of its oxygen.

At the end of each switchback, at the point where the trail turned one-hundred-eighty-degrees, I counted aloud, "Number one." "Number fifteen." "Number twenty-seven." Cappy stayed right behind Zoe, hiking a full switchback below me. We passed one another in the middle of each lap, me one level above. Often, they fell farther behind, so I paused at the end of a row to let them catch up a bit. Though I savored the peace of walking alone out front, I was not yet comfortable allowing too much distance between us. Looking back, I realize I was balancing my need for solitude with my need to remain connected by staying just one length ahead.

When I counted "Number thirty-three" where the trail U-turned, I stopped to wait for Cappy and Zoe to join me for our break. I was tired, but felt for the first time I had mastered the art of climbing with my hiking poles. Being able to use them to gain greater power—on both flats and steep climbs—added to my growing sense of confidence. Scouting ahead, I could see only one or two turns above—after that, the switchbacks disappeared, blending into the mountainside.

That morning, walking ahead of my companions, I was feeling strong and confident. What a change! Somehow, somewhere, in the last few days I had hit my stride—I had gotten stronger, physically and mentally, and I was not feeling afraid anymore, anxious sometimes, but not afraid. And it felt really good.

I found my necklace and rubbed the flat rings between my fingers as I watched Zoe and Cappy approach. To keep up with Zoe's longer stride, Cappy had to take more, faster steps. Three of Cappy's steps carried her the same distance as two of Zoe's.

"Thirty-three!" I called out as they drew close. "We made it!"

They joined me in the wide shady place and began to unbuckle their loads. My pack already leaned against the large pine marking the inside of the sharp turn. I was perched atop the stone retaining wall that ran along the uphill edge of the path.

"That was tough," Zoe said, "but counting the switchbacks made it feel like a game."

"Bear Ridge, ninety-nine—The Three Women, thirty-three and counting," I said.

"You're a real competitive person, aren't you?" Cappy asked Zoe, as she propped her pack near mine. Cappy ran her fingers over the hair around her face. Finding loose strands, she tucked them back into their loose knot.

"Yep," Zoe said. "Growing up with brothers, I learned to turn everything into a contest, whether it's with someone else or just against myself." Zoe's shoulder-length blond hair was in a ponytail that poked through the little hole at the back of her baseball-style cap. "Yosemite" was written in blue thread above the bill, where a team logo might have gone. Her sunglasses straddled her head, atop her cap. In the forest's depths, it was too dim for sunglasses. My own were balanced on my hat.

I pulled out a snack of dried mango, dried cranberries, and pecan halves, a favorite flavor combination. The golden strips of mango were honey sweet, the

167

chewy cranberries tart, and the nuts crunchy. The fruit would carry me uphill until lunch. We all downed gulps of water and slowly savored our food. I leaned back onto the soft duff-covered hillside, putting my sandaled feet high up onto the bark of a tree, letting the blood flow towards my heart, rejuvenating me.

"Zoe, how'd your sores do on that climb?" I asked. She had not appeared to favor either hip when I had watched her approach.

"The ones on my hips are really tender. I've got them padded with that moleskin you gave me. They feel a little better today, but uphill is always easier."

"Thirty-three down, sixty-six to go," Zoe said, as we set off again.

"Stop at number sixty-six this time?" Cappy said. "We ought to get to the top about lunch time."

"Onward and upward," I said, taking my first steps up switchback thirty-four.

We walked together for a time, discussing how to adjust and use the hiking poles more efficiently. Cappy liked to swing hers forward simultaneously and push back with both arms at the same time. I agreed—when the climb was steep that was the best way to use them. I showed how I had learned to move mine opposite one another when the trail was less steep, how that gave me real power by lengthening my stride.

The length of the switchbacks grew as we climbed higher—fifty yards, then a hundred yards a lap instead of twenty-five. Fortunately, the climb remained in the coolness of deep shadow. Absorbed by trees and earth, sounds did not carry in the still forest. But scents were powerful—the sharp, cool, mint-like perfume of the firs and pines mixed with the musky aroma of duff decomposing underfoot.

I stopped to admire a fir sapling trying to get a start on the verge of the trail. Its deep green branches were tipped with two inches of new growth, vibrant pale green and soft as fur. Picking one of the new ends, I rubbed it between my fingers and brought it to my nose. Sharp and cool, it had a heady perfume. I tucked it above my ear, like a librarian's pencil, hoping its aroma would follow me as I walked.

"Thank you," I told the little tree.

I continued to count the laps and call the number aloud at each one-eighty. "Number thirty-nine." "Number forty-six." I kept Zoe and Cappy close—they followed a terrace or two behind—but I did not initiate conversation when my zig passed their zag. Every now and again, their chatty words would drift my way, so I was vaguely aware that they were talking, but I was never tempted to join in.

I liked the way this was working out and hoped Zoe would join us permanently. The first few days of the hike, when Murphy's Law had held sway over everything, I had needed to walk as a trio. I had needed the company, the team, and I had needed the emotional support I found in walking together. But as our trail Fairy Godmothers intervened, pushing Murphy and his Law out of the way and I had gained strength and confidence, I did not need that constant companionship when I walked. On the contrary, I was enjoying walking a bit apart, perhaps inspired by my interactions with the solo hikers, Stella and Max.

During the first leg of the hike, I had enjoyed Cappy's every morning, noon, and night review of the lines and dots on the map, and her exact knowledge of where we were in space and time. "Here's where we are right now. Here's where we'll camp tonight." It helped me to feel safe. I had enjoyed it when she had introduced each and every mountain, river, and meadow by its proper name. "This is Mount What's-It, and this is Lake Something-Or-Other."

After Jane had departed, and it had become just Cappy and me, I came to realize that Cappy had a strong desire to label everything and to know her exact place along the trail at all times. But after I had heard the same peak or pass pointed out several times in one day, I realized my need for labeling was far below Cappy's. In fact, her need to tame the environment through names and labels ran counter to my equally powerful need to gain and maintain a silent kinship with the elements of the natural world around me. Labeling disassociated me from the very nature with which I wanted to "become one." I sought emotional and spiritual connection without the mental interference that words, especially proper names, brought to the experience.

Now things had changed again. So far, Zoe seemed to like walking and talking with Cappy, and they hiked at a similar speed. The thought niggled in my brain that if all went well, if Zoe officially joined us, and we once again became The Three Women, I might have the opportunity to walk alone like this more often. I smiled. It felt liberating.

My walking became a meditation. I remembered and began to chant in a whisper from Thich Nhat Hahn's words, "Peace is every step, peace is every step," which wandered into my morning chant, "Love, life, truth, beauty, abundance, and peace." My mind and heart began to expand into the broad and infinite space extending outwards from my body, merging with the space through which I passed. I felt myself cocooned by the forest, blissfully joining with the trees, the air, the earth, and forgetting my own difficulties with the climb. An alert part of my mind maintained a clear awareness of the path I was walking and perpetuated the count, so I moved efficiently along the trail towards my destination of the sixty-sixth switchback.

Startled, I was brought out of my meditation by a pair of male voices coming from just ahead. Two NOBO hikers, the first we had encountered all morning, were headed my way downhill at a good clip.

"Morning," I said, smiling, as we came together.

"Hey," said a husky, forty-something man with a large pack. His t-shirt was soaked with perspiration. He paused and pulled a bandana from his pocket to wipe more sweat from his red face.

"You comin' from VVR?" a somewhat younger and thinner man asked, pointing downhill with a tilt of his head, blond wisps sticking out from beneath a camo-patterned cap. He came to a sudden stop to avoid crashing into his partner.

"A couple hours ago," I said, then answered their questions about the trail I had just traversed and VVR's accommodations.

Then it was my turn to ask about the trail ahead. "How far is it to the top?"

Their reply surprised me. "You're almost there—maybe eight or ten switchbacks."

As they moved on, I waited for Cappy and Zoe to catch up, excited to share my good news. Once again, a Trail Legend had turned out to be just a legend. From where I stood, firmly on switchback number fifty-eight, ten more switches would be only sixty-eight, not the dreaded ninety-nine! The Legend of the Ninety-Nine Switchbacks was nothing but a fairytale.

From the top of Bear Ridge, we looked southward into an emerald valley crisscrossed by thin rivulets meandering their way towards Bear Creek. The path, a long series of downward switchbacks, skipped ahead of us through lush green grasses and tier after tier of hanging gardens. Swaths of wildflowers, in splashes and puddles and falls of color—yellows and blues, reds, pinks, and purples—spilled down the hillside. Swept up in the jubilation of colors, I fairly rolled down the hill.

The bright sun heated the ground and air around us, pulling perfume from flowers and filling my nose with scent. Butterflies, some small and pale yellow, others a black-violet sprinkled with spots of gold and sapphire, fluttered and paused, moving gently from bloom to bloom. Fuzzy black bees and their smaller yellow-and-black-striped cousins hummed and vibrated about their work, their hind legs packed with golden pollen. Intent in their purposes, the flora and fauna alike ignored the humans moving past like just another puff of breeze.

This leg of our journey was one I would have extended if I could. I imagined lingering in this vibrant Eden to meditate in what was a natural temple, but I kept moving, concentrating on the physical sensations of walking through the space. Molecules of moist air brushed like velvet against my skin. My nose pulled in honeyed aromas with each breath while my eyes bathed in a shifting tapestry of colors and shapes. I could not resist singing the few lines I knew from *The Sound of Music*, "The hills are alive with the sound of music, with songs they have sung for a thousand years." Though I did refrain from dancing through the greenery like Julie Andrews.

I was startled by Cappy's voice, which came from above me. I stopped and turned to see her one full switch behind me, but only eight or ten feet directly above me. She had paused in that spot to wait for me to approach from the opposite direction. I had been about to walk right by her without seeing her. I asked her to repeat herself.

"I wish Jane were here to tell us their names," Cappy said. She was squatted down, looking closely at a small purple blossom at the top of a long slender stem.

"Is that a delphinium?" I suggested. "Or maybe a blue dick?" I had no idea what I was talking about but wanted to contribute to her game of flower *Jeopardy*. Cappy was most content when things had names. I reached out and stroked one of the long stems with my fingers. I know lots of flower names and recognize numerous blossoms—I just do not know which goes with which.

Cappy gave me a raised-eyebrow look I interpreted as, "You're kidding, right?"

I shrugged and smiled. I had done my best to play along, but the naming was not important to me. I strolled away, trying to recapture my communion with Mother Nature.

Zoe did not join in the game. Her abrasions, which seemed only this morning to have lost their power to pain her, were aggravated by the steady descent, each step causing a mini-crash of her oversized pack onto her hipbones. Even with moleskin padding, the pounding bruised and tore her skin. She never complained but went silently into herself. Amidst the beauty, Zoe was not having a good time.

The sun was low in the sky—only about an hour of daylight left. We had climbed upwards over two thousand feet and then back down an equal amount, covering about seven miles, a good day. I waited for my trail-mates at the point where our path met Bear Creek.

"Our campsite should be right along here," Cappy said, as she got close. I knew she'd know exactly where to go.

"You want to lead us?" I was ready to call it a day.

We had not walked one hundred steps when the designated campsite appeared on our left on a shelf of land just above the trail opposite the river. I slipped off my backpack, which had grown heavy. Cappy and I stood in the middle of the campsite stretching and twisting to loosen hike-stiffened muscles.

Zoe remained mid-trail, wearing her pack and looking unsure of herself.

"What're you doing, Zoe?" Cappy said. "You're not thinking of hiking on to where Nemo might be waiting, are you?"

Zoe looked ahead down the trail, then back at Cappy. "It's only a couple miles," she replied. "Besides, he has the tent."

The mother in me came flying out of my mouth unbidden and uncensored. "A couple of miles! Zoe, you are not hiking off down the trail by yourself at sunset. It's going to be completely dark in a little while. It'll take you an hour, at best, to get there." I walked in her direction, remaining inside the campsite's perimeter a few feet from where she stood in the trail. I had thought we had gotten past this decision, but apparently Zoe was having second thoughts.

Cappy joined in, equally distraught over the thought of Zoe hiking off into the darkness by herself. "You don't even know if he's really there. Given the snit he was in this morning, he could easily have hiked on another five miles, just to get a little closer to his destination. Zoe, we can't let you do this!"

"What choice do I have? Where will I sleep?" She stood unmoving in the middle of the trail, but she did not look quite so determined as before. The starch had gone out of her posture.

"You'll sleep with us, of course. We three can squeeze into our tent. It'll be tight, but for one night we can handle it," I said.

"Oh, I couldn't do that to you." Zoe still resisted with her words, but her body communicated she was on the verge of giving in. She had moved off the trail and onto the smooth dirt edge of the campsite, her hand resting on the buckle of her pack's hip belt.

"Oh, yes, you can. We insist!" Cappy said with finality.

Zoe dropped her pack on the ground next to mine and sagged down onto a fallen log bench.

"Let's get camp set up. We can talk solutions over dinner," I said.

The campsite was well-established, clearly marked with logs and stones set in a semi-circle around a smooth cleared space. Yet, it was technically way too close to the trail and river, only a couple dozen feet from the fast-moving water, less from the trail. The backcountry rule, as the rangers had made clear to us when we had picked up our permit, requires camping and peeing one hundred feet, about ninety paces, from water and trails. "We'll just go up the hill a hundred feet to pee, and call this spot perfect," I said.

Bear Creek, really a broad and swift river, made a sharp ninety-degree turn just across the trail from our vantage point. Then it headed west, straight as a tree-lined boulevard, sailing off into the setting sun. When the sky turned yellow and orange with the sunset, the river did too, appearing more like polished metal than flowing water. The fractured surface reflected each and every color hundreds of times over, in each and every facet that was a wave or a ripple, splitting the water's kaleidoscope surface into a series of dazzling Impressionist images worthy of a master.

With camp quickly assembled, we cooked and ate perched on rocks facing the river, content to watch the dynamic light show in companionable silence, though we had much to discuss. Even after sunset, the sky glowed silver and the broad creek reflected that remaining brightness as quicksilver.

In the fading light, Zoe wore the straight-backed posture and quiet-eyed countenance of resolve, having shed the pinched look of anxiety that had taken over her face and shoulders when we had arrived at camp.

Out of this gentle twilight, a specter appeared on the trail. Where everything else—path, trees, water, rocks—was illuminated by the last of the sun's photons in

173

various shades of pewter and chrome, the approaching figure seemed to absorb the light and stood out as pure black, like a shadow, against the lighter background.

A hiker still on the trail this late was unusual. Our three heads swiveled to observe. Conversation ceased. I leaned forward, anxious to know who approached, my eyes struggling to find focus. Eventually the figure drew close, and Nemo materialized from the blur. Wearing a black jacket and cap, he stopped on the path exactly where Zoe had earlier stood.

After a moment, Zoe rose and walked to the edge of our site. Her toes just touched the perimeter—the boundary line that would have been a wall or fence were we in a civilized neighborhood. They stood in loud silence, simply looking at one another.

Neither Cappy nor I moved or spoke. This was Zoe's conversation to have. Inside my head, though, I repeated, *Don't give in, Zoe. Stay with us.*

Nemo spoke, then Zoe. I could hear their voices, but not their words.

After a few minutes, he pivoted on his heel and walked back the way he had come. Zoe returned to her seat with us, and we were The Three Women.

"So?" Cappy said after a few moments of silence. "What'd he say?" We watched her closely in the gloam.

"Nemo's camped a couple of miles ahead. He's really pissed that I stopped here with you and didn't hike to where he'd set up camp."

"If he walked back two miles to find you in the dark, he can't be all bad," I said. "He must have been worried about you, after all."

"I guess so," Zoe said. She swiveled her head to look down the trail in the direction he had disappeared.

"But if he was really worried," Cappy said, "he wouldn't have walked off leaving you so far behind in the first place."

"True," I agreed.

"I told him we'd find him in the morning to divide up the equipment." Her tone of finality was mixed with a pinch of sadness.

As dark settled around us, the air grew cold. We had yet to figure out how to stretch a two-person tent to fit three. It would be a tight squeeze, but I was sure we could sleep three abreast for one night. We stood arrayed around the tent, each trying to visualize how to arrange ourselves inside. Cappy's hands rested on her hips, head cocked, as she surveyed the situation. I could practically see gears turning in her head.

"I can just sleep outside next to the tent. I don't want to displace you gals." Zoe sounded anxious; her voice small.

"No," we replied in stereo.

I bent to look at the inside space. "We'll all be fine. We'll lay out the sleeping bags head to toe. That'll give us more space."

"Zoe, do you get up in the night to pee?" Cappy asked a practical question. Zoe shook her head. "Joan and I both do, so we'll put our heads by the door. You can be in the middle, with your head at the other end."

I reached inside and began arranging the thin inflated sleeping pads, the synthetic fabrics swishing and rasping against one another. I spread the sleeping bags out over the pads. Zoe and Cappy knelt by the fabric door, reaching in to help.

With all three of us inside, wrapped in mummy bags and pressed like sardines into one another, it was quickly uncomfortable. It was too hot, too stuffy, and the slightest movement set off a cacophony of swishes. Zoe's head was crammed into the foot of the tent, and she lay in the trench created by the overlapping pads. I lay on my side, as still as I could, trying to be as narrow as possible. Eventually, I had to roll over. Like dominoes, my roommates readjusted their own positions. The rustling was deafening in the silent night, and I was not any more comfortable in my new position.

An hour after climbing into our tiny home, when it was clear that none of us was sleeping, Zoe announced she would sleep outside. "We'll all get a better night's sleep," she said as she struggled to climb out of the tent. We attempted to dissuade her, but neither of us argued real hard. Zoe put her pad on the ground next to the tent's wall so it would block the breeze coming off the water. She donned cold weather gear—jackets, gloves, socks, and hat—slipped in and pulled her bag up over her head, cinching the drawstring tightly so that just her eyes and nose showed. Cappy and I rearranged ourselves into familiar sleeping positions. And we all fell asleep quickly.

That was the only night we attempted converting our two-person tent into a three-person tent. The failed process, though humorous in the moment, made clear how vital it was going to be for Zoe to get all or part of the tent she and Nemo had shared. Without shelter, she would be in trouble when we entered the true "High Sierra" where camping high above timberline in the clear, cold sky would mean sub-freezing temperatures even in August.

Starting Point — Vermilion Valley Resort (VVR) — 7670 feet
Ending Point — Bear Creek Junction — 8985 feet
Highest Point — Bear Ridge — 9880 feet
Distance Covered — 7.6 miles
Cumulative Miles — 67.6 miles

Serial Encounters

The world is made up of stories, not of atoms.
~ Muriel Rukeyser, *The Speed of Darkness*, 1968

Day Twelve
July 30, 2006

Starting Point — Bear Creek Junction — 8985 feet

Perhaps we dawdled in camp to savor the river's splendor. Perhaps, we lingered, anxious to postpone fording Bear Creek—Trail Legend Number Four. Or perhaps it was the impending confrontation with Nemo waiting up the trail. Whatever the reason, we were tardy that morning.

The JMT stuck to the edge of boisterous Bear Creek—really a river bounding along in its narrow channel, like a wild animal trapped within rock walls trying to get free. The roaring and growling of the water made talking impossible, but that did not keep my mind from perseverating on both upcoming challenges.

A small group of hearty NOBO hikers at VVR had described Trail Legend Four, the Ford at Bear Creek, as perilous. How deep *was* the river? We heard the river was hip deep, but it might be waist deep for us. How fast *was* the water flowing? They said it was so swift people were getting knocked down by the river's force.

But *you* made it through okay, right? Just barely, they confessed, while standing six-feet tall. Cappy and I were short and especially troubled by the tale of depth.

One person said to watch for an orange plastic bag mounted on a stick by a nameless ranger, a warning of danger. Over breakfast at VVR, we heard two middle-aged women (just like us) had been swept a quarter-mile downstream before they were able to overcome the force of the water to crawl out onto the rocky ground. They had spent hours combing the river's edge to find all their possessions, some of which had been ruined.

That morning, a NOBO gentleman-of-the-trail we came across—a broad-shouldered, well-built fellow, with the cat-like stride of a long-distance runner and a palpable air of confidence—painted a different picture. At a wide spot in the trail, he explained the Bear Creek Crossing Legend was "a bunch of BS, excuse the expression." He advised us to leave the trail and walk downstream "a little ways" to find a spot where the creek widened out and became shallower.

We had left the conversation confused and anxious.

There was nothing I could do about the river crossing—it would be what it would be—so I aimed my anxious energy on our other obstacle. I hoped Cappy and I had succeeded in convincing Zoe she needed to come away from her negotiations with Nemo with all or part of her tent—at the very least, the ground cover. It seemed so obvious to me—she carried the permit he absolutely needed to remain on the trail, and he possessed the tent she needed to survive nighttime temperatures in the high country—but I wondered if Zoe would be assertive enough to win what she needed. I was certain my hiking partners were having similar inner conversations on the level and shaded trail. I kept my eyes ahead. I wanted to see him before he saw us.

Long before we found Nemo, we met two National Park Service Rangers where the trail left the winding creek to cross through a meadow. The young men, dressed in the green-and-gray uniforms of the NPS, were out maintaining trails and campsites. When we drew near, they were breaking up an illegal camp, scattering the rocks of a fire ring someone had built too close to the trail. They took our arrival as an opportunity to pause in their hot, dirty work and set aside their tools.

One ranger, the elder of the two, was of the mountain man variety—tall, deeply tanned and freckled, with a thick copper-colored beard. His boots and uniform looked like they had seen several summers in the backcountry, and he looked like he would go completely feral with a little encouragement. His younger partner was of the Eagle Scout mold, with closely cropped black hair and a tidy uniform despite the heat and dirt all around him. So properly "put together" was he that his neatly trimmed mustache stood out as a badge of nonconformity.

Pleasantries finished, they explained the work they were doing and gave us the requisite speech on the One-Hundred-Foot Rule: hikers must camp at least one hundred feet from water and trail. Our well-used campsite the previous night had clearly broken that rule, but we did not mention it.

The older ranger, who was barely older than Cappy's kids and my son, said, "We're also checking wilderness permits today. Can we see yours, please?"

"Sure." I slipped my pack to the ground. Zoe did the same. I pulled our permit from deep inside my pack and extracted it from its Ziploc bag before handing it to Mountain-Man-Ranger.

"This permit is for the three of you?" he asked after he scrutinized the document.

"No, that's just for Cappy and me," I said, pointing back and forth to the two of us.

Cappy explained that we carried a permit for three because we had started as a trio, but Jane had left us at Red's.

"Then where's yours?" he turned to Zoe, who pulled her permit from a waterproof wallet.

When he saw it was for two people, a light of recognition went on in his pale eyes. He looked up and asked Zoe, "Is your hiking partner up ahead? A guy named—" He paused before turning to his partner to ask, "What was his name?"

"Nicodemo," Zoe offered. "His name is Nicodemo."

"Right. That's it." Eagle-Scout-Ranger nodded his head.

Mountain-Man explained how they had stopped Nemo several hours earlier. Without a permit, Nemo had been unable to substantiate his right to be in the backcountry, let alone on the John Muir Trail. The men-in-green had instructed Nemo to wait where he was until they could check out the veracity of his story. "We're glad to know that he was telling us the truth."

"He's waiting for you where the trail turns towards the creek crossing," added Eagle-Scout.

We went on to discuss the weather, the trail, the impact the late snowmelt was having on the wildflowers and the high water. Then Cappy asked specifically about the dreaded Bear Creek Crossing. "How deep is it? Is it safe to ford?"

"You're early in the day—it should be fine. The later it gets, the more snowmelt there is, and the higher and faster the rivers run. It can run five or six inches deeper in the evening than in the morning," Mountain-Man explained. "You're short, so it's good you'll get there early."

"We've heard so many scary stories. Do you have advice for crossing safely?" I asked.

"Be sure to unbuckle your pack, just in case you fall down, so you can get out of it quickly," advised Eagle-Scout.

"You have hiking poles. Use them. And go slow," added Mountain-Man.

We bade them farewell and continued down the trail, knowing Nemo and the river lay just ahead.

Sure enough, barely a half-hour after chatting with the rangers, I saw Nemo sitting in his studied casual manner on a large, angular, trailside rock. To give the two of them some privacy for what would surely be a contentious conversation, and hopefully a successful negotiation, Cappy and I greeted Nemo and then proceeded another fifty feet down the trail. We stopped and settled into a restful snack time, while we waited for Zoe to conclude her business with Nemo.

We observed them closely while trying to appear disinterested. Though the sounds of their voices drifted our way, we were too far to hear their words. We tried to decipher their body language. First, they stood far apart, an uncomfortable gap like a solid thing between them. Nemo kept his arms crossed over his chest, leaning one hip against a boulder. The affected casualness of his lower body's lean was at odds with the firmly closed stance of his upper body. He looked directly at Zoe's face. Zoe, hands in pockets, alternated between looking at his face and looking at the ground. As the conversation progressed, they both began gesticulating, pointing and gesturing towards the trail, equipment in the packs, and one another. Zoe shook her head several times.

It had to be painful. They had started the hike, not two weeks earlier, a team of friends with a common goal. We were watching a divorce. Eventually, they began digging around in their packs, tossing equipment onto the ground. I watched Zoe give Nemo her water pump and her stove. Nemo handed over some tools or equipment too small for me to identify at that distance. Then, she hesitated before holding out the permit. Nemo took it and stuffed it into his pocket. What I did not see change hands was the tent—not even the fly—not even the groundcover.

"I didn't see him give her any tent pieces. Did you?" I asked Cappy. Zoe and Nemo had turned their backs on one another while they repacked their backpacks on opposite sides of the trail.

"Nope. I think he got it all. He must have one very silver tongue," she said.

"And one very ungenerous heart," I added. "All she needed to get was the ground-cloth. We could have jury-rigged a tent from the two ground-cloths. What are we going to do now?"

Zoe walked our way. Nemo still fiddled with his pack.

"I don't know," Cappy said. "We'll have to figure something out." We stood and readied our packs to move on.

"We sure will," I agreed.

Zoe's face was a pale blank wall as she walked silently past us following the trail.

We fell in behind her. I could not think of any other time when Zoe had taken the lead. She did not walk far, not even a quarter mile, pulling up shy of Bear Creek Crossing.

"Well?" I asked.

Zoe explained Nemo had relented to breaking up their team. He would walk on alone, freeing Zoe to continue the trek with us. In exchange for his magnanimous generosity, he took the stove, purifier, permit, and the whole tent!

Just as we had feared. Zoe was more disappointed than angry, disappointed she had so misjudged the quality of her friend. She was determined to solve the tent problem without a tent.

While we discussed the results of one obstacle within sight of the next, Nemo walked by, heading south. He acknowledged us with a slight nod of his head. I wondered if he was gone for good, or if we would run into Nemo again. I know Cappy was as thrilled as I was to have Zoe with us permanently, but we worried about her sleeping arrangements. The weather was cold at night, and we had yet to reach the "High Sierra" to the south—nights of frost and below-freezing temperatures were coming. I was not sure if Zoe realized how viciously cold it was going to get.

Then, I set aside my tent worries to focus on my river worries.

With trepidation, we approached the point where Bear Creek bisected the trail, slicing it deep and wide like a backhoe had been at work. The power of the water was channeled into a narrow, fast-moving current, which gave off a splashing, roaring noise that was unnerving.

Standing at the intersection was a gray-haired man in full hiking gear—and a llama. Yes, a llama. The llama was laden with two bulky packs, hanging one on each side with a third piled atop. The man, sans backpack, held securely onto a stout lead rope attached to the animal's muzzle. Facing the animal, with his back to the river, the man was pulling his end of the rope firmly towards the water. At the same time, he used gentle coaxing words to encourage the animal into the rushing current.

The llama stood stock still, refusing to take even one step in the direction the man wanted it to walk. The more the man pulled, red faced and leaning deeply into his pull, the more stubbornly the pack animal resisted, pulling in the opposite direction, the rope taut. Slowly, the tug-of-war turned into a dance. Man and llama began moving around, circling one another. As the stronger animal twisted and turned its backside towards the ford, the man vainly attempted to spin it around. Round and round they spun, face to face, connected by the thick line between them. Finally, the man quit pulling, and they came to a stop, still facing each other, no closer to the water than when we had first arrived.

The man sighed, sagged a little bit, and let the line go slack. He stepped to the llama's side, reaching out his free hand to pat the animal's flank. Eyes wide, the llama stepped back. The man spoke softly and reached out again. The animal relented, stood still, and allowed the man to rub its shoulder. Finally, it nuzzled the man's arm. Reconciled, the two walked back up the trail away from the water to rest and come up with a new plan.

Cappy used the opportunity to make a new trail friend and get the scoop on the llama. "Are you hiking alone?" she asked.

"Yep," said the man. He tied the lead to a tree branch. "I'm meeting my son in a couple of days." The man took a red bandana from around his neck and began to mop beads of sweat from his creased face and neck. "I came from Tuolumne Meadows. My son is flying out from Colorado and is going meet me in Sequoia in two days—*If* I can get across the river!" The man removed his broad hat and wiped his head and gray hair.

"You walked all the way from Yosemite with a llama?" I chimed in. "Why did you choose a pack animal rather than a backpack?"

"I used to backpack often, but hurt my back a couple of years ago and can't carry a full pack anymore." He touched his lower back and did a twist-stretch. "Until today, it's been great to have the llama do all the heavy lifting." He went on to explain the art of packing and setting up camp and keeping both he and the animal well fed.

"I may have to camp here tonight and wait until the morning when the water's at its lowest."

"Good luck," we said and turned towards Trail Legend Number Four, wondering what the llama knew about the river that we did not.

We stood at the water's edge and surveyed the path forward. The water was moving swiftly from left to right in front of us. The river topped its banks, straying among shrubs growing alongside, exposing their roots as it pulled moist earth away. The bottom of the creek, hard to see because the surface of the water was alive with bubbles and ripples, was lined with smooth rounded stones varying in size from tennis balls to footballs and half-inflated basketballs. The stones would be slippery, but there was no moss or algae growing in that fast current.

"Let's talk this through before we start," I said. We stood shoulder-to-shoulder looking at the water and thinking aloud.

"Yes," Cappy agreed. "First, we all unclip our belts." Each of us reached to undo the buckles at belly and chest.

"And lengthen our poles," I added. "We'll want to plant them wide to broaden the base and keep steady."

Zoe said, "Like the Ranger said, we should go across one at a time. Only one in the water means there's only one to rescue at a time."

"Right. And those on shore should take off their packs, but keep their poles. That way we're ready to come to the rescue immediately," I said.

"I want to go first," Cappy said, not taking her eyes off the water. "I'll go real slow—one step at a time." She looked from me to Zoe. "Are you both okay with that?"

We agreed and removed our packs. I leaned my load against a rock and returned with poles to the water's edge. Cappy stood scrutinizing the path underneath the water, her face intense with concentration. Zoe came up beside me.

"You ready?" Cappy asked.

"Ready whenever you are," I responded.

"Then let's do it," she said, placing her hiking poles into the water, like a pair of steel support beams, a foot from the edge.

A full five minutes later, she was on the other side. With both feet firmly on dry ground, Cappy threw her arms, still gripping her poles, into the air and gave a loud "Whoop!" Zoe and I cheered and returned her victory salute.

"One down, two to go! My turn," I said and went to fetch my pack, while on the other side, Cappy removed hers.

I strode to the water's edge, planted my feet firmly, and scanned the river's bottom for the smoothest, most direct path across. Reaching forward, I placed my hiking poles in the water, giving them a broad stance for better balance. Step one: right foot, left foot, feet side-by-side. Barely ankle deep, but I could feel the force of the flow trying to push me downstream.

Second step: I lifted and placed my poles ahead one at a time to maintain a tripod of stability. I took another step forward, right foot, left foot. The river's bottom dropped sharply—I was already in to mid-calf. Buffeted by the current, I leaned upstream.

I lifted my downstream hiking pole, intending to place it just ahead, but the water yanked it away, nearly pulling it out of my hand. Thankfully the wrist strap held the pole securely, or it might have sailed downstream. Twice I attempted to place the tip of the pole down among the rocks, and twice it was nearly swept away. On the third try, I aimed for a spot well upriver from my target, so when I stabbed downward, the tip was carried to the perfect spot. After jamming in the other pole, I took another step forward. The water was above my knees.

Pausing to survey the step ahead into deeper water, I teetered. The cobble I stood on rocked back and forth. I leaned upstream, pressing firmly on both poles, like a quadruped with limbs splayed. I sucked in breath and let out a gentle "Wooooah!" My ankles and knees worked independently to find a stable angle while my hips and upper body strove to remain balanced.

Step three: the hem of my shorts dipped in the frigid foaming water. Step four: I was in up to my hips. The deeper I walked, the more the water pushed and the more I had to lean into the oncoming flow. To place my foot meant plunging it upstream, aiming for a spot far upstream of where I actually intended to step.

I was halfway across the creek and climbing out before I realized how cold my legs and feet had become. My skin was numb in the snowmelt, and my bones ached. The final steps in shallower water were quicker, and then I was standing beside Cappy on dry land.

I raised my poles high and mimicked Cappy's earlier "Whoop!" She lifted her poles to meet mine—a clanking, celebratory high-five. My toes and knees tingled sharply, defrosting in the air, and a wave of warm relief began at the crown of my head and rolled down the length of my body.

"Your turn, Zoe! Slow and steady!" I said, removing my pack.

"On my way," she called back. Her longer natural stride and longer reach (not to mention her youth and strength) carried Zoe across Bear Creek swiftly. We greeted her "Whoop!" with another round of enthusiastic clanking high-fives.

"Another Trail Legend bites the dust," Cappy said, as we collected ourselves.

"Were we lucky to arrive after the season's peak floods? Were the waters that much crazier a few days ago? Is that how these rumors get started?" Zoe wondered aloud.

"I don't know. Could've been. The snow's been melting really fast the last week," Cappy said.

"This was Trail Legend Number Four, right?" I counted. I had my pack on my shoulders again. "First, we conquered the sun cups and snowfield before Silver Pass. Second, we walked right through that amazing waterfall."

Cappy said, "Yesterday's ninety-nine switchbacks that turned out to be only sixty-eight was Legend Three."

I finished the count, "And fourth, we've forded the *impossible* Bear Creek."

"The Three Women, four—Trail Legends, zero," Zoe agreed.

We walked along the track, following the river we had just crossed, tightly spaced to continue our conversation.

"It's interesting, that with all these Trail Legends, we've spent so much time and energy worrying about the next *monster challenge*," I said over my shoulder, "and none of them have lived up to their reputations. For me, crossing Rush Creek on that log back on our misty third morning was *far* worse than any of these Trail Legends."

"How 'bout our very first river crossing—when we thought we were lost on the way to Donohue," Cappy said. I nodded, remembering how shocked we had been at having to wade through water that deep.

"Aren't the swarms of blood-sucking mosquitoes worthy of their own Legend? Maybe we should start some crazy rumors of our own!" Zoe's voice was full of laughter.

"We could spread our own tales." I turned my head so my voice carried back to Cappy, third in line. "When some northbound hiker starts to warn us about an awful obstacle ahead—"

"We'll throw in our own warnings! I love it!" Zoe finished my thought. "How 'bout a washed-out bridge?"

"Or a new landslide?" I laughed at the absurdity.

"Of course, we'd never really—" Zoe and I dissolved into laughter. Cappy shook her head, but smiled at us.

Feeling light of heart, I picked up the pace, and a peaceful silence descended on us.

Lying on a granite slab in the warm sun, resting after lunch alongside Cappy and Zoe, I was still thinking about Zoe's backpacking equipment. Thoughts of tents and stoves reminded me of my first backpacking trip thirty-seven years earlier.

I was fifteen, and had backpacked into the Yosemite backcountry with a group of ten boys and girls, all members of my swim team. We were led and chaperoned by two fathers, one who had been a NPS Ranger in Yosemite in his youth so was intimately familiar with that wilderness. We hiked and camped for a week in the high country around Tuolumne Meadows.

It would have been August of 1969, when backpacking was a lot different. Unlike in 2006, we carried aluminum and canvas backpacks and walked in heavy leather boots. We wore denim jeans or cotton shorts and t-shirts during the day, then layered ourselves with cotton long underwear, wool sweaters, caps, and gloves in the evenings. A thick plastic rain-slicker with a hood served as my final layer.

Back in the day, we used stainless steel Sierra cups to drink directly from the lakes and streams—no water filters. I remember just dipping my shiny silver cup into the clear water of a running stream and how sweet that water tasted. We built fires to cook our meals—no compact stoves. One evening I was given the chore of collecting fallen wood. Then I watched as our leader chopped one branch into kindling with a small hatchet he carried before he started a fire in a circle of stones.

We ate the most god-awful food ever created. Pork-n-beans, still in the cans, the best offering on the menu, was cooked directly in the fire, then served half-burned, half-cold on aluminum plates. Freeze-dried food was in its infancy, a spinoff from the NASA space program like the Tang we drank. The cooking process was far from perfect and results were nearly inedible. The pale-yellow scrambled eggs were rubbery and tasted like chalk. Powdery chunks floated like curds in the chocolate milk we drank. As a kid, I was a picky eater, highly sensitive to textures, so I could barely swallow the food without gagging. The only thing that kept me from refusing to eat altogether was not wanting to appear foolish in front of the cute boys in the hiking group, and the fact that I was famished.

Clean-up may have been worse than eating. I remember being assigned the chore of cleaning the egg remains out of the cast iron frying pan. Our leader showed me how to scrub out the dried egg that clung to the inside of the pan with sand. I buried the slimy mess in a hole, before rinsing the pan with fresh water right in the stream. I look back on that now with disgusted wonder.

My younger sister, Diane, hiked on that trip, too, which meant we were stuck sharing a tent. On nights with fair weather, we all slept outside under the stars, a wonderful experience for a city girl. Those nights Diane and I shared the ground-cloth without arguing. But on the one night it rained, we squeezed ourselves side-by-side into something called a tube tent—an eight-foot long, bright yellow tube of thin plastic, like a giant trash bag without a bottom. We tied a rope high on one tree, slipped the line through the tube, and tied the other end to another tree. We ended up with a sagging, triangular tunnel suspended from the rope, wide open at both ends.

The tent would have worked better if we could have moved the trees to position them properly. Barring that, we had to make do with our tent aimed down a slope. With the sky pouring buckets all night, a seasonal gulley found its way in the tent's backdoor and out the front. My sleeping bag and I were drenched from head to toe in the stream of cold water. My sister snored through the whole event until I woke her to share my misery. We argued until the sun came up.

The next morning, I spread my bag and clothes out on rocks to dry in the sun and watched while everyone else swam in the frigid lake. I had had enough of cold water during the night, so I sat on the rocks to watch my teammates frolic like otters.

We might have been the largest group on the trails back in 1969, but we were not the only group. Camped near us one evening was a young couple on their honeymoon. They had set up their tent in the early evening, but before they could properly hoist their food supplies into the branches of a tree, which was considered best-practice back then, they became amorously distracted with one another inside the tent. Unfortunately, a mother black bear and her cub, out foraging at dusk, happened along at that exact moment, drawn by the aroma of food.

The bears attempted to join the couple and their food bags inside the tent. Thinking quickly, the groom used his pocketknife to slice a hole in the wall of the tent, allowing the two of them to escape, terrified, but otherwise unharmed. They took refuge with us and spent the last days of their honeymoon camping and traveling in the company of ten children and teens. They even shared our meals, as the bears had eaten everything they had carried in their packs, right down to ripping open cans of tuna to lick them clean.

I was grateful for the scientific improvements to backpacking food and equipment that had taken place in the intervening years. Modern freeze-dried foods were savory and easy to cook. There were no icky dishes or pans to clean, no heavy pots or cans to tote, minimal trash to carry out, and no firewood to gather or chop.

By 2006, everything was much more compact and lightweight. Our tent and packs were pounds lighter, so was our clothing. My modern shoes weighed nothing compared to those old brown leather boots. On top of all that, this time around, our food was stowed safely away inside bear-proof containers, not hanging about in a tree like a smelly piñata luring bears into camp.

We could have forced our six tired feet up and over Seldon Pass that afternoon, but confronting the towering dark clouds atop the mountain ahead was another thing entirely. Though we had come through one high-elevation electrical storm unscathed, and lightning is not supposed to strike someone twice, chasing it to a new place and expecting it to avoid striking us a second time seemed foolhardy. Wisely, we stopped to make camp at Marie Lake.

We had a second more immediate reason to quit early. Before the approaching deluge began, we needed to jury-rig a solution to our three-people-and-one-tent problem. I remember little of our post-lunch hike, because, with every step, I had been puzzling over our tent conundrum. We had no "chewing gum and baling wire," but between us we did have an assortment of tools and supplies we might use to assemble the three big puzzle pieces—the two-person tent, its rainfly, and its "footprint" ground-cloth—into a makeshift shelter. We had no extra poles or cloth, but we carried nylon line, black plastic trash bags, and a miscellaneous assortment of nylon straps and various connectors.

As I walked, I shuffled the available ingredients around in my mind like an oversized tangram puzzle, turning them first one way then another, trying to conjure an arrangement that would produce a sheltered sleeping space for Zoe. Eventually, in my mind's eye, the various pieces assembled themselves into a lean-to. I was sure it could work and eager to try it.

"I have an idea for the tent," I blurted the moment we pulled to a stop. "I think we can make a lean-to with the footprint." I sloughed off my pack and was unstrapping my half of the tent.

While Cappy and Zoe removed their packs, I checked on the darkening clouds still growing outward from the pass ahead. Dark gray dashes reached downward from the flat bottoms of storm clouds, a vivid display of water pouring from the sky onto the craggy mountaintops.

"It's already raining up there." I pointed and the others swiveled to look.

"We need to get this up quick." Cappy bustled about, unstrapping her half of the tent parts.

"Zoe, you must have shelter tonight," I said. Cappy was as concerned as I was, both of us more aware than Zoe of her need to be protected from the elements. Despite being August, at well over ten thousand feet, the night was going to be wet and frigid.

"First, let's get the tent up. Then I think I can jury-rig the footprint onto its side," I explained as I unrolled the tent.

Cappy and I moved quickly—having built the tent so often we could have done it blindfolded. I flipped the body of the tent out like a bed sheet, and we threaded the long, flexible tubes into their cloth sleeves. Pressing each pole-end into a corner pocket forced the tent upward into a dome.

"We'll be okay without the ground-cloth as long as we're careful where we position it," I said as we arranged the tent on the level stone, leaving a wide space along one side for our construction project.

Zoe was ready with the tent's footprint. At a growl of thunder, we turned our heads in unison to see the clouds grown both taller and broader. Lightning bloomed into an asymmetric web against the blackness of the clouds, urging us to hurry.

I pulled my attention back from the sky. "Here's my idea."

I pointed and gestured as I explained. "We can use the ground-cloth to make a triangular-shaped tunnel for Zoe to sleep in, like a lean-to on the side of our tent," I began, pointing along the ridge that ran along the top of the tent's dome. "If we attach one of the long sides along here and stretch it out to the left until it just touches the ground over here, it will be like a half of a tent."

"There won't be a floor to her space," Cappy said, "just walls that meet at a point above her. Is that how you see it?"

"It is. If we had both ground-cloths, she could've had something between her sleeping pad and the ground," I confirmed, "but we don't."

"What about the rain?" Cappy wondered. "I don't think this material is waterproof." Cappy took the black nylon rectangle from Zoe and felt its texture with her fingers.

"I don't think it is either," I said. "I was hoping, after we build the lean-to, that we could stretch our rainfly out to the side to cover both structures—but I'm not sure." I used my hands to show how far the rain fly might reach.

"I'm game," Zoe said. "Let's try it." She took one corner of the black cloth Cappy held, and between them, they spread it out.

"Let's use a couple carabineers to connect the high edge to the tent, then tie lines to each of the lower corners as tie-downs," I said. We each carried line and spare clips in our packs solely for solving problems. After some trial-and-error with the connections, Zoe found a pair of football-sized rocks to use as anchors.

The tightness of the cords and clips had to be repeatedly adjusted and secured. It was a matter of equilibrium, not too tight, not too loose, but a Goldilocks-style "just right." Finally, we stretched the rainfly at an awkward angle over both the dome and the lean-to, hoping it would keep both sleeping shelters dry.

It had taken several tries and a handful of false starts, but we did it. Though it looked flimsy, it stood steadily. We stepped back and took in the final result. We had created a taut triangular tube along the length of our tent, just as we had envisioned.

"We are women. Hear us roar!" I said, throwing my hands into the air. In return, my teammates cheered. It was satisfying to have tackled the problem with teamwork—another victory, one of many that day.

"We need a bottle of Champagne to christen it!" Cappy's face held a full smile that reflected my own sense of pride and accomplishment. We walked around the tent and its sidekick, admiring our slightly lopsided contrivance.

"Or at least a bottle of beer," Zoe agreed, then extended her arm to sprinkle a few drops of water from her Nalgene onto the rainfly and said, "I christen thee Franken-tent!" We all laughed.

I nodded my approval. "Appropriate name for something so cobbled-together."

"Take a really good look at it," Cappy said. "Remember exactly how it's built, so we can reconstruct it tomorrow."

Good idea, I thought. I scrutinized our handiwork, trying to memorize every detail. Solving the problem once had been kind of fun, but reinventing it would not be.

"I think the storm is moving away." Zoe's words interrupted my concentration. I turned to look at the approaching black storm clouds, but they had nearly disappeared! Either they had rained themselves dry and shrunk to nothing, or stronger winds higher up had blown them away. All that remained were puffy white cumulous clouds playing chase across a bright sky.

Suddenly, there was a gift of time—a reward for a job well done. Instead of battening down the hatches, we had the afternoon and evening for leisure. Taking the time to really look around, I discovered we had staked our claim in a beautiful stone stadium-shaped basin. Our fifty-yard-line seats, located on a broad granite shelf tilting gently towards the lake, provided us an unobstructed view. The sprawling, dark-blue lake was littered with tiny islets and snake-shaped peninsulas made from rocks cast aside when a glacier had scraped the lake's basin out of the mountain.

I took off my hat and massaged the back of my neck. I studied my partners as they began to relax. Zoe sat, her lanky body bent over her pack, rifling through its contents. Long strands of tawny hair fell into her face, so she tucked them behind her ears. She pulled out soiled clothes, gathered them into a small colorful pile, and made her way down to the lake for a bit of laundry and water pumping.

Cappy sat with our topo map spread across her legs and the trail guide at her side. We had pulled up a little short of our planned destination, so she was recalculating the next day's mileage and memorizing our path. Her face relaxed in deep concentration, she trailed her forefinger across the map's face and then checked the directions in the guide book.

Cappy looked my way. "Tomorrow, just before we get to Muir Ranch, we'll be at the symbolic halfway point."

"Really? How can that be?" I was surprised we had traveled so far already. I was removing my sandals and socks, but stopped at her announcement.

"One hundred miles." Eyebrows raised, she nodded slowly, ensuring me she was giving me the facts. "Half the distance between Happy Isles in the Valley, where Zoe and Nemo began, and Whitney."

Cappy, Jane, and I had begun hiking in Tuolumne, skipping the twenty-two-mile climb from Yosemite Valley to Tuolumne Meadows. Each of us had made that climb before, so had not felt the need to do it again, especially with full packs. Many JMTers make that same choice. So Cappy and I would have covered eighty-some miles when we reached Muir Trail Ranch the next day, when Zoe counted one hundred.

"We're just getting into the rhythm of the walk," I said. "I don't want this to be half over. I want to keep walking." My feet were nearly healed, my leg and back muscles were strong, and I really felt I could keep walking forever.

"It's getting easier, don't you think?" Cappy looked as contented and relaxed as I felt.

"I do. We've worked out the kinks—it feels natural." I stretched out on the boulder I had chosen as my chaise longue. "It's so different from the first week, when everything was going wrong."

"It wasn't *that* bad," Cappy said, cocking her head like she had no idea what I was talking about.

I sat back up and looked at her. "Cappy, don't you remember? Have you forgotten it all? It started with my sprained ankle and blisters. Then we lost the trail and ended up in the lightning..."

"After that it got *way* better!" Cappy insisted, sitting up straight and meeting my gaze.

I was incredulous. "*Better?*" I continued. "Then I drowned my camera and had to cross the river on that awful log. The rivers ran scary high. Red's lost your food box—"

"Yeah, but *then* it really got better," she insisted again, creases forming between her brows. She actually believed what she was saying.

"—and that horrible snowfield at Silver Pass. And all those evil mosquitoes!" I wanted to laugh, but could not, it was so unbelievable. I know I rolled my eyes in disbelief at her steadfast insistence. "Those first five or six days were like Biblical plagues—we were just missing frogs in our packs and blood in the rivers."

She shook her head and smiled. I do not think she could come up with another argument, but she was not going to relent either.

"It's more than *better* now," I assured her. "Everything went wrong early, but now everything is right in the world—perfection. And I'm *not* ready for it to be half over."

"We need to savor it, because, like it or not, Muir Ranch is the traditional halfway mark!" Cappy stood to join Zoe at the lake—pump, water containers, and tiny towel in hand.

I pulled my necklace free from my neckerchief and read the words on the rings—courage, spirit, strength—for the first time in a while. They made me smile.

Cappy was right about one thing. I needed to savor the current moment. While the two of them worked and played in the water, I sat cross-legged on my slab of granite, surrounded by immense natural beauty—infinite blue skies, sparkling water, towering peaks in silver and gray, green splashes of vegetation, the sweet perfume of fresh air, and pure silence—and I set about intentionally savoring the great fortune of my place on Earth.

I lay back to bask. Heat radiated from the rocks beneath me, joining in my core with the warmth traveling through the thin air from the sun. I closed my eyes, intending just to relax, but instead napped.

No moon illuminated the night, the thin crescent having abandoned the sky to billions of twinkling stars. The Milky Way coalesced into a thick stripe of white brilliance arching overhead, like headlights of a traffic jam on the freeway to Heaven. Celestial light spilling onto Marie Lake's still ebony surface puddled into a twin Milky Way and transformed our gray granite stadium into white-hot silver.

When it became too cold to remain outside, Cappy and I held the lean-to's edges steady, while Zoe slipped feet first and fully clothed through the entryway of the Frankentent directly into her mummy bag. Then we snuggled into our own sleeping bags next door.

Lying next to me, Cappy said, "If only we still had my one-man tent—"

"One-*woman*," I interrupted.

She chuckled. "If only we still had my one-*woman* tent. If only I hadn't sent it home with Jane, we wouldn't need the Frankentent."

"If only—but we didn't know we'd need it. Sending it home was the right choice at the time," I assured her.

"I know, but I have an idea." Her enthusiasm grew as she talked, words coming fast. She rolled over to face me. In the low light, I could barely make out her features. "When I talk to Jim on the phone tomorrow at Muir Ranch, I'll ask him to ship it overnight to the packing company that's delivering our last food boxes."

"Brilliant!" I immediately understood how that would be the perfect solution to our lingering problem. "Do you think there's time? Don't they only collect their mail once a week or something?"

"We can only try," Cappy rolled onto her back and adjusted her jacket-pillow. "I just hope Jane got the tent to Jim before she left for her mom's house."

We both went quiet, thinking, breathing.

"I'm so glad you thought of that." I picked up our book, switched on my headlamp, and turned to a new chapter.

With the tent flap open wide, and billions of stars as witnesses, I read aloud from our bedtime story. In the *White City*, women were naive and helpless creatures in the face of the "Devil". By contrast, The Three Women were strong and resourceful, successfully meeting all challenges to body and mind.

Starting Point — Bear Creek Junction — 8985 feet
Ending Point — Marie Lakes — 10,575 feet
Highest Point — Marie Lakes — 10,575 feet
Distance Covered — 6.6 miles
Cumulative Miles — 74.2 miles

Centerpoint

The idea of a sacred place... is apparently as old as life itself.
~ Joseph Campbell, *The Power of Myth*, 1988

Day Thirteen
July 31, 2006

Starting Point — Marie Lake — 10,575 feet

When we started climbing towards Seldon Pass, we had that entire mountain to ourselves. After a while, though, a dark spot far below us began working its way up the trail, eventually growing into a man hiking just fast enough to catch us as we crested the pass. The mystery-spot-turned-man revealed himself to be Wade, a trail friend we had met during breakfast at VVR just a few days earlier.

"Heck of a climb." Wade joined us where we stood facing north, surveying the way we had come. He pulled out a bottle of water and turned to enjoy the same broad view of Marie Lake and the mountain peaks and passes beyond.

"You made it up in good time," Cappy said. The breeze flowing up from the valley caught her stray gray curls, making them bounce around her face.

Wade chuckled. "I was working hard to catch up with The Three Women." He hoisted his water bottle high, making a toast to conquering the mountain.

"Thought it would be fun to have company on the trail for a while. Sometimes I get tired of hiking solo." His mouth spread into a wide grin that pushed his cheeks up until they bumped into his eyes, scrunching them into an endearing whole-face smile.

Forty-ish, Wade was a muscular man, compact, about the same height as Zoe, but well-built for mountain walking and carrying heavy loads. His goatee and mustache, freed from civilization's demands and razors, were spreading into a full beard that was coming in golden brown. That happy expression always resided amongst the whiskers, and his eyes emitted a bit of a twinkle.

"You're kind," I said, "but I doubt you had to work very hard to catch us. We walk at a tortoise's pace—you're much more the hare."

"Let's get a group photo next to the sign," Cappy said. She had already retrieved her camera and was pointing at the pass's wooden sign.

SELDEN PASS — ELEV. 10,900 FT.

"True," Zoe said. "We're slow hikers and *proud* of it! All the hikers we meet along the way pass us by."

"Some quickly, some slowly, but all eventually leave us in the dust," Cappy added.

"Cappy, you get in the photo this time." Zoe exchanged places with her for a second picture.

Those photos could be a page right out of a hiking equipment catalogue, Patagonia or Cabela's, each of us sporting a different example of a fashionable hiking outfit. Wade's was certainly the most unusual—ultra-light trail runners, neoprene sleeve-braces on his knees, a loose green t-shirt, and what looked like calf-length, army-green yoga pants.

I had guessed it. Somehow, teachers recognize other teachers even in disguise. Wade taught fifth grade, and I imagined his fun-loving nonchalance and that twinkle in his eye were huge assets in keeping and directing the attention of a gaggle of energetic ten-year-olds. He definitely kept all three of us in the thick of interesting conversation during the short interval he remained with us.

We began our descent as a foursome—The Three Women and Wade—and remained so during our morning snack-n-rest in one of several alpine valleys that hung terraced one above the next. After a bit of chatty R-and-R, Wade left us with a wave and bounded down the trail at a jaunty pace by himself. We watched his shape shrink back into the dot it had been earlier that morning as he crossed the valley and disappearing over its open edge.

I arranged myself on a lichen-decorated stone shelf at the head of the hanging lake, legs dangling over the edge. Beside me stood a cairn built by a previous traveler from seven flat, carefully balanced stones. Like a huge infinity pool, the far edge of the lake met the sky in a thin straight horizon line—the edge of the world.

Perched on that rocky shelf, I contemplated the natural beauty spread out in front of me. The air was silent and still. Light and shadow played across the surface of the water. My eyes followed the footpath as it wound its way through that little paradise towards its infinity-edge. In that sacred moment, I was simultaneously relaxed and vibrant.

That day, that moment, on that rock, beside the cairn's balanced sculpture, I passed through a turning point in my JMT odyssey. Looking back, I realize my entire journey can be meaningfully divided into the days that came *before*, and the days that came *after*, that moment.

The hike had been conceived as a challenging adventure in nature, but in that critical moment, beside the cairn, it shape-shifted into a pilgrimage. That day marked the center of the trip—the gyre of my inner journey, and simultaneously, the physical centerpoint of the trail.

I was aware only of the noticeable change in my comfort level—of feeling entirely at ease in my body and in my surroundings. I ascribed those differences to stronger muscles and shifting seasons. I *was* stronger, so the challenges were easier, and my fears, along with my aches and pains, diminished. Spring was turning the mountains over to Summer, taking away with her the rain, the thunder and lightning, high water, mosquitoes, and much of the remaining snow.

In this new state of ease, I experienced fewer distractions and could devote more energy to taking in the details. My eyes absorbed more—more and brighter colors and textures, more depth and breadth. My other senses took in more sounds, aromas, and flavors, as well. It was like a veil was being lifted from between me and the world around me, allowing us direct contact. It seemed I had found my place. I felt at home—I belonged.

The words on my necklace had become manifest, and I looked forward—with strength, spirit, and courage—to the inviting and precious mystery of what lay ahead. Joy bubbled close to the surface. Before, I had felt way too small for the space I occupied, but now my body was strong, and my heart expanded fearlessly into the vastness of the world around me. Before, I had secretly wanted to go home. That day, I *was* at home, right there on the trail, and wanted to stay forever.

To this day, when I reflect back on my grand JMT Odyssey, it is that spot, just south of Selden Pass, that comes immediately to mind. I can close my eyes and bring it all back with perfect clarity—the small rock tower, a miniature monument built to mark the way; the thin silver line in the distance where Earth touched Heaven; and the golden-hued trail connecting them like a long slender arrow pointing towards the horizon and the future.

Each time my mind wanders back to that iconic memory, my heart returns to the sense of awe I felt sitting on that rocky ledge. My chest swells, my breath catches, and I yearn to return to that place of peace and extreme well-being.

All morning and into the afternoon we descended from terrace to terrace, pond to lake, each bigger and broader and lusher than the last. The trail crisscrossed Sallie Keyes Creek repeatedly. The first crossing we made in a single step—the creek was so slender. But as water gathered water on its way downhill, the crossings became more interesting—we skipped atop a scattering of cobbles, strode across large steppingstones, and balanced along the narrow backs of fallen logs.

"Wait! Stop!" Cappy commanded. "We need a picture of this."

"Of what?" I paused, bewildered.

"Of you—on that log! Don't move." Already across the creek herself, Cappy stood at the water's edge aiming her camera at me with one hand, her other hand signaling, Halt!

I stood midway across on the fallen tree serving as the bridge over fast running water. My sandaled feet were positioned solidly on the smooth top of the log, and my hiking poles, fully extended, stretched to the bottom of the streambed. I glanced down at the log and the racing water, and it dawned on me—Cappy was documenting my newfound confidence.

I looked directly at Cappy's camera, wearing a satisfied smile. There I was, striding sure-footed and balanced on the narrow beam, feeling no hint of the phobia that had previously held me prisoner.

Once across, I jumped from log to riverbank with a triumphant shout, sharing a metallic, hiking-pole-high-five with Cappy. "We've come a long way, baby!" I said.

A dog, big and white with a retriever's chunky body, greeted us with a wagging tail as we approached the wooden gate guarding the entrance to Muir Trail Ranch that evening.

"Hey, Buddy, are you the official escort?" Zoe bent down and petted the friendly animal. As she unlashed the loop of rope holding the gate closed, the dog slipped under the lowest rung and waited for us on the inside. Zoe swung the broad split-rail gate wide for us to pass before closing it securely behind. The dog, tongue lolling and tail wagging, led the way downhill towards a cluster of buildings.

One small, ageless building constructed of rough stone stood a little apart from the rest. Its wooden door, leaning from its hinges and reinforced with rusty metal straps, gave away its age, the way crow's feet beside a woman's eyes belie her youth. Built of local golden-brown stone, that outbuilding had served as storage for a long, long time. Scores of five-gallon buckets, standing shoulder-to-shoulder, filled the dark interior and spilled out onto the surrounding green grass, a rainbow of plastic—white, yellow, pale blue, red—each sporting an owner's name and anticipated arrival date in bold print.

Muir Ranch, our third re-supply stop, was unlike the first two. Being in a remote spot, it offered few amenities to thru-hikers—no showers or toilets, no phone, no store, no restaurant. Thankfully, they did provide re-stocking support, an indispensable service. Extrapolating from the number of giant paint cans stuffed in the little stone building, they did a good business with JMT and PCT travelers.

The woman managing the office came out to greet us where we stood gawking at the avalanche of paint buckets. She saw order in what appeared to us a chaotic jumble and spent mere moments searching labels before locating ours exactly where she expected them. I dragged mine over to a wooden bench where I could sit down, pry off the lid, and reacquaint myself with what I had packed six weeks earlier. Cappy did the same with her own bucket.

Nemo had already visited Muir Ranch and gone on. We hoped he had taken his fair share of the contents and left Zoe her half, as she was totally dependent on that food for the two weeks that remained. There were no places like Red's, VVR, or Muir Ranch further south on the trail where food supply packages could be held for hikers. Cappy and I had paid a pretty penny for our fourth and final food drop to be delivered by packhorse to a trail junction halfway between Muir Ranch and Whitney Portal. Zoe and Nemo had not chosen that expensive option, so whatever food waited for Zoe at Muir Ranch was all she would have to eat for fourteen days.

The woman clearly remembered Nemo passing through and located Zoe's paint can. Zoe opened the bucket to find her full share and a new problem—two weeks of food was too bulky to fit into her bear canister. For a while, she just stood and surveyed the mountain of food, unsure what to do.

Meanwhile, Cappy and I were rifling through our own buckets and extolling their contents. "Clean underwear!" I sighed. I would throw away the pair I had been wearing for multiple days. Sending myself new underwear and a supply of disposable panty liners had been my best packing idea ever—pure luxury.

"Chocolate!" Cappy lifted a Ziploc bag of M&M's from her pile of food.

"*The White City*, continued!" I waved the fourth installment of our bedtime story.

"And dried mango!" One of my very favorites. I opened the Ziploc bag and put a golden slice in my mouth right then and there.

It took a long time to unpack all of my supplies and then reorganize them into my canister and backpack. If I held back that night's dinner, I could, with a combination of careful organization and brute force, just barely stuff nine breakfasts, lunches, and dinners, nine days of snacks, and my sweet-smelling care products into my bear can and still secure the lid. Cappy was able to do the same, keeping only that night's dinner on the outside. But try as she might, there was no way Zoe could force fourteen days of meals and snacks into her canister. That was going to prove a problem later, but for the moment, she put the overflow into two hefty stuff sacks she could tote to camp.

In addition to a food drop, Muir Ranch did offer, for a fee, brief use of a computer with an excruciatingly slow dial-up internet connection for sending emails and a free campsite for JMT and PCT thru-hikers. Leaving our packs outside the door of an old, hand-hewn cabin, we arrayed ourselves on three mismatched chairs around the old desktop computer, anxious to make contact with the outside world. Our families were expecting us to check in via phone, but they would just have to be content with emails.

Using email for this purpose was very utilitarian. I could assure my family I was safe and confirm our location, but I could not indulge in any storytelling. I had been making a mental list of the fun tales I might share on the phone, but they would have to wait. After those messages, my son and parents would not hear from me again until we reached the end of the trail—they would just have to trust we were where we were supposed to be. Dean and Dad would be confident of our steady progress, but Mom would be imagining every possible disaster that might befall us.

We did, however, make two important arrangements via email. First, Cappy sent a message to Jim, asking him to ship her one-*woman* tent back to us via USPS to the same packhorse delivery service that already had our food boxes, explaining the urgency of acting quickly. At the same time, she updated Jim on our progress. He would be meeting us at Whitney Portal, so he needed to know we would be a day late arriving—*and* that we would be The Three Women, rather than two.

Cappy read the email aloud, to confirm it was complete.

I nodded, "It's good. Everything's there. Let's hope your plan works."

She hit Send.

Zoe sent word to her folks, too, so they would know when and where to meet up with her after we all drove back to Yosemite. She did *not* mention the absence of Nemo in those plans. That could wait until later.

Retrieving our newly food-heavy packs and Zoe's extra stuff bags, we walked the quarter-mile path to the very primitive campground. I confess I had been expecting Muir Trail Ranch to be similar to Red's or VVR, so I was disappointed when we arrived to find the rustic buildings, no phones, and no showers. Despite lowered expectations, I was further let down by the backpackers' campsite. Granted, it was free, but there were no bathrooms, no bear boxes, just a wide patch of packed earth under the widespread boughs of a giant evergreen tree. We shared the site with one other camper.

Our friendly campmate introduced himself with his trail name, Redwing, after the chirpy, scarlet-shouldered blackbirds who hung out among the reeds and cattails in marshes and meadows at lower elevations. Scarecrow would have been a more apt moniker for the very tall, very slender gangly young man, with a bushy, clumsily trimmed dark beard, and hair that stuck out like dark straw from under his wide-brimmed hat. When he removed his sunglasses, his warm and expressive eyes, deep set and brown, peeked out beneath dark brows. Twenty-something, he was Zoe's age.

In an It's-A-Small-World moment, we discovered he hailed from our own Grass Valley neighborhood. We invited our new friend to join us for dinner. Eagerly, he dashed off, all limbs and angles, to fetch his food, his red-and-black-plaid flannel shirt flapping loosely around his thin frame. He returned with a freeze-dried entrée in his long, knobby fingers, and we spent a leisurely evening exchanging adventure stories—his being way more "adventurous" than ours.

"I started on the PCT at the Mexican border the first week in March," he told his eager audience, his animated voice communicating the excitement of those distant first days. "There were ten hikers who started that day. Four of us teamed up and stuck together through the desert. Those guys are long gone, probably to Lake Tahoe by now." Disappointment leaked out with his words.

"What happened?" Cappy asked.

"I don't know how I picked it up, but I ended up sick with giardia." Scarecrow—I could not think of him as anything else—talked like he was confessing a sin, spitting out the last word.

"That's horrible!" I said. I was familiar with that awful infection. Giardia is a tiny, aggressive parasite, common to Sierra rivers, which backcountry travelers can ingest with inadequately filtered water. A rigorous regimen of anti-parasitic medication is required to beat the wily infection that wreaks havoc on its victims' digestive systems, zapping them of strength.

"I was *always* careful to filter my own water. But sometimes in the desert people share their water. You have to trust they've filtered it." His voice stopped. He looked down and shook his head like he still could not believe it had happened to him.

"I got really sick. Had to go home and rest in bed for a couple weeks to get well. My mom had to take care of me—I was so weak." He sounded defeated. "My guys had to hike on without me." My heart went out to him. "Once I was better, I went back and picked up the trail where I'd left off."

"Today, I took a zero day," Scarecrow explained. "I needed to rest and recoup some." He appeared to rally, sitting up straight and speaking with optimism. To me, his day off sounded more like a last-ditch effort to regain his traveling strength than a little R-and-R.

Observing him closely as he talked, I suddenly saw hollow cheeks, where earlier I had seen angular features and a healthy slenderness; boney wrists and ankles, where I had seen youthful lankiness. Perhaps Scarecrow was not as recovered as he wanted to believe. Perhaps his illness had knocked the stuffing out of him. The mother in me wanted to ask some personal questions, offer some sage advice. But I was not *his* mom, so held myself back.

The number of NOBO hikers had dwindled—PCTers were long gone, and most JMTers moved SOBO—so Scarecrow was nearly alone on the long trail, two-thirds of which still stretched out ahead of him all the way to Canada.

"I'm behind on my miles but ahead on my food." He confessed to running low on food.

I offered him a cup of my hot chocolate to accompany his dinner, and he accepted with the eagerness of a puppy. I was food-rich right then, and wished I could have donated more to him, but I had only enough to get me to the packhorse and my next cache.

"I'm going to dig through the ranch's barrel of leftovers and take whatever they'll let me have." Like Red's and VVR, Muir Ranch had a supply of abandoned food left by hikers who had oversupplied themselves. If our slow-and-steady tortoise pace burned more than three thousand calories a day, his jackrabbit speed required much more.

The Three Women rarely indulged in cooking desserts, which tended to be messy affairs, opting instead to eat the candy we had packed. That night, to celebrate our arrival at Muir Ranch, we had something special. Cappy had packed a dehydrated concoction—a gooey just-add-water chocolate mousse, large enough to satisfy several people. She divided it up four ways, and though we all savored the creamy richness, it was Scarecrow who seemed to most relish the extravagance, scraping every last drop from the container and licking his fingers.

All evening he had given off a jolly attitude, laughing heartily at his own well-told stories, but his smiles tended to highlight the dark circles under his eyes. Redwing intended to resume his solo hike the next morning, hoping to make up time, hiking fast and furiously. But Scarecrow did not seem so sure of success.

While listening to his stories—a modern day Greek myth of trials to bear—I was filled with compassion for him. At the same time, I felt gratitude for my own situation. I had experienced numerous difficulties, and especially the first week, I had felt overwhelmed by pains and fears, but nothing I had struggled through remotely compared to Scarecrow's experiences. He was young and strong and should have been at the peak of his fitness. Cappy and I were over fifty and, though far from weak, we should have paled compared to him. He was hiking the two-thousand-mile PCT compared to our two-hundred-mile JMT hike. Yet, there we were, plodding along, at our measured speed toward our ultimate goal—growing daily in strength, courage, and confidence—while it appeared as though, despite his optimistic words, Scarecrow was at risk of abandoning his ambitious adventure and heading home. Perhaps if he had been traveling in our direction, Cappy and I would have adopted him like we had adopted Zoe, but he was not, and we could not, so we just wished him godspeed.

Dusk was settling in, and Zoe's overabundance of food lay arrayed around her bear canister, which could *not* expand to accommodate one more iota of food. She had whittled the pile down, pressing every ounce of space out of the can by leaning her full weight on its compressed contents. What was left, however, still filled one stuff-sack the size of a basketball.

"That's it. Now what do I do?" she leaned back on her heels, appealing to Cappy and me.

"Hang it in the tree," I said, thinking that was the best of the bad ideas available. All JMTers carry a bear canister for a reason—hanging food had long been proven more attractant than deterrent to bears.

"I've never done that," Zoe confessed. "How do I get *this* up *there*?" Zoe stood holding the over-stuffed nylon bag in one hand and a length of thin nylon line in the other. She studied the branches in the tall pine standing flagpole straight in the center of our encampment.

"I haven't done it for years," Cappy said, "but it's pretty straightforward." She stood up from the log she had been using as a chair and walked to Zoe's side, offering to help.

"I've done it a few times, but it's never as easy as it sounds," I said.

Cappy and I tied together the coils of line we each carried, making one long rope. "You'll have to use a rock to carry the rope over the tree limb," I said, searching the ground for a tennis-ball-sized rock.

Cappy offered an oblong stone to Zoe. "You're the rock climber. You better tie the knots."

With a chuckle, Zoe began wrapping the thin line securely around the rock—first in one direction, then the other. When she had finished, she held up her gift-wrapped stone and said, "Now what?" looking directly at me.

"First rule, be careful. I know some very funny stories involving people hitting themselves in the head with rocks when attempting this process," I said with a smile. "But they're only funny in hindsight," I added. "The idea is that you throw the rock over the branch, so that the line follows it up and over and back down. That gives you a primitive pulley system for raising the bag high in the tree and, just as important, a way to get it back down in the morning."

The process sounds so simple, but I have never found it to be so. The choice of branch is critical; it must be high enough that a full-grown bear, standing on its hind legs, cannot reach the bag. The branch must be long enough for the bag to hang far away from the trunk, so that even a baby bear cannot climb out along the branch to reach it. Bears are good puzzle-solvers, so if it can be reached, they will patiently work until they find a way to get the food. The process always seems to involve repeatedly throwing the rock towards the chosen limb, missing multiple times, and dodging the plummeting stone between throws. It was no surprise when that was exactly what happened that night.

Cappy and I stood back as Zoe stepped forward and sighted her target. "Here goes nothing!" She had chosen a long branch a good fifteen feet in the air and aimed at a spot about eight feet from the trunk. The first two pitches fell short, missing the branch entirely. Each time, Zoe dodged the dropping rock.

"This is not easy!" Zoe said. Her next three attempts sent the rock higher but ensnared smaller branches growing off the main branch, which bent, sending the rope and rock downward again. Only once the rock hit Zoe, glancing harmlessly off her shoulder, and falling loose from its rope wrapping. Finally, out of pure luck, the rock and rope sailed over the branch in just the right spot. Success.

Hoisted in the air, the food-stuffed piñata dangled from the tree.

Starting Point — Marie Lake — 10,575 feet
Ending Point — Muir Trail Ranch — 7600 feet
Highest Point — Selden Pass — 10,900 feet
Distance Covered — 7.9 miles
Cumulative Miles — 82.1 miles

Fourth Leg

Muir Trail Ranch to a Nameless Pond
Day Fourteen to Day Twenty-Two

Monsters In Paradise

Courage doesn't always roar.
Sometimes courage is the little voice at the end of the day that says
I'll try again tomorrow.
~ Monika Anne Radmacher, *Courage Doesn't Always Roar*, 2009

Day Fourteen
August 1, 2006

Starting Point — Muir Trail Ranch — 7600 feet

Despite my fitful, bear-filled dreams, no actual bears showed up during the night. Zoe's food bag hung unmolested from its limb high in the tree. However, there were worrisome visitors of a different kind in the morning.

While Zoe retrieved her food, the quiet was broken by a strange thunk-thunk vibration that permeated the air. We stood, eyes skyward, searching. I cocked my head as I turned this way and that, trying to isolate the rhythmic noise, but in the hilly terrain, it echoed, making its source difficult to locate.

The metallic sound was out of place, so it was not until the machine itself came into view that I identified the distinctive vibration of a helicopter. This was not the big city, where it could be NewsCopterFour reporting, an emergency medevac airlift, or even a police chase—but a helicopter still meant trouble.

"What could it be?" Zoe cupped her hands around her eyes, shielding them from the bright morning sun. A green National Park Service chopper sailed directly over the tree that had minutes earlier held Zoe's extra food. It headed southeast, the same direction we would be walking. We packed up in a focused silence punctuated by short bursts of anxious speculation.

"A rescue?" I suggested. "Maybe someone got lost or hurt."

"A forest fire?" Cappy said.

Breakfast eaten and newly heavy loads settled onto our shoulders and hips, we headed out the dirt path. The camp's big white dog escorted us as far as the gate, where he watched to make sure we had latched it properly before heading back to his guard station in the shade.

The JMT grew wider as it followed alongside the roaring San Joaquin River, climbing a gentle incline deeper into the mountains. The water to our right hurried seaward, tumbling over the large angular rocks that made up its banks and kept it in its bed. The deep V of the river's canyon was filled to the brim. Water pushed and shoved itself downhill, muscling its way from snowy peaks toward the lowlands. No gentle eddies clung to the shore. No fish lurked in calm pools. This cold, swift water did *not* welcome wading—swimming would be deadly.

"One slip and you'd be lying on a beach at the coast tomorrow!" I joked.

"Actually, your many broken pieces would probably be floating in some reservoir downstream," Cappy informed me. "I don't think the San Joaquin makes it all the way to the ocean anymore."

"All this water runs out before it makes it to the Pacific Ocean?" Zoe was as surprised as I was.

"Hard to believe," Cappy assured us. "Big Ag farms gotta water their crops."

Our little parade stretched out along the path, the JMT carrying us towards Kings Canyon National Park, deep in the heart of the Sierra. Again, we heard the approaching high-pitched worrying whine of a helicopter as it merged with, and then broke through and above, the water's rumbling. The copter flew low over the river, following its path like an unobstructed highway into the wilderness—so low the pilot's head was level with ours, and we could see into the passenger area. As it disappeared ahead, the sound dropped to a deep-throated foreboding thrum.

"That wasn't the same helicopter," Zoe pointed out. It was not the small green machine with the NPS symbol—its logo was unfamiliar.

"Was it the sheriff?" I asked. "CalFire?"

"What could be happening?" Cappy wondered. We had stopped center-trail to watch the machine zip past. "I don't smell smoke, do you?" We all turned to survey the whole sky, but saw no evidence of smoke.

"They're definitely on a mission," I replied, "not sightseeing." The helicopter had been flying fast and low, nose down and tail slightly elevated in an angle of intensity.

As we speculated, a *third* copter zipped past in the same direction. Striding along the riverside trail, anxiety walked with me. With each step, I watched the sky and craned my ears for other sounds that might provide clues to what lay ahead. For the next hour, helicopters flew back and forth above the river, transporting people and gear deeper into the mountains.

Rather than spreading ourselves out along the trail, as had become our wont, we walked clumped together. Curiosity was tempered by anxiety—one pulling me forward, excited to know what was happening—the other holding me back, fearful of what we might encounter. Was there a bad guy out on the trail? Had someone gotten lost or been hurt? Was this a search and rescue mission? A manhunt? A fire? Maybe the helicopters were carrying EMTs with emergency medical gear. Or gun-toting rangers and sheriffs. Or squads of searchers or firefighters.

A pair of uniformed rangers, guns strapped to their hips, appeared on the trail in front of us. They stood side-by-side, looking towards the river and talking. I expected them to greet us and ask for our wilderness permits; but as we approached, the two serious-faced men only paused their conversation and nodded. When we were out of earshot, they resumed talking. We walked on; curiosity piqued.

Initially, I had thought I might ask them what was happening, but their stiff posture, crossed arms, and bare acknowledgement of our presence radiated the message, "Do not interrupt our important business," as clearly as a bright red Keep Out – No Trespassing sign.

"If there were danger ahead, they would have stopped us," I said after we had walked twenty yards.

"Or at least warned us," added Zoe.

"That eliminates an axe murderer!" Cappy said, pulling a nervous laugh from us all.

"Probably fire, too," I said.

"Still a mystery!" said Zoe.

After a quarter-mile, we came upon more uniforms—two sheriffs, both male, and a female ranger. They stood at the edge of the trail—armed and serious. As we approached, they were pointing and gesturing toward the trail and mountains ahead, deep in their own animated discussion. Like the pair before them, their sober conversation stopping abruptly as we passed, they acknowledged us with slight nods, the ranger nearly whispering, "Morning." Again, their demeanor did not invite questions, so I kept walking. Their conversation resumed after we had passed.

A little farther along, we found a lone female hiker sitting on the verge of the trail, leaning on her pack. "Hey," she said, looking up from where she was digging through a small stuff bag.

We greeted her and slowed to skirt her feet, which stuck out into the path. She asked, "So have you heard?" Forty-something, small but muscular, her eyes shone.

We stopped. "Do you know what's happening?" Cappy asked as we formed a semi-circle around her.

The woman sat a little straighter, pulling the bag tightly into her chest before speaking. "I heard that someone drowned. Fell in."

"In that?" I said, pointing to the wild water right beside us.

"That's what I heard. A woman," she clarified. Her bronzed face crinkled.

"Really?" and "My god!" Zoe and Cappy said.

My eyes were pulled to stare at the white, angry water like magnets to iron. When I gathered power enough to pull them away, I saw the other three were staring at the river, too.

Thoughts tumbled round in my brain. *How did she fall in?* I could not imagine even getting close to that fast water. *Where did it happen? Was she alone?* Her last moments must have been terrifying. *Did someone see her fall?* But the only thing I said aloud was, "Where? Was it near here?" My head swiveled back to watch the water roar past. My stomach churned as I imagined a person caught in that flow.

Our whole JMT adventure was an escape from civilization and all its messy human problems and issues, from traffic and bills to work and politics. It was a retreat to the wilderness à la Walden Pond or the trampings of John Muir. The natural world was our Utopia—Civilization symbolized all the evils we were temporarily escaping. Right at that moment, however, it seemed the river had become evil. Rather than neutral, Nature had a wisp of evil in her.

The woman stood and pointed farther ahead on the trail. "I heard it was near where this river and another meet near Kings Canyon, but I'm not sure exactly." Her short brown hair framed her tanned face, making her dark eyes prominent. They were ringed with tight worry lines that matched the distress tightening her voice.

"I've been just sitting here a while. The news sort of knocked the energy right out of me," she admitted. "Hiking solo, I'm mostly confident, but now and again, I worry about something bad happening, me needing help. This really hit me, like it could have been me."

"I was just thinking—it could have been any of us." Hands on hips, Cappy drew herself up to full height.

"I can't imagine what would possess anyone to get close enough to fall in," I said.

"Nobody would try to wash their hands or filter water into a container." Zoe nodded.

"That water is so furious you'd be beaten to death before you had time to drown." I shook my head.

I was finding the idea of someone venturing to the edge of what was more like a ferocious wild animal than a usable body of water to be incredible. At the same time, I was shocked by the woman's revelation. The utopian natural world I had conjured for my own blissful meandering was suddenly shaken by a temblor of reality. The wilderness was wild. We were not. We needed to be careful.

We bade farewell to our informant and headed on our way, retreating into complete silence to ponder. I found myself hugging the left edge of the trail, the side farthest from the river. It was a wide, flat trail, very safe, with no danger of the river reaching up to swipe at my feet, no danger of falling in. Yet I could not help edging away. The woman's story had painted the rushing water in evil hues.

Our plan was to stop for lunch at the ill-fated point where the San Joaquin River was joined by Piute Creek—the point which marked the boundary between the Sierra National Forest's John Muir Wilderness and Sequoia-Kings Canyon National Park's Wilderness Area. At the confluence and boundary, we found an impressive steel bridge spanning the Piute and a welcoming sign.

YOU ARE NOW ENTERING
KINGS CANYON NATIONAL PARK

The morning was hot at this lower elevation, so shade provided by a copse of trees on the far side of the Piute called to us. Stopping halfway across the span, we leaned on the railing, witnesses to the power of the water speeding by beneath us. The river and creek that met at this point were each filled to capacity—their gray and green waters converging, swirling, then racing on with even greater combined strength. Looking down on all that power, I could not imagine the horror of being trapped in its frigid violence. No amount of strength or courage could overcome that raging force of nature.

We ambled off the bridge and spread our gear around the shady spot under the small collection of trees, settling ourselves on the ground. I laid my provisions out on my cross-legged lap, using the lid of my bear can as a tray.

I was finishing the last bites of my Fig Newtons when two groups of uniformed rangers and sheriffs converged on the near side of the bridge, the Kings Canyon side. Just beyond our hearing, they talked over a map that one held out for all to see.

One ranger broke away from the group to walk our way. He wore the classic NPS Smokey-the-Bear hat and a pair of aviator sunglasses, revealing little of his face.

His mouth, nearly buried in a thick mustache, gave away no more information. Greeting us in the shade of the trees, he asked to see our wilderness permit.

I dug deep inside my pack for the priceless paper. *Finally*, I thought, *we're going to get a chance to ask questions.*

Cappy did not wait one second. "We've just hiked over from Muir Ranch," she said. "We've been watching the helicopters all morning. What's happening?"

I stopped searching to watch his face.

"Ma'am, there's a search for a missing woman." The ranger removed his glasses, revealing dark brown eyes fringed by the deep creases that come with spending years in sun and weather. "We think she fell into the Piute." He paused a moment, as all four of us glanced towards the rushing river. "You can see it's running real high."

"We heard rumor of that," Cappy said, "but found it hard to believe."

"It's terrible," I said, emboldened. "Do you know how?" I stepped forward and held out our three-person-permit.

He took my paper and scanned it while answering. "We're not sure. People underestimate the water's power, get too close, slip. We just do not know. She may've gone down to replenish her water supply and slipped on wet rocks. Her husband found some of her things by the river when he woke this morning."

"Thank you," he said, handing me back the form. Then he added, with genuine concern, "You ladies be safe out there." He pushed his sunglasses back into place and turned to rejoin his group.

We returned to our rest period, filling it with anxious conversation instead of our usual silence. It was anything but restful. Like rubberneckers, we could not take our focus off the fatal accident that had taken place along our peaceful highway through the Sierra.

Months later, long after Cappy and I had returned to home and work, we would learn the drowned woman had actually been murdered by her husband. He had pushed her, staged the scene to look as though she had fallen, then hiked out to call for help with a concocted story. A "civilized" man was found guilty of the evil deed. Even deep inside the boundaries of the wild, natural world, a human had been more dangerous than the elements, choosing to use the river as his weapon. It was a relief to learn that Nature, a benign, neutral force, was found innocent of all wrongdoing.

A dark cloud hung over us as we set out after lunch. We bore along the morning's somber mood as surely as we carried our backpacks. Though the Kings Canyon sign had greeted us politely, the neglected condition of the trail was less than welcoming. The walkway was a narrow alley between walls of vegetation as tall as our shoulders, confining and claustrophobic under the hot sun. Shrubs on both sides reached into the dusty trail, grabbing at our arms and legs, leaving scratches, pulling at clothes.

Then we trudged through a stretch of dead forest as foreboding as any fairytale woods, giving life to the haunted thoughts swirling through my brain. It was easy to imagine wolves and witches lurking in the shadows, lying in wait for girls in red hoodies who strayed from the trail, or hikers in ruby boots.

The trail emerged from the black forest to walk beside the San Joaquin River far upstream from our lunch spot. Cut into granite and hanging on the rock face, our path once again paralleled the speeding water's trajectory, climbing while it plunged. The river's sounds bounced off the canyon walls, reverberating until individual crashes and splashes were no longer discernible within its bellow. The trail climbed until we were perched on the granite cliff face looking far down on the river, its size made miniature by the distance.

I hiked close to my trail-mates that afternoon. Their companionship was a comfort after the morning's troubling events. I was not frightened, but a low-level anxiety seemed to shroud us like a mist. My "everything is wonderful on the JMT" balloon had popped.

Our day's final destination sat far above the water. However, it waited atop the towering cliff on the far side of the canyon from where we stood. To get there, our path would pull us down to the bottom of the slender canyon to the water's edge, carry us across a bridge, and then drag us all the way back up the other side.

Far upstream, a graceful span came into view, delicate as lace from that distance and the only visible trace of human influence. While the trail we trod was barely a scratch in the hard gray stone, the bridge was an engineering feat, a sculpture.

"How'd they build that in this canyon?" I wondered aloud. "It must've been a massive effort." I was impressed with the human ingenuity and dedication that had gone into carving the JMT out of the heart of the granite Sierra.

We paused in the center of that old bridge and looked straight up at the switchbacks climbing the canyon's eastern face toward Evolution Meadow and our campsite. The first three were marked by distinct horizontal lines across the rock face, but beyond those the trail disappeared into the stone curtain like an optical illusion.

"Cappy, do we know how many switches there are?" Was I stalling? Hesitating to begin? I was exhausted for some reason. It was not late—there were several more good hiking hours left, but my body was sagging.

"Nope. That info wasn't in the guidebook," she said, "but I'll bet there's lots." Cappy seemed eager to climb, practically bouncing on her toes.

I pulled a Ziploc bag of hard candies out of a pack-pocket. Maybe a sugar infusion would help. I put a red cinnamon ball in my mouth, then selected five more pieces to put in my pocket for later when I began to droop again—a Werther's in gold foil, two butterscotch, a red-and-white peppermint, and another cinnamon.

I held the bag out to Cappy, nodding to signal an offering. She took a couple candies and smiled her thank you.

"We better count 'em on the way up," said Zoe. "I'm extra tired this afternoon, so we best get started."

I held the bag her way. "Want some?" The spicy sugar coated the inside of my mouth. "I'm tired, too. I wish I could inject this stuff directly into my bloodstream."

Zoe made her selections. "Thanks. These little booster rockets should help."

I stuffed the little bag back into my pack and started up the first switchback. "Number one," I announced.

I counted aloud each time the trail turned. At the even-count end of each switch, the trail was dry and dusty, the air holding the chalky aroma of decomposing granite. The odd-count end of each switch made its U-turn where Evolution Creek fell from the sky. Whether it was really cooler near the waterfall I was not sure, but a sense of relief came from the water and foam tumbling past.

At the tenth turn, I leaned against the canyon wall where the trail clung to the stone. I thought about taking my pack off while I waited for my partners to catch up, but decided it would require too much effort—I would use up more energy taking it off and putting it back on than I would just standing and leaning. I let the wall take as much of the weight as it would.

Slow and steady Cappy, putting one foot in front of the other, came striding up. She did not appear any more tired than usual as she stood sipping on her CamelBak. Zoe, though, had a slack-jawed, pale expression that suggested she was as tired as I felt. She half-sat, half-leaned on the rock wall beside me and pulled out her water bottle. Leaning her head back against the same wall, she drank deeply.

"I'm exhausted," I said. "How are you two?" I took off my hat and wiped my face with my bandana. My curls were damp and flattened from the heat. My head itched. I poured a little of my water down the front of my shirt. It was not cold, but it was cooler than my skin.

"Totally whipped. I'm not sure why, but I am." Zoe had pulled off her hat, freeing her limp ponytail, and head tipped forward, trickled water on the back of her neck, letting it roll off her shoulders.

"I'm just dragging myself up this mountain," I agreed.

"I'm feeling great," Cappy said. "Why don't I take the lead and set a little slower pace for a while."

"How much farther do we have to go?" I asked.

It was like the poppy field scene from *Wizard of Oz*, where Dorothy and the travelers, within sight of the Emerald City, breathe the perfumed air and are suddenly overwhelmed by the need to lie down and sleep. Only Cappy, our Tin Man, was immune to whatever in the air was zapping our strength.

Patiently and with the enthusiasm of a cheerleader, Cappy answered, "We just have to get to the top of this climb." She pointed up the cliff face. "Our campsite is practically perched on the edge. We can do this!"

I took a step back to look up. From beneath, switchbacks are impossible to judge; they just merge into the mountainside. The distance down to where we had begun had grown steadily as we had ascended. The San Joaquin was far below. But the distance to the top of the wall seemed unchanged, the sky receding with every step we took.

Cappy took off first. I slouched after her with Zoe bringing up the rear. I focused on the path in front of me—my tired legs were dragging my feet, unable to lift them as high as usual. The last thing I wanted to do was stumble and fall.

More than halfway up, after I had lost count of the switches, a huge boulder— tabletop flat and as broad as my living room floor—hung out like a shelf over the canyon. We stopped there for a picnic in the sky. Zoe dropped her pack and herself to the ground, emitting a groan. I let my pack fall from my shoulders and then plopped down, unsure if I would ever get back up. I leaned back, feet propped up on my pack. I took a crazy photo—my sandaled feet in the sky, with only the tiptops of black mountain peaks suggesting the earth. A pair of hawks, directly out from where we were perched, circled on updrafts and called to one another in high-pitched voices.

Cappy was a good sport, doing her best to encourage Zoe and me to renewed strength. I tried to indulge her, tried to soak energy from the sunlight, from the natural beauty surrounding us on all sides, from the pecans and dried cranberries I inhaled. I was beyond that kind of renewal. The only thing that would restore my strength and energy was a hearty dinner and a good night's sleep—luxuries still many steps ahead.

At the time, I had no idea why I was struggling with a physical limpness that felt like my body had been drugged. Looking back, I doubt my exhaustion was completely physical. Certainly, my pack was several pounds heavier—I had added all that new food at Muir Ranch. And the previous night's fitful, bear-dream-interrupted sleep had not been refreshing. But might the morning's emotional shocks have deflated my energy? Might the massive emergency response we had witnessed and the ultimate news of the woman's drowning have zapped me of my usual afternoon second-wind? Perhaps my earlier adrenaline-rush had been replaced by an adrenaline-crash. I cannot be certain from this distance. I just remember how horrible the news had been, how unusual that level of exhaustion felt, and how surprised and confused I was by my weakness.

"All I want to do is get to camp," I said, rising at the end of our allotted rest. I stretched my arms above my head, twisting and bending to extend my back and shoulder muscles, trying to loosen knots and get blood flowing. "Let's get this behind us." I lifted my pack and carefully swung it round my shoulders, willing it to feel lighter than when I had set it down twenty minutes earlier.

I walked in a dream state, counting my steps. One, two, three, four. My legs swung like the heavy weights, the bobs on the end of pendulums. Left, right, left, right. Five, six, seven, eight. My arms worked in rhythm with my legs, swinging my hiking poles forward and back, in an opposite motion. In my dream state, the rhythm of my body's pendulums pulled me slowly forward. No thinking required. Just movement. One, two, three, four. Back and forth, my body moved across the canyon face. First toward the falling water, then back to the dry end of the switchback. To the water, then back to the dust.

Conventional time disappeared. Once the sun had moved beyond the narrow strip of visible sky. Once everything lay in shadow. Time shifted. Only the swinging pendulums counted time. There was only the time between steps. When accumulated, their sum was the time between the water and the dust. Accumulate enough of each to get time to the top.

One, two, three, four. Left, right. Right, left.

Back and forth. Water, dust. Water, dust.

Cresting the cliff wall with the final switchback, we discovered the waterfall we had followed upward had changed. At this higher elevation it broke into a series of cascades. The water charged towards the edge, falling and tumbling over several small drops, foaming and dancing with each bounce. This was the river as it approached the edge of the mountain. Atop the cliff, it flowed flat and smooth, coming directly at us as we stood perched on the crest, the trail running right next to the streaming water. Then Evolution Creek careened over the last few yards of rock before it ran out of earth and plunged to meet the San Joaquin far below. In seconds, the water covered the fifteen hundred feet we had taken so long to climb.

We had seen hanging valleys from a distance before, across canyons and wide glacial valleys. This time, we stood right at the mouth of the valley, at the spot where it ceased to exist and simply vanished into thin air. Water rushing down the valley from the higher peaks that surrounded it simply fell off the edge of the Earth.

"Our campsite is only a short distance ahead, less than a half mile. It's under trees and not far from the river," Cappy said, breaking our reverie, quoting the guidebook to lure us along.

"I have *sooo* hit the wall." I allowed myself to speak aloud what I had been thinking now that we were near our final destination.

I tipped my body forward, shuffling my feet to keep up with my torso, to keep myself from falling on my face. Ahead, trees stood back from the water, and grass carpeted the space between them and the trail, which paralleled the river. The water, flat and smooth as glass, gave the illusion of peacefulness.

Without a word, Zoe stooped to pick up a small cone and tossed it into the center of the river. We all paused to watch as it was swept along into the cascade and over the cliff in just seconds. A little gasp escaped me.

After just a few more steps, we found a lonely campsite—we had that remote valley entirely to ourselves. I quickly discarded my pack and flopped down onto a log. Zoe joined me. The two of us were spent. Not so Cappy. She was full of energy. I leaned my elbows on my knees to support my limp body.

"Come on, girls. Gotta get the tent up before you two collapse completely." It was supposed to be a joke, but it was too true for a laugh.

She was right. I dragged myself to my feet and got out my portion of the tent. Cappy began to clear away a group of river-smoothed rocks piled in the middle of the site, only to discover the dirty fingers of civilization had penetrated even into wilderness this remote. Crammed beneath and hidden among the rocks was trash—plastic bags, paper towels, and wrappers from the dehydrated food that the previous occupants had carried in but could not be bothered to carry back out.

"How disgusting!" Cappy stepped back and pointed to insects crawling among the trash heap.

"Haven't they heard about 'Leave No Trace' camping?" I said as Cappy bent to pull the yucky garbage from its hiding place.

"Obviously they didn't get that message!" Zoe shook her head in disgust, but knelt down beside Cappy to help. "What are we going to do with all this?"

"Pack it out, of course." Cappy spoke without hesitation. It gave me the heebie-jeebies to touch someone else's refuse, but I followed Cappy's lead.

"This is appalling!" I said. "Who the hell goes backpacking and leaves crap like this behind? How can you be someone who loves the wilderness and also someone who desecrates it?" As they pulled out the junk, I consolidated and compressed it so we could divide it up and spread it among the trash bags we each carried. We *would* pack it out.

"It doesn't even make sense," Cappy said, her face squeezing together around her wrinkled up nose as she looked at her now filthy hands. My own were sticky and blackened by grease, and I wanted to wash them in soap and water before I touched anything. I could feel my face shrivel of its own accord, like I was biting into something bitter.

We found a place where the rushing river eddied into a calm pool and were able to safely wash our hands and fill our water bottles. Still, we stuck close together and stayed well back from the faster water. Even Cappy would not consider swimming.

After inhaling dinner, we crawled into bed early, skipping our bedtime story. We fell one-by-one into unconscious slumber so deep that we were oblivious to all the midnight noises stealthily visiting our little island of civilization in the woods.

Starting Point — Muir Trail Ranch — 7600 feet
Ending Point — Evolution Meadow — 9260 feet
Highest Point — Evolution Meadow — 9260 feet
Distance Covered — 9.0 miles
Cumulative Miles — 91.1 miles

Walking On The Edge

The aim of life is to live,
and to live means to be aware,
joyously, drunkenly, serenely, divinely aware.
~ Henry Miller, *Tropic of Capricorn*, 1939

Day Fifteen
August 2, 2006

Starting Point — Evolution Meadow — 9260 feet

Today, I will wear my boots, I decided as I lay snuggled in my down-filled cocoon. I was feeling refreshed and energized by my long, deep sleep.

I had been hiking in sandals for two weeks, since blisters had forced me on Day Two to abandon my hiking boots for my kinder and gentler Tevas. For nearly one hundred miles, they had shirked their duties, dangling from the back of my pack by their laces. I had been carrying my boots, rather than my boots carrying me, and it was time they started doing their job.

We were moving into the High Country, where we would spend most of the remaining journey. We would be living and traveling above timberline—the climbing would be steeper, rockier, and harder on my feet. Little of the trail would be made of soft meadow soil or duff-carpeted forest floor. From here on out, much of the JMT had been chiseled and blasted from granite or built across talus slopes of scree. Boots would offer better protection and support than sandals. That was assuming I could convince my feet to tolerate the same monsters that had torn them to shreds and planted the original blisters.

That morning, even though my hotspots had finally healed, as a defensive strategy I taped my feet as if they had not, wrapping them from heel to toe, like burritos, in a protective layer of duct tape. When we stopped for lunch, I would give my feet a rest and retreat to sandals for the afternoon. After lacing up, I walked around in small circles testing the unfamiliar feel. Though apprehensive about walking in my *evil* boots, I thought giving myself two footwear options during days of rock-hard climbing was prudent.

Using a carabineer, I clipped my Tevas onto the back of my pack. "I think my pack just dropped two pounds!" I hefted it smoothly up onto my back in one quick swing.

"Those two pounds are now on your feet, though," Zoe said. "You're not really carrying less weight."

"Better near the ground, than up on my shoulders," I said, holding a booted foot up to admire.

I liked to think I could evolve as a hiker and an outdoors-woman to become "one with nature." Perhaps my profound appreciation of nature's beauty would someday allow me to transcend my role of outsider, mere traveler. However, my blisters and their bandages were a daily reminder that I was, in truth, simply a sojourner passing through—I did not really belong.

I needed special shoes to protect my civilized feet from the earth. I needed lots of expensive equipment to stay warm, sheltered, and fed—things any self-respecting squirrel or deer could do without assistance. I had to resupply myself with caches of food sent ahead to way stations. I could not live off the land.

I did not want to think about it that way. It sounded like I was just walking on the edge—the edge between civilization and wilderness. Perhaps I was not really walking through the wilds, just along their fringe. Even though it felt like I'd been immersed in nature for two weeks, perhaps the JMT was just a narrow ribbon of civilization laid down through the natural world, and I was still comfortably within its embrace.

Ready, I buckled my pack and reached for my hiking poles where they had leaned overnight against a tree. Gripping the handles, I discovered one had been roughly cut. "Hey, these are bite marks!" I said. "Some little varmint has been chewing on my poles!" Several pairs of parallel gouges, the incriminating teeth-prints of gnawing incisors, pointed directly to the culprits. "Squirrels!"

Cappy checked her own poles which leaned against the same tree and found similar destruction. "What little sneaks! Definitely squirrels. After the salty sweat from our hands." She spun around as though she would spy the villains watching us from behind rocks or peeking from around the backside of the broad tree.

"I didn't hear anything last night, did you?" Zoe asked. Her canes rested against a different tree, and they showed no signs of tampering.

"Nothing," Cappy said. "I heard nothing."

Zoe held up her hat, her finger protruding through the top. "The little rats chewed a hole in my cap!" The gap was dead center above the bill.

"First, it's human scofflaws—now animal vandals! What is the backcountry world coming to?" I inspected the bite marks in the black foam handle, rubbing my finger across the scars, and concluded it would not hamper forward progress.

Cappy donned her own hat, only to discover that it, too, now sported a hole in the center of her forehead! She rolled her eyes and sighed.

In the years since, I have given thought to all this gnawing. The wild creatures chewed on the edge of civilization—venturing in on forays, taking what they needed, then dashing safely back to their side of the line. Was I was just gnawing on the edge in my own way—venturing across the line, pretending to belong, then retreating back to my rightful side of the boundary whenever I ran out of food or equipment or courage?

They say ninety-five percent of all visitors to America's National Parks never venture more than a quarter-mile off the main roads. I had always felt rather smug that that did *not* describe me. After all, I was one of the five percent who regularly tramped far from the road, deep into the wild. Maybe I had been fooling myself all along. Perhaps in hiking the John Muir Trail, I was just walking along another "main road." I would never be able to truly become "one with nature," no matter how hard I tried. Of course, little of this deep thought registered that morning on the trail.

"Let's get out of here!" Cappy led the way with a determined step, following Evolution Creek upstream deeper into Evolution Valley—a mammoth valley made from lots of little valleys strung together, one slightly above the other, like terraces in an amphitheater.

Before leaving the woods, the trail dove right into the deceptively calm waters of Evolution Creek and popped up on the other side—the same water that would plunge just moments later over the edge of the steep cliff we had climbed the day before. A Trail Legend held that every year foolish hikers naively followed the trail into the creek and ended up being swept to their deaths. Near the spot where the trail submerged itself, a small tattered sign, hand-lettered on binder paper and smeared by rain, was tacked to a thin stick shoved into the mud at the edge of the water.

Cappy read the note aloud to us.

DANGER!
DO <u>NOT</u> CROSS HERE!
GO FARTHER UPSTREAM!

"That's pretty clear," I said. "But it seems a rather flimsy sign—something that could be easily missed." I imagined some poor soul, distracted by the surrounding beauty or sore feet, walking right past the warning and into the water. My eyes followed the moving water downstream towards the muffled roar of the waterfall and shuddered.

Zoe shook her head. "You'd think there'd be a permanent signpost for something this life-threatening—a red sign with skull and crossbones even."

"I guess they figure everyone passing this way has read the guidebook or heard word-of-mouth warnings." Cappy put her hands on her hips and shrugged.

"This is the first Trail Legend that's lived up to its reputation," I said. "All the others fizzled out, but this one feels real."

"I'm glad we took it at face value—didn't second guess it," Cappy said. "Aren't you?"

We found the safe ford, made obvious by scores of footprints entering the shallow water, and crossed through ankle-deep on a wide cobbled riverbed. The transformation of the river from raging monster to stealthy killer to sweet babbling creek in just a short hike upstream was impressive. Grasses spreading out from the riverbanks disguised how the river had spread out to fill the entire valley floor with a thin layer of seeping water.

Evolution Meadow was a soggy-bottomed jungle of grasses and wildflowers—waist or chest high and stretching for hundreds of feet in all directions—that nearly obliterated the muddy trail. A bit like American pioneers crossing the high-grass prairies, we pushed aside the vegetation with our arms to glimpse the path one step ahead. Breaking trail, parting the sea of grass, was hard work, so we alternated taking the lead, sticking close together, so as to not get separated.

Wearing boots had definitely been a good choice, not for the hard-rock reasons I had anticipated, but because the meadow was one giant sodden and spongy maze. The noises released with each step were animal-like—sucking and slurping, squeaking and squishing. In some stretches, the mud grabbed at my boots and held on with a tenacious grip that would have pulled my sandals right off my feet.

The best part of the day's journey began with a short group of switchbacks that lured us upward from one small valley to another, each cradling a pristine alpine meadow—petite valleys so beautiful we stopped in each one to spin slowly, trying to take in the details. Birds called and flitted about, their arrowhead shadows tracing across rocks and shrubs. Butterflies and moths, bees and dragonflies danced and purred in abundance. Flowers clustered in like-colored bunches, painting the slopes in rainbow designs. Ground squirrels popped up and then hid. Marmots strutted from one barely concealed rock to another. Water trickled and gurgled. The trail meandered—winding its way around boulders and splashing back and forth across the water—like it had been laid out by a sprite drunk on fermented nectar.

"Wouldn't this be an ideal setting for A Midsummer Night's Dream?" Cappy said, as we stood in the center of one picture-perfect little terrace. She closed her eyes then slowly inhaled the air, warm and thick with sweet perfume.

"It would be easy to imagine fairies flitting around this flower garden. Or Pan walking out of that cluster of little trees." I pointed at a copse of small trees, stunted and twisted into peculiar poses resembling dancers moving to the unheard music of past winter storms. I, too, took deep breaths, enjoying the sweet scents that hung so thick in the air I could almost taste the nectar.

"It looks more like Narnia to me." said Zoe.

Before leaving that little valley, I broke a budding stem from an aromatic plant with lavender puffball flowers and stuck it into the front of my shirt, hoping it would perfume the air as I walked. I plucked the long narrow scape of wild garlic; chewing its spicy sweetness as we resumed our journey made me wish Jane was still with us.

The JMT was taking us all the way to Evolution Basin, but we stopped short of that goal to eat lunch and bask in the sun on a group of granite chunks overlooking the path.

"John Muir loved the pine forests best," I said, "but I love the moonscapes of higher elevations."

"More than these amazing meadows and all their wildflowers?" Zoe asked.

After moments of thought, I said, "Yes. They're unique, so extreme, they're my favorites."

"Nothing beats an alpine meadow in my mind," Zoe said.

Overhead, the sky was a pale summer blue devoid of clouds. The straight white line of a jet trail worked its way across the sky like a slow-motion arrow, a reminder that civilization was still out there at a distance that grew with each step we took away from Muir Ranch. We had not seen another human all morning, and given we were carrying out the refuse left by the previous occupants of our last campground, we were just as happy to be all alone in the world.

Entering Evolution Basin and climbing still higher, the last of even the smallest trees disappeared, and vegetation gave way almost entirely to granite. The river widened and slowed until it morphed into Evolution Lake, the most beautiful lake we had encountered yet, and we had experienced some beauties. Rocky on one side and lined with hardy grasses and sedges on the other, with spots of snow dotting the stones and peaks surrounding it, the lake rested at almost eleven-thousand feet. The gray harshness of granite stood in contrast to the sparkling sapphire of the water, challenging the eyes to absorb the details.

The trail skirted the edge of the oblong lake, from outlet to source, another stunning sight revealed with each of its twists and turns. If I still had my original camera with its thousand-photo capacity, I would have been clicking photos like a mad woman, but limited as I was by my older cameras' batteries, I guarded my shots jealously. Predictably, I had clicked the shutter three times before we had walked half the length of the lake, so I allowed myself one final photo. I was forced to relinquish my desire to capture my experiences. I was forced to simply experience and let go. *How Zen.*

At the inlet where the lake morphed back to river, the trail crossed to the other side again. The water was still wide, still a lake, but it was shallow. Footstool-sized rocks, tops as flat as drums, had been arranged into a straight-as-a-jet-trail line. Placed one perfect stride apart, a Celtic stone circle tipped on its side and rolled out like a red carpet beckoned us to cross. Each stepping-stone suspended our feet a mere inch above the knee-deep water's surface. The crossing had the beauty and simplicity of a Japanese rock garden. We crossed almost reverently, one at a time, mindfully savoring each step like a bit of walking meditation.

Thich Nhat Hanh's words of guidance came to mind, "Walk as if you are kissing the Earth with your feet."[13] I reached out with my right foot, finding firm stone under my heel, then rolled my body's mass forward onto the ball of my foot, so my whole foot was engaged. I could feel the ground push up through my leg supporting me, like the roots of a tree. I picked up my left foot and reached towards the next steppingstone, first feeling the solidness under foot, before shifting my weight forward to rest there. For just a moment, my weight was exactly split—half resting on each stone—then I began the process again. Each step created the odd pairing of the feeling of the Earth's solidness beneath my feet with the visual

---

[13] Thich Nhat Hanh, *Peace Is Every Step: The Path of Mindfulness in Everyday Life* (Random House, 1995) p. 28.

perception of walking on smooth water. Without a wobble, I reached the opposite shore.

My boots were once again my friends. They had redeemed themselves that morning, supporting and cushioning my feet against the harsh granite path. Going forward, nearly all of our footsteps would be on solid granite, high above tree-line and surrounded by towering peaks and panoramic views of stone and sky.

We set up camp at Sapphire Lake, which lived up to its name in the early evening, and may or may not have been more beautiful than Evolution Lake.

We had been immersed in nature for over two weeks. Like swimmers bathing in water and coming up only briefly for air, we had emerged into the edges of the manmade world three times when we had picked up our cached food. We *would* eventually have to go back, admit our frail humanity, and retreat. But at times like that evening, I found my very soul had acclimated to the natural world, and I was completely in tune with the Earth and the sky and the water surrounding me. Not a single fiber of my being was missing people or worldly comforts. I was content with the vast pleasures of putting one foot down on the stone in front of me and then the other, all day long, then falling asleep to dream on the same granite.

Starting Point — Evolution Meadow — 9260 feet
Ending Point — Sapphire Lake — 10,970 feet
Highest Point — Sapphire Lake — 10,970 feet
Distance Covered — 8.4 miles
Cumulative Miles — 99.5 miles

Lunch At John's Place

Fairy tales are more than true—
not because they tell us that dragons exist,
but because they tell us that dragons can be beaten.
~ Neil Gaiman, *Caroline*, 2002,
paraphrasing G.K. Chesterton, *Tremendous Trifles*, 1909

Day Sixteen
August 3, 2006

Starting Point — Sapphire Lake — 10,970 feet

"Everyone says the climb to Muir Pass is the most difficult climb yet." Cappy's voice was slightly off key and tight with eagerness. "If we want to spend any time at the top enjoying the hut, we need to move out earlier than usual." Cappy bustled about, doing her morning chores at double time. She started to arrange equipment into her pack, only to stop mid-motion, her attention diverted to another important task.

The previous night, just before our bedtime story, Cappy had run through the morning's itinerary for Zoe and me, as was her nightly custom. That morning, she went through the detailed travel plans again. She held the trail map in her lap and pointed out each peak and pass with her finger.

"Here's Muir Pass. There's Mount Darwin and Mount Mendel—" I tuned her out without looking too vacant. She had pointed out the same landmarks the previous day as we had worked our way through the heart of Evolution Valley— thirteeners, all named for pioneering scientists, Darwin, Mendel, Lamarck, Spenser, and Huxley.

"Mm-hmm. Mm-hmm. Okay. Right." I did not really care about the names. I wanted to savor the natural world I passed through. I had patiently listened each of the previous days, but my tolerance level was down that morning. I was determined to be kind, but I intended to walk well ahead to minimize the number of name-that-landmark sessions I would need to mm-hmm my way through. Fortunately, Zoe was interested and was much better at paying close attention than I was.

Without conferring, both Zoe and I had ramped up our morning speed, silently harmonizing to Cappy's high-pitched vibrations. I was going to wear my boots again all morning.

"Cappy," I asked. "Why're you so intent on hitting the trail so early this morning?"

At first, she did not answer, and I was not sure she was going to. Then she stopped to look directly at me. A smile moving across her face softened it to saintly serenity. "I've been dreaming of climbing Muir Pass and hanging out in that historic hut for over thirty years, since I was in college, and I do *not* want to miss a moment of that experience." As though she had just caught herself wasting time, her eyes refocused, her smile disappeared, and she turned to the final assembly of her equipment.

"Let's go!" Cappy pointed the way with her hiking pole.

Aye-aye, Sir! I thought, then stepped out to lead the way in the direction she pointed me. "To the red dot!" I said, referring to the point on the map where Cappy had determined we would pause for our morning break beside Wanda Lake.

We climbed steadily through a monochromatic moonscape painted using every shade of silver and gray available in an artist's palette. No vegetation smoothed the angular lines of the granite landscape, and not a single cloud disturbed the bleached blue-gray sky. From this vantage point, the world was huge and breathtaking. We were specks, mere sand fleas, moving on a tissue-thin crust between earth and sky, following a path that with each step penetrated deeper and deeper into that sky.

When I came over a rise, the view widened. Just steps from the trail, a small lake, the color of a blue topaz, sat glowing amidst the gray rock. Emerald-colored sedge grasses grew in a thin ring around its shoreline like a green lace frill. Its sudden appearance was startling and alien, so vividly colorful in what had been a monochromatic landscape.

I waited for Cappy and Zoe. As my companions approached, I did not speak. I wanted to watch their reactions as they reached my vantage point.

"Oh. Wow!" Zoe sighed. She stood immobile beside me—her focus pulled like a magnet towards the sparkling little lake.

When Cappy walked up, she followed our gaze until her eyes fell on the watery gem. "That's Wanda Lake," she said. "There's something in the silt from the granite that turns the water that unusual blue color." Almost in unison, Zoe and I turned to look at Cappy for a moment, then turned back towards the little lake, unable to pull away for long.

"Wanda Lake is named after John Muir's daughter, Wanda. This is the last lake on this side of the pass. Just on the other side, below the Muir Hut, is Helen Lake, named after his other daughter," Cappy continued.

"It's so beautiful," I whispered.

Zoe had dropped her pack next to mine and was fishing around for a snack. I sat down on a square rock, pulled the bandana from around my neck, and wiped dust from my sunglasses. Zoe sat down across the path from me, settling in to enjoy our ritual morning break. I was thinking how ironic it was that "the red dot" was really a blue dot, a lake that was a blue circle drawn large on the landscape, when I noticed Cappy still stood on the trail wearing her pack. She was looking ahead up the path, rather than at the lake.

"We can't stop yet," she said, looking first at Zoe, then me.

"Sure, we can." I resealed the tube of sunscreen and looked at my watch. It was almost ten o'clock, the perfect time for our morning rest break. "We've walked an hour and a half. It's a great place to stop. It even has a view." I waved my hand in the direction of Wanda Lake. "Besides, it's the red dot!"

"No. We can't." Cappy turned to look up the trail again, and obviously did not get my red-dot-blue-dot pun. "I want to be able to take my time at the hut. If we stop now, that means less time up there. If we snack while we're walking, we can take a longer rest when we get there." She pulled a protein bar from her pocket and unwrapped it, still standing in the center of the footpath, still wearing her pack.

How could I say what I wanted to say and still be diplomatic? Had we not finally learned how to pace ourselves? We covered more distance with less pain when we took long breaks mid-morning and mid-afternoon, in addition to a lunch siesta. Why would we want to change that successful pattern? I was confused. I had not expected her resistance.

"Cappy, this was supposed to be our morning rest spot, right? I want to rest for fifteen or twenty minutes." Not wanting to argue, I kept my voice light and looked right at her. "I need this morning rest. I thought we all did." Displaying patience is not the same as authentically being patient, and inside I was anything but.

"The hardest part of the climb is over. If we keep walking, we can be there in a half-hour. Then we can relax for an extra-long time." Cappy's voice was insistent, rising an octave with determination. She remained standing, occupying the trail.

Zoe usually played the role of silent observer when Cappy and I disagreed. She did the same this time, standing up and taking one symbolic step towards the view and away from the discussion. I was sure she would simply go along with the end result, no matter what was decided.

I felt caught between two negatives—the proverbial rock and a hard place. I could have a serious disagreement with Cappy and insist on taking the morning break, or I could acquiesce, knowing my body would pay for it later. Which was the lesser of evils? Pain and tiredness later in the day or a relationship-damaging argument with my hiking partner?

"Cappy, a break right now will only delay us a few minutes. Surely we can allow that much time for a rest."

"That's less time at the Muir Hut." Her normally expressive face withdrew into a mask of emotionless blankness. "I'm going to keep on hiking. Come now or come later. Do what you want." She spun around and walked off.

Was that a challenge? Is she so confident I'll take the bait? Does she care?

I watched her move steadily away. The breeze played with her curly ponytail and rippled her white shirt. The click-click of her hiking poles on the granite grew fainter with distance.

Dueling emotions of loyalty and independence battled for my heart. *Is my sense of team loyalty misplaced? Why is it all or nothing—no room for compromise?* Why was I so dependably loyal, when Cappy showed no awareness of the team concept? Confusion was joined by frustration, as the thread stretched taut between us grew more frayed the farther she stepped away.

Turning towards Zoe, I saw she was watching Cappy's exit, too. "Well, Zoe," I lifted my shoulders in an exaggerated shrug. "I guess we're hiking."

"Guess so," she replied. Reluctant, I stood. In unison, we lifted our packs and reassembled ourselves to hike.

"Onward and upward," I mumbled. Cappy was about a hundred yards ahead, easy to see in that minimalist landscape. Zoe fell in right behind me. I knew Cappy expected us to follow her. Of the three of us, Cappy was the slowest hiker, so it was only a few minutes before we caught up to her. After walking together for a few steps, long enough for a silent "you won" to pass between us, I walked out ahead at my usual place in our little procession.

The trail snaked along beside Wanda Lake, then climbed steeply under a bright sun towards the twelve-thousand-foot Muir Pass. The landmark hut was visible from far below and made the pass appear much closer than it actually was. We walked and walked, and the hut never grew in size—it seemed to recede a yard for every yard of progress we made.

The hut remained tantalizingly out of reach—a lone, brown snaggletooth taking a bite out of the sky. My energy was flagging. My feet had grown heavy. My reserves were dwindling. Cappy and Zoe lagged yards behind me, so I lowered myself onto the verge on the high side of the trail, resting my pack on the ground to take the weight off my shoulders and hips without unbuckling it. I put a

Werther's Coffee Caramel into my mouth and gulped Gatorade from my Nalgene bottle. My lunch, out of reach in the bear can deep in my pack, called out to me— Fig Newtons and cranberries, peanut butter and crackers.

When Cappy drew close, she looked as tired as I felt. Her steps were slow though determined, and she sagged a bit under the weight of her pack. I began to feel hopeful she might finally agree to stop for a rest.

"We've already hiked another half hour, and we've still got a long way to go. Why don't we stop to recoup for just a little bit?" I suggested.

"Look how close it is! We can't stop now." She spoke with the fervency of a thirsty pilgrim eyeing a watery mirage. "We'll be there in a few minutes." She had paused in front of me, but it was obvious she had no intention of sitting down even for a moment.

How is her reality so different from mine? To my perception, the Muir Hut was still a long, steep hike away. It was a clear day, at high altitude, so the hut appeared close enough to touch, but that was only an optical illusion. It was at least a half-mile distant, as the crow flies, but we were not crows—the trail ahead led back and forth across the face of the steep mountain.

"Cappy, I'm exhausted. I just want to rest." I spoke my rational appeal in my most persuasive voice.

"Go ahead, if you want to. I'm not stopping. I'll rest when I get to the hut." Pointing towards the pass, she added, "Look at all the people already up there. I want to get there while our friends are still there." There were several colorful specks moving about the top of the pass near the sharp-roofed hut. Her matter-of-fact tone signaled her intolerance for argument or compromise.

Frustrated and tired but intent on staying together as a team, I stood up. "All right," I breathed, turning my back on Cappy and walking on. Anger is a terrific motivator. The adrenaline-charged negative energy that surged through me like an electrical current helped to propel me upwards. Bitching aloud to myself with each step, I pushed myself into a rhythm that would get me to the top as quickly as possible.

This is so stupid, I thought. *Exhausting ourselves is not a good idea. Why is Cappy so stubborn? Why do I always compromise?* Bitch, bitch, bitch. Not very mindful, but very effective in finding hidden pockets of reserve energy.

At the time, I saw Cappy's decision to forego a rest as irrational, her willingness to walk away without compromise as abandonment. Looking back over a decade, I realize my own stubborn team loyalty was equally irrational, undermining my loyalty to myself. Were I in the same situation today, I would have stopped to rest for twenty minutes beside the trail. I would have waved goodbye to Cappy, calling, "See you later at the top." I would not have taken her decision personally, but accepted it as her choice. But that is not what I did; instead, I used my throbbing anger to propel myself up the steep, rocky trail.

When my stomach cried out for more food, I fed it Werther's and Gatorade. When my muscles complained and my legs found lifting my feet difficult, I served up another dose of adrenaline by giving into my vexation, "This is soooo stupid! I can't believe I'm doing this!" I said aloud to myself, tossing gasoline on my inner fire.

The last stretch was particularly difficult. I dragged my body along without looking back to see where Cappy and Zoe were. I kept my head down, my upper body angled forward, focusing only on the ground at my feet, like a bull charging blindly through space. I passed under and through gorgeous natural beauty I completely ignored in deference to my general pissy-ness.

Suddenly, I was at the top. I stopped in my tracks when the trail stopped climbing and leveled out. I spun slowly around, dazed like I had just awakened from sleepwalking. I had been watching my feet and the trail, but there at the top I looked up and all around.

Vast expanses of gray and silver granite sloped downward and outward infinitely in every direction, a moonscape broken only by a handful of distant blue lakes. An equally monochromatic pale blue sky hovered overhead, spreading outward towards the same infinite distances.

Two dozen people populated the area near the hut perched on the summit. A buzz of conversation filled the thin air. I had not seen so many people in one place for a week, not since VVR—though it felt longer, like it had been months.

I did not join them. I found a flat outcropping right off the trail and allowed myself to collapse to the ground with my pack still on. Seated, I unhooked it and let it flop onto its side next to me. I dragged out the food canister. My lunch lay on top of the other contents. With laser focus, I stuffed food in my mouth. Ravenous for sugar, fat, and protein, I could not get food into my mouth, chewed, and swallowed fast enough. It was a frantic need. Peanut butter squeezed onto crackers, onto fingers, directly into my mouth. Handfuls of sticky dried cranberries and pecan halves, which normally I would have artfully arranged onto the peanut butter, I simply scooped up and shoved into my mouth. Bite after crumbling bite of fig cookies I washed down with deep gulps of Gatorade.

My hunger finally sated, I leaned back on my pack. My boots unlaced and removed, I propped my feet up onto a rock ottoman with my head on my pack. Looking down the mountainside for the first time, I saw Cappy and Zoe climbing slowly upwards, the last switchback still ahead of them.

I was in no mood to be sociable—I was a little concerned I might actually tell Cappy I held her personally responsible for all my physical aches and pains, for my hurt feelings and sense of abandonment. Instead, like a hermit, I withdrew. I pulled my cap down over my eyes and began my much-needed rest. The ground beneath me was toasty warm from baking in the sun, even though the air at twelve-thousand feet was cool.

"Joan, you awake?" It was Zoe's voice. She had removed her pack and was arranging herself beside me. I sat up a bit and rearranged my hat, tucking my hair behind my ears.

"Just resting," I answered.

"That was an awful climb. How can something be so beautiful and so terrible at the same time?" Zoe rifled through her bear canister, pulling out her lunch.

"How are your hips holding out?" I asked.

"They're fine on the ascents," she said with her mouth full of nuts. "It's the descents that still give me trouble. I'm not looking forward to climbing down from this perch."

"Where's Cappy?" I realized she had disappeared as soon as she had arrived.

"She went straight to the hut." Zoe pointed over her shoulder toward the crowd in and around the primitive stone structure.

Sure enough, when I looked over my shoulder, I could see Cappy, camera in hand, chatting with a small group of khaki-clad hikers.

It was a party atmosphere at the top of Muir Pass. A throng congregated on the wide, flat top of the pass, a stark contrast to the solitude of the trail. Sometimes I found these transient communities attractive, and I wanted to join in the embrace—other times I was repelled by the noise and commotion and wanted to retreat as far away as I could. The group spontaneously gathered atop Muir Pass fell into the latter category, their boisterousness out of place in one of Nature's sacred cathedrals. I remained in my resting spot on the periphery, absorbing the infinite view laid out in front of me, even after Zoe wandered away towards the hut.

One bearded young man, beside a huge pack, stood playing a six-foot long didgeridoo. I wondered what he had had to leave behind to make room among his possessions for that unwieldy luxury. He propped one end on a rock well out in front of himself, and into the other, he hummed fervently. Its husky, melodious vibrations sang out across the vast spaces between the pass and the tall craggy peaks all around us, like the deep vibrating chants of Tibetan throat singers. He stood at the top of the world, and the notes he created traveled uninterrupted for miles and miles and miles.

In the gaps between the musician's Aboriginal songs, another hiker began to serenade the group with alpine yodeling, his warbling voice vanishing into the same vast emptiness. Both high and low notes rebounded off distant granite walls, their echoes floating toward us like answering songs.

My eyes followed the music into the distance. The views from twelve-thousand-feet were amazing. Evolution Valley, which had taken us two days to transect, lay visible at our feet, surrounded by sky-scraping peaks and saw-toothed ridges. The small lakes we had passed on the way up twinkled like precious stones under a jeweler's lamp.

Cappy returned to the little shelf where I rested, sitting down to eat her lunch.

"Nice view, eh?" I said in my most amiable voice. "'On a clear day, you can see forever' comes to mind, doesn't it?" I was not sure if I was ready to be warm and friendly yet, or not. But I knew things would work best if we were a functioning team, so I spoke to convince us both I was friendly.

"It's as nice as I'd hoped it would be," Cappy said between bites. "You can really see where we've been. That's Mount Darwin over there. And that's Mount Mendel." She was pointing at the same mountain peaks. "That one is Mount Haeckel and there's Mount Lamarck."

"I'm going to check out this famous hut of yours." Annoyed again, I rose to escape another naming session as quickly and as diplomatically as I could.

Cappy was right, of course. As the negative energy of my anger seeped away into the mountain beneath my feet, I could clearly see and appreciate Muir Hut's unique beauty. Built by the Sierra Club in 1930 out of bricks cut from local granite, it sits directly on the summit—at eleven-thousand, nine-hundred, and fifty-five feet. Officially christened the John Muir Memorial Shelter, it is a gold-hued cylinder topped by a cone.

I found Zoe talking with a small group of hikers just outside the hut. Together, we entered the cool, dark sanctuary, stepping past the heavy oak door designed to stand guard against the elements. I wondered just how many hikers had passed under that stone lintel in the previous seventy-six years. The temple-like interior felt sacred—a monk would have been right at home.

Overhead, the roof's bricks formed concentric circles. A stone fireplace adorned one wall. Out of respect for its place in history and nature, I moved around slowly, silently, in a state of reverence.

Zoe must have felt similarly, because she spoke in a hushed tone when she pointed over the mantle to a large brass plaque dedicating the shelter to John Muir. It read in part:

THE MUIR HUT IS INTENDED AS

A TEMPORARY SHELTER FOR HIKERS

CAUGHT IN STORMS ON THIS EXPOSED SECTION OF TRAIL.[14]

Zoe wondered, "Can you imagine waiting out a big storm in here?"

Leaping to mind came the storm Cappy, Jane, and I had experienced atop Donohue Pass way back on Day Two. Sheltering in the Muir Hut seemed way better than curling into a fetal position on the wet ground.

---

[14] The Muir Hut was designated a National Historic Landmark in the National Register of Historic Places in 2016, and was rededicated by the Sierra Club at a ceremony at the hut on August 25, 2016, the one hundredth anniversary of the National Park Service. The new bronze plaque, which displays likenesses of John Muir and William Colby in front to the Muir Hut, reads:

> The John Muir Memorial Shelter was erected in 1930 to commemorate America's leading early conservationist and first president of the Sierra Club. Conceived by Sierra Club "High Trip" Leader William Colby, inspired by the Italian Trullo Hut building tradition and designed by Bay Area architect Henry Gutterson, the rustic alpine shelter endures as a fitting tribute to Muir's great passion for reserving wilderness and his legacy for our National Parks. August 25, 2016, National Park Service Centennial Sierra Club

I reached out to touch the flat, cut edges of the stones fitted in the walls. "It would be cozy with enough firewood," I whispered back.

"You would be so isolated. What if a storm lasted for days?" she asked.

"It used to be a thing to do," I said. "People used to plan their hikes so that they could camp here, in good weather or bad. A bucket list check."

"And where did the wood come from?"

"Good question." I laughed. I could not imagine toting a load of firewood up that mountain.

Outside, the didgeridoo's enchanting song was carried on the breeze, while inside we touched the strong old walls, gazed up at the stone halos in the ceiling, and imagined what it had been like in the "olden days".

Using Zoe's camera, we took turns snapping photos of each other at the hearth. Zoe, standing tall, posed like a mountaineer, one booted foot propped on the hearth, one hand on the mantle. I tried the same pose, but being six inches shorter, I could not really pull it off.

When we emerged squinting into the sun, Cappy was waiting there with her pack, looking anxious to leave. "It's getting late, girls, and we've a long hike ahead of us. But first, please, will you take a picture of me in front of the hut?" She held her camera out in my direction and put her pack to the side.

We stood three abreast. The descent before us was buried in deep swaths of white. Decorated with hieroglyphs of pink "watermelon snow" and sparkling innocently under a clear blue sky, the snowy expanse radiated a beauty at odds with its high degree of difficulty.[15] Had I realized the day's journey was to be a series of challenges worthy of a classic questing tale, I would have approached each formidable task we faced with less fear and more awe.

"That's Helen Lake," Cappy announced, "named after John Muir's second daughter." I do not think she saw me roll my eyes. "It's in Le Conte Canyon; Wanda Lake was in Evolution Basin. Isn't that neat? The John Muir Hut is bookended by the two lakes named after his daughters!"

---

[15] Watermelon snow, also called red snow, looks like it has been painted with pink and red watercolors. It is created by a species of green algae with a secondary red pigment in addition to the green pigment chlorophyll. It thrives in near freezing water. Watermelon snow is common in higher altitudes during the summer in the Sierra Nevada.

"What do you think about gaiters?" I asked no one in particular. "Looks like those guys are both using them." I pointed toward two men forty yards ahead making their way across a broad white expanse punctuated with punchbowl-sized pools of water.

"They're having a tough time with those snow cups," Cappy said. "Looks pretty challenging." As we watched, the fellow in the lead lost his footing when the ridge of rotten ice that separated two sun cups shattered, and his leg plunged knee-deep into sun-softened snow and ice water—post-holing. Three simultaneous gasps escaped us. We observed as he regained his balance and extricated himself from the hole his leg had created in the ice.

The Three Women were quiet.

"Gaiters for sure," was Cappy's delayed answer. "Gotta keep our feet dry." Soon we were strapping waterproof fabric shields around our ankles and boots.

"We got this," Zoe said. As an athlete, she tackled every challenge with a sureness I had trouble mimicking. Her firm jaw suggested she was just about to launch herself forward downhill. Underneath, I knew she worried about the punishment the descent would inflict on her wounded hip.

Studying the white terrain ahead, I thought about the serpentine path we would need to follow around and between the cups. I conjured visions of walking across the icy obstacle course with the grace of a high-wire acrobat, balancing my pack as I navigated around the sun cups. Despite my efforts, I shivered at the thought of falling butt-first into a slippery cup of frigid ice water to become the backpacking equivalent of a turtle on its back.

I navigated the descent like I was traversing a minefield, testing each step before putting my full weight on my forward foot. I kept one eye on the path Cappy had taken ahead of me and one eye on the snow beneath my next step. Would it be better to walk where she had walked, where the ice layer had been tested and proven itself strong enough? Or would her passing weaken its crystal bonds, so I should find a different route? I chose to follow her steps. It was a slow process.

From behind came startling sounds—the crunch of shattering ice, followed by Zoe's surprised yelp. With care, I swiveled my shoulders to look. She was just pulling her boot out of the hole it had created.

"You okay back there?" I called.

"Yeah, just dandy," she answered. "Damn, that's hella cold." She adjusted her balance and took a successful step at a small angle to her original path.

I turned back to my own slow progress. Each deliberate step demanded a purposeful choice and a careful shift of weight. My movements resembled Tai Chi practice, where every move is intentional, balanced, and in slow motion.

"Who-hoo!" someone screamed. Three brightly colored comets flashed by to my right, shooting down the hill rocket-fast amidst a cacophony of wild yells. I nearly fell as I whipped my head around to see them pass. At first, I thought someone had fallen, screaming for help. But then I realized three hikers were tobogganing across the icy surface, partly on their boots, partly on their packs, and the whooping and hollering was in celebration of their joyride. As quickly as they had shot into sight, they disappeared far down the slope.

Not in a million years would I have done that. Who knew what lay in wait at the bottom! Frozen hell! I could not even trust the surface of the path to support my weight, let alone a high-speed trajectory.

"Can you believe that?" Cappy called back to us.

"Crazy!" Zoe answered.

We would later learn there is actually a term for that "controlled slide maneuver"—glissade—but it did not appear to be either controlled or rational to me. Once my heart rate rebounded, I returned to my own slow and prudent progress.

Cappy stopped to wait for us where the sun cups came to an end. Ahead, the track cut straight across the face of a slope that slanted sharply down to our right. Should I fall, I imagined an involuntary "glissade" to the foot of the mountain and arriving in multiple battered pieces. Ahead, the depression in the snow that was the trail fanned out into three near-parallel dark lines across the dazzling diagonal surface, none of them more attractive than the others.

"Any wise thoughts about how to attack this?" I swept my arm through the air taking in the way forward.

"Be careful," said Zoe.

"Funny," I replied, thinking she was being ironic.

"No, really," she said again. "Be careful."

That I intended to do. "I was thinking about some practical advice for how to not end up down there in a heap." I pointed.

She had made me smile, which was good. I had been in a pretty crappy mood for most of the day. My anger over the morning's forced march up "The Epic Climb" was mixed with an equal part of frustration generated by the afternoon's cup crossing. Standing there, drips of fear were being added to the recipe one at a time, creating a volatile soup of negative emotions.

"Today continues to be a test," I said, still not realizing The Three Women had been cast in a mythical questing tale. "I think we should adjust our poles. We need to use them on the snow on either side of the trail." I was thinking aloud. "Keeping balanced side-to-side is going to be critical." I began testing different pole lengths against the untrampled snow on either side of the path's trench.

"Good idea." Cappy began adjusting her own sticks. "Other thoughts?"

I did not answer. That had been my one brilliant notion.

"Be careful," Zoe said a third time. This time, I chuckled despite my solidly entrenched dark mood.

Cappy led the way, stepping with care and thrusting her poles into the ice crust on each side.

I waited until she had taken ten steps, then I followed in the same purposeful way—finding solid footing in the wet and ice-encrusted trench, anchoring myself with my poles. My toes gripped the insoles of my boots tightly in an attempt to grab hold of the ground. My ankles shifted, changing angles as the soles of my boots found stability. I slipped and slid like an inexperienced ice skater, but my poles held firm each time.

When Cappy let out a high-pitched squeal, I looked up from my feet to see she'd tipped over and was seated on the downside of the trail. Her feet and lower legs were still in the trail's shallow swale, but her heavy pack was threatening to take her sliding. She twisted and wriggled, arranging herself, and waited for Zoe and me to get close.

"Can I help?" I asked, as she sat on the curb of snow catching her breath and brushing several strands of her loosened hair from her face.

"I'm good," she said and smiled, just as Zoe joined us.

"You scared me, Cappy!" Zoe said.

"I guess I wasn't being *careful* enough," Cappy joked, signaling her full recovery.

"Shall I take the lead for a while?" I asked. "It's tough work being the trailblazer.".

"Good idea," Cappy said.

She was up and I squeezed past. Moving again, we spread out along the trail. It was hard leading in this terrain. When I had followed Cappy, I could rely on the fact that she had already tested the footing. Now, I wanted to test each step with extra care.

Ten minutes later, it was my turn at imbalance. I had planted my poles carefully on either side of the depression, then leaned on them both as I took two steps forward. My right foot slipped in the icy trough and skidded forward like I was attempting to do the splits within the confines of the narrow trail. Then the right pole, which I was now using to keep myself from actually doing those splits, plunged through the frozen surface, deep into the snow, and failed to provide much needed support.

I ended up sprawled much like Cappy had been, legs askew, with my upper body and pack pulling me downhill. I know I let out a noise of some kind, because almost immediately Cappy called out.

"Fine," I yelled.

I lay there for a few moments not moving. I wanted to think out my next moves before I made them.

I do not remember how I recovered myself, but I do remember it requiring quite a bit of reserve energy, an already shallow supply. I remember thrashing around. The problem was the thin crust of ice covering the squishy snow was not strong enough for me to leverage myself upwards. Every time I pressed down on the surface, it cracked and my arm plunged through the rotten ice into the wet mass below. Eventually, I figured out how to push with my full flat forearm, spreading out my weight, and I popped right up and twisted my body uphill. Cappy and Zoe arrived just as I was sitting down on the snow curb like Cappy had done earlier.

"Your turn, Zoe," I said. "But be careful." The joke was getting old, but still elicited a groan of appreciation.

That day, The Three Women had been transformed into fairytale characters in an old once-upon-a-time story—a group of kindred souls out on a quest. In the stories, it is always three tests and then a treasure. We had vanquished our first two very real challenges—The Epic Climb to the hut and The Treacherous Snow-Crossing. By three in the afternoon, we were fully enmeshed in our third test—The Trail Of Glass—and I was definitely ready for that treasure.

For some time, we trudged along a sun-drenched trail largely free of snow and devoid of vegetation. Built from disorganized piles of metamorphic rock shards, the path underfoot shifted and clinked like broken glass. Narrow, the trail took an undulating path up and down across the shifting ground. My ankles and knees endured a strenuous workout as the angular shards rocked and tipped and slipped against one another.

Crossing snow, our complaining had been lighthearted, almost playful. Authentic complaining began in earnest as we wobbled our way across the teeter-tottering glass rocks, our unhappiness coming out in curses.

"This is like a goddamn funhouse in a horror movie!" Zoe spit out her words.

"At least we're too high for rattlesnakes to be hiding in the rocks," Cappy said.

"Maybe we've died and gone to Dante's Hell—doomed for an eternity!" I suggested.

"Damned rocks!" Zoe added.

It was pointless to be angry at rocks, but I had come to the end of my stores of patience. We all had. The sun was hot and reflected off the rocks, glaring at us from above and below. Sweat dripped down my back and between my breasts, soaking my clothes and creating a tangy aroma.

I should have taken my morning rest, I thought. We all should have. We were running out of energy, struggling with the hike and getting crabbier by the step.

In the classic questing tales, the characters pass three tests, find the treasure, and then live happily ever after. The Three Women's quest should have ended as soon as we completed what Zoe called "the ugliest, rockiest, hike-from-hell." We should have gotten our prize right then and there! But fate had something else in store for us. We were given a bonus fourth obstacle to overcome. After vanquishing The Epic Climb, The Treacherous Snow-Crossing, *and* The Trail of Glass, we came face-to-face with The Boulder Monsters.

The wobbly part of the trail ended at a field of large boulders, massive cubes all tossed together helter-skelter. It was an old landslide, but it looked like a young giant's block tower had tumbled down right in front of us, blocking our way. We spent a long while wending our way through, around, and over that pile.

Eventually the mountain ran out of tests. Vegetation began to appear along the rocky trail, first just small hardy shrubs, then grasses and bushes flourished. Stunted trees clustered in groups. Water trickled among the rocks and trees. I had not realized how much my eyes longed for the luxury, the gentleness, of greenery until I felt them spontaneously relax in response to the dramatic change in scenery.

At the first real meadow, a small green space sheltered on three sides, we stopped. Were all our labors going to be rewarded with a beautiful, green campsite?

"Is this it?" I asked, wanting desperately to stop for the night. "Cappy, please, tell me this is our campsite."

"I think so. This stream must be the Middle Fork of the Kings River."

"Thank the gods!" I threw down my pack, then followed it to the ground.

Zoe dropped beside me.

"Don't get comfortable, girls. Let's get our tent up." Cappy took charge.

Our campsite rested in the middle of a glade. The ground was carpeted with grasses and miniature wildflowers. The open space was backed up against a sheer granite wall and enclosed on two sides by copses of twisted dwarf trees. The vegetation was so lush, we might have traveled to a different universe. The air carried the rich aroma of green plants rising from the sun-warmed earth. The open side looked out across a forested valley towards row after row of mountain ridges, the closest ones black and saw-toothed, the most distant ones smooth and misty violet. Behind us, the sky was turning pale yellow.

After a few short hours amidst that lush beauty the day's misery was expunged from my brain. With surgical precision my black mood—the effect of the landscape's ugliness and the trail's difficulty—was excised from my mind. In its place, contentment grew like a flowering green vine. This was our well-earned treasure, our Garden Paradise.

After dinner, Cappy pulled the topo map from its small compartment and spread it on a flat stone. She had the guidebook opened in her lap to the sections we had just covered.

I was leaning against a granite boulder and writing in my journal, when Cappy's voice caught my attention. I looked up from my little spiral notebook, "I'm sorry, Cappy, what did you say?"

She sat up straight. "I said, we're still a day behind schedule. We have to catch up." She pressed her finger into the map and waved the typed trip itinerary she had created back in June. Looking from me to Zoe and back again, she expected a response.

"Okay." I was not really sure what she wanted me to do. We had danced around this problem every evening for a week.

We had gotten off schedule on Day Two and Three, when the storm atop Donohue and the flood of runoff in Rush Creek had stopped us in our tracks. Two weeks later, we were still one day behind the altered plan Cappy had emailed to Jim from Muir Ranch.

"We really need to make some decisions, choose different stopping spots, so we can catch up," Cappy said. Our eyes met and held. "Or we're not going to get to Whitney on time." Worry lines ringed her eyes. Her mouth reduced to a slim straight line.

Get there on time? I thought. I did not feel the pressure of time. Cappy did. It was an end date we had chosen for ourselves, not a deadline we *had* to meet. In my mind, it was flexible.

"Cappy, honestly, I don't care when we get to Whitney." I knew as the words came out of my mouth it was exactly the wrong thing to say. "Can't we just arrive a day late? What's the difference?" I kept my voice calm, hoping to sound open, not indifferent.

What's her hurry? I thought.

Zoe moved around camp quietly organizing her possessions, repacking her food canister and hanging up some damp clothes to dry. She did not say a word, but I knew she was listening and considering.

"Joan, Jim's going to be there on the fifteenth. We need to be there, too," Cappy reminded me her husband would be waiting for us at Whitney Portal when we emerged. "We have to make up ten miles."

"Why don't we just tell him to come a day later?" I asked.

I had asked the same question three days earlier when we were at Muir Ranch sitting at the computer typing emails home. "We could send a message with the packer who's bringing our food to Charlotte Lake," I suggested.

Am I being selfish? I thought, getting up. I began to walk around the glade. I walked towards the mountain view and watched as the yellow to the west darkened to gold and tangerine, and the eastern blue melted into pale yellow.

"I don't want to come in a day late. Jim's already made motel reservations in Lone Pine," Cappy said behind me. "Besides, how can we send a message with the packer if we get to the meeting spot a day late? He'll be long gone." She held her position on the stone, though she had moved all the papers to the ground in front of her. I had not thought this was about seeing Jim, but I began to wonder if her earnestness grew from missing her husband.

Cappy took her ad hoc position of chief navigator seriously, leaving nothing to chance. She had kept us safe and on track for more than two weeks. And I had voluntarily handed over all responsibility for trail decisions after the first few days because it seemed so important to her. Now she wanted me to step back in and help her to make decisions, but I did not want to. Actually, I did not care.

Feeling frustration rise, I knew I was not going to win this argument. I continued to watch the sky, while Cappy waited for my response. The silence was broken only by the whisper of the breeze moving up from the valley and the evening calls of birds invisible in the trees. I wanted to be calm when I spoke, so I took a couple more deep breaths of the sweet scented air before I turned to face her.

"Cappy, seriously, I don't care when we get to Whitney," I repeated. "I know it's important to you, and that's fine, but it's not in the least important to me. So, feel free to make any decisions you want. Change any of the timeline you want. Just point me in the right direction." I had been worried that my words might emerge too forcefully, but they had not. They came out soft and steady. I swallowed and walked closer to hear her response.

"But I don't want to make these decisions all by myself. What if I make a mistake?" Like a conductor, Cappy's hands rose and fell in time with each question. "What if we can't make the mileage? What if we run out of steam in an area where there's no place to camp?" Cappy's questions revealed how heavy the weight of responsibility had become for her. Her eyes were wide in an appeal.

I was beginning to understand. I had let her shoulder this extra load because I thought she wanted that control, not realizing how hard the job had become and how worried she was about letting us down. "Show me," I said and walked over to sit beside her on the rock.

Zoe had finished her organizing efforts and, sensing the shift in the conversation, she walked over and joined us around the map. Cappy explained the dilemma and a variety of solutions, all of them with problems of their own. I did my best to listen with care and describe my preferences.

We agreed to walk a little farther each day—an extra couple of miles a day would be enough. Some days, the distance would have to be much longer than others, as camping spots dictated where we could stop. Those extra daily miles meant we would meet the packhorse bringing our next food cache on the day he arrived. Those extra daily miles meant we could get to Whitney Portal on the fifteenth, as planned—a happy ending.

Before beginning the trip, I had been impertinent enough to ask the Universe to use my upcoming JMT adventure to provide me with challenges that would push me to my limits—physical challenges, of course, and mental, emotional, and spiritual challenges as well. A romantic notion on a collision course with the reality of the trail's challenges.

Thank you, Universe.

Starting Point — Sapphire Lake — 10,970 feet
Ending Point — Lower Lake at Tree Line in Le Conte Canyon — 10,400 feet
Highest Point — Muir Pass — 11,955 feet
Distance Covered — 6.5 miles
Cumulative Miles — 106.0 miles

Hidden In Plain Sight

The mind can go in a thousand directions,
but on this beautiful path, I walk in peace.
With each step, the wind blows.
With each step, a flower blooms.
~ Thich Nhat Hanh, *Peace is Every Step:*
The Path of Mindfulness in Everyday Life, 1992

Day Seventeen
August 4, 2006

Starting Point — Lower Lake at Tree Line in Le Conte Canyon — 10,400 feet

The morning began with a glorious sunrise. Our little alpine meadow-in-a-bowl's open side faced eastward, and we watched the sun rise behind the distant row of mountain peaks. Their black silhouettes cut a ragged fringe across the bottom of the raspberry-lemonade-colored sky. The carpet of grass glowed emerald, each blade spotlighted by the horizontal rays of light. As the sun floated higher, the mountains separated themselves into distinct ranges, each a different color—slate, tan, and dove gray. The sky became first turquoise, then a clear blue. Before us down the mountain, the stream that was the Middle Fork of the Kings River twinkled in the morning light.

Sitting cross-legged on the grass-cushioned ground, I meditated. I concentrated on my breathing, following the air as it flowed in and out of my lungs. The morning sunshine warmed my skin, and a wisp of a breeze feathered my curls. I relaxed my mind and my body. The earth supported me. The air surrounded me. I felt embraced.

The morning's walk carried us alongside the descending Middle Fork. First a trickling creek, it merged with cascading tributaries to swell into a giant, rushing river overflowing its banks. The trail tracked close to the water on a long, gradual downward climb through Le Conte Canyon. We passed through a series of ecosystems—thick shadowy forests, cool damp fern grottos, and several alpine meadows overflowing with flowers—finally arriving in a thick forest in the canyon's depths. The descent was in every way opposite to the previous day's slog. There were no snowfields to cross, no boulders to scale, no ankle-twisting shale to traverse; the trail was gentle on our bodies. Vegetation was voluptuous, cool air perfumed. We stopped for a break beside the bounding river and for lunch on duff-carpeted ground in the shade of a thick stand of conifers.

As I walked, I reflected on the previous days on the trail. I began to giggle, and chuckle, then laugh aloud until tears came. I had gotten *exactly* what I had asked the Universe for—an abundance of challenges that pushed me to my limits on so many levels. The predictable physical trials of the trek were joined by interpersonal challenges, tests of inner courage and strength, and so many more. I pulled out my necklace and fingered the rings.

Walk your own walk, hike your own hike, I coached myself with that old hikers' adage as I found myself bristling at Cappy's repetitive identifying and labeling.

Looking back, I believe Cappy needed to speak aloud the day's plan, the place names and feature labels, as a way of feeling in control and at ease. I think, having the power of knowledge brought her a familiarity with our surroundings, and that brought her comfort and confidence. But at the time, living in such close proximity, I was not able to understand the therapeutic nature of her name-giving rituals. Instead, it was making me crazy. To feel that same sense of comfort, control, and ease, I needed the peace and calm I found in silence and solitude. And I needed to savor my environment, not analyze it.

I wanted to experience a flower at a sensory level. I wanted to see it and smell it and touch it, not label it. I touched the stems and blossoms, running them through my fingers, noticing their texture. I brought a lavender one close to my nose, inhaling its aroma, noticing how different it was from the yellow one.

Somehow, I needed to find a way to overcome this very different challenge to get beyond my own reactions and to find peace in our different ways of being.

Earlier that morning while meditating, I found that Cappy's morning review of the day's events and landmarks slid past me without stealing away my focus from my breathing, from my internal calm. Cappy seemed content to share her knowledge and observations with Zoe, and Zoe seemed to enjoy the conversation. They did not need me to take part or even to listen to them.

My hiking would become a walking meditation, I had decided that morning. I would just let the constant talk dissipate while I focused only on my own steps, my own path. "When walking, walk." Thich Nhat Hahn's pithy wisdom spoke to me that morning.

I walked ahead as usual but began extending the distance between us. Staying close enough to be aware of my hiking partners behind me, I created more space around myself. I walked all alone along the path in pure and peaceful solitude. I stopped every now and again, at turns in the trail and crossroads, to wait for Cappy and Zoe, to touch base, make contact. Then I would walk on ahead again, resuming my meditative pace. They strode together, chatting and happy, experiencing the journey in their own ways. With my changed perspective, with the spacious sense of peaceful aloneness that change created, my morning walk was a pure, uninterrupted delight.

I walked in solitude as we passed through a series of meadows—Big Pete, Little Pete, and Grouse—each bordered by woods and a smattering of silver boulders. Water trickled and meandered everywhere, and ferns unfurled themselves in the cool shade of rocks fuzzy with green mosses and orange circles of lichen. Wildflowers danced in the up-flowing breeze that sent rainbow waves and ripples across the meadow and filled the air with perfume. Bees, butterflies, and dragonflies bobbed and buzzed individually, while gnats swooped in swarms. I could not stop smiling.

I was so content that when we paused to find the perfect lunch spot among the trees along the edge of Grouse Meadow, I laughed aloud with appreciative glee when Cappy pointed out the bird, standing still-as-a-statue, observing us from the side of the trail.

"Look," she said, pointing into the shadows of the trees. "We have a welcoming party. A grouse has come to say, 'Welcome to Grouse Meadow'!" The delicate stripes and spots of its feathers mimicked the dappled shade in the undergrowth where it stood hiding, making it next to invisible only inches from the footpath.

The canopy of tall trees provided deep shade for our lunch spot. Lying back on my pink pad, stockinged feet propped up on my pack, I watched as red-headed woodpeckers flitted among the branches. The trees' needles, silhouetted against the pale sky, overlapped one another, creating changing patterns as they were nudged around by a light breeze. The gentle movement was mesmerizing, and I slipped away into a dreamy state.

I was brought wide awake by a repetitive tattoo that vibrated through the ground beneath me. I tipped my head up to listen more closely, and the sound became, not a drumbeat but shod feet pounding rapidly down the dirt path next to our shady oasis.

Eyes fully open, I sat up and swiveled just in time to watch as two young men flew by, oblivious to our existence, jogging down the trail. They wore running shoes rather than boots, and were shirtless, wearing only lightweight running shorts that sat low on their hipbones. They carried ultra-lite packs that were nothing more than silk-thin daypacks. In mere moments, they had disappeared phantom-like around the bend in the path.

"Those guys are crazy!" Zoe whispered from her sleeping nest.

"They certainly aren't smelling any roses," I chuckled, shaking my head, "or pine trees, for that matter."

"They didn't see us, and I bet they missed the grouse, too," Zoe said.

"They remind me of those two guys we met at Red's, the ones who were intent on doing the whole two hundred miles of the JMT in five or six days," Cappy said.

"They've already finished—probably back at work, too," Zoe added.

"Poor fellas," I said. "They're missing all this." I swung my arms skyward to encompass the trees, mountains, and sky overhead.

I resumed my supine position and my pine needle-gazing. "Look up. Doesn't that look like black lace on white satin?" I asked. An occasional breeze stirred the needles in the umbrellas of branches above us, creating dynamic Fibonacci patterns in ebony and pearl, and the wind's shushing lullaby ushered me towards my nap.

If the morning had been a beautiful color photograph, the afternoon was an undeveloped negative. We shuffled along hot and dry stretches, through partly burned forests, and over poorly maintained meadow trails.

Dark gray storm clouds were moving in. For the first time in days, we heard the foreshadowing rumble of distant thunder. Large raindrops plopped on the trail, making miniature craters in the powdery dust, first slowly, one at a time, then more quickly. Lightning scribbled lines across the dark sky.

We huddled to talk. "Do we go on?" I asked. "Or look for a place to camp?" Personally, I wanted to stop, not walk in the rain, but the surroundings were some of the most uninviting we had encountered, making walking on and stopping equally unattractive options.

"We're still a couple miles from where we'd planned to camp," Cappy said.

Stopping will put a cramp in Cappy's plan to cover extra mileage today, I thought. I wondered if that was what she was thinking.

While we talked, I removed my pack. Balancing it on a log, I dug for my waterproof jacket deep in its bottom and for my pack's rain cover, too. Whether we hiked on or found a campsite, my pack and I needed to stay dry.

"This is such a gross spot. Maybe if we walk awhile, the storm will pass by," Zoe was donning wet weather gear.

"More than likely it's just a quick afternoon storm and will be gone in a bit," Cappy added. We moved deeper under the forest canopy edging the trail.

No sooner had she spoken than the rain became a pelting deluge. The ground was wet, and the trees around us no longer offered effective shelter of any kind.

"Check that," Cappy said. "Let's find a reasonable spot to set up camp and hunker down. This storm is here to stay." After the previous night's conversation about being "on time," I was glad it was she who suggested we cut the day short.

"We'll make up the distance tomorrow," I said. "Just a couple miles, right?"

"Right," she answered.

Decision made; we selected a flat spot near where we stood. It was not the requisite one hundred feet from the trail, but we convinced ourselves this was a *minor* emergency and our transgression was forgivable. We were in a part of the forest that had burned fairly recently, so the ground was as much ash as it was dirt. By the time we finished, my arms and legs and clothes, but especially my hands, were streaked with soot. I dared not touch my face. We were a trio of Cinderellas.

It took a while, but we managed to crawl into the tent and its sidekick without bringing in too much ash. It was way too early to eat or sleep, so I read aloud. While the storm pummeled us, we laid back and distracted ourselves by once again visiting *The Devil in the White City*.

Voices approached. I paused reading. Cappy unzipped the tent, and we peered out to see who was still traveling in the rain.

I still wonder if I should have believed my eyes. Dressed in the brightest and most fashionable leisure clothing, more suitable to the yoga mat than the trail, three young women chatted happily as they passed us by—billed caps over their blond scrunchy-captured ponytails, tight spandex capris paired with snug pullovers, one colorful layer over the next, bright socks poking out the top of their boots. They were walking-and-talking rainbows—in vivid aqua, electric pink, and lime green. They could not have been more incongruent in that bleak and soggy place if they had been mounted on unicorns.

They were the second group of hikers who had walked unseeing past us that day. Had we become so immersed in the wilderness, shed so much of our civilized selves, that we blended in? Were we feral humans? Perhaps we had become as naturally camouflaged as that grouse had been in Grouse Meadow. Like the early afternoon's fast-walkers, these rainbow-clad women seemed not only unaware of our presence beside the trail, but of the entirety of the wilderness that surrounded them.

Starting Point — Lower Lake at Tree Line in Le Conte Canyon —10,400 feet
Ending Point — Palisades Creek just before Deer Meadow — 8,432 feet
Highest Point — Lower Lake at Tree Line in Le Conte Canyon —10,400 feet
Distance Covered — 9.0 miles
Cumulative Miles — 115.0 miles

Stairway To Heaven

Life ought to be a struggle of desire toward adventures
whose nobility will fertilize the soul.
~ Rebecca West, *The Young Rebecca*, 1982

Day Eighteen
August 5, 2006

Starting Point — Palisades Creek just before Deer Meadow — 8,432 feet

Dorothy's haunted forest in the Land of Oz had nothing on *our* haunted forest. Emerging from the tent, I half expected a flying monkey to pop out from behind the fire-blackened trunk of a dead tree. Fallen branches and small rocks were stained black. I picked my way towards what remained of trees, avoiding thin stems of the recovering brush, yet my clothes were streaked black by the time I finished my morning toilet. The more I brushed at my shorts, the more the black spread. Grimy fingernails and cuticles made my hands look like a car mechanic's.

Returning, I found Cappy armed with a comb, wrestling her hair into control. Her once-white shirt had become a canvas for an abstract charcoal drawing. She brushed a wisp of curl from her face, leaving a smudge across her cheek. Zoe emerged from her bedding, knees and shins streaked with gray. By the time the tent was deconstructed and packed away, we were a trio of chimney sweeps, sans chimneys.

"Let's eat breakfast after we get *out* of this place," Zoe suggested, stuffing her sleeping bag into her pack.

"Good idea." I was relieved by the thought of escape.

We bade adieu to the night's impromptu campground. It had served its sheltering purpose, allowing us to ride out the rain in dry tents but without beauty or ambiance. The storm was long gone, and the morning's gray skies were breaking up, leaving only a sparse scattering of clouds fleeing east across a blue sky.

"Keep a lookout for the Tin Man and the Cowardly Lion," Cappy said, as she stepped onto the narrow trail.

"Lions and tigers and bears! Oh, my!" I sang out, joining her.

"Oh, my!" Zoe smiled and shook her head.

If there had been room for us to walk two or three abreast, we might have linked arms to skip and sing "We're off to see the Wizard." But as the trail barely accommodated a single-file procession, I satisfied myself with humming the tune, which became a persistent earworm.

In a half-mile or so, the fire-scorched woods came to an abrupt end. Like a magic spell had been cast, the environment was transformed in an instant into an open meadow, lusciously green and spotted with wildflowers. Like time travelers, in one step we had moved from a grainy, black-and-white silent film into a Dolby Surround Sound, 3D, Technicolor blockbuster. A languid trickle of water snaked through the green with the tiniest of gurgles and splashes, beckoning us to sit down for breakfast and offering us water for our pumps.

While we ate, Cappy brought out the topo map, and the topic of The Golden Staircase bubbled to the top of our conversation. She placed her finger beside the spot where the bold line marking the JMT crossed a score of thin contour lines bunched so tightly together they looked like a smudge of black ink. It was as dramatic as a map can get, the equivalent of a flashing red light warning of radical elevation change. "The Staircase looks practically vertical," Cappy said.

"Remind me. What's the elevation change?" I prepped my mind for a big number and an arduous climb.

"It's about fifteen hundred feet of climbing," Cappy answered quickly. "Straight up."

"Look, practically every Trail Legend we've heard about turned out to be a dud," I said. "The river crossings, the waterfall crossing, the sun cups, the ninety-nine switchbacks, all of them. Why would this one be any different?" I watched Cappy.

"It's not that I think it's *going* to be bad," she explained. "There's the *potential* for it to be really bad." Cappy's ponytail of curls was wrapped into a bun, but the down of gray around her face had all sprung loose, and, backlit by the morning sun, it glowed like a silver halo.

"Hope for the best and prepare for the worst, right?" Zoe said.

"Right-eyo," I said. *Right out of the Boy Scout Manual*, I thought, approving.

Finished eating, I wiped the last vestiges of the haunted forest from my mind as I scrubbed the soot from my skin. Sacrificing one of my precious face-cleansing cloths, I meticulously cleaned under each fingernail and around each cuticle. As my hands regained their natural freckled tan, the white cloth turned black.

"Listen to what the guidebook says." Cappy read from Tom Winnett's book again, "'The steep, rocky switchbacks of the Golden Staircase, [are] built on the cliffs of the gorge of Palisade Creek. This section was the last part of the Muir Trail to be constructed, and it is easy to see why.'" She looked up at me. "It was the last built because it was a sheer, impassable cliff."[16]

"Cappy, we've climbed a lot of switchbacks. Why's this different?" Zoe asked.

---

[16] Thomas Winnett and Kathy Morey, *Guide to the John Muir Trail* (Wilderness Press, 1998) p. 38.

Zoe was always willing to engage with Cappy when she worried over the next challenge. She was way more patient than me. It is not that I did not worry, but I wanted to keep my anxiety in check until I was certain what I was up against.

"It's supposed to be a really hot and dry climb, very exposed, not sheltered by trees," Cappy re-explained what we had heard from hikers we had crossed paths with, who had all heard it from somebody, who had heard it from someone else.

She looked at me using water from my drinking system to wash my hands. "And there's no water source anywhere along the way, so we need to make sure we have full containers when we leave here." Cappy was stressed, and I wanted to avoid absorbing any of that energy.

I took a couple breaths before speaking again. "So far, the rumors and Trail Legends have been intimidating and overblown."

"I know, I know. I don't want to cry wolf—I just need to *feel* prepared." Cappy refolded the map and slipped it back into its pouch.

We headed off across the meadow, which grew thicker and more luxuriously tangled with each step. Grasses and flower-topped stems stretched for the sky, competing for the sun's rays. We had to push our way through the lush hip-, waist-, and sometimes shoulder-high jungle, like Hepburn and Bogart in *The African Queen*. We wound our way through the unkempt maze, keeping our noses pointed towards the line of trees ahead, ultimately arriving at the edge of the woods. There, in the shade, the trail settled itself down and escorted us through the cool, quiet forest.

We came to a halt. The wall known as The Golden Staircase loomed ahead. From where we stood admiring the obstacle at a comfortable distance, the trail seemed to disappear into solid rock, the switchbacks invisible on the rough vertical canyon wall. It was spectacular.

A vertical drapery of gold-colored granite rose from the base of the river valley clear into the sky, like a golden canvas where a fearless graffiti artist had risked life and limb to spray paint just a handful of hunter-green slashes to suggest solitary trees. The towering barrier was larger than life, larger than even the Trail Legend had suggested, "impossibly steep— dreadfully exhausting—"

Like Ali Baba stymied by a rock wall, we needed a magic phrase to provide a way through: "Open Sesame!"

It was midmorning when we began our ascent. The sun was climbing towards its zenith in a sky unmarked by clouds. I took the lead and set the pace at a slow and steady rhythm, using my hiking poles to help lift my body with each step. I had gotten efficient at this kind of climb.

"One, two, three, four—love, life, truth, beauty," I counted and chanted as I took deliberate steps up the ramped switchbacks.

The trail possessed an inherent beauty invisible from below. It was smooth and wide despite hanging like cantilevered shelves stacked one above the other on the cliff wall. Chiseled from the granite by craftsmen using the power of dynamite and the precision of mason's tools, it was both a marvel and a testament. It felt like we were climbing up the glowing walls of a majestic cathedral. The trail swept in graceful arcs back and forth across the rock, offering panoramic views that extended farther and wider with each new level. I wondered if this was what eagles saw when they flew in slow circles in these High Sierra valleys.

Though steep and strenuous, the way was far from impossible—neither was it dry and desolate. In many places water trickled down the face of the cliff, seeping out of cracks, and wandering along the trail where we placed our feet. The trail's narrow edges were lush with wildflowers and aromatic plants, mimicking the colorful parkways along a city sidewalk in the sky. The warm rays of the sun pulled moist aromas from the blooming plants. Sweet perfumes of flower nectar mixed with the sharp and spicy scents produced by aromatics.

I was pulled up the steep trail by my nose, moving from one flowering plant to the next, oblivious to the difficulty of the climb. More than once I paused to run my fingers along the feathery petals of the small plants. I broke leaves from a pale-green pennyroyal plant, with its sage-like fragrance and puffball flowers, and brought them to my nose.

We paused for our late-morning snack a third of the way up the Staircase, at a spot wide enough to allow us to sit three abreast against the rock wall that held up the next switchback. Before us hung a breathtaking panorama of the canyon where we had started the day.

Cappy surveyed the flowering plants that grew nearby as she bit into a Clif bar. "I wish Jane were here—she'd know the names of all these plants." We were able to agree on the identities of the bold red paintbrush and deep violet penstemon flowers and the compact pennyroyal aromatics, but there were others, like the familiar yellow blossom in Cappy's hand, for which we could conjure no names.

"This Golden Staircase is nothing like I expected." Zoe smiled. "It's beautiful! And there's so much water!" Her long legs were tucked under her body, and she cupped a handful of granola dotted with bright M&M's.

"Is this when I resist saying, 'I told you so'?" I chuckled and raised my eyebrows.

"I know," Cappy met my laugh with a smile and a shake of her head. "These aren't even the hardest switchbacks we've climbed."

"Either that, or we're just so much stronger they *seem* easier!" I suggested.

"They *are* pretty steep, and we're only part way to the top." Zoe pointed upward over her shoulder. "Don't jinx the climb by calling it easy!"

My own mood had climbed with every step up the trail. "Do you think this spot seems even more beautiful because this morning was so ugly, or is it really this amazing?"

"Is that a koan, like the tree falling in the woods?" Cappy answered.

"*I* think it's so beautiful because we timed our trek perfectly." Zoe wore a satisfied smile.

That was true. If we had left Tuolumne earlier in July, we would have been struggling through deep snow at all the higher elevations. A couple weeks later, the water and the flowers would have been dried up and gone.

"*Then* the Trail Legends would have been true." Cappy added the last word on the subject, then rose to resume the climb. I picked up a golden stone chip, thin like an arrowhead, to add to my pebble collection.

We continued upward, but rather than becoming "impossibly steep—dreadfully exhausting," it remained a heavenly climb through a garden. Successfully tackling an obstacle of that size and reputation builds confidence. I could feel myself swelling with the knowledge that I was strong alone, and we were even stronger together. There were more tests to come, certainly, but The Golden Staircase was iconic, almost as significant to me as bagging Mount Whitney would be.

Lunch placed us under one of the few trees that clung to the granite wall—a huge and ancient red-barked evergreen that towered like a sentry over a small patch of ground at the wide spot where the switchback reversed its course. In the lead, I had been eyeing that tree with its promise of shade and rest for twenty minutes of steep climbing, making it my goal to attain before I brought our little caravan to a halt for lunch. I kept telling myself, *Almost there. Almost there. Just a bit farther.*

After lunch, we laid back, feet propped up, for our afternoon siesta. Relaxed, we fell into a peaceful silence. I closed my eyes and listened to all the small noises, needles rustling in the moving air, insects buzzing around the aromatics, an occasional bird calling, and my own breathing.

After long restful minutes, Zoe whispered, "Do you realize, we haven't seen another human being this whole day?" Her cap lay across her eyes.

"You're right," Cappy said. She rearranged her legs and crossed her arms behind her head.

I rolled my mind back over memories of the day. "The last people we saw were those rather odd women who hiked past us in the rain last night."

Our pleasant silence resumed.

The high-pitched call of a hawk pulled my eyes toward the vast expanse of space beyond our Staircase. I searched the sky for the caller, hoping to see her in flight. An answering call, farther away, came a minute later. Then they, too, were quiet.

Looking back, many of my most memorable experiences come from stretches of the trail, like the Golden Staircase, where we had encountered no one, where we had the earth and the sky, the beauty, all to ourselves.

"How old do you suppose this grandmother tree is?" I wondered aloud, "Do you think it started growing here before or after they carved the trail?"

Cappy answered. "This section was built last, in the late Thirties. If the seed fell and began to grow the following spring, the tree would be, what, a little over sixty years old."

"Too big and old for that, right?" I ran my eyes from the fir's broad base, up its rough red bark, to where its highest branches probed the sky. "So, it must've been standing sentry right here while they were constructing the trail, and they maneuvered around it."

Zoe broke her silence, "I bet the guys who built these switchbacks sat right here and ate their lunch in our shady spot."

Years later, I learned that the red fir had been anointed with the apt scientific name *Abies magnifica*, because of its sheer magnificence. The tree that towered over our trailside lunch spot that day will live for hundreds of years and will still be encouraging and sheltering hikers on their heavenward climbs up the Golden Staircase for many generations to come.

When we crested the last of the golden switchbacks, we stood at the lip of the canyon and looked back the way we had come—toward the rows of peaks and ridges across the canyon and the valley floor far below—I felt euphoric, my confidence buoyed by our accomplishment.

Cappy and Zoe took photos from that vantage point, digitizing the scene for future reference. I watched camera-less, my cameras' batteries already dead. All I could do was attempt to absorb the beauty into my purely analog mind for my own future reference.

"Ladies, we've still got a lot of walking to do." Cappy tucked her camera safely away. The early, rainy stop of the previous afternoon had put us farther behind, so we still had quite a distance to cover.

The trail climbed gently through Palisades Canyon. Palisades Creek was full, flowing in the opposite direction but along the same general route as the JMT. We stopped climbing in a glacier-carved cirque surrounded by numerous peaks, several of them thirteeners. Down canyon, the way we had come, lay the two deep blue Palisades Lakes we had hiked past—up canyon stood the imposing mass of Mather Pass, which we would ascend first thing in the morning.

We set up camp amidst a scattering of angular rocks and boulders, erratics, about the same size as the tent. Apart from a thin rug here and there of hardy greenery, the environment was composed entirely of gray and silver rock and clear blue sky. The sharp thirteeners and their broad saw-tooth shoulders threw shadows across the granite floor. The stark landscape was magical and lunar, nearly devoid of color, yet it contained a myriad of shades between black and white.

Tent up, dinner eaten, water containers filled, we arrayed ourselves on slabs of granite still warm from the sun and watched as puffy clouds sailed across the sky and the sun sank behind the towering peaks.

"Cappy, how far did we walk today?" Zoe lay on her back, knees bent, head resting back on her hands. She had taken her hair out of its ponytail and it lay fanned about her head.

"About seven-and-a-half miles," Cappy answered. "Most of it uphill."

"A good day then," Zoe was satisfied.

"We made up some of that lost time." I rolled on my side to look at Cappy. "Was it enough?"

She turned her head my way. "We're still four or five miles behind schedule."

I nodded. "Good. That's only a few good hours of walking."

The problem was all about space and time. Passes needed to be tackled early in the day when we were fresh and the sun was not so high in the sky, rather than at the hot and tired end of the day. Mather Pass was set up perfectly to be our morning hurdle. Distance was important, but so was positioning ourselves. It was a little like billiards; it was great to bag one climb, sink one ball, but one needed to leave oneself in a good position to climb or sink the next to ensure a successful game.

"I find it interesting, all these Trail Legends. We have spent so much time worrying about the next monster challenge," I said. "There was the waterfall to walk through that really had us scared. And then, when we got there, it turned out to be almost easy and really fun."

"So true." Cappy joined my reminiscing. "Remember Evolution Creek and the handwritten sign on that stick: 'Abandon Hope All Ye Who Cross Here!' or some such warning. I wonder if someone ever really did get swept over that waterfall?"

"You just don't know what to believe. In any case, we sure have been fortunate. We seem to come upon each and every Trail Legend when it's done being legendary!" I said.

"Listen to the confidence in our voices." Cappy sat up. "We've overcome so much."

"And faced our fears," I said.

"Like crossing rivers on logs?" Zoe teased me.

"Yeah. Like that." I laughed, remembering how I had scooted across that big log on my butt.

The sun was long gone, but its last horizontal rays were painting the eastern mountains the cotton candy pink of alpenglow. Though the rock beneath me still held and radiated considerable warmth, the air above was growing chilly fast. I reluctantly rose from my granite chaise longue to don my evening layers—fleece pants and jacket, gloves and warm hat.

Turning back around, I spied the moon rising above the ridge the alpenglow had just vacated. "Look at that!" I pointed. "It's almost full, just one sliver missing."

My friends turned from their own layering processes and reacted in unison, "Wow!"

"What an amazing day," I said. "I give this one a perfect ten!"

"Yep. It's an A+ campsite on an A+ night." Cappy was smiling widely.

As evening drifted into night and the sky grew darker, the moon grew even brighter. Without city lights to interfere, without the thick curtain of a lower elevation atmosphere, the lunar face was spotlight bright, illuminating all the objects and surfaces around us. I would be able to read our bedtime story without the aid of my headlamp!

In the wee hours of the morning, I crept from my down cocoon and slid quietly out of the tent for my nightly pee. I had pulled on my jacket and fleece bottoms and wore my socks, half-dressed against the subfreezing cold. Though the moon was gone, my path away from the tent was vivid with starlight alone.

The Milky Way, a brilliant white line, curved like the stripe on a skunk's tail clear across the deep black of space. Rather than returning immediately to the warmth of my down bag, I stood in a pool of light, tipped my head back, and stargazed. At more than eleven thousand feet, standing alone in a black-and-white world made of granite, space, and light, I had the sensation that I was standing *in* the sky, not under it, one speck of light among the many. I felt at once both huge and infinitesimally small, a part of the universe and apart from the universe, integral and separate—a paradox, opposites both true. When meditating, I sometimes attain a sense of dissolving into, becoming one with, the space around me. That night, my eyes wide open and fully present, I felt that same sensation.

Starting Point — Palisades Creek just before Deer Meadow — 8,432 feet
Ending Point — Palisades Canyon, Past Upper Palisades Lake,
Just North of Mather Pass — 11,200 feet
Highest Point — Just North of Mather Pass — 11,200 feet
Distance Covered — 7.5 miles
Cumulative Miles — 122.5 miles

Climbing With Sisyphus

Wildness reminds us what it means to be human,
what we are connected to rather than what we are separate from.
~ Terry Tempest Williams, From "Statement before the Senate Subcommittee
on Forest & Public Lands Management," 1995

Day Nineteen
August 6, 2006

*Starting Point — Palisades Canyon, Past Upper Palisades Lake,
Just North of Mather Pass — 11,200 feet*

We had spent the morning climbing, climbing, and climbing some more. Switchback after switchback drew us upwards, through ever thinner and colder air, towards the top of twelve-thousand-foot Mather Pass.

Having surmounted one of the more challenging "landslide repairs" in the trail, I stood resting at the end of a switchback, drinking water, sucking on a Werther's candy, and waiting as Zoe and Cappy joined me. Though I liked to hike ahead in solitude for long stretches, it felt good to rejoin and reconnect with them. I managed the distance between us like a yo-yo string, extending the distance to my comfort limit, then pausing to pull it in tight, before extending and pausing, balancing my dual needs for independence and community.

"That rough spot was hard on my feet," Cappy said, "but the rest of me is feeling strong this morning." Her face was stretched into a satisfied smile. This was the second time in two days Cappy mentioned sore feet, yet it barely registered at the time. While Zoe and I had suffered early in the journey from a variety of sores and pains, Cappy had walked more than a hundred pain-free miles, so I did not give her feet any more thought.

"I don't like walking over scree. I have to really focus on my footing," Zoe said.

That, coming from the rock-climber, made me chuckle. "You and your pack are so tall you're probably more top heavy than we little people are."

I was getting chilly, despite the sun's steady rays, as my sweaty, resting body cooled down. A rising breeze added to the chill, so I turned to move on. I continued to lead our ascent, sticking to my rhythm and pace, using my arms and poles to help pull my body up the challenging slope and steadily eating up the distance to the top.

All of a sudden, the steep ramp ended, and I was standing on top of the pass. "As the crow flies," I had covered only a half-mile distance from the campsite, but as the switchback turns, I had walked almost a mile-and-a-half and climbed nearly a thousand feet. I took off my pack and stood to admire the infinite view, turning a slow circle, attempting to absorb its sheer size. Within that immense panorama stood several distinct peaks—thirteeners, even a couple of fourteeners—the only earth that reached higher than my twelve-thousand-one-hundred-foot vantage point atop Mather Pass.

I was perched above the spaces where eagles flew!

Oh, what a photographer could do with that view. If only. I shook my head to banish the lament and savored the measureless beauty.

My reverie was interrupted when I heard Cappy arrive with a shout. "Amazing! Did you see this? A Sierra primrose! I can't believe it." She was pointing at flowers!

It was hard to believe anything could grow there, at over twelve-thousand feet in the air, unprotected from sun and wind, rain and snow. There was no soil, no dirt, just a thin layer of decomposed granite settled into cracks and sheltered at the base of rocks. Yet, there they were, tucked into a crevice on the crest of Mather Pass, the bright pink Sierra primrose, bold five-petaled flowers, standing an inch above a supporting green-gray mat.

"A little garden in the sky!" Cappy tossed aside her pack and squatted down for a closer look.

I had walked right past it, but once she pointed it out, I spied several other patches of the tiny primroses hiding in plain sight. They stood dwarfed by the outsized rock on which they grew—the giant mountain we stood atop, granite gray all around, poking into a clear sky that was everywhere blue.

"On a clear day, you can see forever," I said. Though I knew it ended at some distant horizon, the three-hundred-sixty-degree view appeared infinite.

We had Mather Pass entirely to ourselves. Not a soul was there when we arrived, and no one interrupted our high-altitude morning snack break. But before we began the south-face descent and just as we had begun to pose for the requisite mountaintop portraits, a father-son team popped up from the north side, the same way we had come.

"Hey! Welcome to the top of the world," Cappy called the moment their heads were visible. Already on our feet, we waited as they strode our way.

"Good morning. I'm Jeff," said the older of the two. "My son, Mark." He indicated the younger man with a nod of his head, then extended his hand. We greeted one another with the warmth of good trail friends.

Jeff was in his mid-forties, a decade younger than Cappy and me, and his son twenty-something, younger than Zoe. Both men were tall, certainly over six feet, and athletically slender. They wore the standard trail attire and carried the universal gear.

Before they offloaded their packs, I asked, "Would you mind taking our group picture? Then we could take yours."

Mark used both Cappy's and Zoe's cameras to capture us as we posed, packs on, poles poised, backs to the vast northern panorama, faces shielded by hat brims and sunglasses.

"You doing the whole JMT?" Zoe asked, as we traded spots.

The men replied while they posed and I took their photo. "Yep. I wrangled a month's vacation, and Mark's on summer break from the university. Been planning this for a year. Figured it might be the last chance to get Mark all to myself for a while." He cast a warm smile his son's way.

"Where're you from?" Cappy asked. "Not California." We were ready to start down, but it had been days since we had been with people long enough to talk, and I think we were all hungry for conversation and new stories.

"Minnesota originally," said Mark. "I'm in school at Northwestern—Chicago area—and think that's where I'll stay." He was out of his pack and already pulling out food and water while we talked. If we had to eat three-thousand calories a day to keep our little bodies going, I assumed a "growing lad" like Mark might have to double that on a trek like this.

"He's turned into a city boy," said his father. "His mother and I have trouble getting him back home to visit. This trip, I have him trapped, all to myself, and it's wonderful. Bonding time." He looked at Mark, obviously teasing him. His son blushed a bit and smiled, his mouth already full.

"We used to do Boy Scouts together, when we were both much younger," Jeff said. *He carries himself like one of my son's old Scoutmasters*, I thought, *calm and confident*. It was not difficult to picture him standing erect in his old khaki uniform and broad-brimmed hat. "But it's been a long time. I wanted to recapture some of that sense of adventure together."

"Just like in the olden days," Mark interjected with a generous smile. He was obviously a willing participant in his own kidnapping and seemed to be very at ease in the wilderness, his "city boy" transformation not entirely complete.

I thought about the myriad reasons that people put their lives on hold in order to take on the long, challenging adventure of hiking the John Muir Trail—to conquer the physical challenge or witness the natural beauty, to sink into the solitude or discover spiritual meaning, to escape life's responsibilities or simply enjoy the romantic adventure of the journey. I would have to add bonding time to my list.

I believed Cappy was on the trail for the beauty and the adventure, completing the JMT having been a goal of hers since the Sixties. Zoe reveled in the physical challenges of the trek. I was less sure of my own aspirations, as they seemed to be evolving with the miles. Before we had embarked, it was both the allure of the adventure and the promise of a healing spiritual experience that called me to the trail. During the first rough days on the JMT, however, the physical and emotional challenges of the trail were all I could focus on. Once those dragons had been bested, I had been able to immerse myself into the natural beauty and the solitude, allowing them to work on my wounded spirit. Maybe I was on the trail for *all* the reasons on that list.

Before we bade the pair farewell and slipped over the edge, Cappy pointed out the colorful primroses she had discovered. They oohed and aahed, and waved goodbye, though with their long strides and youth, they were sure to pass us by soon.

I led us over the rim of the pass, my nose pointed south—hiking poles fully extended, muscles and mind newly rested—onto the steep downward trail.

The climb down into Upper Basin was markedly different from the climb up the north slope, through a different set of ecosystems owing to the south-facing alignment. It began dry and dusty, desert-like. Every step kicked up a little cloud of white decomposed granite dust, making the back of my legs gray with a gritty powder.

The granite path felt precariously steep under foot, and the thin layer of dust and pea-sized gravel on the stone underfoot was like walking on ball bearings. My feet wanted to skid out from under me and send me to my butt. I placed my poles with purpose before each mincing step—if my strides stretched too long, my pack and I would be doing the splits. Once during that descent, my mind wandered for a moment to the stark lunar landscape around me, and I found my arms windmilling and my feet doing a soft-shoe to keep myself upright. I stopped in place. *Breathe*, I told myself, willing the pace of my pounding heart to slow. *Focus, focus*, I commanded. *You do not want to fall.*

An ironic image popped into my mind as I stood looking back up to the pass and then forward into the basin. Climbing eleven- and twelve-thousand-foot passes, the milestones that marked our way along the JMT, we were manifesting a Sisyphean challenge. We were like poor Sisyphus of Greek legend, who was condemned for eternity to push his boulder to the peak of a mountain before falling back down and having to start again. Like him, we pressed our way up the north face of each pass, pushing and pulling ourselves up endless switchbacks. Then, hiking poles at the maximum setting to prevent a slide, we rolled ourselves and our burdens back down to the bottom to start anew. Each of us was doomed to repeat the endless exercise of lifting and toting ourselves and our load skyward, only to tumble back down to Earth before starting the process all over again at the next pass. The analogy and its imagery made me giggle, washing away the last vestiges of the fear that had gripped me when I had almost fallen on the marbles.

My partners approached, heads down, concentrating on their own measured steps. So many times in the last ten days, I had paused and watched them approach, sometimes ascending a slope, sometimes descending switchbacks, sometimes crossing a broad flat meadow, always under the weight of their packs. The daily effort of hefting heavy loads up and over several mountain passes was molding their bodies and gaits. Cappy's calf muscles bulged and flexed with each step, clearly defined beneath her short hiking skirt. Zoe's bare arms were tan, her biceps contracting and releasing as she worked her hiking poles in support of her legs.

The story of Sisyphus is supposed to represent the futility of persisting at doomed endeavors. Our version of the tale was the opposite of futile, the opposite of doomed. We made progress every day, in miles crossed, in passes bagged, and in the transformation of our visibly stronger bodies.

We gathered for a moment on the trail to compare our slip-n-slide experiences and grab a gulp or two of water. With her hiking pole dangling from its loop on her wrist, Cappy pointed far across the basin below us to where the trail would carry us to the next pass.

"From Mather, at almost twelve-thousand-one-hundred feet, we're headed down to where we'll cross the South Fork of the Kings River. That's at about ten thousand feet," she instructed. Zoe and I looked where she pointed across the valley. "Then we'll start back up again. We'll stop tonight at Lake Marjorie, at about eleven thousand feet. Then tomorrow morning, first thing, we'll be set to go up and over Pinchot Pass, which is only a bit taller than Mather, twelve-thousand-one-hundred-and-thirty feet. Isn't that amazing!" Cappy's eyes shone.

I attended to her words and gestures with one half of my brain, so the other half was free to concentrate on my feet and my balance. Simply standing on the steep gravel-strewn trail required my focus.

"Eleven to twelve to ten to eleven, all in one day! That's something!" said Zoe.

I looked back and up to see a small cloud of dust hovering over the path just below the pass. "I think we're being pursued," I said, shifting everyone's focus towards the mountain we had left behind.

The white cloud with two dark dots at its center appeared to be rolling down the trail and was making good time. Father and son would be striding past us on their long legs quite soon.

As we descended, bits of vegetation began to appear along the trail, hardy plants, low to the ground, fewer than we had encountered at the same elevation on the north side. Lower still, we strode through meadows with stunted trees and meandering streams. In the lowest parts of the basin, we crossed the South Fork of the Kings River and numerous feeder streams. Around them, lush meadows spread out, wildflowers bloomed, birds and squirrels traded songs and calls.

We stopped for a long lunch break when we came across a collection of flat granite slabs in the middle of one of those broad green meadows. We took that lunch break seriously, readying ourselves for the afternoon climb.

"I think the JMT Diet is working," I said. I was sitting cross-legged and munching with abandon. I'd taken off my hat, my boots, and my long-sleeved shirt. I was down to tank top, shorts, and socks, my daily napping attire.

"What do you mean?" Zoe asked. She glanced up from munching turkey jerky. Her hat and boots were off, too.

"In the early spring, Cappy and I attended a talk at the local community college about the JMT, given by a couple who'd done it," I told her. "They shared their photos and their stories. They used the term JMT Diet to describe how, no matter how much they ate and ate and ate, they each still lost weight on the trail."

"I think she lost twenty pounds, and he lost ten, or vice versa," Cappy added from her corner of the polished granite slab.

"I think it's working, because my hiking shorts are really loose around my waist." I used my thumb to pull the waistband out from my hip. "In fact, they're so loose I don't even have to unsnap them to slip them down when I pee!" I laughed.

"If my pack's hip belt weren't strapped around them, I think they'd fall off while I walked."

"Really, Joan!" Cappy laughed with me. "My shorts are pretty loose, too. I won't be able to keep up this exercise regimen when I get home, though, so I'll have to slow down the eating."

"Not now, though," Zoe said. "I'm always hungry. It's like I can't ever get really full." She punctuated her statement by taking a predatory bite of jerky.

Descent finished, it was time to lug our loads up the next ridge. Goodbye, Mather. Hello, Pinchot. The lower part of the ascent to Pinchot Pass climbed through thick forest on the north-facing ridge. Switchback after switchback in the shade of the trees carried us uphill at a snail's pace. Near timberline, the trees shrank in size and number to be replaced by alpine meadows dotted with small lakes and ponds and filled with scattered erratics. The trail kept rising, wandering back and forth through one meadow after another.

The sky was clear, the green carpet decorated with a rainbow of wildflowers. Trickles of water—rills and rivulets—crossed and re-crossed the meadows. The sounds of moving water mixed with the shush of the breeze through the grasses and shrubs. Ponds glistened. The occasional marmot lay sunbathing on a rock. Birds called.

The afternoon climb, designed to put us in a perfect spot to start the final climb up to Pinchot Pass, was challenging. I was growing tired when I arrived at the wide, shallow lake well ahead of the other two. I remembered, from Cappy's earlier description, that it bore a woman's name. Was it Monika? Marie? No, we had passed Marie Lakes days back. Maybe it was Marguerite. Margaret? Something like that, I was sure.

Lake What's-Her-Name sat center stage in her own terrace. Water gurgled deep-throated in narrow channels, crisscrossing her emerald meadow in maze-like geometric patterns. Very narrow, just a few inches across, each straight stripe of water could be crossed with a single stride. Peat dyed the water in the thin channels a burnished bronze.

Ahead, the trail wended its way up yet another long, steep route, which we would surely be tackling in the morning. Looking back the direction I had come, the meadow resembled an emerald tabletop, its edge straight and sharp as a knife's, above it only empty pale sky.

I had been sitting for ten minutes or so when the miniature silhouettes of my trail partners appeared above the edge of that green horizon. First came their hats and heads, then torsos made broad and square by their packs, and finally their booted feet. They arrived a few minutes later at my side, panting and exclaiming over the terrace's beauty.

"Isn't this amazing?" I said.

"The water changes color depending on which direction you look." Cappy pointed first left then right. "This way it's golden, and that way it's black." She began unbuckling her straps to let her heavy pack down.

"Look back to the north," I said. "It's like we're perched on the edge of a flat world."

Zoe set her huge pack next to mine and turned the direction I pointed. "It reminds me of the *Lord of the Rings* movie, so uber-natural. Doesn't it look like someplace where you'd run into elves and hobbits on the trail?"

"Maybe we should be on the lookout for trolls," I laughed. Beginning to feel rested, I was eager to set up camp.

I stood up from my stone resting spot and walked a few paces towards the eastern edge of the meadow, where the flat ground was fractionally higher and drier, and said, "Don't you think this is the perfect spot for our tent?"

Cappy, who had been scanning our surroundings, turning this way and that, stopped, turned to face me directly. "This is *not* Lake Marjorie, Joan." She spoke with the authority of absolute, scientific fact, like she was talking about gravity, like she had said, "Rocks fall *down*, Joan. Not up."

"Our campsite is another mile or so up that hill," she added, pointing to the gray granite trail leading skyward towards the treeless heights of the next mountain pass. There was no doubt in her voice.

My heart sank. My body sagged at the thought of another mile, all of it obviously uphill.

"So what lake is this, then?" I quizzed. It was the best I could do in challenging Cappy to prove her much greater and better-labeled knowledge of the trail and its landmarks. I was tired and disappointed, and I did not want to hike any farther.

"It's just some nameless lake," Cappy said, sweeping away my question with a careless gesture. She sat on the rock where I had recently rested and began to fish around in her bag for a snack.

Knowing any challenge of Cappy's trail knowledge would be futile, I swallowed my disappointment. I waved towards the water, "Goodbye Lake What's-Her-Name. Lake Marjorie, here we come," then grabbed my pack and turned to go.

"Are you leaving? We just got here," Cappy stopped digging in her bag to look at me and frown.

I turned my head to look over my shoulder at her. "Yep. I'll see you at the campsite. I'm tired. All I want to do is get to where I can stop," I said before heading up the trail. I knew I was being a pill, but I did not have an ounce of energy to waste on patience. I would need it all to get up that hill.

Looking back, the irony is clear. I was doing to Cappy exactly what she'd done to me on the way to Muir Hut. Abandoning. But at the time, I was sure I was in the right both times.

One mile. I can do that in a half hour, I assured myself.

"Even uphill," I insisted, speaking aloud now that I was alone.

I mustered my energy. "I will be at Lake Marjorie in thirty minutes," I said again, just to make sure I had heard myself.

"At least I'm in the shade," I whispered.

I shook my head, turned my mental dial to my climbing mantra, and focused on my steps. "One, two, three, four. Love, life, truth, beauty, abundance, and peace—" Arms and poles swung to complement feet and legs. Boots pressed the earth, poles pulled through space. "—five, six, seven, eight. Love, life, truth, beauty, abundance, and peace."

Without warning, the forest ended.

I stopped counting—and chanting—and walking.

The space in front of me opened up to another beautiful meadow dotted with more beautiful wildflowers, dominated by yet another beautiful lake, fed by more beautiful meandering trickles and streams.

Can one become immune to beauty? My eyes were tired, over stimulated by colors and shapes, light and dark. One view eclipsed the last. I was losing the ability to appreciate each individual gorgeous object, each stunning scene. Beauty was becoming like white noise, drowning out my comprehension.

Maybe I needed vitamin A to restore my vision. Maybe I needed to close my eyes to rest them. Maybe I needed sleep in order to replenish the chemicals in my retinas that registered greens and blues. That day, that week, I had used them all up. Maybe in the morning I would have a new supply.

Assuming I had found the *real* Lake Marjorie and not another imposter, I located a lovely place to set up camp. There was a small ledge east of the lake, almost like a royal dais, looking out over Marjorie and her meadow.

Waiting, I lay back on my pad, closed my eyes, and took deep breaths, recalibrating my attitude. I let my impatience float out into the sky with each breath, my frustration drip into the earth as my muscles relaxed.

I was awakened when I heard Cappy and Zoe call my name from just steps away. That little nap had both energized and quieted me. I sat up and smiled a greeting. "What do you think of putting our tent on this shelf?"

"It's perfect," Cappy said. She removed her pack and was digging out the tent-half she carried.

The joke was on us. The next morning, we would walk a quarter-of-a-mile before discovering we had not actually spent the night at Lake Marjorie after all, but on the shore of another imposter, another nameless tarn. Even Cappy had been fooled by her own wishful thinking, allowing us to stop just short of our intended destination. We would laugh at our mistake and decide it came with a purpose, for we made an inspiring new friend at the second Faux Lake Marjorie.

Zoe strung a clothesline between the tent and a small tree. I carried only two each of underwear, sports bra-tank tops, and hiking socks, and needed to "freshen up" one of each. This leg of the hike—between Muir Ranch and our packhorse meetup—was longer than previous legs, so my clothes needed to be washed and dried along the way. And I would not be able to just mail home the dirty ones when new ones arrived.

In addition to my water bottle, I carried a small, collapsible fabric bowl, about eight inches in diameter, that I filled with water from the lake. I used a biodegradable soap, but it did not please me to put my dirt or the chemicals into the lake, so I carried it all several long strides away from the lake's edge. I sat on a small rock stool on a broad glacial-polished slab of granite to do laundry.

"Pull up a seat," I said to Zoe, who had strolled over with her own dirty clothes and water containers.

"Don't mind if I do." She folded her long legs to sit down and spread her clothes out beside her.

"You can use my bowl when I'm finished." My socks soaked in soapy water while I twisted the water from my tank top. "It's so chilly—I don't think everything is going to dry tonight, so I'm only doing half my stuff."

"Nothing worse than hiking in wet panties!" Zoe agreed.

"You doing laundry, Cappy?" I asked. "Or going for a swim?"

"It's too cold even for me," she said, carrying her water our direction. "It's not late, but I'm just about ready for another layer." She set her armload down in our makeshift laundry room and went to retrieve her jacket.

I rinsed my socks and passed the soapy bowl towards Zoe. Then I hung my wet clothes on the line by the tent. I was just retrieving my jacket and fleece pants from my pack when I heard a male voice call out, "Hello, neighbors!"

I turned to see a mature gentleman, older than Cappy and my fifty-something, dressed in JMT fashion standards—khaki hiking pants (the kind that can be reduced to shorts with the zip of a zipper), a moss green shirt, and hiking boots—standing at the edge of our little dais campsite.

"Permission to enter?" He wore a wide, genial smile.

"Permission granted," Cappy answered.

She and Zoe stood. I slipped on my jacket and walked over to greet our visitor. Other than the father and son Scouts at the top of Mather Pass, we had not seen anyone to talk to for days, making him a welcome sight.

"Name's Bob." He entered the campsite proper. His handshake was a warm, firm grasp that matched his smile.

"Nice little spot you have here. Where do you all hail from?" he asked. "Which way are you headed?" We filled in our answers, then followed with all the expected trail queries.

In his sixties, Bob had a gray fringe of hair surrounding a balding pate. Bushy white eyebrows bounced above his pale eyes as he talked, and a multitude of laugh lines stretched and relaxed in an animated way as he told his stories. And a storyteller he was.

"It's certainly cocktail hour by now. I wish we had a nice bottle of Naggiar Sangiovese to share, but we can only offer you a rock to sit on so we can visit for a bit." I gestured towards our little oasis on the dais.

We circled around and sat on stones to share our stories. My lament about having no wine prompted Bob to tell a trail tale from his younger years. It seems that he and his buddies used to carry full bottles of wine and a corkscrew into the backcountry. "That'd add too much weight to my pack for me to do that now," he said. "I was much stronger and crazier then!" Again, that chuckle. He had us all laughing.

It turned out that Bob had hiked the JMT several times. "In fact, I try to do it every summer," he said. "Though I don't know how many more times I'm going to be able. Every year I wonder if it will be my last. Then I tell myself, 'Just one more time, one more time.' I'll eventually be reduced to just doing small pieces of it." His laugh was contagious.

What an inspiration, I thought. *I hope I'll be as healthy and strong as Bob ten years from now, so I can continue to hike and camp in the Sierra in my sixties.*

When I described where Cappy and I lived, he said, "Then we really are neighbors! I live in wine country, too, over in Sonoma."

"It's a small world after all," I chanted more than sang.

It was such a comfortable domestic scene—companionable conversation with company on the front porch, laundry drying on the line out back, dinner waiting in the kitchen.

"This has been delightful, but it must be supper time, and I best be going." Bob rose. "We must do this again next year," he said, tipping his make-believe hat, and heading off the front porch towards his own home next door. He disappeared into the high-altitude twilight behind a small copse of trees, and, as he was heading north and we south, we would never see Bob again.

Starting Point — Palisades Canyon, Past Upper Palisades Lake,
Just North of Mather Pass — 11,200 feet
Ending Point — Lake Marjorie — 11,132 feet
Highest Point — Mather Pass — 12,077 feet
Distance Covered — 8.8 miles
Cumulative Miles — 131.3 miles

Golden Touch

I felt my lungs inflate with the onrush of scenery—
air, mountains, trees, people.
I thought, "This is what it is to be happy."
~ Sylvia Plath, *The Bell Jar*, 1963

Day Twenty
August 7, 2006

Starting Point — Lake Marjorie — 11,132 feet

I do not know if the landscape had actually grown more magnificent every day or if my eyes had recovered overnight from their overawed immunity to beauty, but this day seemed like the most beautiful I had ever experienced. Once again, the profusion of color, of light and shadow, registered in my happy brain.

Sapphire blue lakes sparkled in golden cirques. Wildflowers splashed rainbows all along the path's fringes. A breeze made the small grasses and dwarfed shrubs dance. And our footpath zig-zagged its way in and out and around the gold-tinged rocks, sparking pools, pale green shrubs and swaths of small flowers—all the while heading ever upward.

The climb to Pinchot Pass was entirely different from any other. This mountain had been molded of a golden metamorphic stone that glowed in the sun. The rock, which broke and crumbled easily, had disintegrated into a thin layer of soil that held more moisture, so even at eleven thousand feet, vegetation grew along the trail.

Switchbacks swept left and right, lifting us towards the top of the twelve-thousand-ninety-foot pass and taking us past numerous small lakes and ponds. Ribbons of snowmelt, often mistaking the trail for a streambed, meandered downward as we took steady steps upward. Grasses, sedges, shrubs, and wildflowers galore, finding comfort in numbers, populated the mountainside and the trail's boundary wherever the soil had accumulated and there was even the smallest protection from the wind.

The passes were growing taller as we walked southward. Of the seven passes along the Muir Trail that stretched above eleven thousand feet, today's Pinchot was our fifth. In the next few days, we would be surmounting the final two—Glen Pass and the tallest of them all, Forester Pass, which measured over thirteen thousand feet. The passes soared higher and higher, and so did our strength and endurance.

We'd climbed quite high when I came around a bend in the trail to an unexpected sight. A string of horses was making its way down from the pass and coming our way. First, I paused, thinking I would wait for my hiking companions, who were a few minutes behind me, to catch up. But, where I stood, the trail was narrow and would *not* be a good spot to cross paths with the pack train. I did not want to be standing on the outside, the open cliff side, of the switchback when they passed, but neither did I want to be squeezed against the wall on the inner side of the trail by the passing animals.

I am not particularly fond of horses. To be truthful, they scare me. I find them huge and intimidating, so I wanted as much distance as possible between them and me. This journey had brought me face-to-face with a number of my fears, those I had known I had—lightning and crossing water on logs—and some I had not realized I possessed—walking through waterfalls and crossing steep snowfields. I had faced them all with varying levels of grace and discovered I was braver than I realized. In having to share the trail with a string of horses, I was unexpectedly gifted with yet another opportunity to face something that frightened me.

I surveyed the path ahead, looking for a wide spot that offered enough space for me to step aside and let the packhorses pass safely. Twenty yards ahead, the trail wrapped itself around the remnants of an old landslide. Several gaps had been created where the fallen rock met the footpath, small alcoves alongside the trail where the three of us could stand aside and let the creatures take their right-of-way.

Cappy and Zoe found me waiting for them in one of those rocky alcoves. They had been eyeing the horses, too, and noticed I had stopped walking so hurried to join me where I stood. The horses had disappeared for a moment behind a rocky outcropping that hid a section of the trail ahead.

When they re-emerged, they were quite close, kicking up dust as they trotted rapidly along. The first and last horses in the string carried female riders. Between them, five sturdy animals were laden with boxes and canvas bags—one strapped to either side and one centered atop—that swayed with each step the horses took. Their steps, sounding like metal on rock, were out of rhythm with one another, so they moved forward, swaying and lurching in a random pattern. The horses bunched together, heads overlapping tails, feet finding purchase on the rock-strewn trail.

The first woman barely acknowledged us with a curt nod. The other raised her hand and offered a quick, "Thanks." Neither smiled. Each sat erect in her saddle, a broad-brimmed hat on her head and dark glasses hiding her eyes. They clicked and talked to their mounts, urging them to hurry. In moments, they were out of sight.

Where were they headed? Why were they rushing their animals? Like other long-distance travelers, we were planning to meet a pack horse in a couple of days, and pack trains kept numerous out-of-the-way ranger stations and backcountry camps stocked with supplies, so it was hardly unusual to encounter packhorses in the backcountry. What struck me as odd was their intensity, their effort to hurry. It was a heavily loaded train, carrying lots of supplies—the kind of regular load scheduled well in advance. So why the rush? The encounter left me wondering.

We climbed higher and higher, leaving all but the hardiest little plants and colorful patches of lichen behind. At that altitude—nearly twelve thousand feet— we were wrapped in the peaceful silence of space. Save for the wind and ourselves, there was nothing to make a noise. Just as there was no sound, there was no smell, only the pristine odorless scent of air—clear and clean.

Despite the steep climb, I did not need to downshift into my climbing mantra nor will myself up the hill. I simply placed one foot in front of the other, over and over again. Suddenly, I found myself popping up among the rocks at the top of the pass, like one of the Sierra pikas that populated the high country poking its head out of its rocky tunnel.

Pinchot Pass could have been mistaken for a castle at twelve-thousand-ninety- feet. Piles of gold-hued scree—made from shattered metamorphic rock and the oddly shaped pieces of unbroken rock that remained standing—resembled castle turrets ringed by ramparts. Wind poured over the top of the pass, shockingly cold, so the first thing I did was dig out warm garments and begin layering them—fleece jacket, gloves, and hat, windbreaker, too.

"Brrrrr!" Cappy, then Zoe, joined me at the top. They quickly pulled on outer layers, and we hunkered down, using the castle's defensive features for shelter. The panorama was complete, a full three-hundred-sixty-degree, horizon-to-horizon view of the world below and beyond. I munched on a Clif Bar, my eyes surveying the northern view. Mather Pass stood tall on the far side of the lake-dotted basin we had crossed the day before.

"Good news and bad news," Cappy began. Leaning back on the castle wall, she was munching on handfuls of homemade granola, rich with nuts and dried fruit.

"I'll bite," I laughed. "Start with the good news." Zoe and I pulled our gazes from the view to concentrate on Cappy.

"No more climbing today. We just climbed over a thousand feet in two miles, and we made really good time." Cappy smiled. Her golden-brown eyes, hidden by dark glasses, were undoubtedly sparkling. I shared her pride of accomplishment.

"At this rate, we might just make up all our lost time soon." I knew that made Cappy very happy, but still could not get excited about making up lost time. In fact, I rather liked the idea of stealing extra time in order to return late.

"And—? That bad news?" Zoe asked.

"The next leg of the trail is going to be a different kind of challenge."

"How so?" I asked.

"Tonight's campsite is at eighty-five hundred feet. We're sitting at over twelve thousand right now," Cappy let the difference sink in.

"Whoa! We have to drop almost four thousand feet today?" I took off my hat and studied her face.

"Almost. It's closer to thirty-six-hundred, actually," Cappy said. "It's going to be tough on Zoe's hips and your ankle. We'll need to take plenty of breaks along the way." I knew she was worried about Zoe's abrasions—they were always exacerbated by downhill marches.

Zoe, the youngster, spoke. "That's a lot of pounding on the old joints." She was smiling, trying to make light of the potential problems.

"Do you have anything to pad your hips?" I asked Zoe. "I'm going to retie my bootlaces, to keep my toes from getting jammed into the tips of my boots." I began to unknot the laces.

"I'm glad we're not doing this hike NOBO, or we'd be *climbing* up those thirty-six-hundred feet instead," Cappy said. "I'm going to re-lace my boots, too."

Zoe stood, stretching her long body, twisting, turning, and reaching upward, taking the measure of the tender new skin stretched across her hips.

"Show me what you're doing there." Zoe sat down beside me.

I demonstrated, and she started to change her own lacings.

"How are your hips and shoulders? Do you have anything to pad them with?" I repeated.

"They're lots better, but this worries me a bit." she said. "I think I'm going to try padding my hips with my extra socks."

"Clever idea."

Woods Creek Basin, south of Pinchot Pass, was massive—a deep and long valley curving south and east from our lofty height. The rocky trail ahead crept down through talus slopes similar to those on the north side before opening up into broad meadows. Expansive forests carpeted the basin's distant floor. Hidden from view, Woods Creek and its tributaries flowed through the heart of the basin.

We took off down the hill, grouped together for the first couple switchbacks. Long poles, careful foot placement, and total concentration made the walk very quiet, save for the rhythmic clicking and scratching sounds of poles and boots on stone. I could not look up while I walked. The tight switchbacks were littered with rock fragments that could easily trip up an unobservant hiker. Instead, I stopped frequently for short moments to satisfy my need to take in my surroundings. If I had had a camera, I would have called them Kodak Moments.

When the switchbacks began to lose their steepness, the trail left the naked rock to sweep through one alpine meadow after another. Occasionally, sandy talus fields from old landslides interrupted the meadows. The trail crossed myriad rivulets, all running downward with us and rambling among the meadows' erratics and wildflower patches.

After a couple of miles and more than a thousand-foot drop, I stopped in a lush field of grass carved into geometric patterns by crisscrossing, golden streamlets. My feet had been complaining for a half-mile; the balls of my feet and the pads of my big toes burned. *Are blisters forming again?* The water called out to those tender spots, so before Zoe and Cappy could catch up, I pulled off my boots, socks, the protective layers of tape, and plunged my feet into that liquid gold. I wiggled my toes and flexed my ankles, making circles in the gilt water. I would not have been surprised had I heard the hiss of flames being extinguished by the cool water.

"Don't you want to rest in the shade?" Cappy asked when she arrived. I am sure I looked like I was planning to stay awhile, my pack tossed to one side, shoes off, eyes closed in pure pleasure. I had long since removed my jacket and was thinking about abandoning long sleeves as well.

"Normally I'd say yes, but it's not exactly hot," I said, "and this water feels too amazing to leave." I was reclining on my back, looking straight up at both her and Zoe silhouetted against the sky.

"I'd highly recommend it. It might be magic water. My feet were on fire—now they're only smoldering. A little more time, and they just might be healed and ready to keep on trekkin'." I laughed, but I was close to serious.

"I could *use* some magic." Zoe promptly dropped her pack, sat down, and began to unlace her shoes. "I don't know how it will help my hip, but I'll take whatever I can get."

"You're outnumbered." I smiled at Cappy. "Join us."

She hesitated a second, then had to admit the water had restorative properties and might've been enchanted.

"See how golden the water looks? I think that's where it gets its magical powers," I teased. "Zoe, you should baptize your hips with it."

An hour later, as we packed up again, Cappy said, "We're still over fifteen miles from where we need to meet the packhorse." Anxiety clipped her words like it always did when she talked deadlines and destinations. She pushed the long sleeves of her once-white shirt up to her elbows and pressed her lips together into a fine line.

"We still have the rest of today, all of tomorrow, and the following morning," I said lightly, determined to avoid absorbing any of the nervous energy she projected. "Don't you think that's do-able?" I turned to face the path, ready to move on from both the magic water and our conversation's topic.

My pack on, I tightened the hip belt and chest strap, a process that had become so automatic I barely needed to think about it. During the first days of our trek, I had had to search through several pack-pockets every time I needed to find an object. It had taken focused attention and several moments to get my pack's straps adjusted just right each time I donned it. But by Day Twenty, I could find anything quickly, knew precisely in which pocket and how deep to dig. And I could pull on my pack and be properly adjusted and ready to hit the trail in just a few seconds. I was definitely becoming *one* with my meager possessions and my pack.

"I think we can," said Cappy. "I think we'll get there in time. But we have to keep moving." Her agreeable words did not exactly jibe with the anxiety that leaked out through her voice.

"You sound like 'The Little Engine That Could'! 'I think we can, I think we can—'" I laughed and stepped onto the trail, cutting the discussion short. She could worry with every step if she chose, but I intended to return to my little bubble of walking bliss.

Woods Creek Basin had *looked* gigantic from the top of Pinchot Pass that morning, stretching way off into the distance before disappearing under a dark canopy of trees made minuscule by the distance. By the afternoon, it *felt* gigantic, too. We had been walking for hours and still had miles to go before we slept. The scenery all around was stunning. The meadows gave way to thick forest with a deep shade that kept us cool during the heat of the afternoon.

And still the trail kept taking us down. I wrote in my journal that night that "we walked—up and down and up and down, but mostly definitely down." Below nine thousand feet, manzanita and chaparral scrub brush replaced the forests, making the trail dusty once more. Without tree cover, it was suddenly a hot, dry August afternoon.

What we had not seen while under cover of the woods were the cliffs that rose behind and on either side of us all along the length of the wide canyon. When we emerged from the shadows, the towering cliffs stood as tangible proof of the distance we had come. That morning, we had stood at the top looking down, and now we gazed upward from the bottom. The imposing walls rose over three thousand feet above our heads.

On entering the valley floor, we crossed an invisible boundary and reentered civilization's fringe. An easily accessible entry point to the heart of the Sierra brought weekend campers and casual day-hikers in from California's Central Valley to the west, so the JMT and the several small cross-trails were teeming with all manner of humans. Old and young, in singles and pairs, parades and swarms, families towing children, all played Follow The Leader into Sequoia-Kings Canyon National Park. Like Wood's Creek, which had grown with the contributions from its many tributaries, the trail population swelled at each onramp onto the wide and busy JMT highway.

Not wanting to be swept away to drown in the flow of humanity, The Three Women drew together into a compact group on the widening thoroughfare. Only at Red's Meadow two weeks earlier had we come in close contact with so many people who were not JMT or PCT thru-hikers. We had encountered a crowd at VVR and another atop Muir Pass, but those had been smaller flocks of fellow sojourners. Members of the sorority of the trail, they had looked and smelled like us, acted and sounded like us.

These people were different, alien. They dressed in bright summer fashions and smelled of shampoo and soap. They were loud and hurried, moving about in chatty groups. They were less openly friendly, too—few made eye contact, and those who did gave a quick nod or smile before disconnecting. Perhaps they were uncomfortable, thinking we looked rough. I missed the instant camaraderie we had found with travelers in the backcountry. I felt like a stranger in a strange land, and my wary antennae perked up.

Woods Creek had grown into a deep, broad river pushing its way out of the highlands. Though not traveling with the howling ferocity of the wild-animal-river, Piute Creek, that had a few days back claimed the life of a sister hiker, Woods Creek moved with the firm and steady progress of a fully laden freight train.

"The guidebook said the bridge over Woods Creek is very unusual," Cappy had told us while we sat soaking our feet earlier in the afternoon. "It's a suspension bridge called the Golden Gate of the Sierra."[17] It had been part of one of her more fascinating mini-lectures. Approaching the river crossing, we were on alert.

"Look! There it is," Zoe announced, smiling. She stopped abruptly and pointed ahead, her blond ponytail still swinging.

A stately bit of architecture—a wooden sculpture far from roads and toolsheds—stood unique and apart from the surrounding trees. It was graceful, made of simple elegant lines.

Standing beside Zoe, admiring the bridge, I said, "It looks so out of place, but at the same time, it's so—attractive." I had trouble assigning the descriptor *beautiful* to both this human engineering product and the products of the natural environment surrounding it, but it was plain that it was accurate for both. The suspension bridge was like a pen-and-ink drawing, while the natural landscape surrounding it was like a vivid oil painting.

A supporting tower stood at each end of the bridge, one on the river's north bank near us, the other on the south bank. A pair of thick cables connected the tops of the two towers, hanging in broad drooping U's over the water-filled gorge between the banks like a pair of Double-Dutch jump ropes. Two additional cables supported a footpath made of wooden slats, which was suspended in another graceful inverted arc over the water far below.

"Wow! How cool is that!" was my immediate response.

"This will be fun." A broad smile spread across Zoe's face, mirroring mine, I am sure.

---

[17] Thomas Winnett and Kathy Morey, *Guide to the John Muir Trial* (Wilderness Press, 1998) p. 40.

The structure drew us forward until we were watching from just a few feet away while a youngster crossed ahead of us. The girl, dressed in bright shorts, t-shirt, and tennies, first tested the bridge floor with a tentative tap-tap-tap of her foot. Then she walked quickly, one hand on each of the thick ropes that served as handrails. The boardwalk seemed to roll gently in a sinuous wave that followed her across to the other side, her feet making a clapping noise on the wooden slats that was swallowed up by the sound of the flowing water passing below.

Drawing right up to the entrance ramp, we stood to read a sign posted on an upright.

ONE PERSON
AT A TIME
ON BRIDGE

Cappy hesitated when I waved her ahead of me. "No, you go first," she said, her face blank.

I could not tell if she was being gracious or was concerned, but I stepped ahead of her and walked up the wooden ramp that was the bridge's northern terminus. The first steps onto the narrow span, only three-feet wide, were like stepping onto a pirate ship's plank, except that it extended far out over the water and then kept going to dry land on the other side. The narrowness afforded a curious view of the water speeding along far beneath.

I let my hiking poles dangle from their wrist loops, so I could use the rope railing to balance myself. The span jiggled and swayed under my feet just enough to make it fun and interesting, not enough to be scary, or even exhilarating. The sinuous movement I had noticed when the girl had crossed began under my feet, too, spreading forward and backward from where I stepped, so that the ground seemed to gently rise and fall like ocean waves with each stride. When I got to the center, I tried bouncing a bit, bending my knees and straightening them quickly a few times to see if I could make the span bounce or swing. The bridge responded with a jerky little wriggle, then immediately returned to its snake-like waves. My body weight, even with my pack attached, was just not enough to have any impact.

I turned to look at my hiking pals, waved and smiled. "It's fun!" I called back to them, then quickly finished my crossing and waited for them join me.

Zoe came next. She stopped in the middle, like I had, and attempted to make the bridge bounce, too, but had the same experience. She arrived by my side with a big smile and a bounce in her step. "Definitely a very fun bridge."

I raised my brows and nodded in agreement, "No kidding."

I am sure we looked an odd pair, as we stood side-by-side waiting and watching for Cappy to begin her crossing. Zoe towered over me. I barely came to her shoulder and had to look up to her face when we talked.

As we watched Cappy's careful beginning, Zoe said, "I think she's feeling uncomfortable about the crossing.

I observed Cappy closely. She was doing fine, just a little hesitancy, and definitely no bouncing in the middle. I am sure she was holding the railings tightly, but that is what they were there for.

She arrived with a smile. Her eyes revealed it to be a smile of relief. We high-fived like we used to do with challenging river crossings back when we were only JMT beginners and each crossing had seemed a major accomplishment.

"I didn't like that," Cappy stated rather emphatically and with a slow-motion shake of her head. "I don't like unstable ground."

I could identify with that kind of unbidden fear reaction. I had started the hike unable to walk across single-log bridges, my confidence in my own ability to remain upright completely undermined by unreasonable terror. Now it was steady, unshakable Cappy who was a bit shaken.

"One woman's suspension bridge is another woman's log crossing," I said and was rewarded with a small smile.

"I was surprised by how much it bothered me." Cappy blew out a big puff of breath, like she had been holding it.

We moved away from the bridge to search for a camping spot. Campsites, lined up cheek to jowl, lay alongside the river, with more spread out in great swaths farther from the water. Large metal "bear boxes"—distinctive permanent fixtures that reinforced how immersed this place was in civilization—were positioned among the campsites. Most sites were occupied by tents and a colorful assortment of camping accessories. After days of quiet solitude, accompanied only by nature sounds and our own noises, human sounds were strangely disorienting. Mothers called to children, kids called to one another and laughed as they played, men and women chatted over the rustling and rattling of coordinated camp assembly tasks. The cacophony caromed around inside my brain uninvited and threatened to take over all the quiet spaces.

In silent accord, we walked to the end of the row, unified in seeking out an isolated corner in that bustling little frontier town. We moved into the very last riverside campsite. It was still within sight of the bridge but shared only one tree-lined boundary with human neighbors. The vast campground had been cut from the thick woods growing along both sides of the river. Towering pines and firs encircled and shaded all the sites, growing right down to the water's edge and filling the air with their tangy scent. We set up the Frankentent between two large boulders that could have been mistaken for tents themselves and settled in.

As Cappy and Zoe swam in the cold water, I waded in up to my knees, gave myself a "bandana bath," then sprawled out on a sun-warmed boulder beside the creek. From my perch, I watched them play like a couple of river otters, diving and splashing and floating on their backs. Their delight in their own antics made me smile. Closer to the bridge, a gaggle of kids frolicked and splashed, their shrieks of laughter drifting our way.

Despite the injection of civilization's sights and sounds into our previously isolated existence, the singular day was drawing to a close. By any number of measurements, that day had been our most challenging, yet our most successful. Unhurried, we had traversed ten miles of endless and constantly changing landscape. We had climbed up and over our highest pass yet—a vantage point that had afforded us a three-hundred-sixty-degree, infinite view of our universe. We had then descended more than thirty-five-hundred feet through one strikingly beautiful ecosystem after another. At less than eighty-five-hundred feet, Woods Creek Camp and its welcoming Golden Gate were nestled a tad lower than Tuolumne Meadows, our great adventure's starting point twenty days earlier. In one day, we had traveled from the highest point to the lowest point thus far, and then celebrated by relaxing beside dancing and singing water.

Starting Point — Lake Marjorie — 11,132 feet
Ending Point — Woods Creek — 8520 feet
Highest Point — Pinchot Pass — 12,090 feet
Distance Covered — 9.7 miles
Cumulative Miles — 141.0 miles

In A Different Light

Come Fairies, take me out of this dull world,
for I would ride with you upon the wind
and dance upon the mountains like a flame!
~ William Butler Yeats, *The Land of Heart's Desire*, 1894

Day Twenty-One
August 8, 2006

Starting Point — Woods Creek — 8520 feet

Morning came early. I was awakened neither by dappled sunlight filtering through the tent's nylon walls nor by the chirping of birds. It was not the musical gurgling of moving water that brought me to consciousness. It was not even Cappy rustling in her sleeping bag beside me. It was the unbridled noise of humanity that startled my eyes open. At first, I had no idea where I was or what those foreign noises were. I lay for a few moments, confused, until my mind cleared.

I looked to my right toward Cappy. "What the hell?"

"People," she replied, rolling her eyes and exhaling sharply.

I remembered where we were, camped among the masses in Kings Canyon. In my dreams, I had been somewhere far from civilization. "I guess it's time to get up." I laughed.

"My alarm clock seems to have gone off." Zoe's disembodied voice came through the fabric wall.

"It's pretty obnoxious," I said. "Couldn't you have chosen a nicer alarm bell?"

"Like bird calls?" Cappy said. Like me, she was shifting around, stretching to reach the pieces of clothing she had set aside at bedtime.

With little discussion, The Three Women arrived at a consensus. We were going to make a quick escape from that miniature tent-city and slip back into the unpopulated wilderness. To that end, we packed with swift and focused determination, breakfasted while we worked, and made a beeline for the southbound trailhead.

At the sign pointing the way south out of camp, we met a thirty-something couple also making haste for the wilderness. We walked a short way together. Younger and stronger, they would outpace us as soon as the pleasantries and ritual information exchange were completed. But for the moment we talked weather and trail conditions, shared our aversion to crowds, and compared notes on passes past and future.

"Did you happen to run across a group of packhorses on the trail yesterday?" the tall, tanned woman asked.

"We did. On the north face of Pinchot. In the morning. We had to get out of their way." Cappy described our encounter in detail.

I perked up. The pair must have thought the incident curious, too, or they would not have asked, so I added, "They seemed to be rushing. We thought it a little odd."

"They were stopped, watering their horses, when we came across them." The fair-haired, bearded man filled in more details.

Zoe asked the big question, "Any idea why they were in such a hurry?"

"One of the women said they were on a rescue mission," the woman explained. "A guy was hiking the trail with some sort of fake leg, a prosthetic, and it broke, snapped in two, so he couldn't hike out. Can you imagine?"

"I'll bet it was that guy we saw up by Muir Hut. You remember him?" I said to Cappy and Zoe. "He had one of those new curved metal prosthetics like that Olympic runner. It didn't look like a leg, just a bare piece of metal that curved from knee to shoe."

"Wasn't he one of those guys who skied down the snowy side of Muir? The ones who scared us when they whizzed by hollering?" Zoe reminded her.

"Oh, *that* guy." Recognition blossomed on Cappy's face.

"I talked with him and his buddies for a few minutes on top of Muir Pass," Zoe added. "He was all jazzed about his new leg. Called it his peg-leg."

"He must have been awfully frustrated," I said, "stuck in the wilderness, legless. I wonder how they got help."

"His friend hiked out to contact the rangers," the fellow continued. "The packers were already on the trail to deliver supplies somewhere but got diverted for the rescue."

"I'm so glad we ran into you," Cappy said. "Mystery solved."

We parted ways, and though they suggested we would see one another at a campsite that night, I was pretty sure, even with our stronger, faster Hiking-Version 2.0, we would not.

Having part of a leg break off was certainly an extreme situation, but any serious backcountry injury could put a hiker out of commission, keep her from being able to walk out to safety. A fall resulting in a broken wrist or ankle or a deep cut could quickly become a dangerous situation if you were hiking solo. Sometimes I got frustrated with my hiking companions. We did not always see eye-to-eye on our progress or our plans. But I always appreciated how The Three Women were able to work out problems as a team and support each other when fears or pains arose. I felt safe and secure hiking with steady partners, even as I savored my solitude while walking out in front.

The morning's hike was a mirror image of the previous day's descent, with a gradual climb out of the chaparral and through the forest. Forest trails are easy on the feet, soft with soil and duff. The silence was welcoming, interrupted only by the music of birds and the occasional squirrel making a mad dash across the footpath.

A couple hours after leaving the crowded campground, we stopped for our morning snack and rest break in peaceful isolation alongside a small creek.

"We are just about to enter the Rae Lakes Basin." Cappy's face was dreamy, her voice tight with excitement. She told Zoe what she had told me six months earlier when we were deep into our preparations. "It's been one of my life's goals to see Rae Lakes, ever since I was first backpacking during college."

"It's a land of many lakes." I was looking at the map Cappy had pulled out. I could see that directly ahead lay Rae Lakes Basin. Just to the west was Sixty Lakes Basin, and to the east were many more of the blue ovals symbolizing lakes.

"I'm disappointed we can't stop for the night," Cappy said, "but I'm thrilled we get to spend a few hours there. Someday, I will come back to stay longer." With that, she stood, ready to see if the mythical place she had created in her mind resembled the real thing.

Each charming lake enticed us to stop and visit a while—swim in its pure waters, hike around its perimeter, lounge on its sunbaked shoreline. We declined every invitation, albeit reluctantly, until we could justify a pause by labeling it lunchtime. With Lower Rae Lake to ourselves, we sat on a huge granite boulder overlooking the water and savored our midday meal.

Living up to her reputation, after lunch Cappy was in the water. She claimed the shallow water near the shore was warm and inviting. She waded in to her knees, called back to Zoe to join her, dove headlong into the lake, and resurfaced twenty feet out sputtering, her long hair like a rope dangling down the center of her back. Zoe stripped down to sports bra and shorts before wading in. Both of them stroked back and forth, splashing and laughing. They insisted it was refreshing and called up to where I sat on my rocky perch.

Content where I was, I waved.

Cappy climbed out to lie on a sun-heated rock. I was sure she needed to heat her core back up after time in the frigid snowmelt. Zoe continued to swim back and forth in front of our picnic site, looking for all the world like a misplaced dolphin.

As pretty as Lower Rae Lake was, and Dollar and Arrowhead before her, she paled in comparison to Middle and Upper Rae Lakes. The conjoined lakes shared a narrow isthmus of land barely above the waterline that provided a slender path between them. The slight land-bridge was the only thing that kept the two lakes from merging.

We were feeling pressured by our schedule and knew we could not linger at either the Middle or Upper sister. But their Eden-like beauty dazzled us and slowed our pace from a ramble to a traipse. Then, we were loitering, pointing, and oohing and aahing.

Golden fish played in the shallow water. Birds twittered in the shrubs and small trees. A little frog leapt across the path and dove into the water. Flowers bloomed along the track. Berries, pink and red, decorated one of the shrubs.

"Bear food," Cappy said, pointing them out.

"I'd live here if I were a bear," Zoe said. "This would be a great spot." She turned around in a slow spin, taking it in like she was considering placing an offer on the real estate.

I watched the water, following the shoreline with my eyes. Narrow rocky peninsulas pointed to the center of the lake, while small crescent-shaped coves cut into the land. The water took on colors that were ever changing—pale and sparkly from one angle, bright and reflective from another, clear enough to reveal the lake's rocky bottom from yet another. The lake glowed sapphire and turquoise, periwinkle and azure.

"Cappy, you were right," I said. "I could stay here a week. There's so much to investigate."

Feeling the pull of Glen Pass and the next day's packhorse meet-up, we turned to walk on. Near the land-bridge, I almost stumbled over a man crouched down, studying something in the water.

"Hey. Name's Arnold," he said, rising. No sooner had we finished introducing ourselves than another man appeared, walking our way across the little isthmus. "That's my friend Hank."

Neither young man carried a full backpack, though both had belt packs stuffed with camera gear and a daypack. They wore the standard JMT uniform along with broad-brimmed hats. Their beards showed more than a week's growth.

"You ladies staying or just passing through?" Hank asked. He leaned his little tripod against a nearby rock and drank from a water bottle.

We explained our dilemma, our desire to stay forever, our original plan to stay a night, and our immediate situation.

"Unfortunate. This is paradise—and perfect for photography," Arnold said, lifting his black Nikon. "Between here and Sixty Lakes Basin, I've taken a thousand shots."

"And that's only in his spare time. He's supposed to be counting fish and looking for frogs." Hank laughed a soft chuckle. That, as I am sure he intended, generated confused looks on our faces.

"Why are you counting fish?" I asked, looking from one man to the other.

"We're trying to determine why the yellow-legged frog, an important native species to the Sierra, is going extinct. People have considered a lot of different reasons—disease, climate, predators, pollution. We're of the mind that it's because the non-native trout, introduced by people, are killing them off by eating their eggs," Arnold explained. His whole demeanor had changed, from casual backcountry hiker to serious professional scientist—this was a passion for him—and he stood a little taller.

Hank added, with the careful cadence of a teacher, "So we're comparing what's happening here in Rae Lakes, where we have trout, to what's not happening in Sixty Lakes, just over the ridge, where there are no trout—and we hope there never will be."

"Counting trout and looking for frogs. That makes more sense, now," Cappy said. "I find scientific studies like that really fascinating. What are you finding?" Her face mirrored Arnold's seriousness.

"All the data thus far seem to support our thesis," Arnold said. "That's good, but it's also bad. Good, because we know what's causing the problem. Bad, because the trout aren't going anywhere, and they're decimating the frog populations."

"How long are you out here doing this?" Zoe asked.

"We've been here all summer and just about finished collecting data. Next, we have to go back and analyze it and write our report," Hank said. "But first we're taking some time for a little vacation."

"Hence all the photos!" Arnold interjected. His face went instantly from serious to playful, a big smile crossing it, and he held up his camera again.

I asked what he was photographing.

"A little of everything," he said. "Yesterday, all I did was take close-ups of flowers and rocks. The only lens I used was my macro. But there's a full moon coming, and I'm hoping to see something interesting to shoot tonight."

My heart ached a little. Cappy's desire was not the only one thwarted by the indifferent demands of the trail. My original plan to document our journey with thousands of photographs had drowned with my new little Nikon. If only.

Hank pointed out an unusual multicolored peak made of metamorphic rock standing regally above the two lakes. "I took an interesting series of portraits of the Painted Lady in all different lights. I got up in the dark one morning to catch her at dawn and later snapped some great shots of her silhouette at dusk."

"You're making our departure very difficult," I said, "but if we stay and talk, I'm going to start crying because we can't stay overnight." I laughed.

I bent to pick up a small jade-green stone, satin smooth from years in moving water. I placed it with my pocket collection. We waved our farewells and allowed the path to guide us away from Middle sister and past Upper, too.

We had not intended to climb Glen Pass that evening. We did it on a whim. It was a spontaneous unanimous decision. After departing from Upper Rae Lake, the trail veered upward through a tall shady forest interrupted by wide patches of heather growing where the sun came through gaps in the canopy. As the forest gave way above timberline to smaller plants and open views of the looming pass, we paused on the trail to survey the area and talk about finding a campsite. We stood in a perfect spot to bed down for a first-thing-in-the-morning assault on the pass.

"How do you gals feel?" Zoe asked. "I mean, are you tired? I'm feeling really strong right now." She hitched up her pack as she spoke.

"I'm good." I paused between sips of water. "My head's telling me I'm supposed to be tired, and the plan says I'm supposed to be ready to stop, but my body's telling me otherwise. I could walk for a long while." Despite already having hiked seven miles and climbed over two thousand feet that day, on the heels of our two most accomplished days, I was feeling fresh, raring to go even.

"I don't even *want* to stop," Cappy said. "I want to go on. But, and it's a big but, Glen Pass is right there. Do we want to go over it this evening? Now? Right now? Or wait until the morning? We could go a little closer and camp, but beyond that, we can only go all the way and camp on the other side."

"So, you're saying we have to choose between maybe a half-mile and camp on this side, or we have to commit to going up and over," I said. I looked at my watch. It was almost six o'clock. "How many miles? And what's the climb?" I wanted to really know what going on would mean. I dug a plastic bag of hard candies out of my pocket. If I was going to walk farther, I was going to start a sugar drip now. I popped a cinnamon in my mouth and held the rest out as an offering. Zoe took a pair of peppermints.

The pass towered above us, a wall of naked rock that poked its nearly twelve-thousand-foot, pointy head into the sky. Switchbacks crisscrossed its face, I was sure, but they were camouflaged by its roughness and the talus slopes that fanned out from top to bottom.

"It's about two miles from here to the top, and we'll gain about fifteen hundred feet," Cappy provided the statistics. "Not an easy hike." She selected a caramel.

I chimed in again. "Funny. Ten days or a week ago, I'd have said, 'No way,' but right now, I say, 'Piece of cake!' Let's do it."

Together, we had grown so strong these last few days that it was empowering. The physical learning curve we had faced in the beginning had been really steep, but we had tackled it, and now we were reaping the benefits.

"Okay, ladies. Onward!" Zoe pointed the way with her right arm and pole.

The switchbacks grew steeper and steeper, their precariousness demanding my constant attention. Yet I did not have to downshift or stop and rest. I just kept walking at that same steady pace with no huffing and puffing. The trail underfoot was sometimes sandy, sometimes smooth, and sometimes buried under piles of scree. I hugged the inner edge of the trail, keeping my hand on the high side like a staircase banister.

No greenery softened the harsh beauty of the bare rock. We were way above tree-line and nothing grew there. Snow bunched in patches to the side of the trail. A chill wind picked up as we gained elevation, coming at us from the west. I stopped to dig out my windbreaker. Even the heat my muscles generated was not enough to keep me warm.

The eastern end of each switchback wrapped around a long vertical ridge that ran up and down the face of the mountain. That ridge acted as a windshield, so it was warm in the evening sun. On the west end of each switch, though, it was really cold, buffeted by the wind that whistled against the sharp angles of stone. Walking west, the wind was directly in my face, working against my forward progress, grabbing my big square pack where it stood over my head like a sail, trying to force me backward. I had to lean forward at the waist, and press into the wind to maintain forward motion. Walking east, the wind pushed at my back, helping me like a ship running before the wind, though sometimes a gust felt like it was trying to throw me right off the edge of the narrow path. Then I would pass the vertical ridge and be warm again.

Despite the challenge of the climb, I felt exhilarated. I paused now and again so I could take my eyes off my boots and the trail to admire the panoramic views. Row after row of peaks and ridges—eleven-, twelve-, and thirteen-thousand-footers—spread out into the distance, and below, the lakes we had visited that afternoon dazzled.

A long, slender knife-edge of granite rising up to slice the sky, Glen Pass was unlike any of the other passes we had surmounted. The sliver of rock, only wide enough to accommodate the single-file trail that ran along it, reminded me of walking atop the brick wall that separated my childhood home from our neighbors' yards. A traveler pausing to stand in the middle of the trail, with arms outstretched, could drop a pebble from each hand so that both stones would plummet hundreds of feet before bouncing and dropping again and again, one into the Rae Lakes Basin to the north, the other into the Bubb's Creek Canyon to the south.

We arrived on the eastern end of the nearly twelve-thousand-foot Glen Pass and stopped together where the final switchback led out onto its razorback.

Glen Pass was skinny. There was nowhere to sit and rest, but it was just as well. It was late, closing in on seven o'clock. We were on the trail later than ever before. The earth around us was naked and steep, and we had a distance to walk before we would find flat space to set up our tent. The sun was low enough in the western sky that, even from our perch, it had disappeared behind the next row of peaks. Though the sky would remain light in the extended high-country gloaming, it was getting cold quickly. We needed to keep moving.

The trail turned sharply through a notch in the rock just wide enough for one person to slip through and dropped at a sharp angle to a series of steep descending switchbacks.

"We need to find somewhere to stop for the night," Cappy said after just a few minutes.

"I know we need to hurry, but we also need to be careful," I said. I had been so exhilarated by the spontaneous way we bagged the pass that I had been oblivious to the passage of time. The sky was inching towards darkness. Though only a couple hundred feet below the almost twelve-thousand-foot pass, we were deep in its shadow. I could feel anxiety nibbling around the edges of my mind.

The stone walkway dropped at a steep angle and was dusted with sand and small stones. Hurrying increased the chance that one of us would skid and fall. I focused entirely on where I placed my feet, each step deliberate. I was not going to fall.

"Pretty quick here we're going to have to choose between putting on headlamps and just stopping on the trail," Zoe said after a few more minutes. "I do not want to walk this trail in the dark."

"There aren't any official camping areas up this high," Cappy remembered from the guidebook. "Let's just look for a flat spot, any flat spot."

No sooner had those words been spoken than we came around a bend in the trail to find a nameless shallow pond, just a dip in the rock floor smaller than the average backyard swimming pool and not nearly as deep. It was surrounded and sheltered by vertical walls and large boulders. Beside it lay a smooth flat space about the size and shape of my bedroom, perfect for our tent and its lean-to. I quickly removed my pack and took out my share of the tent.

I looked up and gasped. The entire space was suddenly bathed in the spectacular orange and pink light of an intensifying alpenglow.

Over the years, I have stood many an evening in the Sierra admiring the spell cast by sunlight's last hurrah, the way it first coats the whole west-facing mountainside with bright color, while the rest of the world goes gray. As the long unseen sun sinks below the sea, the colorful glow shrinks, its bottom line creeping up the mountain canvas, like an upside-down hourglass filled with an ever-shrinking volume of salmon-colored sand, until only the tip of the tallest peak remains in the colored light. Finally, the color is completely extinguished as the last grains of glowing sand fall upward into the sky.

As amazing as I find the alpenglow phenomenon every time I witness it, that night's experience was singular. Our little camping room was bathed in an alpenglow spotlight. We were immersed in pink and orange. The pond reflected it, and the room's vertical walls and boulders glowed as though illuminated from within. It was like being inside a magical snow globe filled, not with white snow, but with glowing photons of fiery light that swirled all around us. We stopped our work to watch the colors and shadows shift and change around us like colorful fluids spreading and mixing and flowing away.

Alpenglow is always fleeting. After too short a time, we stood witness as the darkness chased the last of the vivid colors across the space to leave us behind in the dullness of night's full shadow.

I blinked my eyes. "I didn't even know that was a thing you could experience."

We stood in near complete darkness, punctuating the silence with words that only served to expose our tongue-tied awe. There really are no words in English to describe the experience clearly. I wonder if the Tibetans or the Nepalese, who live high in the Himalayas, have words in their languages to describe what we saw and felt that night.

Donning headlamps, we quickly finished the tent we had abandoned to watch the lightshow. Then, bundled in several layers against the high-altitude cold of the clear night, we fixed our dinners, filtering and boiling water from the snowmelt pool to make our hot entrées and cups of hot chocolate.

We deserved a good rest and to wallow in the day's accomplishments and the contentment left behind by the light show. That day, we had hiked over ten miles and gained thirty-five hundred feet—a new team record! For the third day in a row, we had hiked longer and harder than ever before. Without Champagne, we used the hot chocolate to toast our accomplishments.

Little did we know the show was not over. The Sierra, John Muir's "Range of Light," had yet another surprise up its sleeve that night.

"Moonshadows! You've got to see the moonshadows!" I was whisper-shouting.

The swishing of Cappy's sleeping bag was her first answer to my call. "What?" She mumbled her way to wakefulness and poked her face between the tent's flaps.

"Hmmm?" Zoe sat up, already alert inside her multiple layers and lean-to, her head emerging to look at me.

"You've got to see this. The moon is casting shadows!" I said. I had hesitated waking them from their sound sleep, but only for a moment. I could not let my partners miss this.

The air was frigid. I had pulled on a fleece jacket and bottoms, a hat and socks, to go out for my nightly pee, but I was still cold. There were sure to be ice crystals on the outside of the tent when it was time to get up in the morning. But beauty trumped cold, and this was too auspicious to miss.

The full moon, a "super moon" I would later learn, appearing uber-bright and huge from our high-altitude perch, was an intense white spotlight in the cloudless night. Every wrinkle and pimple on the man-in-the-moon's circular face was precisely visible. Intensely brilliant, it cast shadows, making my headlamp redundant. I stood admiring the sky and playing with my shadow, while the others put on enough clothing to come out and play with me.

Zoe turned around and around, looking first skyward, then at the black-and-silver shapes around us. "The moon is gigantic!"

"What's going on?" Cappy emerged, then went silent, taking in the second light show of the night.

Our little camping room beside the pond was populated by glacial erratics large and small. Earlier in the night, they had glowed with the colors of flame; then they'd disappeared into the deep blackness. Now, they were brightly illuminated and casting fat inky shadows. Every grain of sand and pebble glowed silver, its shadow a tar black puddle behind it. The moon's twin floated like a blob of mercury—quicksilver on the onyx black surface of the campsite's petite pool.

"First an alpenglow fiesta and now a moonshadow party," Zoe said. "And to think we just stumbled on this site by chance."

"It's magical, like a black-and-white fairyland. Next thing we know, the fairies themselves will come dancing out of the shadows!" I said, twirling in an exaggerated dance among the standing stones and shadows.

Starting Point — Woods Creek — 8520 feet
Ending Point — Nameless Pond, Just South of Glen Pass — about 11,700 feet
Highest Point — Glen Pass — 11,926 feet
Distance Covered — 10 miles
Cumulative Miles — 151.0 miles

A Cowboy, An Egg, and A Question

The power of imagination makes us infinite.
~ John Muir, *John of the Mountains:*
The Unpublished Journals of John Muir, 1938

Day Twenty-Two
August 9, 2006

Starting Point — Nameless Pond, Just South of Glen Pass — about 11,700 feet

Unable to sit still, I rose to pace in a small circle in front of my seated companions. *Where was our courier?* I wondered. Had they forgotten about us? Had we missed the horse and rider somehow? It was past noon, and a gray fog of uncertainty hung in the air around us.

I reviewed my resources. I had two power bars and one freeze-dried dinner left in my near-empty food canister, and it was a very long walk to the closest outpost of civilization. What would we do if the food delivery never arrived?

"We don't even have a backup plan," I said. Hands on hips, turning to look at Cappy, I tried to sound calm, but the squeak in my voice gave me away.

We had arrived an hour earlier at the intersection of the JMT and the Charlotte Lake Trail, the location where we were scheduled to meet up with the courier who was packing in our food packages. The wide, flat space was absolutely deserted, not a soul in sight.

Because Cappy and I had experienced so much trouble in our original attempts to arrange for the courier service, we had never been one hundred percent confident about that food drop. Phone calls had gone unanswered for weeks in the spring and early summer, and we had never received a satisfying confirmation that our shipped boxes had been received until the very last day before I had left home. Cappy had called to tell me she had received a message from the packing service, "The packer will meet you at the trail junction no later than August ninth. If you're not there, he'll take your food down to the Charlotte Lake Ranger Station and leave it in one of the steel drum storage containers out back where animals cannot get at it."

It was August ninth, so we figured the packages had probably already been delivered. Rather than waiting at the junction, we hiked down the steep spur trail towards the Charlotte Lake Ranger Station.

The ranger will be able to help us, I thought. *We are not the first hikers to set up this arrangement, so certainly the ranger will be familiar with the routine.*

We had been told Charlotte Lake was a popular camping spot accessible to the civilized world along a popular backpacking route that climbed up and over Kearsarge Pass. That was confirmed when we walked down the mile-long trail towards the lake, so I envisioned a bustling NPS office and visitor's center, where we would hang around and chat for a while with the helpful ranger and then fetch our boxes.

Partway down the mile-long trail towards the lake, Zoe brought us to a sudden stop. "Why are we carrying our packs all the way down only to carry them back up again?"

Why indeed? All three packs were off in seconds and leaning against trees just off the trail. "What goes down must come back up," I said. And off we went towards the Ranger Station feeling much lighter.

Instead of the bustling station I had imagined, we found the door to the tiny one-room cabin padlocked, the windows shuttered for winter snows in midsummer. The Charlotte Lake Ranger Station had not been opened up for the season.

There was no Charlotte Lake Ranger.

Worry rose to my knees, like a slow flood.

That's okay, I thought, in an attempt to recover. *They'll be in sealed steel drums behind the station.*

We each lifted the lid of one of the three metal barrels—rust seeped through the peeling NPS ranger-green paint.

"Empty," Zoe said, her voice flat.

"Empty," said Cappy, her voice a little squeakier than usual.

"Ditto," I said. Only random pieces of trash lay on the rusty bottom of the barrel.

Worry turned to fear and rose to sour my stomach.

My partners slumped down onto the river-rock-and-concrete steps that led to the locked cabin door while I paced. Silence hung around us. Cappy twisted back to look at the deserted building, shook her head and let out a sigh. "I want to find my papers, review my notes. They're up in my pack."

I stopped pacing. "Let's not wait here. Let's go back up to the junction to wait." But feeling deflated, I was slow to move to my own suggestion.

"This is depressing," Cappy said. "What if we have to hike out to a store? It's a long walk in the wrong direction."

"Don't let your imagination run wild. Let's think positively," Zoe said. "The delivery will come. It's just a bit late. Let's be at the junction when it arrives." Zoe unfolded her long body and stood.

"What if..." Cappy started, then stopped herself when both Zoe and I threw stern looks her way.

"Think positively," Zoe repeated.

"Right. I'll just put on my happy face," Cappy pasted an exaggerated grin on her face. It resembled a grimace.

We retreated back up the steep trail, stepping in our own footprints all the way to the spot where our abandoned packs waited. Hoisting mine, it felt featherlight. I was too aware that the canister inside held few bites of food.

As I walked, I silently ran through the short list of possible scenarios. Best choice was the difficult twenty-mile hike out over eleven-thousand-foot Kearsarge Pass and all the way into the town of Independence located out on Highway 395, where we would probably find a store. A second possibility was hiking eight miles out the same way, also over Kearsarge, to Onion Valley Campground, a car-accessible campground, where I imagined we might find someone with a working cell phone. There, we could call the packing company.

Neither was a good option. The hikes would be difficult and time-consuming with no guarantee of success. That is where my mind stopped, refusing to venture further.

Cappy, who was leading the way, let out a shriek, startling me out of my futile thoughts back into the present moment. She pointed up the trail. "He's here!" Her whole body vibrated with excitement.

In one move, I dropped the worry I had been carrying up the hill and filled my lungs with enough air to float me the rest of the way.

The three of us stood frozen on the trail watching the slowly approaching rider as he emerged from an old Gunsmoke episode. He was pure cowboy, from the top of the ten-gallon hat that shaded his face and half his body to the pointed toes of his well-seasoned boots. His horse's gait was set on mosey. A lead rope stretched from the horn of his saddle to the head of a packhorse that followed closely behind.

The cowboy brought his horse to a stop and greeted us with a rich and gravelly, "Howdy, ladies." He even tipped his hat.

"We've been waiting for you." Cappy's greeting was almost an accusation. The grimace she had worn earlier morphed into a real smile.

"This your food cache?" he asked, turning his shoulders and pointing behind him with his thumb.

"We are *so* happy to see you!" Cappy said quickly, her tone gentler. Her hunched shoulders relaxed, and she stood a bit taller.

"We were worried we'd missed you!" I said. We talked over one another in our excitement. The watery sensation in my gut dissipated, and the ground felt solid under my feet again.

He chuckled in response. "I'm gonna turn these horses 'round. It'll take me a minute or two on this trail. Why don't you gals start up ahead of me? We can unload your boxes at the trail junction up top."

I did not want to take my eyes off him. He might be a phantom who would disappear if I let him out of my sight. Heading up the trail at a newly energized pace, I kept glancing over my shoulder to make sure he was following.

By the time we got back to the trail junction, he had maneuvered the pair of animals around and caught up to us. He pointed to a small copse of trees that offered a bit of shade, and we reassembled there. I propped my backpack against a fallen log.

Our cowboy dismounted, tipped his hat a second time, and said, "I'm Paul."

I offered my hand. I know my smile was stretched clear across my face. I had *really* not wanted to implement a Kearsarge plan.

Paul walked to the pack animal and began unloading cardboard packages from the leather bags hanging on either side. "You gals been waitin' long?" he asked, holding out a large box, its address label in my handwriting.

In my excitement, I fairly snatched it from his hands. I wanted to go directly to the log seat under the trees and open it, but held myself in check and stood to chat with the friendly, grizzled cowboy. While Zoe took charge of Cappy's large food package, Cappy ripped open a third impossibly thin cardboard box she was hoping contained her one-person tent.

Disappointment darkened her face. The box contained no tent, only the rainfly. She held up the small trapezoidal piece of nylon, no bigger than a fitted sheet for a double bed. "Are you sure there isn't another box for us?" she asked.

"Why would there be a fly, but not a tent?" I asked. "Jim obviously got your message. And why would he pack them separately?"

"Jim would *not* have sent one without the other." The look on Cappy's face turned to confusion. She kept looking in the tiny box and back at the horse.

"A real mystery," Zoe said, downplaying the disappointment.

The deliveryman stood beside the packhorse. The saddlebags were empty. "That's all they give me this mornin'," he said, his voice, though sympathetic, was flat and factual.

He gathered the cardboard trash from our hands and folded it into an empty saddlebag. "You ladies have more trash for me?"

Turning to my pack, I pulled out my black plastic trash bag and handed it to him. I would start the final leg of the hike with a new trash bag.

"Thank ya, ladies." Without another word, he mounted up and tipped his hat a third time to signal his goodbye.

We watched for a few moments as the two horses moved slowly eastward, then turned to the job of repacking our bear canisters with our final ration of food.

"Now what do we do?" Cappy asked no one in particular. She shook the thin piece of nylon and looked from me to Zoe and back again. "What good is this little thing?"

"I'll be okay," said Zoe. "Don't worry." I do not know if she believed her own words, but she sure was not convincing Cappy and me. The average nighttime low temperature in the high-country during August is only thirty-one degrees; many nights would be colder.

"The nights are getting colder and colder. Did you see the frost on the tent this morning? I was *counting* on that little tent," Cappy continued to perseverate aloud on the mystery of the missing tent.

The rainfly would be better than nothing, but just barely. It *would* give us a waterproof layer to add to the Frankentent, and it might protect Zoe from the damp and cold as we continued to climb and sleep at higher and higher elevations.

I sat on the log in the spotty shade, the large nylon stuff bag I had pulled from my box balanced on my knees. Opening the drawstring top and reaching in, I tried to remember all the treasures I had packed for myself six weeks earlier.

I knew there would be seven breakfasts, seven lunches, and seven dinners, as well as snacks and candy and Gatorade. There would also be vitamins and small containers of bug spray, sunscreen, moisturizer, moleskin, first-aid tape, and even two pair of clean underwear and a pair of socks.

From the blue sack I pulled a small cellophane package, carefully wrapped inside soft cloth layers of underwear and socks, the backcountry woman's bubble wrap.

"Look what I packed!" I held up a large chocolate Easter egg preserved from the holiday.

"What *is* that?" Zoe cocked her head quizzically when she looked at the dark lump I held aloft.

"A See's Candy Bordeaux egg!" I announced, feeling very proud of myself. I had completely forgotten I had packed it. "I'll bet there's three-thousand calories right here in this little package!" I pulled out my pocketknife.

"I can*not* believe you sent yourself See's candy!" Cappy said.

"Not me, *us*," I cut the half-pound of chocolate and decadently rich sugary filling into three big pieces. "We have to eat it right now before it melts in the sun." I handed a piece to each of them and licked my sticky fingers.

"Heavenly!" I closed my eyes to savor the richness of the melting chocolate.

"This is like mainlining sugar!" Cappy said.

Zoe just whimpered.

"With all this sugar in our blood, we'll be able to run the next couple of miles," I laughed.

It took some time, but I finished the chocolate *and* stuffed all seven pounds of new food into my bear canister and tucked away everything else that came in the delivery, including the last installment of *Devil in the White City*.

From the trail junction, we hiked downward forever through one ecosystem after another—rocky knobs, alpine meadows, forests—to Lower Vidette Meadow in the bottom of the canyon. Once down, we shifted gears and climbed right back up the other side of the canyon, following Bubb's Creek upwards through the same series of ecosystems. The lush Vidette Meadows, filled with acres and acres of fragrant purple lupine and countless other wildflowers, provided sweet breaks from the granite trail.

The extra boost of Easter sugar was not enough to counteract the effects of adding those seven pounds of food and supplies to my pack. Many miles and hours of climbing down and then up on the hard rock trail took a toll on all of us. Every one of the little joints in my feet and ankles ached from the constant pounding. On this fourth day of long rocky hikes, I was feeling every mile, every step.

We had begun the day near the top of twelve-thousand-foot Glen Pass and were headed back up to a point just above tree-line, near thirteen-thousand-foot Forrester Pass. Between those two high points, we had descended twenty-five-hundred feet in the morning only to climb back up thirty-five-hundred feet in the afternoon. It was that Sisyphean challenge in reverse—first we tumbled down to earth, then we climbed back into the sky.

I stopped beside a little creek somewhere above ten thousand feet after climbing beyond the reach of even the stunted trees that populate the edge of timberline. The green space, where I sat to wait for Cappy and Zoe was a small rocky meadow. From my rock seat, I had a tremendous view of giant Forester Pass, a massive wall of granite looming ahead, the way to the top a three-mile, two-thousand-foot climb.

When the others arrived, I wanted to suggest we camp at that very spot. I knew Cappy planned for us to travel farther up the mountain to put us in a better position for the morning's climb. I should not complain. Hers was a good plan. But I was really tired. This fourth hard day in a row felt like too much. We had already walked over ten miles, and my body was begging me to stop there.

I sat eating a nutty Kind Bar and drinking water when my hiking mates came over a rise. "Take a break," I said, thinking that if they got really comfortable, we might end up camping there.

"Just a short one," Cappy said, sitting down a few feet away. "Our campsite is another mile up that slope." She pointed toward Forester. "And it's getting late again."

Zoe had dropped to the ground and was tearing the wrapper away from a power bar. Her long back sagged, and her face drooped.

"Isn't that impressive? Look how mammoth that ridge is." Cappy was gazing at Forester. "It'll be our first thirteener!"

She looked tired, too. Wisps of her curls had come undone and hung limp around her face. But Cappy was determined; I saw the strength in her eyes. We were camping a mile up that hill. There would be no purpose to me suggesting otherwise.

"Where are we camping?" Zoe asked. "This has been a long day." She had taken off her hat and was redoing her ponytail, threading the tail through the little hole in the back of her cap.

"There's a little lake in Upper Vidette Meadow," Cappy explained. "They must have run out of creative lake names, so many up here are nameless. They're labeled on the map only by their altitude. Ours is Lake Twelve-Thousand-Two-Fifty, or something like that."

I rose. If I sat any longer, I could not be sure I would be able to get up and hike. My muscles had started to stiffen while I sat, like rigor mortis was setting in. I stretched my back, reaching up, bending forward, twisting side to side. Satisfied, I lifted my heavy pack and convinced my spent muscles to heft it onto my back.

"Y'all coming?" I said. "I want to get this behind me."

"I need a couple more minutes. Go ahead," Cappy answered. "I'll be right behind you." That proved it, Cappy was as tired as she looked, as tired as I felt.

At the edge of the meadow, the trail immediately began to rise, and soon it was charging up the barren slope. Every muscle I owned was rubbery from overuse. Each step I took, some part of my anatomy complained. If I continued to mentally track the tenderness as it moved up and down my lower extremities and back and forth from side to side, I would never get to Lake #12,250. I would end up curled up by the side of the trail.

First, I tried chunking the climb, taking just one short hike after another, which sometimes served me well when faced with a long, challenging stretch of trail. It's the "I'll hike to that big rock and rest one minute" method that can take me fifty yards, then fifty more, all the way to my destination, sort of like chewing and swallowing a bear one bite at a time.

I paused beside a large granite rock. *Sometimes you eat the bear—sometimes the bear eats you*, I thought. That plan was not working. I would need a new tactic if I was going to make it to our prescribed endpoint and regain my heretofore carefully nurtured blissful, one-with-nature, state of mind. I needed to channel all that negative energy, after all it was just energy, into something productive, like getting my defeated body up that mountain. Leaning against a tall square boulder, not daring to sit down or even remove my pack for fear of the urge to quit, I closed my eyes and took three deep and cleansing breaths.

I let the mute strength of that ancient stone support me. I imagined the thousands of hikers who had passed under the watchful eye of that silent standing stone in the seven decades since that section of the JMT had been cut into the side of the mountain. In my mind's eye, some of those hikers walked powerfully up that hill as if they rode an escalator. Others, like me, struggled to put one foot ahead of the other. But none of them lay by the side of the road. No one in the silent historic parade in my mind complained or faltered. They just moved resolutely onward and upward.

Opening my eyes, I stood up straight, extending my torso to stretch to my full height, all five-feet-four-inches of it. *Mountain pose, how appropriate*, I thought. I raised my arms high over my head to extend myself even farther, then brought them back to my sides.

I adjusted my hiking poles, reducing their length by two full inches. I became a quadruped, consciously using my arms and shoulders to lift some of the stress and strain off my legs. Planting both poles two feet ahead and up the trail, I pulled my body along.

Slow and steady wins the race, I thought. A real musical rhythm developed—the click of my poles on the ground sang along with the scritch my feet made on the decomposed granite that dusted the stone steps, and the scrunch of boots placed on dirt patches. Click-scritch-scritch-scrunch became a four-count dance step as I pulled on my poles to lift my torso upward with my arms, then pressed backwards with the poles, giving them a final forceful shove to propel myself forward and upward.

One, two, three, four, and repeat.

Click-scrunch-scritch-scritch.

As my body found the rhythm, I added the mantra I'd chanted each day of my walk. The eight-beat chant and four-step pattern merged, and I was hypnotized.

"Love..." Step left. Breathe in. Pull on poles.

"Life..." Step right.

"Truth..." Left. Breathe out. Push on poles.

"Beauty..." Right.

"Abundance..." Left. Inhale. Pull.

"And..." Right.

"Peace..." Left. Exhale. Push.

"Give me strength." Right.

Repeat...

I was no longer aware of my surroundings. I had entered the flow-zone, an altered state of consciousness where I felt only the transcending fluid dance movements of bones, joints, and muscles as they carried me indefatigably upward.

Time and space slipped away completely. The trail became a tunnel of light through a blur of colors made from rocks and sky. All that existed was ground, chant, and motion. I was alone and in rhythm with the trail as I pressed down with foot and arm, the earth pressed upward. "Love, life, truth, beauty, abundance, and peace, give-me-strength."

Without warning, the trail opened out onto a wide terrace. I was twenty-five feet onto the flat gray moonscape before I became conscious of the changed environment. I stopped and surveyed my surroundings. I blinked my blurry eyes, stretched my neck to get the cotton out of my ears. Slowly, like a Polaroid picture, the details of the scene blossomed into clarity. Up ahead were people. And a lake. Bits of greenery. A handful of tents.

"This must be the Upper Meadow," I said aloud. I looked at my watch and wondered how long I had been hiking. I assumed my partners were close behind and would show up at any moment.

I sat myself down on a wide rock. Suddenly thirsty and hungry, I sucked the last drops of moisture from my CamelBak before rampaging through pack-pockets to find hard candies. The sun had fallen to the rim of the sky, and clouds gathered far to the west. Growing chilly, I dug for my fleece and windbreaker.

There were a dozen hikers milling around the rocky landscape, all of them having set up their tents much closer to the lake and farther from the trail than me. The stark camping area sat in a broad bowl, its open side facing downward in the direction of the trail. On three sides, bare rock mountain peaks, made silver by the low rays of the sun, stretched beyond thirteen thousand feet, their slopes etched with crags and fissures, their ridges knife sharp with serrated peaks.

I thought about setting up the tent, then remembered I carried only half. Cappy had the poles. The wind picked up as the sun sank below the horizon, so I pulled on fleece bottoms and wind pants over my shorts. Alpenglow was beginning to appear on the broad silver screen of the mountains to the east, painting them in shades of flame. The sun was out of sight, but the colors it cast still crawled up the eastern slope until they, too, vanished.

I bent to pick up a thin sliver of stone, gray and gritty, to add to my collection. When I slipped it into my pocket, it clicked against the copper-colored pebble I had selected at our pond-side perch that morning.

I could not believe that Cappy and Zoe had not arrived yet. I knew I had not missed them—I was waiting too near the trail for them to slip past me unseen. *Where can they be? What on earth are they doing down there?*

For a fleeting moment, I was swept by a sense of irritation at having to wait on their slowness. That was quickly replaced by concern. Had one of them taken a spill? A skinned knee? A sprained ankle? I remembered my own fall, on Day One, and the TLC I'd received from Cappy and Jane. The twenty minutes I had waited already was too long.

Leaving my pack as evidence of my claim over that particular campsite, like a flagpole thrust into the ground, I walked back to the trail. I needed to look down to see if I could get a glimpse of my partners.

Nothing. Absolutely nothing.

Should I walk down to see if they need help? Should I just wait? Never before had I waited this long for them, never. On the other hand, never before had I walked so far ahead of my partners, neglecting to stop and check on them from time to time. I was painfully aware that I should never have allowed myself to get so separated from them.

Without the weight of my pack, but using my hiking poles, I headed back down the steep trail, descending the very steps that I had worked so relentlessly to ascend.

A quarter mile later, I heard their voices bouncing up the trail ahead of them. I sat down in the middle of the path on a stairstep made from a cut slab of rock. Over a hump in the path they appeared, moving slowly. Zoe in the lead, heads down, they did not see me at first.

"Joan, is that you?" Cappy called. She paused to look up at me, but did not wave. Her hands held tightly to the hiking poles planted firmly on the ground ahead of her. She wore her fleece jacket over her white shirt.

"I was worried about you gals." I stood up and took two steps down to meet them.

They continued to walk towards me, and I watched for clues as to what might have held them up. Cappy leaned heavily on her poles with each step. She looked like she was using the last of her energy.

"Where's your pack?" Zoe asked, scanning the ground around me.

They stopped when they got close. Zoe shifted the weight of her pack upwards, rearranging the straps on her shoulders and hips. I wondered if her sores were acting up again, or if it was just the normal stiffness from the climb.

"I left it up at the campsite."

"How far is it to the lake?" Cappy asked, sounding hopeful like maybe it was just around the corner. "I hope it's not far. My feet are really hurting." I was concerned. Was this the third day I had heard her complain of sore feet?

"Quite a climb, eh?" I said. "I think it's about a quarter mile back up." I used a tip of my head to indicate the obvious direction. "Are your feet acting up?"

"They are. Sometimes, on the downhills, they bother me a little, but this last climb was really challenging. Each step up hurt."

"These stairs were made for long-legged giants," Zoe said, referring to the height of the trail's steps, built long before from squared slabs of stone.

"You've already been to our nameless lake?" Cappy wore a confused look, suddenly realizing that I had finished the hike already, come down to meet them, and was now doing this last part of the hike again. "And you came back down? That was nice. I'm not sure I'd have done that for you."

"Oh, sure you would." I knew that was true. "I was getting worried." I still wondered if something had happened along the way. I did not say anything though; I did not want it to sound like I was pointing out how slow they were walking. "I wanted to come down to meet you. It's getting cold and late. Besides, I was feeling lonely up there by myself."

"How long have you been waiting?" Zoe asked as we started to move up the hill again.

"I honestly don't know, maybe twenty minutes." I felt sheepish. "I wish I could help carry something. It's still quite a climb."

Instead of my usual place in front of the group, I waited and fell in behind. Without the forty pounds on my back, I could have skipped uphill, but I stayed in the rear. I did not want to lose track of them again.

"Joan, how'd you climb this so fast? I don't understand." Cappy was still confused.

"I don't really know how to describe it, but I guess I got a second wind," I said. "Like you did on the climb to Evolution Meadows."

I was not ready yet to share the secret story of my chant-induced altered state of hiking. It sounded goofy even to me, so I was going to think on it for a while, experiment with it some more before going public even to these intimates.

When we arrived at the camping area, it was well into dusk. The dark hulking silhouettes of the mountains towered over the granite bowl. With a cold breeze rising, I was intent on getting our Frankentent up as fast as I could. Cappy and Zoe drooped onto the rocks that ringed the spot I had chosen.

Each of us operated within our own energy cycles. A few days ago, I had been the straggler climbing up to Evolution Meadows. That evening, Cappy had run out of energy on the final climb, while I had rebounded.

Taking charge, I insisted that Cappy get out the tent poles. It was déjà-vu with the roles reversed. Zoe, meanwhile, was digging out the odds and ends that were her bedding and shelter, and assembled them into her lean-to.

As a final touch, she and I pulled the newly acquired second rainfly taut across the top of her lean-to, making a second waterproof layer for Zoe's little cave. I hoped it would insulate her from the frost that was sure to accumulate in the wee hours.

The moment the tent was complete, Cappy roused. "Look," she said pointing. "Isn't that Gary and Monika, the photographers?" Sure enough, over near the lake we could see the older couple we had leap-frogged with for the past two weeks. They appeared to be chatting with a group of young male hikers I did not recognize. "We haven't seen them in a few days."

"Let's get dinner going before it's too dark to see the stove," I said.

"There's Max over by the water, too," Cappy said. "He's talking to Stella."

I paused to look—she was right. Where I had seen a group of strangers, Cappy recognized the faces of trail friends. In addition to Gary and Monika, she pointed out a whole gaggle of people we knew. Max and Stella, solo hikers we had shared deep conversations with over beer and wine at VVR. Bob, the llama guy, had replaced his llama with his grown son, who'd come to meet him along the trail. And there were the sisters, Helen and Hannah, who were celebrating one's fiftieth birthday on the trail. Even happy-go-lucky Wade was there. Serendipity had brought together all those familiar travelers, trail friends with whom we had shared a lunch spot or a campground, discussed the latest Trail Legend, or celebrated atop a pass.

"How did we catch up with all those people?" I wondered. "I thought they'd all left us behind days ago, way before Muir Ranch. Either they've been lollygagging, or we've been making even better time than I thought."

"Wouldn't it be fun if we all met again at the top of Whitney?" Cappy said.

Halfway through my Peanut M&M dessert, Gary and Monika, the photojournalists from Nevada City, wandered our way. Swallowing a chocolate mouthful, I smiled to welcome them to our spot on the rocks and slid the rest of my dessert into my pocket.

"Hey, ladies. Nice to see you again!" came Gary's greeting. They amazed me. Sixty-something, they were in remarkably good shape. They were walking the trail a little faster than we were while toting along a good deal of extra camera gear.

"Hi. How are you?" we answered in unison. Cappy and I rose and stepped closer. Zoe was working on adding layers to her outer gear, a hat and gloves, but came over just in time to join in the hugs.

"Only a few days left, can you believe it?" said Monika. She was a gregarious, yet businesslike woman with short, dark hair and a serious smile.

"It seems like forever since we left Tuolumne, and yet it feels like only a moment, too," I said. "When do you two expect to hike out?" I looked from Monika to Gary.

"We've actually been dawdling the last few days, so now we have some time to make up," said Gary. "We hope to be in Whitney Portal by the eleventh."

"You're going to have to get moving aren't you? That's only a couple days," Cappy said.

"That's actually why we're going around to all the campsites tonight. This is really our last day of interviewing fellow hikers. We want to make sure we have pictures of everyone we've spent time with," Gary said, pulling his camera strap off his shoulder and bringing the black Nikon around in front of him with both hands.

"We also want to collect some end-of-the-trail thoughts from everyone we talked with along the way," added Monika. "Would The Three Women be willing to answer a couple questions for us?" She brought out a small spiral pad and pencil from the big pocket of her jacket and flipped the pad open. Their journalistic project intrigued me, and I intended to check out their website when I got home, hoping to see The Three Women featured in their story.

We followed Gary's directions, arranging ourselves in front of a stunted shrub growing from a crack in a rock shelf. Cappy, the smallest of us was in the center, with Zoe and me as bookends.

Years later, that prized photo stands framed in a place of honor on my bookcase and practically screams, "JOY!"

Our faces are weathered, tanned, and completely aglow. My eyes are ringed in white sunglass shadows, while Cappy's squint in delight. We are bundled up in an odd assortment of all-weather gear in mix-matched colors. My windbreaker is apple green, my fleece cap black. Cappy's knit hat, a day-glow green, is pulled down past her brows and peeks out from her navy hood. Zoe's beanie is red.

But it is the smiles that make the photo. Our eyes are smiling. Our cheeks are smiling. Our mouths are smiling so broadly they take up our entire faces. We are cuddled closely together, looking like a strong, bonded team, with no hint of exhaustion or disharmony.

"So, ladies," Monika said, "our final questions are these: Why did you choose to hike the John Muir Trail? And has it been worth it?" She held her pencil poised over her pad.

Those were simple questions with complex and multilayered answers, because what she was really asking us was what were our motivations and our goals? And had we reached our goals?

What were my answers? I'm not sure! I know I would never have shared my personal grief over Krei's death and its motivating power with journalists who might publish it.

Standing just below the mighty Forester Pass, I might have made any of the following statements. Every one of them was true then and remains true now.

It sounded like a great adventure!

I wanted to spend a month in the wilderness becoming one with nature!

I love a challenge, and this challenge is an iconic one!

It was on my bucket list, and I wanted to do it before I got too old!

It was a personal test to prove to myself I possessed strength, courage, and resilience!

Unfortunately, I do *not* remember what my answers were that evening.

Starting Point — Nameless Pond, Just South of Glen Pass — about 11,700 feet
Ending Point — Lake 12,250, Just North of Forester Pass — 12,250 feet
Highest Point — Lake 12,250, Just North of Forester Pass — 12,250 feet
Distance Covered — 11.3 miles
Cumulative Miles — 162.3 miles

Fifth & Final Leg

A Nameless Pond Just North of Forester Pass to Whitney Portal
Day Twenty-Three to Day Twenty-Seven

Lost In Translation

We all live under the same sky, but we don't all have the same horizon.
In an instant age, perhaps we must relearn the ancient truth
that patience, too, has its victories.
~ Konrad Adenauer, quoted in
The Atlantic Community Quarterly v.14-15 (1976-1978)

Day Twenty-Three
August 10, 2006

Starting Point — Lake 12,250, Just North of Forester Pass — 12,250 feet

Bundled in layers of fleece against the frigid cold of morning at over twelve thousand feet, I hugged my mug of coffee-laced chai close to my chin. The rising steam warmed the exposed flesh of my face. Each sip of the hot liquid awakened a bit more of my body and mind. I watched the leading edge of the sunrise, its reflection in stone, as it crawled down the flanks of the slate gray peaks to the west, turning them first pink, then gold.

"I'll move when I can see the sun," I said aloud to myself, too cold to move.

Cappy smiled at me and nodded. I knew she would hold me to that declaration. The moment the tiniest slice of the sun was visible, I would have to move.

Zoe, having awakened frost-covered once again, even with the new rainfly layer added to her lean-to, was wrapped up in every piece of clothing she owned. While Cappy and I squeezed ourselves into dense insulated balls to maintain warmth, Zoe moved back and forth across the rocky space of our campsite, attempting to generate heat. Nose and cheeks pink from the cold, she rubbed her mittens together, then up and down her arms, and stomped her booted feet.

On the far side of the camping area, industrious hikers were already moving about, packing for the morning's assault on Forester's northern flank. "The early birds are already heading out." I pointed with my mug towards a pair of hikers suited up and marching in our direction on their way towards the first switchbacks.

Cappy had been watching them, too. "That's Stella and Max," she said in her matter-of-fact tone.

When they drew close, Cappy called out, "Good climbing!" and waved.

The pair took a small detour off the path to walk our way. "Hey!" said Stella, the more outgoing of the two. Her extremely short hair had grown out just a bit since we'd last seen her. It looked like brown cat's fur, soft and silky, above her oval face. "Have you ladies heard the advice going 'round about climbing Forester?"

"Not a thing." Cappy stood to move closer.

"What's the word?" I asked, also rising.

"Apparently, a NOBO hiker came through yesterday saying there was still lots of snow on the approach—enough that the trail is impossible to follow," Stella continued.

"Really?" Cappy and I looked at one another and then back at Stella and Max.

Max spoke in his calm, gentleman's voice, "The word is—keep left. When you come to the snow and lose the trail, go left." Max's deep dark, always sincere eyes looked serious. I wondered if he was concerned for himself or for us *old ladies*.

"That seems easy enough. Just keep to the left," Cappy said.

"Thanks for stopping to tell us." I smiled, too, and nodded. We had been gifted with a heads-up about an upcoming problem, and that knowledge came paired with the solution.

"At the top!" said Max, as they strode away towards Forester.

"At Whitney!" Stella called back over her shoulder.

By nine o'clock we were on the trail, a long series of steep switchbacks that would carry us one thousand feet upward towards the trail's highest point yet, Forester Pass, scraping the sky at thirteen-thousand-two-hundred feet. Though the sun was bold and beat down on us from the pale summer sky, the constant wind stripped the air of all warmth. I wore my windbreaker over my fleece. Despite the effort of climbing, I never generated enough body heat to make those layers too much.

The trail had been scratched out of the silver-colored rock. Sometimes we walked on a ribbon of fine decomposing granite that crunched underfoot. Other times the trail led across stretches of shifting chunks of shale that gave off a metallic clank with each step. No vegetation softened the angular, lunar features of the mountain.

As I walked, I thought about the advice we had been given by Stella and Max, wondering exactly what it meant. We had not actually gotten specific information. I wondered, in the mountainside game of telephone, if we had gotten the whole story—it seemed possible details had fallen away. It was not completely clear to me what exactly we were meant to do. The longer I mulled it over, the more confused I felt.

This "Mystery of the Buried Trail" did not carry the weight of the ominous Trail Legends we had encountered during the first half of the trip. There was no suggestion we would be facing life-threatening problems ahead, though crossing ice and snow on a steep ascent could be precarious. Best case, it would slow us down and tire us out. Worst case, there would be slipping and sliding on the slope.

We stopped for our mid-morning break at a wide spot created by the U-turn between one switch and the next. There was no place to sit, so we stood in the lee of a rock outcropping, leaning our packs and ourselves against the granite wall to rest.

"So, 'keep left'. When do you think we're supposed to 'keep left'?" I was popping M&M's and cashews into my mouth one at a time, alternating between sweet candies and salty nuts.

"We'll know when we get there. We haven't seen the snow yet." Cappy had removed her hat and was reassembling hair the wind had whipped and tangled during the climb.

"You think there's really that much snow left?" Zoe asked. "We haven't seen much snow in days... It *is* August." She took out her small collection of snack foods, selecting one granola bar before putting the rest back into her pack.

"Forester's a lot higher than we've been before—a real thirteener." Cappy unwrapped a Luna Bar. I could smell the banana aroma.

"It's not very comfortable here. Shall we walk?" I asked. "Or do you want to rest longer?"

"I'd rather take a longer lunch up at the top than sit here," said Cappy.

"Ditto." Zoe unfolded herself from where she had been crouching out of the wind.

We set off for the top. I wondered when we would find snow, and when, as the leader, I would need to make the decision to "keep left."

The switchbacks came to an end, and the trail took a more direct course upward. It wound through the leftovers of an old landslide. Emerging from a pile of giant rocks onto a flat shelf, I could see ahead to Forester Pass, where a number of tiny colored dots balanced on its rim, like sprinkles on a frosted cupcake.

Between the pass and the point where I stood lay a broad swath of thick snow. As I waited for Cappy and Zoe to catch up, I scanned the steep mountainside and the snowy obstacle. *Do we "keep left" here, before we get all the way to the snow?* I wondered. *Do we advance until the trail actually disappears into the snow and then "keep left"? Do we avoid the snow entirely by going left and all the way around it, or just stay towards the left side of the snow as we cross it?* Though people were visible at the top, I could not see anyone moving around or across the hanging field of snow.

Zoe joined me, followed by Cappy. Shoulder-to-shoulder we stood looking upward, as though admiring a museum masterpiece. It was a striking sight. The morning's clear blue sky was now streaked with wispy white clouds scurrying ahead of the wind. The granite behemoth rose skyward, grabbing at the flying clouds and forcing the sky to divide itself in two.

I voiced my questions aloud and Cappy answered, "Let's continue until the trail disappears. Then we can decide what to do." She was using her sure-of-herself voice, which I had learned could not always be trusted for its sureness, sometimes meaning exactly the opposite.

"Okay," Zoe and I agreed. I walked on.

I followed the trail, weaving through the talus heap, turning left, then right, avoiding the biggest of the boulders, climbing up and over the smaller ones. Patches of snow began appearing beside the trail, especially on the shady north side of larger rocks. The snowy expanses became wider and deeper, until the trail dove under the white blanket, disappearing entirely. Looking ahead, the steep incline was one broad white expanse with only the heads of the largest rocks peeking out.

We gathered to make a decision about how to apply "keep left" to what lay ahead. High above us, the miniature people on the pass had grown a bit larger, and we could see them waving at us. We smiled and waved back.

Ahead, a pair of hikers came into view, climbing across the snowfield. Did they know to "keep left"? Were they following that advice? Were they on the right track?

I do not remember which of us said, "Let's turn hard left here and skirt the edge of the snowfield." *It would be easier to walk on the rocks than the snow*, I thought, but it would take us in what felt like the wrong direction.

Or who said, "We ought to aim straight for the spot where the people are standing on the pass; a straight line is the shortest path." *That would be the shortest path*, I thought, but it flew in the face of the advice we had been given.

Or if anyone even suggested, "Why don't we follow those guys?"

I do know we avoided an argument by making a neutral choice that split the difference. We sighted a straight line from our spot to where the people were perched on the pass, cutting the snowfield visually in half. Then we aimed ourselves towards the left quarter of that white expanse.

"That way?" I pointed. I hoped we were making the right choice. I wished I had asked more questions of Max and Stella.

"Looks right," Cappy said.

After fifty yards of climbing and slipping, the hiking turned to bouldering. We were scaling tall rocks, slipping in knee-deep snow between them, finding handholds, and heaving ourselves up and over. We would have been okay if we had not been laden with packs. As it was, we dragged our freight and ourselves over one granite obstacle after another. Still, we saw no trace of the trail.

After nearly an hour of slow progress, I came to an impasse with no way up and over. I turned to Cappy and Zoe several yards behind. "This is not the way," I said. "It's too hard. We need to head more to the left."

Cappy turned hard left and moved in a horizontal line across the face of the mountain and across the snowfield. I climbed down and followed her. It was bouldering all the way, climbing up and over scores of huge rocks. Exhausted, after another twenty minutes of hard scrabbling, I caught up to Cappy at the edge of the icy white layer.

There lay the path, completely clear of snow.

"There you are!" I said to the trail. Then I laughed at the irony.

Looking downhill, the trail skirted the edge of the snowfield. We should have walked on dry land, avoiding the snow entirely. We had wasted an hour and exhausted ourselves in the process. We had wrongly interpreted "keep left."

Up top, only a small group remained to wave at us. Disappointed and low on energy, I walked up the trail towards the top.

An hour later, I arrived at the crest of Forester Pass and plopped down on the hard rocks. We were just in time to say farewell to a handful of trail friends, the last of the morning's "early birds" who had already lunched and rested. They had watched us struggle upward. They had tried to help us. They had not been waving to say hello—they had been trying to signal us to "Keep left. More left! More left!" If only we had been able to interpret their message.

I leaned back against the narrow rocky wall that was the very peak of the Forester Pass, closed my eyes, and took deep breaths. I pulled in the thin, high-altitude air, counted to three, then expelled my frustration.

I gazed down the way we had come. The magnitude of the feat we had accomplished flooded in with the crisp air as I surveyed the vastness of the valley and the distant ranges. Patience and determination had carried us up and over the obstacles to that cloud-high perch, to a view usually reserved for eagles and angels. With the world spread out before me like that, gratitude replaced frustration.

Only a few people ever are given the opportunity, or accept the challenge, to climb a thirteen-thousand-foot mountain. Few ever have a chance to see that sublime view, breathe that pristine air, overcome those formidable obstacles, or feel that joy-filled exhilaration. And I was one of them.

The habitable surface at the top was small, with only enough room for a dozen snuggly arranged people at a time. The sun appeared so close, but wind gusts counteracted any warming it provided. We found shelter by tucking ourselves down amidst the people-sized stones like rock-dwelling marmots. This was not a spot for a long, leisurely lunch break. No matter how tired I was from the climb, or how awed I was by the view, I would need to eat my lunch swiftly, then move on to make way for the next batch of hikers working their way up the north face.

Llama-less Bob and his son were eating lunch. They shifted over to make room for us to join them. I still had one serving of summer sausage left from the cowboy's delivery. The thought of that fatty, salty meat lifted my spirits. I leaned back against the rough rock and slowly indulged in the feast, pulling the energy into my muscles to prepare for the afternoon's descent.

Looking down, I spied four ascending hikers. They were in the process of making exactly the same error we had made. They were struggling up through the snowfield, perhaps following footprints we had left in the snow. We waved at the hikers, trying to signal them to "Keep left. More left!" They waved back and kept climbing the wrong way through the snow.

Bob and son, and the three of us chuckled as we kept pointing and waving, but there was no communicating with the climbers.

"Look at this!" Cappy called out, and we all turned. She was bent over inspecting something on the ground, a plant growing out of a crevice between two rocks. Floating above green, fern-like leaves, pale purple flowers bounced in the breeze.

"They're beautiful! How can they survive up here?" I asked. I saw not a speck of anything else green.

"Sky pilots. They're called sky pilots. I read about them in the guidebook last night. Aren't they wonderful!" Cappy was ecstatic. Upon closer scrutiny, she found half dozen more of the plants peering from the shelter of rocky crevices. She exclaimed each time she discovered another, like they were colored eggs on Easter morning. "Sky pilots are native to the Sierra and only grow above ten-thousand feet."

The heavenly view, little purple flowers, and a lunch of summer sausage had erased all vestiges of negative energy from my system. I was newly energized, eager for the next challenge and the next surprise it brought.

"Would you take our picture?" Llama-Bob held his camera in my direction.

"Of course." I adjusted the camera as they arranged themselves on either side of the elevation sign.

I took a shot of the smiling men. "Will you take ours?"

We traded places. The Three Women, packs on our backs, squatted around the sign, for our picture.

SEQUOIA NATIONAL PARK
FORESTER PASS
ELEVATION - 13,200 FT

Different from the previous night's photo, which had captured the essence of our joy, the image from atop Forester was testament to our strength. Our calf and thigh muscles bulged, as clearly defined as the confidence and power that radiated from our smiling eyes.

Behind us, the view extended northward forever. Blue, cloud-streaked skies and rows of distant mountains provided the backdrop for a long, broad valley marked by lakes, meadows, and rocky slopes. We had come a long way, Baby.

Years later, long after our epic journey had been completed, I look at that image of us on Forester Pass and think to myself, *I* climbed those mountains. *I* crossed those valleys. I *own* that power.

The angle of the afternoon's descent was even more barbaric than the morning's climb had been, like the trail was in a big fat hurry to get down ASAP. A constant wind which blew uphill, pressing into my chest, had the unexpected advantage of helping to keep me upright on the steep gravel-strewn path. This was one of the last sections of the JMT to be constructed, and one could see why. Parts had been chiseled right into the side of the mountain and hung like cantilevered shelves on a wall. In other places, masons in the early Thirties had built vast rock walls to engineer additional shelves for the trail to traverse. There were places where the hanging path was made of stair-steps, allowing the descent to grow even steeper.

I paused to let my leg muscles, the ones controlling each downward step and the ones stabilizing my joints, to rest for a moment. Standing still, I could look away from my feet to admire the view southward where the massive Kern River Basin lay surrounded by thirteeners on every side. We were still well above tree-line, still over twelve thousand feet.

I heard the dull pat-pat-pat of quickly approaching feet. Turning, I was surprised by a lone woman running down the trail right behind me. Yielding the outer edge of the footpath to her, I quickly stepped aside just moments before she flew past. She wore bright aqua running shoes, nylon running shorts, a green jacket, and a pint-sized orange daypack. Tiny earbuds trailed wires from her ears. Barely making eye contact as she whizzed by, she nodded once in what I translated as, "Thanks for moving over to share the trail. Sorry I startled you."

I wondered what would have happened if I, too, had been listening to music and had not heard her approach. Would she have slowed down or pushed me aside? I watched as her figure shrank, morphing into a colorful spot that moved across the rocky landscape ahead.

My partners arrived shortly. "How 'bout that girl who just flew by? Can you imagine running this trail?" Cappy skipped her normal greeting.

"I can't even," I said. "Just standing here, I have to keep my mind on my feet and poles, or they'll skid right out from under me when I shift my weight." It was true. If I shifted my focus from my feet to the view, just a slight shift of my hips or a little turn of my torso could transform the gravel and sand under my boots into marbles. It would be very easy to end up on my butt before my brain even realized I was falling. I had done that frantic dance once already.

"I don't get the point," Zoe said. "Look how beautiful it is out here. Why hurry?" It had been ten days since she'd joined Cappy and me and made us a trio again. She had long since acclimated her twenty-something self to our over-fifty pace, downshifting from the speed-of-youth Nemo had tried to maintain.

"Imagine if we had run through Rae Lakes Basin yesterday. Imagine all we'd have missed—the views, the swim, the scientists, that beauty, all of it." Cappy's voice was tight with incredulity. She had spent half a lifetime looking forward to visiting Rae Lakes, and she had had to satisfy herself with just a few hours. To run through that basin would have been sacrilege.

"Maybe to her, it's just another pretty place to do her fitness training, and the workout's what's most important," I said. "Heck, for all we know, this is the tenth time she's run this course, and its beauty is old news to her." I turned to look downhill. Sure enough, she had disappeared entirely into the rocky landscape below.

"Impossible. No matter how many times I'm in the Sierra, it's special," Cappy countered.

"Agreed." Zoe pointed to the vast basin laid out before us and changed the subject. "So, Cappy, where down there are we headed?"

"We're going to stop at the junction with Shepherd's Pass Trail. There's camping in the first forest. Below eleven thousand feet." I swear Cappy had the map completely memorized.

That was my cue to resume our descent.

Just shy of a mile south of Forester Pass, the trail moved downward at a gentler pace. My leg and butt muscles, which had been clenched tight all the way down, could relax, too. I paused to stretch, to encourage those overworked muscles to calm down. There, where the trail began to coast after its headlong dive, we crossed Tyndall Creek or one of its numerous tributaries for the first of several times.

Bob-and-son caught up, slowing as they passed to wave and call "Happy Trails" and "On to Whitney!" The gap between us grew steadily. Their legs were not moving any faster than mine, but their strides were thirty inches to my twenty-two. They had a fifth gear—I only had four.

The land around us alternated between rocky and sandy. Knobs of granite held the high ground; lower spots became vast sandboxes. Both were littered with rocks and boulders. Hardy plant life hunkered in the safety of leeward corners and spread out like area rugs to wave their tiny flowers in the air on three-inch tall flagpoles. The only animals we saw were insects among the plants, and marmots and pikas in the rock piles.

We stopped for a break in the first meadow we came to—one of those grassy, wildflower-spattered spreads that are sliced and diced into complex mazes by miniature streams. The little waterways were narrow and colored amber by earth made from the underlying golden metamorphic rock. Unhurried, the water seemed to amble, rather than flow.

When Cappy and Zoe arrived, I was already removing my shoes, intending to soak my feet in the water, as I had done the last couple of days. The wind was still chilly, but close to the ground, it was not so penetrating. Having been deprived of a long lunch break atop Forester, we extended our afternoon break. For the first time that day, lying close to the ground in the full sun, I was warmed through.

"I hope we really do get to see everyone on top of Whitney. Wouldn't that be fun to celebrate together at the end of the trail?" Cappy had spread herself out on the grass, her feet hanging into the slowly moving water.

"It *would* be fun," I agreed. "They're all moving so much faster, though. They might be a day ahead by that time." I did not want to start trying to keep up with the faster walkers—I liked our comfortable pace.

"Because Whitney is such a huge climb, lots of people launch from Guitar Lake. People can sort of pile up there the night before," Cappy said. "That's what I've read." She'd crossed her arms behind her head, her hat tipped forward.

"Zoe, how're you doing on these downhills?" I asked, knowing there were plenty more to come.

"The sores are gone and bruises have almost faded," she said. She pulled up her shirt and inspected the skin under the waistband of her pants with the tips of her fingers. "Padding my hips with socks was the trick."

"Good to hear," I said. "My blisters are gone, too."

"These downhills are hard on my feet," Cappy said, "like I'm hitting them with a hammer each step."

Again, Cappy's feet were giving her trouble. "What's happening? Blisters?" I asked.

"Not blisters. Tender on the inside, like each of the little bones and tendons and muscles in my feet are in pain," she said. "Every step hurts." She had pulled her right foot out of the water and was massaging it with both hands.

"That's not good," I said. "Is the cool water helping? I've got Advil and Tylenol."

"I'll be okay. I'm just glad we're not going quite so far today. I think I just overdid it the last few days." The skin around her eyes tightened in a silent wince, and she switched feet, putting the right one back into the cold water and kneading the left.

That evening, we picked a site on the edge of the campground, with humans to one side and a sunny glade to the other. We established our camp, then ate dinner sitting on a fallen log out in the late sun. The wind had softened to a breeze, and I soaked in the last of the low sun's heat as I warmed my innards with a dinner of piping hot chili.

"I want to stay here forever." I gazed back across the landscape we had covered that day.

"Here specifically or here on the trail?" Zoe asked. She had finished eating and stretched her legs out in front of her.

"Here in the wilderness. I feel so at peace out here," I said.

"A wonderful dream," Cappy said. "Impractical, though."

The sun sank behind the mountains, sliding us into dusk. Objects gave up their colors for various shades of gray.

"I know, but I don't want to go home." I spread my arms out, taking in everything I could see. "I think I've fallen in love with all this."

Tears rose behind my eyes, as a warm flood of emotion filled my chest. The impending end of our journey had sneaked into my thoughts, and my emotional reaction took me by surprise.

Starting Point — Lake 12,250, Just North of Forester Pass — 12,250 feet
Ending Point — Shepherd Pass Trail Junction on Tyndall Creek in Upper Kern
Canyon — 10,930 feet
Highest Point — Forester Pass — 13,200 feet
Distance Covered — 7.1 miles
Cumulative Miles — 169.4 miles

The End Is Nigh

I have crossed the Range of Light,
surely the brightest and best of all the Lord has built.
~ John Muir, "My First Summer in the Sierra," *Atlantic Monthly* (1911)

Day Twenty-Four
August 11, 2006

Starting Point — Shepherd Pass Trail Junction on Tyndall Creek in Upper Kern Canyon — 10,930 feet

"Only six miles? Piece of cake!" Zoe said.

That was the plan. Somehow, we had actually made up all the time and distance Cappy had once been so worried about—and then some. On this day, Day Twenty-Four, we began the first of two easy-peasy walks. They would position us to make the final audacious climb to the official terminus of the John Muir Trail at the summit of Mount Whitney. We needed Cappy and her feet to be hale and hearty for that arduous assault, and this gentle interlude would give her tender flesh healing time.

Giving ourselves permission for a lazy start that morning, we delayed takeoff until almost ten o'clock. The day's hike was a slow-motion rollercoaster ride—up we climbed five hundred feet, down we strode a thousand, then up again five hundred, with lots of littler ups and downs along the way. For much of the hike, the trail took us through shadowy fir and pine forests on dirt paths carpeted with needles. On occasion, a granite knob interrupted the forest, and the trail emerged onto a dry and open space.

For weeks, the only directional signs we had encountered were posted at the tops of mountain passes—where they announced the elevation—or at the intersections of the JMT with side trails—where they guided us in the proper direction. But that day, several signs appeared.

First, in an open sandy spot, we came face-to-face with a simple metal sign that marked a cross trail. Information had been etched into the sign's brown surface, exposing shiny silver letters.

← CRABTREE RGR. STA. 4.4
← MT. WHITNEY 11.7
TYNDALL CREEK 4.4 →
FORESTER PASS 9.4 →

Zoe announced the distance to Whitney like she was speaking into a megaphone, "Mount Whitney—eleven-point-seven miles!" and gestured like a backcountry Vanna White.

Cappy and I affected a cheer, "Yay! Wow! Hooray!"

It was exciting, our final destination so close. We had momentum, moving fast toward our end goal. I felt effervescent with excitement. *Look what we had accomplished!* I thought. *We're almost there!* I visualized myself standing triumphant atop the summit, arms raised and shouting to the heavens.

Ahead, visible through a narrow slice in the forest, a wall of dark mountains beckoned. The trail, bordered by long dotted lines of cobblestones, was guiding us ever closer to the end of the trail.

After an hour, another metal signpost stepped into our path. Standing in the center of a trail intersection, it pointed us in a new direction. The post held a pair of signs. One confirmed that Forester Pass stood behind us. The other pointed us hard left toward Mount Whitney.

← CRABTREE RGR. STA. 1.0

← MT. WHITNEY 8.3

Zoe announced in her dramatic voice, "Mount Whitney—only eight-point-three miles!"

"Single digits!" Cappy said.

"Yippee!" we all sang.

A lump rose from my gut to my chest. I felt a sudden desire to stop. *Turn around. Go back.* Alarm bells rang in my head. *Warning! Beware of civilization ahead!*

Had I forgotten? I had wanted to stay there in the wilderness forever. Now, I was running out of time!

For days, weeks, I had submerged myself in the experience of walking, of the wilderness, of simply being one with nature. I had welcomed the daily challenges that honed both my body and my mind and was feeling completely at home and content living in the wilderness. Thoughts of home and cars, soft mattresses and electricity, jobs and family, or anything else that smacked of civilization had rarely entered my consciousness. My hiking had resembled a walking meditation for days, with distractive thoughts only occasionally passing through like faint whispers.

Like a countdown to blastoff, though, the mileage signs had triggered the power of anticipation. Something was shifting within me. Anticipation and aversion battled in my mind. I found myself looking ahead. Not just to Whitney, but beyond Whitney to home.

With each mile we traversed, my mind wandered home. I thought of all the comforts and conveniences of my sweet little house, of the eight-hour drive home on 395, and of all I had to do to my classroom to be ready for school to start in just one week. In one corner of my mind, I even began to compose the great stories I would tell family and friends. First Whitney, then home, pulled on me like super-magnets.

I tried to keep the mental invasions at bay, to stay focused on the present, on the trail beneath my feet, on the trees and sky and rocks and flowers I was moving amongst. I counted my steps, "One, two, three, four." I called forth my trusty walking mantra, "Love, life, truth, beauty, abundance, and peace," to stave off the invasive thoughts.

But, a little crack in my mental windshield had begun that day—with those mileage signs—and little by little, the crack began to spread.

The JMT and the PCT split up and went their separate ways that day, the latter heading south through the Mojave Desert to the Mexican border hundreds of miles distant. While the former veered east towards Mount Whitney. Thru-hikers on both trails had shared the same track for nearly two hundred miles, but the time had come to meet our separate destinies.

← JOHN MUIR TRAIL
PACIFIC CREST TRAIL →

The Three Women and the John Muir Trail had a date with a mountain. We were on a mission. Under the hypnotic spell of so many signs, we walked farther that day than we had planned, covering nearly nine miles instead of six.

In the afternoon, just before arriving at Crabtree Meadow Campground, we officially entered The Whitney Zone. Standing guard at the boundary was a handsomely carved wooden sign, words burned into its surface.

ENTERING THE WHITNEY ZONE
SPECIAL PERMIT REQUIRED FOR
ALL HIKERS, DAY OR OVERNIGHT

They meant business. The fines for permit-less hiking were steep. The permit we had picked up back in Yosemite, which I had been carrying for twenty-four days, included our march through The Zone all the way out the other side at Whitney Portal. We were covered.

Another sign, just inside The Zone, pointed once again to our ultimate destination, as if we could have forgotten.

GUITAR LAKE 2.7 →

MT. WHITNEY 7.5 →

I felt giddy at each new sign-sighting. It was like a game, and we were winning. But walking along between signs, eating up the shrinking distance, my sadness at having to leave bubbled to the surface.

Beside that sign, completely out of place in the pristine environment, sat a large Rubbermaid tub, scarlet red with a green lid. Its garish existence in that spot marred the beauty and disrupted the tranquility of the surrounding wilderness as surely as visions of the hot showers and bacon-cheeseburgers waiting for us at Whitney Portal cracked my inner tranquility.

A paper sign printed in big, bold letters was taped to the container's top:

WAG BAGS

YOU ONLY NEED ONE

"The mere thought of using one of these freaks me out just the littlest bit," I said, as I reached into the container for my *one* WAG bag and held the lid open for my companions. I got a sour taste in my mouth, and I could feel my nose crinkle.

I thought about taking two, just in case I produced more than the average hiker and really needed it. But I did not. I followed directions.

I translated Zoe's silence on the matter as an agreement. She reached into the bin, pinched the corner of her WAG with two fingers, and lifted it out with particular care. She held it out in front of herself, away from her body. Her squinted eyes and cocked head communicated a silent, "I'm not so sure about this."

"Oh, it might not be that bad. I read on the Internet they work pretty well," Cappy said, as she grabbed hers with a bit of bravado.

I pressed the plastic lid back in place.

"*Pretty* well' is not the same as *well*. It's something *less* than well. And I'd prefer this worked *really* well," I said.

We stepped to the side of the trail and secured the WAG bags inside our packs before going in search of our campsite.

WAG bags (Waste Alleviation and Gelling Bags) had been elevated to the level of Trail Legend—their story carried along the JMT by NOBO hikers. Of all the Trail Legends we were to encounter, this was to be the only one where my actual experience turned out to be as bad as the Legend predicted. In fact, it was far worse.

Throughout the summer months, the Whitney Zone is crowded with people from all over the world, all wanting to secure bragging rights for summiting Mount Whitney, the tallest peak in the Lower Forty-Eight states. Those swarms of people put a huge strain on the environment, especially when they relieve themselves. A hiker who has to "go" cannot dig a hole in the granite to bury her leavings, and there is nowhere to flush it either.

WAG bags were invented as the solution to that problem. They are the ultimate in Leave No Trace, what-goes-in-must-come-out, backcountry hiking. Beyond Pack It In, Pack It Out, The Whitney Zone required that we carry out not just all our own trash, but all our own human waste—in what everyone called a Poop Bag. They were the harbingers of the crowds massing ahead. Nothing says, "Welcome back to civilization!" like your very own personal Poop Bag.

The WAG bag, actually a pair of thick sealable plastic bags, one inside the other, contained a chunky dry powder, which turned to a thick gel when wetted. The theory was that one's poop would be encased in gel, which would then harden into an odorless brick securely wrapped in plastic. Each WAG was designed to be used more than once over the course of the two or three days it took to traverse The Zone. Unfortunately, I would find that the system did not work as elegantly as described.

Long before our three days in Whitney Zone were over, my WAG would be filled to the brim with a reeking mass the consistency of chocolate-chip cookie dough. Fearful it might leak into my backpack, I swaddled it in an extra trash bag and strapped it on the outside. Still, the aroma hovered around my pack. It was unnerving to be stalked by the invisible stench.

The instructions said we could rid ourselves of the ghastly things only in "the designated human waste dumpsters located at the trail head" at Whitney Portal, ten miles beyond Whitney summit. I would carry the malodorous lump for three days, a powerful motivator for making haste up and over the mountain and toward the Portal with its designated dumpsters.

Any trepidation I had about reentering civilization was magnified by the knowledge that a WAG bag sat in my pack that night. It was the perfect symbol for the growing impact people were having on our vulnerable wilderness areas and for the teeming masses that awaited us on the other side of Whitney. This was not going to be a gentle reentry. We were going to walk headlong into a wall of people. I was more intimidated by that challenge than the challenge of climbing to more than fourteen thousand feet.

Our campsite above Crabtree Meadows afforded us a perfect view of the emergency helicopter hovering over the peak of Mount Whitney. We had just been raving to one another about our campsite's vast panoramic view of the broad backside of California's tallest mountain, our ultimate goal. The granite behemoth looked close enough to touch. Distances in the mountains are deceiving, though. We would not even be climbing Whitney for two more days, not until after we had positioned ourselves at Guitar Lake at the foot of the long ascending trail.

The helicopter was like a wasp buzzing round the head of an elephant, too far away for us to hear the rotors thumping. Had we not been looking and pointing at the massive mountain, talking enthusiastically about bagging the peak, we would have missed the whole event. The chopper, a dark silhouette against the white summer sky, hovered for several minutes, moving only slightly in the afternoon westerlies, before setting down.

We stood up from where we were relaxing and stepped forward to better observe between the trees.

"What do you think's going on?" Zoe asked, pointing, while still holding the nylon bag she had been rummaging through moments before.

"What *could* be going on? What would prompt a rescue up there?" I wanted to look toward my hiking partners but could not tear my eyes from the high-altitude crisis.

"It's like watching a movie with the sound off," Cappy said. "I want to *hear* what's happening."

"Do you think someone fell?" Zoe suggested. Her rock-climbing-trained mind immediately went to an accident.

"It might be a severe case of altitude sickness," I said. "What do they call that, Cappy?"

"Edema," she filled in the word for me. "At high altitude, fluid accumulates in your brain or your chest. It can be fatal—in hours."

For days, I had been trying not to worry about our climactic trek to the JMT's southern terminus at Whitney's fourteen-thousand-five-hundred-foot summit. I had experienced no problems with altitude sickness our entire trip, not even while tackling the twelve- and thirteeners of the last week. My body seemed to have acclimated to the higher altitudes of the Southern Sierra.

BUT.

This was not the first time I would attempt to climb to the top of Whitney, and memories of that previous experience had been following me along the trail for a couple days. Watching the helicopter, I felt my chest tighten with a rush of anxiety, as the memories returned again.

A week before Labor Day in 2004, my friend Sue had called me. Because of last minute dropouts, she had a pair of extra places on a small-group permit to climb Mount Whitney over the three-day weekend.

"Wanna come?" Sue asked. "Do you know anyone who'd want the other spot?"

"Of course, I do! That's wonderful!" I did not hesitate. "And I'm sure I can recruit another friend!" I was in good physical shape and confident that climbing Whitney was do-able.

"It's short notice." Sue's voice was energetic and confident. "We're driving down Thursday, camping at Whitney Portal, then hiking in before daybreak on Saturday. That gives us one day to acclimate to the altitude."

School had just started, so I was not that flexible. I would have to wait to make the six-hour drive on Friday and skip that extra acclimation time. I did not worry— I had spent much of that summer camping in eighty-five-hundred-foot-high Tuolumne Meadows and hiking all over Yosemite's backcountry.

When asked to join me, Rene said, "Yes!" even faster than I had. She was a younger teaching colleague and always up for an outdoor adventure. We would take Friday off, drive down Highway 395 together along the eastern edge of the Sierra, and meet Sue's group that evening.

Rene and I arrived at dusk to find the parking lot and campground full. I heard Sue's musical laugh before I saw her. She is a soft spoken and gentle woman, but that evening her laughter was our locater beacon. She greeted me with a warm embrace, then reached out to include Rene.

"There's room here for your tent." She gathered up equipment that had served as place markers. "We had to beat people back to save this spot," she explained with another warm laugh. "People keep pouring in."

The overflow campground was a dirt parking lot under tall pines. Small tents and sleeping bags covered nearly every speck of ground. It looked like a refugee camp, where everyone's clothing and equipment had been donated by REI and Patagonia. The sheer number of people created a constant background hum.

The plan was to hit the trail before 4AM, so Rene and I decided to save time by sleeping under the stars without the tent. We toted our backpacks from the car, laid out our sleeping bags, made a quick meal, then stowed our food in the large metal bear boxes. I could not imagine any self-respecting bear venturing into that crowd of loud and smelly humans, but I followed the rules and put everything edible or fragrant into the locker.

Shortly after ten, we crawled into our side-by-side sleeping bags, our backpacks near our feet. Exhausted, I hoped for a good sleep before my watch alarm woke me at three-thirty.

All night long, more vehicles pulled in. The dull rumble of their engines arrived before the brightness of their high beams. Each one circled the parking lot, its occupants looking for a place to stop, its headlights making bright sweeps between the trees. I do not know which was more annoying, the hissing sound of newcomers' whispering or the rasping sound of nylon fabric being unfolded and arranged on the ground. Just as one group settled into silence, another car would approach. The parade went on all night, and I grew more frustrated. My own tossing and turning did not help me settle into sleep.

I was sure I had not slept, but I must have because I was awakened in the wee hours to the insistent rasping sound of nylon rubbing on nylon, like someone was arranging a sleeping bag on a pad, over and over again. In my frustration, I whispered, "For god's sake, just finish already!"

I heard Rene mumble something, and the sound stopped for a moment. I sighed at the welcome silence, but the rustling noise began again.

Rene jerked into a sitting position. "Stop that!" she snapped sharply at a barely visible shadow near her feet.

I felt around for my glasses, put them on, and sat up all in one frantic motion. Gaping, I watched as Rene slapped at a small brown bear sitting on its haunches at the foot of her sleeping bag. Its forepaw rested on her backpack. "Go away!" she whisper-yelled and swiped at him again. The cub froze for an instant, then bounded off into the darkness.

Rene turned on a flashlight and inspected her pack where the cub had been worrying it. The bear's claw had sliced a small hole in the nylon fabric. "That mischievous little monster!" she said. "He was trying to get into my pack."

I was wide awake. "What time is it?" I asked, looking at my watch. "Three o'clock."

"Not much point in trying to sleep now," Rene sighed, pulling her legs free of her bag and gathering her boots and jacket.

Mirroring her, I was out of my bag and donning my jacket and shoes.

Saturday's plan was to carry full backpacks from Whitney Portal, at eight thousand feet in elevation, the six miles up to Trail Camp, which sat at twelve-thousand feet. We would leave our packs there. Then, we would scale the last and steepest part of the climb to the fourteen-thousand-five-hundred-foot top of Mount Whitney, after which we would return to Trail Camp for the night. After a good night's sleep Saturday night, we planned to hike the rest of the way back down Sunday and drive home.

Piece of cake.

Wearing headlamps to pierce the dark, we climbed and climbed through the predawn blackness on one switchback after another. Above and below were parades of hikers visible only as slow-flying fireflies moving up the mountain. By the time the sun showed its face, framed in the deep V created by the walls of the canyon we ascended, it was already hot, and we had a long way to go.

From the beginning, I felt sluggish and had difficulty keeping up with Sue and Rene. The group was strung out along the trail in the dark, and once it was light, I found myself at the tail of the pack. Rene walked just ahead, waiting whenever I fell behind.

"I don't know why I'm so tired," I said when I caught up at a turn in the switchbacks. I stopped, allowed myself a long drink of water and some deep breaths. I felt the beginnings of a headache, so swallowed a couple Advil.

"Don't worry," Rene said, "I don't mind walking a little slower than the group." She wrapped stray blond strands behind her ears and readjusted the long ponytail that hung straight down her back.

"It's getting late, almost eight o'clock," I said. "I want to get to the top with time to get back down." I made ready to start walking again.

"I think this is a good day to be a tortoise, not a hare." Rene turned and began a slow, deliberate pace. I followed, weary and working hard to keep up.

We arrived at the ten-thousand-foot Outpost Camp, a small, green valley meadow encircled by trees and rock walls. I am sure I was encircled by beauty, but I had pulled into myself, aware of only how physically uncomfortable I was and how distressed my weakness was making me.

I pulled off my pack and let it thud to the ground. We had only walked a few hours, but I felt beaten. My muscles were like jelly, and I was keenly aware of the effort it took each time I lifted a foot. I sat on the soft grass and leaned back against the trunk of a large pine. I was glad we'd planned for a quick breakfast stop there. Rene sat beside me, looking fresh and in no need of a rest.

My head throbbed dully. My brain felt swollen and bruised inside my skull and seemed to press against the backs of my eyeballs. I took more Advil and drank lots of water. I was hungry, but my stomach complained with a hint of nausea, so I ate only a granola bar and some peanut M&M's. I closed my eyes, cupping my hands over them, while I chewed and rested my head back onto the tree. A vague sense of panic was rising. *I will not be sick, I will not be sick.* I willed my body to cooperate.

"Why don't we leave our heavy packs here?" Rene suggested.

I opened my eyes and slowly rotated my head to look at her. There was concern in her pale blue eyes.

"What?" I asked, confused.

"Why don't we leave our packs here—just carry our daypacks with water and food?" she repeated.

"You mean camp here tonight, instead of up at Trail Camp? That'll mean a longer walk down tonight." I was trying to wrap my addled brain around her alternative plan.

"Sure. But it will be a lot harder carrying this extra weight uphill three miles than walking downhill three extra miles with only daypacks," Rene explained. "I'm tired, too."

I knew she was not as exhausted as I was. She had suggested Plan B purely for my benefit, but it did seem like a good idea. I was grateful and readily agreed. We shuffled bare necessities into daypacks and left our backpacks behind.

My ballooning headache attacked anew after we left Outpost Camp.

"Drink lots of water," is the advice everyone gives when hiking in high altitudes. "It'll prevent altitude sickness." So, I drank extra water and took more Advil. Within a mile, my head was pounding, daggers of light stabbed my eyes, my stomach turned upside down, and my rubbery legs could barely hold me upright. I had a powerful urge to sleep. The two of us fell farther and farther behind the group. Really, I was the one who was faltering, while Rene graciously chose to slow her pace and remain with me.

We had a pair of walky-talkies in those pre-cellphone-in-the-wilderness days, so when we stopped again to rest in the shade of a huge red fir, I spoke. "You go on,

I'm holding you back," I pressed Rene. I stood in the shade, trying to catch my breath.

"I don't want to leave you alone," Rene insisted. "What if this gets worse?" Her face showed concern, the skin around her eyes and mouth drawn tight.

She was truly torn. Rene is a highly competitive person who was determined to bag this peak, yet she's also compassionate and deeply caring.

I held up my little blue walky-talky. "We'll keep in contact with the radios. If anything happens, I'll call you and ask for help. I'm not going to make the top, but there's no reason you can't." I affected confidence.

Decision-making gears turned in her head. "All right," she said slowly, wanting to trust the plan. "I don't want to abandon you."

"You're not abandoning me. I'm making a choice," I insisted, trying to smile, but even that hurt. "Look, I'll make my way slowly to Trail Camp. I'll find Sue's tent and wait there. I'll meet you on your way back down." No longer standing, I had sat down, intending to stay there for a while.

"O—kay," Rene drew out the word as she finally agreed. "But you have to call me if you get worse."

"I will. I promise." I leaned back on a rock shelf and smiled at her. "Take some pictures from the top for me—and radio me when you get there."

She waved goodbye and walked up the stone trail. I remained in the shade of the fir tree. I took more Advil and drank more water. Then I lay down. My brain felt squeezed inside my skull. My stomach threatened to pitch. And I was dizzy. The sun stabbed my eyes right through the dark lenses of my sunglasses. Shiny iridescent spots spun and darted across in my field of vision, so I closed my eyes and pulled my hat over my face. Altitude sickness can be dangerous when it is bad, and I felt bad. Neither the water nor the Advil seemed to help. I tamped down my rising fear. It dawned on me that I might not even make it to Trail Camp.

I started awake, not sure where I was. I checked my watch. It was well after noon. I had been lying by the side of the trail for almost two hours! My shady spot was now in full sun, and I felt hot all over. Worse, though, I was embarrassed thinking about all the people who had walked by me while I was unconscious to their passing.

After sleeping, my head was a little better, a little clearer, though it still hurt like a giant bruise the shape of a wide headband. I decided to continue climbing up to Trail Camp, probably a mile farther and less than a thousand feet higher, where I was sure to find Rene and Sue on their descent.

I do not know how long it took me, but it seemed like hours. I dragged myself upward, one wobbly step at a time, stopping to catch my breath over and over every few steps. I was alone on the trail. Even the late starters had long since passed me by. I walked, oblivious, looking only at the ground where I placed my feet.

Trail Camp was not a pretty place. It was crowded and dirty. Tents grew like mushrooms among the rocks. Camp sat at the base of the infamous ninety-nine switchbacks that carried hikers to the top of the ridge. From where I stood, Whitney's broad peak was invisible behind the hulking wall of granite.

I found Sue's familiar tent behind a rock wall built by climbers long ago to hold back the steady winds. I felt like I had found an old friend. Tears of grateful relief rose in my eyes. I crawled in, wrapped her sleeping bag around myself, and conked out. I held the walkie-talkie in my hand, close to my chest, so I would not miss a call from Rene or Sue.

Much later, in the dusk created by the bulk of the mountain, I woke to a voice calling my name. It took a moment for me to realize it was coming from the radio in my hand and not a person.

Rene's voice crackled. She had made it to the top, signed the logbook, shot some photos, and was on her way back down. My misery retreated a little at the sound of her voice. I was happy she had succeeded. I was not even disappointed for myself, just relieved I had not ruined her adventure, too.

Head still throbbing with the remaining shadow of the earlier pain, I sat outside the tent on one of the protective rock walls and watched for her yellow jacket to appear descending the switchbacks. Rene had told me she was entirely out of water, so I pulled myself together long enough to filter water from the scummy pond, filling my two empty containers to the brim. I planned to greet her with the water, so we could descend to our backpacks before it got completely dark.

I was flooded with relief when her lemon-colored jacket appeared as a bright dot against the gray mountain. I had not realized how alone I had been feeling until her familiar figure drew close. Like Olympic relay runners in ultra-slow motion, I fell into step with her and handed her a water bottle like a baton. "You made it," I said.

I felt better with every downward step.

Standing alongside Cappy and Zoe and watching as the rescue helicopter lifted off, having retrieved some poor soul from the very top of Whitney, added fuel to my fire of anxiety.

"Sometimes you eat the bear, and sometimes the bear eats you," I thought. Two years earlier, the bear had eaten me. This time, I was determined to eat the bear.

I was determined to reach the very top of that monstrous mountain. I was determined to stand with The Three Women on that peak and sign my name in the famous logbook. Then, we were going to celebrate.

Starting Point — Shepherd Pass Trail Junction on Tyndall Creek in Upper Kern Canyon — 10,930 feet
Ending Point — Crabtree Meadow Campground — 10,700 feet
Highest Point — Shepherd Pass Trail Junction on Tyndall Creek in Upper Kern Canyon — 10,930 feet
Distance Covered — 8.8 miles
Cumulative Miles — 178.2 miles

Sauntering Towards Whitney

To live is the rarest thing in the world.
Most people exist, that is all.
~ Oscar Wilde, "The Soul of Man Under Socialism", 1891

Day Twenty-Five
August 12, 2006

Starting Point — Crabtree Meadow Campground — 10,700 feet

"Come on in, Joan!" Cappy called. "The water's fine!" This was the umpteenth frigid lake Cappy had found to swim in.

"Thanks. I think I'll pass." We both laughed as I stood ankle deep at the edge of Guitar Lake.

Once waist deep, Cappy dove headfirst towards deeper water. She popped up, eyes wide from the cold shock. Treading water, she swept her wet tangle of curls out of her face. She began to swim, breaststroke style, back and forth parallel to the shore, her face one huge smile. Why that experience made her happy was beyond me. I shook my head.

Zoe took her time wading in, attempting to acclimate her body, impossible in water so recently frozen. Finally, she counted, "One, two, three," and then plunged in to join Cappy in deeper water.

"It feels great," Zoe called back to me, sputtering.

"Yeah, right—to a polar bear."

Directly across the small rocky bowl, a previous camper had turned a large, round patch of snow into a thirty-foot smiley-face. The clever artist had carved eyes and smile down through the white layer to reveal dark rocks below. Melting snow dripped directly into the lake not fifty yards from where they swam.

While they cleaned off sweat and trail dirt in ice water, I ventured in up to my knees, then stopped. My toes ached with the penetrating cold; I could feel chilled blood retreating up my legs towards my core. I splashed my body with handfuls of water, gasping, then scrubbed with my little towel. Dust and dirt trickled like coffee down my legs.

"Joan, it would be easier if you just swam!" Cappy said, emerging clean and shivering. Zoe dashed out, too, bee-lining for her dry clothes warming on the rocks. Her purple lips curved into a smile.

Painfully easy, I thought.

Let them have their fun. Guitar Lake was their last opportunity for a frigid pool party. The next evening, we would be on the eastern flank of the Sierra, and the evening after that, we would be in the flatlands heading home. We had this whole day and the lake all to ourselves—a sweet interlude—before we would emerge from the Alternate Universe we had been inhabiting for weeks and reenter the Real World.

Clean and dressed, we sat like marmots, sunning ourselves on boulders, letting our hair dry in the warm breeze snaking up from the valley far below. I felt almost guilty enjoying such a leisurely day. We had hiked such a short distance in the morning on a trail that meandered along the edges of meadows and creeks and forests. We had not even started walking until ten o'clock. I had not even broken a sweat.

"That's it?!" I'd said when, before lunch, we came over a rise to find ourselves at Guitar Lake. "We're here already?"

The lake, shaped like an acoustic guitar—an hourglass body attached to a long narrow neck—was scooped out of rock at the foot of the granite wall that included Mount Whitney. Boulders the size of stools and chairs and softballs were scattered around the lake's edges. Little vegetation grew at eleven-thousand-five-hundred feet, only low patches of tough green plants mostly flanking the lake's shore. We set up camp in the lee of a shoulder-high rock pile beside the guitar's body and began to enjoy our first holiday from hiking in almost three weeks, the first since our extra day at Red's Meadow on Day Six.

I spent the early afternoon meditating, napping, and catching up on my journal, where I wrote, "All this foreign relaxation is a gift—an extra special treat for body, mind, and spirit!" Repeatedly, I interrupted my writing to glance over my shoulder and stare at the beckoning tower of stone.

"Visions of cheeseburgers are dancing in my head," I said that evening as I boiled water to hydrate my pasta dinner.

We were hunkered down together behind our protective pile of rocks. The wind had picked up—cold gusts swept across the open landscape with nothing to slow them down. I had donned all my layers, including a warm fleece hat pulled snug over my ears, but I took off my gloves to cook dinner.

Thoughts about the famous burgers at Whitney Portal Cafe had visited me often, ever since signs began measuring the shrinking distances for us. Most times food thoughts rolled through my mind, I had kept them to myself, but the ache for real food was becoming so strong that I had to speak it aloud. I poured boiling water over noodles and sauce.

"French fries. I want a huge pile of French fries," Zoe chimed in. "With ketchup."

"I want mustard with mine—and a green salad—a giant salad with tons of fresh vegetables," I added. "And bleu cheese dressing."

"Will you two stop it already!" Cappy scolded from where she sat clutching and sipping her evening hot cocoa.

I laughed. "Are we getting to you, Cappy? What do *you* want most to eat when we're back in civilization?"

"Strawberries and peaches," Cappy whispered. Then louder, "I hope Jim will bring fresh fruit to The Portal." She had a far-away look in her eyes, like she was imagining herself somewhere else.

It wouldn't matter what food he brought, I thought. *Cappy just wants to see her Jim.*

We had morphed into a trio of old stable horses turned toward home, nostrils flared to catch the scent of hay and oats in the barn. Ironically, just two days earlier, I had been fantasizing about living in the wilderness forever, never going home. I had felt a part of the mountains, like I had grown roots into the ground. With two days left, however, my head had whipped around like that stable horse.

I suffered from a love-hate relationship with civilization. One part of me lusted for one of the Portal Cafe's famous burgers with fries, a Dryer's chocolate-dipped ice cream bar, bushels of fresh fruit, a hot shower and shampoo *and* conditioner, clean underwear, and my own soft bed. But another part of me still wanted to linger in the wild. That part wanted to stay far away from people and buildings and highways, to remain among the wild things, with trees and wildflowers, beside flowing waters, where the Milky Way glowed bright as streetlamps.

My food supply was dwindling towards naught. Rattling around in the bottom of my near-empty bear canister were one freeze-dried dinner entrée, four protein bars, and a little bag each of dried fruit, nuts, granola, and hard candies. I could not have remained any longer on the trail. Without the luxury of the civilized food I carried, I would starve. I had enough food to carry me up and over Whitney and out the Portal, and not one bite more. As much as I wanted to believe my own romantic notions, we were not really creatures of the wilderness, we were only guests, and our time was nearly up.

Cappy had an additional motivation for getting to Whitney Portal. Jim was going to meet us there and chauffeur us back to Yosemite. The previous day, she had mentioned his name every time a sign announced the distance to Whitney, her face soft and her eyes full of light. Cappy missed Jim fiercely, I was sure, though she never came right out and said it.

"Jim will be excited to finally meet Zoe," she said, and, "Jim said he was going to drive down the night before, so he'll be at the Portal early in the morning," and even, "I'll bet Jim's barely washed a dish since I've been gone and is hurrying to clean the house up before he drives down here!"

I was looking forward to seeing Jim, too. He had my bag of supplies—fresh clothes, flip-flops, shampoo and conditioner, a razor and deodorant. When last we saw him, he had hinted, with a twitch of his fluffy white eyebrows, that he would be sure to greet us with *real* food. Like Cappy, I hoped that would include fruit, but I also craved bread and cheese. I had tasted neither of those delicacies in a long time.

The wind buffeted our little tent and Zoe's lean-to. We climbed into our sleeping bags early, after the blood-red sun had sunk through the smoky sky to the west, but before night's thick blackness filled the sky. Our plan was to get up early and hit the trail long before the sun peeked over the monster mountain to the east.

Snuggled in my warm bag, I read aloud our last bedtime story, the final pages in *The Devil in the White City*, the Epilogue, where author Larson reflects, "The [Chicago World's] Fair had a powerful and lasting impact... in ways both large and small" on all those who participated.[18]

I knew our sojourn in the wilderness was similarly having both large and small impacts on my companions and me. Some were obvious—I was stronger, braver, more confident, and my body was in the best shape it had been in twenty years. I would need to allow for the distance of time to provide a fuller perspective on what the larger impacts might be, but I knew I had grown.

Starting Point — Crabtree Meadow Campground — 10,700 feet
Ending Point — Guitar Lake — 11,473 feet
Highest Point — Guitar Lake — 11,473 feet
Distance Covered — 2.4 miles
Cumulative Miles — 180.6 miles

---

[18] Eric Larson, *The Devil in the White City: Murder, Magic, and Madness at the Fair That Changed America* (Knopf Doubleday Publishing Group, 2004) p. 373.

Sometimes You Eat the Bear

Promise me you'll always remember:
you are braver than you believe,
stronger than you seem,
and smarter than you think.
~ Christopher Robin to Winnie-the-Pooh,
in Disney's video *Pooh's Grand Adventure*, 1997
(inspired by the Winnie-the-Pooh books by A.A. Milne)

Day Twenty-Six
August 13, 2006

Starting Point — Guitar Lake — 11,473 feet

"Can you see Hitchcock?" Cappy pointed with her hiking pole.

"Wow! It really looks just like him," Zoe laughed.

She was right. From our vantage point that morning on the trail far above the distinctive shape of Guitar Lake, we could see a second lake, its form the spitting image of Alfred Hitchcock in profile, the left-facing, black silhouette used as the logo for *Psycho* and *The Birds* and all of his other films.

"The cartographers must have been standing up here when they named those two lakes," I said. "The guitar shape wasn't so obvious when we were on its shoreline." From high above, the guitar's hourglass body and slender neck were unmistakable. The big, white smiley face on the lake's far shore was now just a small white circle.

We had paused for a few minutes on a wide granite bench to take our morning break and enjoy the expansive view westward far out over the Central Valley. From that elevation, I imagined, if it were not for the smoky haze on the horizon, we'd have been able to see all the way to the Pacific. I ate one of the last protein bars in my dwindling stash while we admired the spectacular view.

A couple of hours earlier, we had waved farewell to the grinning snow sculpture and been climbing ever since. We had filled our water bladders and spare water bottles to the brim. There would be no water sources on the rocky ascent, nor on the descent—none until we arrived at our destination campground, nearly ten challenging miles away on the far side of the mountain.

We had been giddy that morning, nearly as excited as the day Cappy and I had begun our great JMT adventure. On Day One, we had linked arms with Jane and skipped across the wooden bridge behind Tuolumne Lodge, singing, "We're off to see the Wizard!" as though embarking on a magical path. We had not departed Guitar Lake singing that morning, but I was eager to conquer Whitney and standing at the top of the world would be magical.

"Can you believe it? We are about to complete the mighty John Muir Trail." Cappy had been bursting to be on the trail.

I had wanted to say, "On your marks—Get set—GO!" and watch her dash off. Instead, I said, "Hard to believe the adventure's almost over! Soon, we'll be standing atop that!" I pointed in the direction of the wall that was Whitney and its neighbors.

"Ready?" Zoe asked, and we were off. Cappy did not sprint. But had she, I would not have been surprised.

The steady morning climb traversed the backside of Whitney and the broad ridge that stretched south from the peak. During the first half of the three-thousand-foot climb, the trail took us across gravel-and-stone-strewn rock. The climb was steady, not difficult, though that would change.

The trail then morphed into a relentless series of switchbacks. The ground was cracked and broken. Talus was scattered across the trail in several places, evidence of landslides that swept nearly to the bottom. Our eagerness to get to the top made the monotonous trail feel endless. Could it be around the next corner? The next? But it was not.

A pair of ravens, sitting together on a ledge above the path, was deep in discussion as I walked by. Whether they were muttering about the weather, or arguing about dinner plans, or gossiping about the humans walking by, I am not sure, but their deep voices were distinctly conversational. They nodded their heads and fluffed their feathers when making a point. They were the only signs of life, other than the occasional hardy sky pilot we encountered all morning.

That peaceful solitude would change soon. At thirteen-thousand-four-hundred-thirty feet—two miles and a full thousand feet below the Whitney crest—the trail splits. To the left, the JMT continued to the top of Whitney and its own conclusion. To the right, the spur trail headed over the ridge and down the other side towards The Portal and the parking lot. On that trail, day-hikers climbed up from The Portal to summit Whitney, only to merge onto the JMT for the final climb to the peak. At a wide sheltered spot beside the intersection, a half dozen backpacks stood, lined up against the rock wall. JMTers dropped their heavy packs in that little rock alcove before continuing to the top with a lighter load.

We added our three packs to the waiting group and downsized for the final approach. I took out my fanny pack, loaded it with my lunch and a bottle of water, and tied my windbreaker around my waist. I wished I had a camera.

While we assembled ourselves, a steady stream of summit-bound day-hikers walked past us, heading up from the eastern approach. About one-hundred-fifty people are issued permits to ascend Whitney from the east every day. In the short time we had stood there, a dozen passed by. It promised to be crowded at the top.

"We've definitely reentered civilization," I said. Already sounds of conversation were buzzing through the air.

"Just you wait. There'll be more people at the top than we've seen in a month," Cappy said, taking the lead up the path.

The trail was steep and narrow, in places just hanging off the side of the mountain. In other stretches, it was covered with scree that made the footing precarious. Despite those obstacles and having to share the footpath with so many others going in both directions, we fairly flew up the mountain. Liberated from my heavy pack, I seemed to be walking a foot above the ground.

"Do you feel like you're floating up this hill?" Cappy said.

"Levitating," said Zoe.

"I think I could run all the way to the top." I was not exaggerating. I could have jogged. "To think I was worried about the altitude!"

For a while, the trail ran alongside the crest of the ridge, a long, slender vertical wall notched with eroded window-like holes, talus falling from them both east and west. Looking east through the mountain windows, the White Mountains near the Nevada state-line were visible rising out of the desert. In places, the thin wall rose into pinnacles. The tallest, christened Mount Muir, was substantial enough to be a fourteener. We paused to admire the mountain-turned-monument named for many a Sierra hiker's hero, John Muir. Though tall and pretty, it was *not* impressive. Really just the tallest tooth in a whole row of teeth, it was dominated by the massive head and shoulders of nearby Mount Whitney.

"John Muir did so much to explore and preserve the Sierra. I wonder why the powers-that-be chose this humble little peak for him?" I asked. Not even Cappy had an answer, but we decided it was probably political.

A few more switchbacks took us to the broad expanse that was the top of Whitney. Unlike Mount Muir and the other sharp pinnacles, Whitney was an upside-down soup bowl, a vast rounded chunk of granite. It does not seem right to call it a peak—it was more a dome. Even when we were close enough to see the metal-roofed hut that sat beside the highest point, we still had fifty yards to travel across the curved granite top. A crowd had gathered, some at the hut, some at the plaque that marked the tippy top, others spread out all across the expanse.

Cappy led us straight to the hut, where a short line of people waited to sign the register. Built for shelter, the hut remained locked up, no longer used for its original purpose. Years ago, it was deemed too dangerous to hunker down in a place that high with a metal roof during a Sierra thunderstorm. A flat metal box attached to the side of the stone building held a large thick registration book. Previous pages were filled with the names of those who had come before us.

Zoe held up the heavy protective lid so Cappy could sign the ledger. I did the same for Zoe, and Cappy for me. Besides my name and hometown, I am not sure what I wrote in the area provided for comments. I imagine I wrote, "Sometimes the bear eats you, and sometimes you eat the bear," but I am really not sure I had the presence of mind to be that clever. I recently asked Cappy, and she does not remember the words she wrote either. You would think that would have been a detail we would have both committed to memory, or at least written in our journals that evening, but all the excitement of the moment must have swept the words away.

From there, we made our way through festive throngs to the highest point on the great dome. Waiting our turn, we stood witness while others posed for pictures on the crown of Mount Whitney. The plaque, marking both the mountain's apex and the trail's terminus, described the elevation as 14,496.811 feet. Modern measurements now put the height at 14,505 feet. Somehow, since 1930, the mountain grew eight feet!

National Park Service

U. S. Department of the Interior

Mount Whitney elevation 14,496.811 feet

John Muir Trail — High Sierra Trail

September 5, 1930

This tablet marks the construction of the highest trail

in the United States. Begun in 1928, it was completed in 1930

under the direction of the National Park Service working with

the United States Forest Service.

We took our turn and captured a group photo, the three of us standing side-by-side on the tallest rock atop the grandest peak of the Sierra. I placed my hand on Cappy's shoulder; her hand was on Zoe's. We wore our JMT uniforms, huge satisfied smiles, and a mantle of confidence across our tanned and muscular shoulders.

Turning over that prime spot to new arrivals, we wandered away to find a perch where we could relax over lunch. I felt like dancing, like singing, like jumping up and down and shouting and screaming. I wanted a horn to blow, a flag to fly, confetti to toss.

"We did it, Joan. We *did* it!" Cappy bounced along. "We walked the whole thing!" Cappy and I hugged and spun around in each other's embrace, laughing. "We did it," she said over and over.

"My face hurts from smiling," I said. "It's surreal—a dream." I threw my arms out wide and my head back, expanding myself to take in the whole world.

Then Zoe joined us for a Three Women circular hug. Again, we spun around, dancing beside the highest point in the sky.

"I'm glad I'm wearing these heavy boots," Zoe said, "or I might float off into space!"

We found a couple wide rectangular blocks of granite, tall as coffee tables, wide as area rugs, and away from the masses. There we spread ourselves out for a picnic in the sky. Waiting beside my seat, I found a nearly square, black-and-white-speckled chunk of Whitney granite, the perfect final piece for my collection. I stood to slip the dice-sized rock deep into my pocket.

The view was a surround-sound-three-hundred-and-sixty-degree panorama of infinity. Nothing stood between us and the distant horizon except wide open space. To the east lay the Nevada desert and the White Mountains; to the south and north, row after row after row of ridges separated by invisible valleys; to the west, the Central Valley and maybe, just maybe, the sea. The cloudless sky glowed azure, rich and bright, except where smoke in the west smudged it dirty. We sat to eat, surrounded by that inverted blue-sky bowl. The sun, directly overhead, felt close enough to touch.

Out came the food. I was hungry, as usual. But distracting myself from celebrating that climactic moment long enough to eat was difficult. It is actually difficult to chew and swallow when you cannot stop smiling. I did manage to finish off the last of my pecans and dried cranberries and one more Odwalla bar.

"I'd never have finished if you two hadn't adopted me." Zoe's mood had turned sober. *Are those tears pooling in her eyes?*

"We are so glad you joined us!" Cappy assured her, beaming like a proud mama.

"We made a great team!" I agreed. "I wish we had Champagne! But let's toast, anyway." I held up my half-full Nalgene. The others joined me. "To The Three Women! Cheers!"

"The Three Women!" they repeated.

It was silent for a few moments, then Cappy spoke again, "It wouldn't have been the same adventure without you, Zoe!"

We spoke from the heart. It was important that Zoe believed what we both knew to be true. She had added an important ingredient to our experience—a different perspective, youthful energy, and humor. Our whole experience was richer for her having hiked with us for two weeks.

I could have focused the whole of my attention on the amazing views that surrounded us—the sky, the mountains, the horizon—but instead, my attention was magnetically drawn to what had become peculiarities in my world of late—the people.

It was an interesting assortment that had congregated at that altitude, at least fifty of them. There were couples and families, pairs of buddies, groups of friends, and solo hikers. They talked and laughed, snapped pictures and lounged over lunch like we were doing. Most looked like us, seasoned hikers attired in proper hiking clothes, carrying daypacks and hiking poles. Others were dressed in summer shorts and tennies, like they were out for a day at the lake.

There was a constant line at the registration book and another at the photo spot at the top of the top. As fast as one group walked away, another joined the line. Among all those faces that surrounded us, however, not a single one was familiar. No one from our four weeks in the wilderness was present with us in the crowd on the summit.

Though we still had several downward miles ahead of us to get from Whitney to the cafe and parking lot, for the John Muir Trail itself, this was the end of the line. Mixed emotions tumbled around inside my chest, while my mind worked to untangle them. It was a bittersweet point on the trail. I was floating with excitement, positively effervescent. It thrilled me to think of what my partners and I had accomplished. My smile felt permanently stretched across my face. The previous four weeks had all been aimed arrow-straight at that point, and it was a celebratory moment, sitting atop the crown jewel of the Sierra. At the same time, it was the JMT's terminus. The trail was finished, and our adventure would come to a close in twenty-four brief hours and ten short miles.

"Let's take more pictures." Zoe leapt up, her playful nature taking over. "Let's do some Wonder Woman poses." She threw her arms up and her legs out, like she had stopped mid-jumping jack, and smiled proudly. She shifted position to show off her flexed biceps, then tipped forward, both arms and one leg stretched out like her superpowers allowed her to fly through the sky like Superman.

Cappy and I joined in Zoe's game. We took turns posing in triumph. It was foolishly fun, and we laughed ourselves silly. I was giggling so hard, at one point, I had tears rolling down my cheeks.

Pulling ourselves free from the mountaintop's magnetic field was difficult. Meandering reluctantly towards the trail, taking in the vistas one last time, we were enveloped within the parade of day-hikers vacating Whitney's crown. We backtracked along the JMT—past the pinnacles and the eroded windows and Mount Muir—to the intersection of the spur trail, where our resting backpacks waited. There were two dozen packs there now, squeezed into the alcove space, and we had to wade through and shift some of the new additions to get to ours at the back of the pile.

There we left the Muir Trail behind. The spur trail began through a narrow gap in the mountain, a topless tunnel, which took us from the western side of the Sierra to eastern side. It carried us over Trail Crest, which turned out to be the highest pass we had surmounted during the entire journey. At thirteen-thousand-six-hundred-and-forty-five feet, it stood higher than Mather and Forester and all the rest, though it was not officially part of the JMT.

The eastward trail immediately became truly treacherous. Very steep, it was the most poorly maintained trail I have ever seen anywhere. There were sections where pieces of the trail had fallen completely off the mountain, leaving behind a sliver of the path clinging to the mountain, barely wide enough for one person to walk. I had to lean into the cliffside, practically sliding along the wall, to get past.

The rock surface of the walkway was sometimes satin smooth, other times crumbling into chunks. Some segments were strewn with roly-poly sand or buried in shifting talus fallen from higher up.

"How am I supposed to cross this?" Cappy had stopped at the edge of a wide patch of ice.

Zoe and I were piled up behind her looking ahead in disbelief. Cappy's eyes broadcast her anxiety, stretched wide and encircled with tight lines. We stood for some time surveying the obstacle in front of us. Ice drooled down the rock wall beside the trail in solid drips and spread across the trail in frozen sheets before it dripped off the other edge creating giant icicles.

Stepping aside, we allowed a pair of young men wearing small daypacks to cross the miniature glacier ahead of us. Rather than crossing slowly, they pushed across the obstacle quickly, using their lanky legs to take six long loping strides, minimizing the number of foot-ice contacts they made. Cappy and I looked at one another.

"So is fast the best way to cross?" I asked her. I was dubious. "I think I'm going to take slow, solid, flat-footed steps—and use my poles."

"I'm not sure I want to rely on my poles," she said. "Will they even grip the ice if I need them?"

"Let's go one at a time, like we did with river crossings," Zoe said.

I cautiously tested the icy surface with each mincing step, looking for spots that were more gritty than glassy. My flat-footed gait worked to keep me upright. My heart was still pounding in my chest and echoing in my ears long after I had crossed. I took a deep breath, watching as Zoe crossed last. Incredibly, the ice would not be the worst section of the trail we traversed that day.

A long section of the trail had been hit by a landslide from above sometime in the past. Parts lay buried under piles of unsteady rocks, while other segments were missing entirely, having been shoved over the side with the rockfall. A long series of metal poles had been set into what remained of the trail, right along the drop-off edge. Then a metal cable had been strung between the poles, many of which were rusted or leaned at drunken angles off the edge. I did not know which was worse, the state of the trail or the state of the safety cable.

I tried not to rely on the guardrail too much, not lean my whole weight on it. But if I slipped on the rotten surface, I wanted to be holding onto the cable to keep myself from following the previous landslide to the bottom. So many people take that trail every season, every weekend, a significant number of them minimally experienced hikers, that it is a wonder more people are not severely injured or killed on that harrowing trail.

"I'd hate to have walked the two-hundred miles of the JMT, only to die on the last stretch, just trying to get home," Zoe commented when we stopped to rest part way down.

"Very anticlimactic," I agreed.

Her irreverence made me laugh, good medicine for anxiety.

The trail was crazy crowded. The last of the day-hikers still heading up to the top were passing us going one way. Other day-hikers, the ones who had already summited, passed around us going the other way. None had the burden of a full pack, so they wanted to move faster than we could go. A few individuals were descending at what I considered a reckless speed, rushing to get to the bottom, and I did not want them, in their haste, to put me in danger. When someone approached me from either direction, I would stop, step aside, lean against the solid wall of the cliff to claim the inside of the trail, and yield to them the narrow outer edge to pass.

The final part of the day's descent, widely known as the "Ninety-Nine Switchbacks," was perhaps the only series of switchbacks on the whole trip I did not attempt to count. I was too busy watching my step and planning my route through the rubble and slick spots, so I cannot confirm the number.

Trail Camp, two-and-a-half miles below Trail Crest and only six miles above Whitney Portal, was our destination. The camp had remained invisible to us for most of the downward climb. Only after the switchbacks carried us around a corner created by a long vertical ridge did it come into view.

A small pond, really a large snowmelt puddle served as the only source of water for all the visitors. Radiating outward from the pond, hundreds of small tents stood jammed against one another. It looked like a refugee camp had sprung up on the side of the mountain. Still above timberline, at over twelve thousand feet, there were no trees and no vegetation. It was base camp for most hikers climbing Mount Whitney via the Portal. It was the same place where, under the influence of altitude sickness, I had waited, sleeping in Sue's tent, for Rene to return from the summit, two years earlier.

No one would have chosen to camp there except for the access it provided to Whitney. It offered no amenities. Even the solar-powered pit toilets that had been semi-operational two years prior had been removed. It was a hideously ugly place to camp. The WAG Bag drop-off station was filled to overflowing. Despite a sign instructing people to not leave their poop bags beside the overfilled bins, scores of people had done just that. Mounds of reeking plastic bags were piled all around the canisters, which swarmed with flies, the only living things besides humans that seemed willing to survive in that environment. I was very tempted to add my own WAG to the malodorous pile. I had wanted to be rid of it all day. It was completely full and unusable. I had hoped to pick up a second one at the Wag-Bag station, but there were none to be had. The sign said the next drop-off station was three miles downhill at Outpost Camp. We would be passing that way in the morning.

Zoe found a protected spot amidst the masses where we could position our tent behind a stone wall built as a windbreak. Water filtered and bottles filled from the small pool, we sat on rock stools inside our tiny space and made dinner.

I had one last dinner entrée left. It was the first time during the whole trip I was going to be completely out of food. After dinner, all that was left rattling around in my food canister would be a Ziploc bag of granola for breakfast, two power bars for the next day's six-mile hike down to The Portal, and a handful of hard candies.

"It's either perfect planning or pure luck, but this is my last meal," Cappy said. Back to the wind, she was bundled against the penetrating cold. She looked comfortable sipping a hot cup of cocoa, while her dinner steeping in her cooking mug beside her. Steam rose from the cup in her gloved hands, surrounding her face with a small white cloud.

"A little of both, I suppose." I was wrapped in all my warm clothes and sitting beside her, my back to the wind. I had finished my hot tea and was working on the steaming pasta and meat sauce in my mug. "We did plan well, especially that part about packing one extra meal in every food box." I held up my mug. "This is my last leg's extra meal."

"That *was* a good idea," Cappy agreed. She had moved on from cocoa to curried something-or-other.

"For me," Zoe said. "It was *pure* luck and negligible planning." She had eaten her last entrée the night before at Guitar Lake, so she was eating power bars and snack food for dinner, some of which Cappy and I had contributed. It was a strange combination, not one she would probably have chosen, but we had made sure she had plenty of calories. It was like eating cereal and milk for dinner or cold leftover pizza for breakfast. Not one's first choice, but it would do in a pinch. And this was certainly a pinch.

Trail Camp was housing so many hikers—those planning to go up early the next morning and those, like us, heading down after summiting—it emitted a cacophony. For weeks, the loudest night noises we had been exposed to were our own voices, the gentle swish of nylon against nylon, and the crunching of our own footsteps on the ground. At Trail Camp, the din was constant and raucous. The wind roared through the camp all night shaking our tent despite the windbreak. Yet the boisterous and celebratory human noises—clanking equipment, tents going up, dinners being cooked, boots on rock, talking, calling, arguing, and laughing—were louder than the wind. We were immersed in humanity, and it was deafening.

I tossed and turned in my sleeping bag. Cappy was doing the same beside me. "You awake?" I whispered. It had to be after midnight.

A whispered, "Yeah," came from both directions.

"Welcome to civilization," I said softly. "There are way too many people around here."

"Too many loud people," agreed Zoe.

"Why aren't they sleeping?" Cappy asked. "Don't they have to get up early, too?"

"I'm not sure I like people anymore," I said, rolling over again to the soft shushing of nylon on nylon.

"Goodnight, Joan," Cappy mumbled.

"G'night."

Starting Point — Guitar Lake — 11,473 feet
Ending Point — Trail Camp, Whitney Zone — 12,040 feet
Highest Point — Mount Whitney summit — 14,505 feet
Distance Covered — 9.3 miles
Cumulative Miles — 189.9 miles

Somewhere Over the Rainbow

Somewhere, over the rainbow, skies are blue,
And the dreams that you dare to dream really do come true.
~ Dorothy Gale (Judy Garland) in *The Wizard of Oz* movie,
lyrics and music by Harold Arlen and Yip Harburg, 1939

Day Twenty-Seven
August 14, 2006

Starting Point — Trail Camp, Whitney Zone — 12,040 feet

Morning came with crashing and banging. The upward-bound hordes were on the move. They had begun traipsing through Trail Camp in the wee hours of the morning. Assuming everyone in camp was as eager to get to the top as they were, they showed no restraint.

"Good morning," Cappy chirped, loud enough to include Zoe in her nylon lean-to. Jim awaited us at the end of today's hike, and she bubbled with pleasure. She dressed fast and pushed out through the tent flap, leaving me to follow.

"Still cold out here," she called back.

I took the hint, scrambled into all my layers, and popped out right behind her.

"Look at that." She pointed to the massive wall of granite a few yards to our west.

"Whoa!" It was a breathtaking sight.

The towering east face was ablaze in light that reflected the rising sun, a "Good morning!" version of alpenglow. The low-angle light emphasized the rough texture of the rock, making every crack and crag a black crevasse. Every chunk of talus cast a shadow. Above the sharp spikes that fringed the top of the ridge, the sky was the intense Pacific Blue found in the big Crayola sixty-four-color box of crayons. The mountains themselves glowed Atomic Tangerine, a rarer color found only in the larger ninety-six-color Crayola box. Scattered patches of dirty snow near the top glistened pink.

Cappy dove back into the tent in search of her camera and came out clicking. Our excited voices brought Zoe out of her many coverings, bootless and still pulling on her hat and gloves.

After breakfast, while I applied the usual single layer of precautionary tape to my feet, Cappy said, "I wish I could fix my feet by taping them. I don't know if there's anything I can do so they won't hurt."

I looked up from where I sat on the rock stool. Zoe turned from her packing.

"How much did they hurt you yesterday?" I asked. "I don't remember you mentioning them." She had not said anything until the last few switchbacks, and then only that she had wanted to rest a moment here and there.

"They're really tender this morning. All these days climbing on hard rock have really taken a toll." Cappy sat down near me, removed her left boot, and wiggled her toes. "It's like every little bone and joint in my foot is sore."

I turned my attention from my foot to hers and watched as she massaged the ball of her foot. I could see no swelling, no bruises, no redness.

"I'm sorry. I hadn't realized you were in pain yesterday," I said. I put down the tape and scissors I had been using. "Somehow, I thought they'd gotten better after resting at Guitar."

"That rest *did* help," she said, taking off her other boot. "Yesterday's climb, though, really aggravated them again. Especially that final downhill." She carefully began to rub that foot, causing a flicker of a wince to cross her face.

"Tape has worked for me. Pads worked for Zoe. But I don't know how to protect your feet," I was thinking aloud. "You can use anything I have in my first-aid kit," I said, lifting the blue pouch from the ground and digging through it for inspiration. "Any ideas? What about moleskin? Advil?"

"Are there sores on your skin? Or is the pain all internal?" Zoe asked.

"It's all inside," Cappy said. "Every time I take a step, a sharp pain shoots through my foot."

"We're almost to the end. Can you do these last six miles?" I tried to mask my rising concern, while my mind fruitlessly pawed through ideas.

"Do I have a choice?" Cappy laughed, turning her focus to replacing her boots.

"You will tell me if it gets worse, right?" I watched her attend to her feet.

Cappy is a stoic type. Never say die! Somewhat like me, I suppose, she would never admit defeat or show weakness, not until she had no other choice. I wondered if she was being completely honest about how much pain she was feeling. I would have to keep an eye on her.

In six miles, the trail would drop almost four thousand feet. Cappy's feet would have to endure a lot of hard-rock pounding.

Scads of people climbed past us, heading up to take their turns at the top, while yesterday's mountaintop crowds were heading down. The footpath was like a freeway with traffic jams at the narrow spots. Because we carried big packs and moved slower than those with less luggage, we were constantly stepping aside to let those with smaller loads skitter past.

Soon after passing Mirror Lake, we came to the day's halfway point, Outpost Camp, which marked the outer limit of the Whitney Zone. There were no toilets available, but we followed an overwhelming stench to the large WAG Bag drop off bin.

I heaved my plastic bag into the half-full bin. "What a relief to be rid of that!" I crowed.

We moved away from the bin toward a grassy spot in the shade. The plan was to rest for a few minutes and nibble on our very last powerbars.

"Are you two tired? Do you need this break?" Cappy asked. "If we skipped it, we could get to the bottom faster—to showers and real food."

And Jim, I thought. "You sure you don't want to rest your feet, Cappy?"

"No. I don't want to prolong this. I just want to get to the bottom," she insisted. "My feet are not going to stop hurting until we finish at the Portal, so I'd rather not sit down." Her face and voice were steady; she sounded determined.

"Okay, then," I said and turned back to the trail.

Less than three miles remained of our nearly two-hundred-mile journey.

Those three miles dove two thousand feet in elevation and were going to be particularly punishing on Cappy's feet.

The crowds of hikers had thinned out, so there was plenty of room to spread out on the trail. But on that descent, I wanted to stick close to Cappy, just in case she asked for help. Zoe had the same plan, so we reduced our normal walking speed to keep pace with Cappy's slowed steps. Walking just ahead of her, we found keeping that pace surprisingly difficult. After just a few moments, we would turn around to discover a huge gap had opened up between us. We would pause and wait for Cappy to catch up, observing her closely as she approached.

A wince traveled across her face with every step. She was trying to walk just on her heels, allowing them to take the burden away from the front half of her feet, but on the steep switchbacks, that was just about impossible. She leaned heavily on her hiking poles, each step taken gingerly, like she was walking across burning coals. Her face was creased with concentration.

When Cappy caught up, we waited so she could take a few deep breaths.

"Is there anything we can do to help?" Zoe asked.

"Not really," Cappy said, then added, "On second thought, talk maybe. Distract me a little."

We talked about real food and hot showers. About seeing Jim and what he might have brought in his car. About good shampoo and clean clothes. About shaving our legs and slathering on body lotion. About sitting in a real chair and sleeping in a real bed. We joked about what we would see when we looked at ourselves in a mirror. Zoe and I even ventured into the topic of work and how weird it was going to feel to go back to our jobs. The conversation, however, kept circling back around to real food and hot showers.

"I cannot stop thinking about bacon cheeseburgers with fries," I said. "Do you think I could get double bacon?" The idea of fatty, salty meat was heavenly. Talking about it made my mouth water and my stomach gurgle.

"Stop it!" Zoe laughed. "Now my mind is going to be filled with thoughts of greasy French fries for the rest of the hike."

"That's a bad thing?" I said. "Ketchup or mustard?" I teased.

"Ketchup. And pickles. I want dill pickles on my burger."

"What about you, Cappy? What are you looking forward to most?" I turned to her. "Besides Jim, I mean."

"Jim would be the first thing, for sure."

It's good to see her smile, I thought.

"Then a shower. Then food," Cappy concluded.

"I hadn't thought about that!" I said. "Do I want to shower or eat first?" I paused to let the alternatives run through my imagination.

"Food is my first choice," Zoe decided without hesitation.

"I'm going to spend some delicious time imagining both options for a while," I said.

Cappy was a real trooper, hardly complaining the entire way, though it was obvious she was in constant pain. With less than a half-mile to go, we paused one last time to rest. Cappy leaned back against a large rock that bordered the trail, taking the weight of her pack off the balls of her feet. She closed her eyes and sighed, taking deep breaths. I wished I could take her pack, but that was impossible.

It was sadly ironic that more than either Zoe or me, Cappy wanted to hurry downhill to see Jim, but her body could not cooperate. She had not had any injuries on the whole trip, yet here on the very last day, her body was giving her fits. Thank goodness her pain had surfaced only at the end of the trek, only on the very last day gotten this severe. I do not know how we would have dealt with an injury like that in the heart of the trip. It might have brought it to an early end.

We emerged from the trail like we had stumbled onto a stage. From the wilderness, enter stage left, we stepped into the civilized space of Whitney Portal. The trail turned concrete. The trees backed off. The curtain rose. The space opened up. A parking lot. With cars. A building sat on concrete. Chairs, tables, umbrellas. People. Civilized people, who entered and exited the stage every which way. We were wild people. We had gone feral for a month. We held back, stood close together, surveying the space.

Could we remain wild for a little while longer? I wondered. *How long do we have? Civilization is contagious, like a virus. We're sure to catch it*, I thought.

I pulled off my pack, setting it beside a chair, then leaned my hiking poles against the table. I suddenly felt filthy. I looked down at my dirt-streaked shins. At the grime beneath my fingernails. The aroma of cooking meat filled the air. It wafted from the door of the grill.

"I want to find Jim," Cappy blurted while yanking off her pack. On a mission, she stepped into the parking lot. I followed her. Zoe followed me.

Across the blacktop, Jim waited by his car. I recognized his brilliant white hair and tall slender frame immediately. In a scene reminiscent of every Kleenex-worthy romance movie ever made, freed from the weight of her heavy pack, Cappy hobble-ran on her sore feet across the asphalt towards him, calling, "Jim! Jim!" Her arms were already outstretched to embrace him.

Seeing her, he dashed forward to meet her halfway. And in what could not have been better even in slow motion, she flung herself into his arms. In the middle of the parking lot, they embraced and kissed, tears running down both their faces. They pulled back, looked into one another's smiling faces and teary eyes, and then did it all over again!

It was better than the movies!

That could have been the final scene, the resolution of our story. Except I still had not gotten the hot shower or the double-bacon-cheeseburger I had been lusting for. Until those last two events took place, we could not yet say "...and they all lived happily ever after."

Zoe and I hung back to give them a few moments alone. Feeling a tad awkward, we observed the kissing pair from across the parking lot.

"Think she missed him?" Zoe asked.

"Think he missed her?" I responded. We both laughed.

Eventually, they broke apart and waved us over. Jim and I did a quick hello hug, his long lanky body bending down while I stood on tiptoes. Cappy introduced Zoe.

"I am so glad to see you ladies," Jim's pale eyes twinkled. He was impatient to show us his surprise.

"I have a car full of goodies I brought for you." He was over-the-top excited, ready to burst with pride. He opened the back of his car to reveal coolers and grocery bags full of fresh food. "I imagined you'd be craving fresh fruit, so I brought lots." He showed us baskets of cherries and berries, bags of peaches and apricots. He glowed, smiling as we groaned with pleasure. "There's more, but I'll bet you want a shower first."

I grabbed a basket of strawberries, brought it to my nose to inhale the rich, honey-sweet scent, and then munched down four in quick succession. The red sweetness was intoxicating. I held the basket out to the others. Zoe took a handful, but Cappy shook her head, her mouth full of cherries.

"We've been talking for a couple of days about the burgers in the cafe," I told Jim. "I may die if I don't get one very soon."

I grabbed my bag of fresh clothes and my bath towel from Jim's car and headed back towards the cafe. Cappy grabbed her own clothing bag. All four of us carried fruit towards the table where our packs waited.

I could smell the bacon the moment I entered the cafe, which doubled as a small store. We each ordered food and paid for a turn in their single shower facility. Cappy called first dibs on the hot water. I did not even compete. I was content to sit at one of the plastic picnic tables on the patio, eating berry after berry while waiting for food order number-eighteen to be called. My turn with the shampoo and hot water would come—anticipation was half the fun.

Zoe had no bag of clean clothes waiting for her. She and Nemo had planned to take the shuttlebus back up to Yosemite Valley, where her clothes and supplies sat waiting in her car. Fortunately, I had packed two outfits for myself, just in case, so I loaned her something fresh to wear.

Jim asked questions. And Zoe and I told stories, sometimes talking over one another. When the food came, though, I ate in total silence, focused only on the flavors and the textures—meat, cheese, four pieces of bacon, fresh tomato, dill pickle, and mounds of spicy mustard. I savored every bite of that burger. Then I washed it all down with an ice cold, fizzy Diet Pepsi.

Cappy rejoined us, looking squeaky clean. She finished working her comb through her long ringlets before sitting down. Jim had already retrieved her burger. Seeing it, she dropped her comb on the bench beside her and dug into her fries.

After a couple of enthusiastic bites, Cappy turned to Jim, "You know, we never did get the tent. We got the fly, but not the tent. You did mail it, right?"

Jim stopped eating mid-bite. "What!? Of course, I did."

"I wonder where it ended up," Cappy said.

"The mystery deepens." Zoe laughed.

"On that note—my turn!" I said. Jumping up, my bag of clothes and bottles over my shoulder, I left them telling stories.

The shower was a tiny curtained stall in the corner of a miniature bathroom, but the water was deliciously hot, and there was plenty of water pressure. I lathered my hair with the hydrating shampoo. Three times. Then I layered on the conditioner, letting it soak in while I washed the rest of me. Dirt swirled down the drain. I used a moisturizing cleanser on my face, shaved, rinsed my hair, and reluctantly turned off the water.

From nowhere, the rousing melody from the movie *Chariots of Fire* filled my head. As it looped round and round, a growing sense of triumph swelled in my heart. We had done it! I had done it. I had walked the entire John Muir Trail. I found myself humming the movie's victorious music of Olympic champions as I dried myself with the thick terry towel, then wrapped it around my head. "La la-la, la la-la. La la-la, la la—."[19]

My clothes, cotton-soft against my weathered skin, felt baggy. The shorts hung loose off my hipbones. I did not know just how much weight I had lost, but it was significant. My body shape had grown sleek, muscles firm and defined, bones visible through taut skin. I would step on my bathroom scale in two days to discover I had lost eleven pounds.

I wiped condensation from a small mirror mounted high on the wall, so I could see only my face and neck. It was the first time I had seen my own clear reflection

---

[19] *Chariots of Fire,* Academy Award-winning musical score composed by Vangelis Papathanassiou for British film *Chariots of Fire,* 1981

since the even smaller mirror in the dark shower room at VVR. My curls were pale sun-lightened blond, my face bronzed, my cheekbones prominent. Noticing my silver necklace in the mirror, I touched its three rings and paused my humming to whisper to myself, "Strength. Courage. Spirit." I closed my eyes for a moment and whispered, "We did it, Krei, we really did it."

My body was not the only aspect of myself that had been altered by my experience. Not visible in that mirror was a whole array of inner changes I had experienced. I could not have articulated them that afternoon at Whitney Portal. It would take time and a deeper reflection for me to thoroughly appreciate all I had gained from my JMT adventure.

Hiking
Starting Point — Trail Camp, Whitney Zone — 12,040 feet
Ending Point — Whitney Portal — 8,360 feet
Highest Point — Trail Camp, Whitney Zone — 12,040 feet
Distance Covered — 6 miles
Cumulative Miles — 195.9 miles

Driving Back To The Starting Line
Starting Point — Whitney Portal — 8,360 feet
Ending Point — Tuolumne Meadows Wilderness Ranger Station — 8680 feet
Highest Point — Tioga Pass — 9,943 feet
Distance Covered — 153 miles

The Other Side of The Mountain

In every walk with nature, one receives far more than [she] seeks.
~ John Muir, *"Mormon Lilies"*,
San Francisco Daily Evening Bulletin, July 19, 1877

Much Later
2023

Home Sweet Home, Colfax, California

"Why did you choose to hike the John Muir Trail?" Back on Day Twenty-Two, the two photojournalists, Monika and Gary, asked each of The Three Women this question. It is only with the distance of time and much thought that I have come to know just how multilayered the answers are to their two simple questions: "Why?" and "Was it worth it?"[20]

The goal of completing the John Muir Trail, with its finish line atop Mount Whitney, began with the urgent nudge of loss and grief. My desire grew with the encouragement of wise advice about the healing power of being in nature. But it became more than that, taking on broader meanings. My motivation arose partly from the instinctive human desire to test myself against one of the universe's supreme challenges. With midlife came a need to prove to myself that I possessed the strength to embrace and overcome whatever challenges the second half of my life held for me.

My heart was drawn to the John Muir Trail's sublime pairing of difficulty with beauty, exertion with peace. Two-hundred demanding miles taxed my strength and courage, while the same two-hundred miles bewitched my spirit with its sometimes-charming elegance, sometimes-stunning grandeur, always-hypnotizing wildness.

Not many people on Earth ever take the opportunity to really leave civilization behind for more than a weekend. Yet, along with my hiking partners, I was able to live in the wilderness, immersed in its wild beauty for almost a month.

"Was it worth it?" Most certainly.

Succeeding at such a huge personal challenge changes a person. My JMT experience stripped away much of the power that fear-of-the-unknown once held over me. When we take on the *nearly* impossible and succeed, the impossible begins to look approachable.

I could see farther—literally and figuratively—when I stood on top of mountain after mountain. From that perspective, the horizon grew wider. Distances shrank. After walking two hundred miles carrying all I needed on my

---

[20] Photojournalists Monika and Gary Wescott of Nevada City, CA. *The Turtle Expedition, Unltd.,* https://turtleexpedition.com/contact/

back, the difficulties of life's daily struggles were diminished. Balancing the many parts of my life became less complicated once I learned to ford rivers and walk across narrow logs.

Fear loses its power in the face of someone who has known courage.

May you find the strength, spirit, and courage to embrace your dreams and goals.

Acknowledgements

It turns out writing is harder than hiking! Creating this book has been an adventurous journey more challenging than our two-hundred-mile trek along the John Muir Trail. I could never have accomplished either goal without the companionship, encouragement, and support of many others.

First, of course, in the long list of those to whom I am indebted, are **Caroline "Cappy" Hickson** and **Jane Riedel**, my JMT hiking companions whose stories are woven deeply throughout this book. Without them, the journey would not have begun, let alone finished. I have pestered them with questions over the years and they have patiently answered them, as I verified the accuracy of my memories. We three remain "sisters of the trail," our friendship burnished by the challenges we encountered and overcame together during the summer of 2006. We are heroes in each other's lives. As The Three Women, we continue to hike together on local trails and enjoy one another's company immensely. I cherish my friendship with these strong, courageous, and spirited women.

"Zoe" is now a National Park Ranger working in Yosemite. I'm thankful for the added dimension of youthful exuberance that she injected into our JMT adventure. It would not have been the same journey without her.

Sue Abeloe, my longtime hiking partner, was never actually able to hike with The Three Women, but without her, there would never have been the original goal nor the plan to hike the JMT, and I would have never invited Cappy and Jane to join the adventure.

Writing is often portrayed as a lonely, isolated endeavor. In my experience, nothing could be further from the truth. Developing as a writer and creating a manuscript involves interacting with and learning from or alongside countless others. To each of those colleagues I am uniquely indebted and grateful.

First among those writers, I must highlight the spectacular and unparalleled **Willow Valley Writers** (WVW), my beloved critique group of many years. This dedicated group of skilled and eloquent writers are also the very best critiquers in the writing world. They have provided me with the wisest and richest possible feedback! **Patricia Dove Miller** was originally our teacher and guide. Her gentleness and deep knowledge of style and storytelling have been indispensable to my growth as a writer. **Barbara Olson Lawrence** and I, previously Pat's students and now her colleagues, have worked our way along this writing path side-by-side from the beginning, much as Cappy and I walked every step of the JMT, helping one another to grow stronger and nimbler as we developed our storytelling skills. Without my WVW, seriously, this book would not exist!

The Auburn area's **Gold Country Writers** (GCW) is a community of writers who encourage one another, share resources, and sponsor educational opportunities for writers. I have learned and grown as a writer through my membership in this welcoming group that includes veteran published authors and brand-new writers. I bow in gratitude to all the fine people who make this organization so valuable and so unique.

I have received unwavering encouragement and brilliant support from a lovely circle of dear friends. Some gifted me with their detailed reactions as insightful early readers and outdoor enthusiasts, the very people for whom this book is written. My adventure partner and personal cheerleader, **Bill Currie**, could not have been more encouraging. Sadly, he passed away in 2020, so will not see this project to its fruition, which makes me sad. Others will, and we shall celebrate together when the first books are printed and tip a glass to Bill. **Sandra McPherson**, BFF of nearly 40 years, hiker, and stellar clarinetist. **Pamela Adams**, fellow teacher, longtime friend, and my "reflective-voice whisperer." **Jodi O'Keefe**, teaching partner, loyal friend, powerful outdoorswoman, and JMT veteran. My chosen family and go-to sounding boards, **John and Janiene Lynch**. **Holly Bundock** and **Mack Shaver**, outdoors enthusiasts and close friends, who stood beside my writing trail with constant encouragement. And two creative writing friends, who always remind me how much joy comes out of writing our stories, **Del Dozier** and **Philip Jacques**.

My folks, **Louise and Wally Griffin**, adopted me when I was an infant way back in the Fifties. I was a lucky child and I am a lucky adult. (And that's another story waiting to be written.) They encouraged me in all my endeavors, clever or foolish. By example, they set me on the road to loving books, writing, traveling, and the great outdoors. Honest and generous to a fault, their life philosophy, which I enthusiastically espouse, was that life's purpose is to leave the world a better place than when you found it. They have both been gone several years now, but I know they would be awfully proud of me and this book, and that makes me happy. Deep bow to Mom and Dad. And another deep bow to my brilliant and loving son, **Dean Griffin Eckles**, the center of his grandparents' universe and my own personal hero, who has inherited their generous spirit and joie de vivre. Dean and his wife **Marta Franco** have embraced and encouraged all my writing endeavors. I could not be more thankful for the cards I was dealt.

I am grateful to all of my students, past and current, who over the years have taught me more than I have taught them. I polished my explaining and storytelling abilities, and my writing and editing skills, while working with seventh and eighth graders at Colfax Elementary School for twenty-five years and continue to do so alongside my retired students in Sierra College's OLLI and UC Davis' OLLI programs (Osher Lifelong Learning Institute). Each year, I promised my eighth graders, as we all participated in NaNoWriMo together, that I would make sure to include my deep gratitude for them in my Acknowledgements when my book was published. Here's to keeping promises to fellow writers!

Another deep bow of gratitude must go to friend and gifted artist **Laurel Mathe** of Mystic Designs for the gorgeous book cover design she created for this book. She nailed down my shifting vision and captured the aweing majesty of the Sierra Nevada.

My editor, book coach, and fellow GCW member, **Rebecca Inch-Partridge**, has worked with me for several years. This book would not have crossed the finish line without her loyalty and dedicated efforts. She has played more than her officially assigned roles, becoming my friend, collaborator, and confidant. Especially during the pandemic, when my enthusiasm faltered, Rebecca cheered and cajoled, as together we pushed the final draft of this manuscript up the path towards the mountain peak. I am deeply grateful and forever indebted to her unflagging support and wise advice.

I am honored that **Reagan Rothe** and the staff at **Black Rose Writing** chose to include my story in their collection. I am grateful for their guidance in walking my manuscript those final steps of its journey from digital bytes on my computer to a printed book in my hand.

Author's Note

I have tried diligently to be both honest and accurate in my storytelling. The rendering of places, times, and events is my responsibility. Any errors I claim as my own. The specific elevations of various mountain passes and other locations are tricky, as the numbers on old signs and maps disagree with newer books and internet sites, but I found no one definitive source. I have changed the names of many of the people I encountered along the trail in order to protect their privacy. In a couple instances, I changed some minor, but specific, identifying details for the same reason.

Throughout *Force of Nature*, I describe taking photographs. Be sure to check out the *Force of Nature* Photo Album on my website at www.joangriffin.us/book

Note from Joan M. Griffin

Thank you for reading *Force of Nature*. I hope you enjoyed joining in the adventure.

Word-of-mouth is the best kind of recommendation and crucial for any author to succeed. Please consider supporting me by leaving an honest review online on your favorite store or book-centered website.

With gratitude,
Joan

We hope you enjoyed reading this title from:

BLACK ROSE
writing™

Subscribe to our mailing list – *The Rosevine* – and receive **FREE** books, daily deals, and stay current with news about upcoming releases and our hottest authors.
Scan the QR code below to sign up.

Already a subscriber? Please accept a sincere thank you for being a fan of Black Rose Writing authors.

View other Black Rose Writing titles at
www.blackrosewriting.com/books and use promo code
PRINT to receive a **20% discount** when purchasing.